AF692327

Yangzi Waters

China Studies

PUBLISHED FOR THE INSTITUTE FOR CHINESE STUDIES, UNIVERSITY OF OXFORD

Series Editor

Rana Mitter, *University of Oxford*

VOLUME 44

The titles published in this series are listed at *brill.*

Yangzi Waters

Transforming the Water Regime of the Jianghan Plain in Late Imperial China

By

Yan GAO

Cover illustration: Hubei sheng Changjiang, Hanshui di gong tu 湖北省長江、漢水堤工圖 [The embankment map of the Yangtze River and the Han River in Hubei Province] (1821–1850). The map is adjusted to fit the cover. The orientation of the map is south at the top, and north at the bottom. Library of Congress, Geography and Map Division, Washington D.C., gm71005075, http://hdl.loc.gov/loc.gmd/g7822y.ct003422.

Library of Congress Cataloging-in-Publication Data

Names: Gao, Yan, author.
Title: Yangzi waters : transforming the water regime of the Jianghan Plain in late imperial China / by Yan Gao.
Description: Leiden ; Boston : Brill, [2022] | Series: China studies, 1570-1344 ; volume 44 | Includes bibliographical references and index.
Identifiers: LCCN 2021046466 (print) | LCCN 2021046467 (ebook) | ISBN 9789004505278 (hardback) | ISBN 9789004505285 (ebook)
Subjects: LCSH: Water resources development–China–Jianghan Region–History. | Water-supply–Political aspects–China–Jianghan Region–History. | Human ecology–China–Jianghan Region–History. | Yangtze River (China)–Environmental conditions. | Jianghan Region (China) –Environmental conditions. | Jianghan Region (China) –Politics and government. | China–Politics and government–1644-1912. | China–History–Qing dynasty, 1644-1912.
Classification: LCC HD1698.C52 .G36 2022 (print) | LCC HD1698.C52 (ebook) | DDC 333.91009512/1–dc23/eng/20211014
LC record available at https://lccn.loc.gov/2021046466
LC ebook record available at https://lccn.loc.gov/2021046467

Typeface for the Latin, Greek, and Cyrillic scripts: “Brill.” See and download: brill.com/brill-typeface.

ISSN 1570-1344

In memory of my mother, Zhu Jinlian (1948–2018),
and my aunt, Gao Ziyun (1935–2020)

Contents

Acknowledgments

This book represents a journey of more than ten years. During the gestation of this project, I received help from many people, to whom I owe my thanks. First, I am grateful to my doctoral adviser, Professor Emeritus Donald S. Sutton at Carnegie Mellon, who mentored, helped, and supported me throughout the journey. Without his constant encouragement and support, I would have accomplished much less. I owe him a lifetime of gratitude. Professors Joel Tarr and John Soluri have always been there for me and they deserve my deepest appreciation.

My postdoctoral superviser, Professor Prasenjit Duara at Duke University, granted me the freedom to work on the manuscript. In addition, he offered opportunities for me to present my ideas on various occasions and to network with scholars in related fields. I also owe tremendous thanks to Dr. Giovanni Zanalda, the director of the John Hope Franklin Center, for support and advice on moving forward. I was also fortunate to have great colleagues at the center who encouraged, comforted, and helped me whenever possible.

This book started as a small project with Professor Steven Schlossman at his research seminar at Carnegie Mellon University. In my first year of research and writing, his confidence in the project steeled me through the initial stage of exploration. During the subsequent period of field work and writing, Professor Lu Xiqi at Wuhan University gave me unreserved support and granted me generous access to sources in his own collection—which became the basis of this book. Luo Dufang at the Chinese University of Hong Kong and Professor Xu Bin at Wuhan University accompanied me on field work around Dongting Lake and on the Jianghan Plain. I owe them great thanks for their scholarly insights and fun company!

The turning point of this project came at the Rachel Carson Center (RCC) in Munich, Germany, a truly intellectually inspiring place. I thank Professor Christof Mauch, who not only reviewed the outline of the book and met with me to discuss the theme but also coined the title of the book, *Yangzi Waters*, which I find poetic and inspiring. I greatly appreciate his open-mindedness and positivity. I enjoyed the interaction with fellow scholars at the RCC, who offered me great intellectual stimulus and made my time at the RCC invaluable and memorable: Amanda Boetzkes, Cao Mu, Pey-Yi Chu, Saskia Beudel, Han Zhaoqing, Chihyung Jeon, Alan MacEachern, Ruth Odenziel, Paul Sutter, Robert Wilson, and Wang Zhen. Special thanks are due to Paul, Ruth, Alan, and Zhaoqing for reading parts of the manuscript and giving me insightful advice on how to advance the project.

I also thank Dr. Dagmar Schäfer, who gave me the opportunity to do research on digitized local gazetteers at the Max Planck Institute for the History of Science (MPIWG) in Berlin. Shih-Pei Chen and Che Qun provided wonderful support and guidance on my research at the institute. Some of my favorite experiences there were discussions at the institute colloquiums. I thank Masato Hasegawa, Fan Fa-ti, and Christian de Pee for enlightening conversations on research, writing, and life.

Over the many years spent developing this book, I received assistance from many scholars in the field. They helped me stay focused and redirected me, when necessary, in one way or another. I am deeply indebted to David Pietz, Peter C. Perdue, Robert Marks, John McNeill, Micah Muscolino, Bao Maohong, Han Zhaoqing, Hou Shen, Brian Lander, Peter Lavelle, Xiaofei Kang, Jianhua Xu, Li Li, Zhang Lianwei, Jeff Nicolaisen, Liu Jiacheng and John Weigel. I owe particular thanks to David Bello, Ling Zhang, Pey-Yi Chu, and Christian de Pee for sharing their writing experience with me and encouraging me to address problems. Two anonymous reviewers also offered critical advice about improving the manuscript. Any remaining errors are solely mine.

My friends and colleagues have greatly supported my work. Peter Brand not only reviewed my text at the proposal stage, but also offered me advice on writing and revisions. Jim Blyth and Sheila Martin encouraged me, not least by serving delicious meals and reading a draft of my writing. Lan Zhang graciously accommodated my teaching and has always been a helpful source. Thanks to Elaine Shi and Hubert Chan, who are always there for me.

Several libraries offered me travel funds for research. Harvard Yenching Library and the East Asian Library at the University of Michigan generously granted me days of on-site research that greatly helped me access sources. I also appreciated the AAS Small Research Grants co-funded by the Chiang Ching-kuo Foundation, which enabled a month of research in China in the summer of 2015.

This book would not have been possible without the understanding of the Brill editors Qin Higley, Dove Morissette and Elizabeth You. I thank them for their confidence in me and for their patience as I completed the manuscript. I also thank my copyeditors Debra Soled, Wendy Smyer Yu, Jeremy Hall, Brenda Black, and Barbara Werden, who each tirelessly read at least one chapter, correcting and polishing every detail. Working with them has been a great joy.

My family has been firmly behind me for the entire journey, and I owe them the most. My father Gao Yunhua has always been a strong supporter of my writing. My aunt Gao Ziyun was often concerned about me when I was away from Wuhan but lost her life in early 2020—I dearly miss her. I owe a million thanks to my daughter, Eva—I had to be away from time to time for work, and she endured many periods of separation from me. She is the light of my life. My husband, Raj, has extended the most unreserved support to me throughout the process. He put up with my complaints, frustration, sweat, and tears and persuaded me to keep going whenever I thought about giving up. His devotion to the family deserves a lifetime of gratitude from me. This book is dedicated to all four of them.

Memphis, TN
May 2021

Figures and Tables

Figures

Tables

Introduction

Water, Society and Politics

I grew up on the Jianghan Plain, the alluvial plain at the confluence of the Yangzi River* and its biggest tributary, the Han River. For over twenty-five years, I experienced the subtropical monsoon weather of the plain, with its smothering heat in the summer, chilling cold in the winter, and rather pleasant but short spring and autumn. I grew up in this watery environment, feasting on its variety of fish, aquatic plants, and crops and panicking when the Yangzi and Han Rivers threatened to flood. How, I want to ask, did the ecosystems of the Jianghan Plain shape people's lives, and how was the natural environment transformed in this reciprocal relationship? With several hydraulic megaprojects on the Yangzi River today concentrated in the Jianghan region, one wonders, how have the geography and ecology of the plain shaped the historical trajectory of the region, and how have human politics and cultural practice been written on the landscape and waterscape of the plain?

In this book I analyze the interactions between human society and the natural environment that underlay the developmental trajectory of the Jianghan Plain from the seventeenth to the early twentieth century. To express the central concept employed for interpreting the human-nature relationships of the plain, I use the term "water regime." The water regime here is broadly defined: it includes not only the historical bodies of water (rivers, lakes, and wetlands) on which humans have built structures (dams, dikes, and land enclosures) but also an environmental complex in which various natural elements (including animals, forests, floods and droughts, and diseases) were closely associated with and interacted with bodies of water and the human world. As this book shows, various bodies of water have been a critical part of the transformation of the Jianghan Plain, from a hydraulic periphery in the early Qing dynasty (late seventeenth century), to a core region of hydroengineering in contemporary China.[1] It also demonstrates how this transformation of the plain affected the political and social tapestry of late imperial and modern China and how the interplay between social and ecological conditions intertwined with the ever-changing relationship between people and water.

---

* I have used "Yangzi" throughout the book. Occasionally, "Yangtze" or "Yangtse" is used as a variant of "Yangzi," if the word is quoted directly from other sources.

1 What I mean by a "hydraulic periphery" was a region where hydraulic activities were less intervened by the state. It by no means overlooks the scope and vitality of community-based hydraulic activities on the Jianghan Plain.

© KONINKLIJKE BRILL NV, LEIDEN, 2022 | DOI:10.1163/9789004505285_002

This conceptualization of the water regime aims to construct a hydrosocial approach to understanding water and politics. Prior studies on water conservancy (*shui li* 水利) in Chinese history have predominantly focused on human agency, thus reducing water, or nature in general, to merely the background to human politics. A few important studies that emerged over the past decade have successfully reinterpreted the relationship between water and society but an integrated approach that analyzes the social, ecological, and cultural dimensions of water has been absent.[2] In addition to providing a regional environmental history, this book's hydrosocial approach takes into account the complexity of the water environment as well as of society, exploring the myriad socioecological processes that have transformed and continue to transform the plain.

In this book, I trace the evolution of the water regime from the 1600s to the early 1900s, which could assume a different primacy in in different contexts; it could be a regime highlighting the human conquest of land and water or a regime in which the forces of preservation and encroachment fought and negotiated with each other. It could be a military regime in which water was ignored, and an environmental crisis loomed, or a regime in which water was emphasized as a source of energy. In each regime, human and nonhuman actors interacted, developed complex relationships, and induced changes. The shifts in the water regime underlay the long-term social and environmental transformations of the region. I argue that changes in water systems were the result of an intricate interplay among the local politics, cultural practices, hydraulic engineering as well as the hydrogeomorphology of the rivers, and the geography and ecology of the Jianghan Plain. In this way, the waterscape and landscape of the plain were a kind of "socionature" produced through the interactions between water, state politics, and social powers that acted upon it.[3]

2 See Ling Zhang, *The River, the Plain and the State: An Environmental Drama of the Northern Song China* (Cambridge: Cambridge University Press, 2016); David Pietz, *The Yellow River: The Problem of Water in Modern China* (Cambridge: Harvard University Press, 2015); Micah Muscolino, *The Ecology of War in China: Henan Province, the Yellow River, and Beyond, 1938–1950* (Cambridge: Cambridge University Press, 2014).

3 The concept of "socionature" emphasizes that natural or ecological conditions and processes do not operate separately from social processes, and that they are simultaneously natural and social. Erik Swyngedouw studies the intertwined relationship between water politics, hydraulic engineering, and modernization of Spain in 1890–1930. He emphasizes the hybrid character of the water landscape, or "waterscape" in "Modernity and Hybridity: Nature, *Regeneracionismo*, and the Production of the Spanish Waterscape, 1890–1930," *Annals of the Association of American Geographers* 89, no. 3 (1999), 443.

This book contributes to the broad discussion of the relationship between the state and society in what has been called "hydraulic societies." On one side is total state control within a Wittfogelian "hydraulic empire"; on the other side is a Balinese Geertzian or Stephen Lansing-style democratic irrigation model of power resting on local social organizations. By focusing on the massive community-based water management in the Jianghan Plain, this book reveals the transitional process from local initiative to increasing intervention by state power. As I pointed out earlier, the Jianghan Plain experienced a shift from hydraulically marginal to a hydraulic powerhouse in about four centuries. Hence, this book is a regional history of social and ecological transformations from a long-term perspective.

Furthermore, the large body of literature on water control has not dealt with many factors in this particular region—for example, the Manchu migrants adapting to the environment in China proper, militarization during the age of the Taiping Rebellion, and the rising hydroenergy regime of the early twentieth century. By conducting a hydrosocial analysis of water and politics, this book offers a fresh perspective on those factors and shows that water is not merely a resource that is exploited but a natural condition that informs human relations.

1 Theorizing Water and Politics

The relationship between hydraulics and politics has been an inseparable part of the discussion on water control in Chinese history, reflecting China's long history of authoritarian government administrations. Karl Wittfogel's model of "Oriental despotism" remains an important reference in this respect. In this model, one or a few supreme individuals had absolute control over the common people, just as they did over the rivers that coursed through their territory.[4] States that were built based on large waterworks developed permanent despotic systems. Furthermore, Wittfogel applied his model to China, India, and other "hydraulic states."[5] Many scholars have pointed out two main fallacies, among many, in the theory of hydraulic despotism. First, Wittfogel adopted a totalitarian view of China and emphasized the permanent political

4 Karl A. Wittfogel, *Oriental Despotism: A Comparative Study of Total Power* (New Haven: Yale University Press, 1957).

5 See Karl A. Wittfogel, "Chinese Society: An Historical Survey," *Journal of Asian Studies* 16, no. 3 (1957). In his article, Wittfogel discussed major dynasties in Chinese history and argued that Chinese society was a typical hydraulic society throughout its history.

consequences of water control; second, he ignored diversity and changes in Chinese society (and many other societies) in his theory. Therefore, his view is static, and his argument is ahistorical.[6]

Before Karl Wittfogel, other social theorists had fundamental ideas that resembled those of Oriental despotism. For example, these ideas formed the basis for G.W.F. Hegel's distinction between East and West, and Karl Marx's concept of the "Asiatic mode of production" elaborating Hegel's abstract scheme prefigured the Wittfogelian hydraulic despotism model. Scholars thus emphasized the lack of political autonomy in Chinese society. For example, Max Weber stressed the dominance of the official class over political and economic life and argued that Chinese cities never achieved the economic centrality and political autonomy found in the medieval West.[7] Kung-ch'üan Hsiao stated that prevailing incompetence, corruption, favoritism, exploitation, the inertia of the peasants, and stagnation in nineteenth-century rural China reaffirmed the totalism of state power and that thus the weak peasantry had to rely on local gentry, as representatives of the state, for positive leadership.[8] Joseph Needham, who had been heavily influenced by Wittfogel's idea of a despotic hydraulic society, believed that the expansive bureaucratic system in late imperial China contributed to a rather slow pace of technological innovation, which hindered the onset of a scientific revolution.[9]

---

6 Theodore Shabad, "Non-Western Views of the 'Hydraulic Society,'" *Annals of the Association of American Geographers* 49, no. 3 (1959): 324–325. See a comprehensive critique of Wittfogel's theory in F.W. Mote, "The Growth of Chinese Despotism: A Critique of Wittfogel's Theory of Oriental Despotism as Applied to China," *Oriens extremus* 8 (1961). Donald Worster, in his famous revisit to Wittfogel's theory to examine the American West, points out that although Wittfogel's theory of Oriental despotism has become "far-fetched and prejudiced," his theory does raise important questions about "the link between water and power, … in the hope of understanding more fully the consequences of our behavior toward nature"; Donald Worster, *Rivers of Empire: Water, Aridity, and the American West* (New York: Pantheon Books, 1985), 29.

7 Max Weber, *Religions of China* (New York: The Free Press, 1951), 13–20. For an extensive discussion on oriental despotism, limited state power, and the relationships between state and economy, see Peter C. Perdue, *Exhausting the Earth: State and Peasant in Hunan, 1500–1850* (Cambridge: Harvard University Press, 1987), 2–3. In his classic studies on Hankow, William T. Rowe criticized Weber's "treaty-port view" of Chinese cities, and he emphasized the long-term trend towards the privatization in the Chinese economy as well as "the rise of a specifically urban consciousness and the emergence of a true 'urban class.'" William T. Rowe, *Hankow: Commerce and Society in a Chinese City, 1796–1889* (Stanford: Stanford University Press, 1984), 341, 342.

8 See Kung-ch'üan Hsiao, *Rural China: Imperial Control in the Nineteenth Century* (Seattle: University of Washington Press, 1960).

9 Joseph Needham, ed., *Science and Civilization in China*, vol. 4, pt. 2 (Cambridge: Cambridge University Press, 1965). Review articles about Needham's scholarship include Timothy Brook, "In Memoriam: The Sinology of Joseph Needham," *Modern China* 22, no. 3 (1996);

Opponents of the Oriental despotism model criticize the assumption inherent in the theory of a lack of any limitations, legal or customary, on the absolute power of the ruler. They propose the opposing model of local self-governance in water management. Works that are representative of this view include those by the anthropologists Clifford Geertz and Stephen Lansing. Geertz conducted an extensive investigation on the irrigation systems in Bali and Morocco and analyzed two contrasting models of water management: the wet rice paddies in Bali, where the irrigation system is largely managed by local farmers associations called *subaks*, and the drylands irrigation in Morocco, where communities developed an individualistic style of water management and an emphasis on private ownership.[10] Lansing's study further asserted the self-governing water management of Balinese local society, which showed that water management, especially of the irrigation system, was organized by "networks of 'water temples' … constituted an institutional system separate from the state."[11] Both Geertz's and Lansing's arguments assumed a largely decentralized model in hydraulic societies; their studies changed the scholarship dominated by Wittfogel's theory of Oriental despotism and contributed to a profoundly new understanding of the relationships between local control of and state power over water. However, limited by the nature of their anthropological work, they also implied that water temples in Balinese society were permanent, a position that poses an ahistorical view of the society by emphasizing its stability and downplaying the temporal changes in state-society relationships.

In China, each model seemed to fit a different region, such that the Wittfogelian model in the politically important northern China and the Geertzian model the economic powerhouse of Jiangnan (the lower Yangzi valley). Wittfogel and Hsiao describe intensive state control, especially in the management of the Yellow River. A variant of this model noted long-term spatial movement of state water control: Ch'ao-Ting Chi described "key economic areas" that shifted from the loess region and the North China Plain to the Yangzi

Robert Finlay, "China, the West, and World History in Joseph Needham's 'Science and Civilization in China,' " *Journal of World History* 11, no. 2 (2000).

10 Clifford Geertz, "The Wet and the Dry: Traditional Irrigation in Bali and Morocco," *Human Ecology* 1, no. 1 (1972).

11 J. Stephen Lansing discussed it for the first time in his article, "Balinese 'Water Temples' and the Management of Irrigation," *American Anthropologist*, n.s., 89, no. 2 (1987). He elaborated his point later in *Priests and Programmers: Technologies of Power in the Engineered Landscape* (Princeton: Princeton University Press, 2007).

valley in the south during the Tang dynasty (618–907)[12] and underlined the state's increasing reliance on this region throughout the late imperial period.[13]

In contrast, water management in southern China, as examined by Mark Elvin, followed a more self-governing model. In the Sanyuan polderland in late seventeenth-century Guangdong Province, he described "regular annual meetings of publicly selected representative and systematic public selection of hydraulic managers" as a sort of "proto-democracy."[14] Japanese scholars also found strong democratic elements in the lineage management of hydraulic projects.[15] This local management model is seen in R. Keith Schoppa's nearly nine-hundred-year history of Xiang Lake, an artificial lake constructed for irrigation southwest of Hangzhou in 1112. Over time, private landowners' interests and lineage feuds slowly drained the lake for agricultural cultivation until it completely disappeared under the Communist regime. But countervailing actions by local officials promoting the common good presaged "modern environmental awareness" in premodern Chinese society.[16]

Such community-level initiatives for managing the commons are emphasized in some anthropological and historical works on southern China. Kenneth Dean and Zheng Zhenman's study of self-governing hydraulic communities in the alluvial Putian Plain of Fujian identified a kind of "second government" that was generated by village temples and the ritual alliances they have formed, and that addresses certain local concerns more effectively than the state and local government officials.[17] Thus, they traced a shift in control over water on the Putian Plain from the state to the local level. They also found a correlation between village temple construction and the formation of ritual alliances among lineages to manage water resources. The idea of ritual alliances within a common irrigation system resonates with Geertz and Lansing's observation of Balinese self-governing water management.

---

12 Ch'ao-Ting Chi, *Key Economic Areas in Chinese History: As Revealed in the Development of Public Works for Water-Control* (New York: Paragon Book Reprint, 1963), 39–45.

13 Chi, *Key Economic Areas in Chinese History.*

14 Mark Elvin, *The Retreat of the Elephants: An Environmental History of China* (New Haven: Yale University Press, 2004), 117–118.

15 Mark Elvin, et al., ed., *Japanese Studies on the History of Water Control in China: A Selected Bibliography* (Canberra: Institute of Advanced Studies, Australian National University; Tokyo: Centre for East Asian Cultural Studies for UNESCO, Tokyo Bunko, 1994).

16 See R. Keith Schoppa, *Song Full of Tears—Xiang Lake: Nine Centuries of Chinese Life* (New Haven: Yale University Press, 1989). A later edition of the book includes a new epilogue; see R. Keith Schoppa, *Song Full of Tears: Nine Centuries of Chinese Life around Xiang Lake* (New York: Basic Books, 2002).

17 Kenneth Dean and Zheng Zhenman, *Ritual Alliances of the Putian Plain*, vol. 1: *Historical Introduction to the Return of the Gods* (Leiden: Brill, 2010), 3, 9–10.

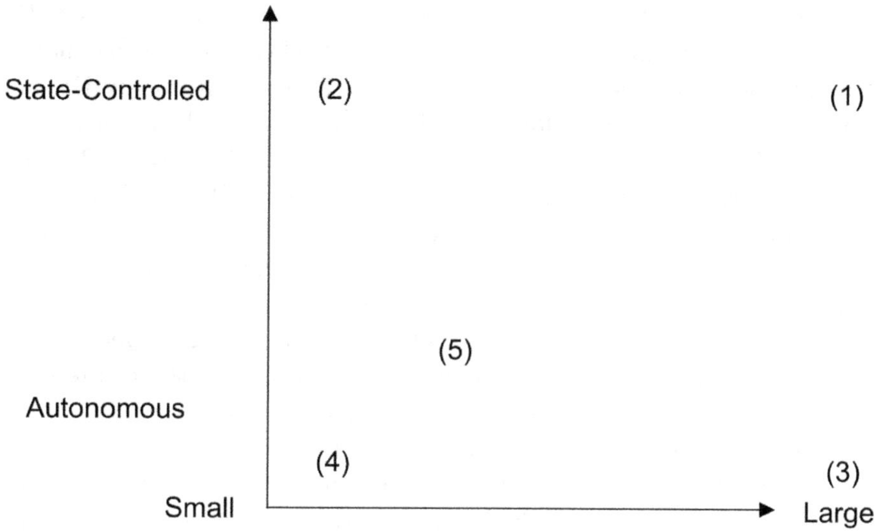

FIGURE 1 Five modes of state control in water management
SOURCE: PERDUE, *EXHAUSTING THE EARTH*, 171.

To evaluate various degrees of state control in water management, in his work on the transformation of the Hunan economy from the sixteenth through the eighteenth centuries, Peter C. Perdue distinguishes five modes of hydraulic organizational structure: "(1) large state-controlled projects like the Yellow River Administration, with its hordes of bureaucrats and military troops responsible for maintenance. (2) smaller state-run projects in nearly every province, like the Jinshazhou works in Wuchang prefecture, Hubei, or the Hucheng stone bank in Jiujiang prefecture, Jiangxi. Relatively autonomous works range from (3) the huge Sanyuan polder [analyzed by Elvin] down to (4) the tiniest irrigation ditch in a peasant's field."[18] The hydraulic works, known as the Hunan polder organizations, fell into the fifth mode "between the extremes of autonomy and official control, but nearer the autonomous pole."[19] The distribution of the five modes indicating the degree of state control is shown in Figure 1.

Perdue went on to discuss the complexity of the polder organizations in the Hunan region. He recognized that "the self-contained geographical units of the enclosures around Dongting Lake must have had a strong shaping effect on the social communities they contained, particularly since the development

18 Perdue, *Exhausting the Earth*, 171.
19 Perdue, *Exhausting the Earth*, 171.

of these polder lands made possible the growth of new marketplaces."[20] He detailed suggestive information on how those "self-contained geographical units of the enclosures shaped local society": in Xiangyin County [Hunan Province] "each polder was dominated by one or two prominent lineages ... identified by the polder with which it was associated."[21] Following Perdue's work, this book further investigates the shaping effects of the "self-contained geographical units of the enclosures," called *yuan* 垸. The story of the *yuan* in the Jianghan Plain is another example of Perdue's fifth autonomous mode of water management in late imperial and modern China.

An analysis of this fifth mode rejects both extremes—the despotic model and the completely self-governing model—and reveals interesting patterns of ebb and flow between the powers of state and society. First, this mode emphasizes the relatively autonomous nature of the hydraulic units in the middle Yangzi. After the Southern Song state initiated the *tuntian* 屯田 (military agro-colonies) in the Jianghan Plain in the 1200s, the hydraulic construction known as *yuan* was soon adopted by the people as an essential structure for survival in a watery environment. Since the imperial rulers' attention to water projects focused predominantly on the Yellow River for political stability and on the Jiangnan agriculture for state revenue, the Jianghan Plain along with the Yangzi River management was then on the margin of imperial rule. Therefore, in its early stage of development from the Southern Song to the early Qing (1200s–1600s), the *yuan* was mostly constructed, financed, and managed by local communities with minimal state intervention. The state presence in the resource management of the Jianghan Plain increased in the early eighteenth century when the population started to exert greater pressure on the arable land, and the Yongzheng emperor (1723–1735) took a more interventionist, though still limited, approach in this region.

The self-governing hydraulic communities of the Jianghan Plain never succumbed completely to state power, because of their peculiar nature. Shaped by the flood-prone environment of the plain, the community members were inward looking. They were both inclusive and exclusive, engaging in constant conflict and collaboration with one another and struggling with neighboring *yuan* over waterworks and flood control. Likewise, they were both transient, because the *yuan* flooded easily and dikes broke easily, and permanent, because *yuan* communities persisted even after dike boundaries vanished. Their peculiar nature caused the *yuan* communities to develop their own

20 Perdue, *Exhausting the Earth*, 174.
21 Perdue, *Exhausting the Earth*, 174.

mechanism for discourse with the powers above—they developed a stable managerial system that persisted from the late Ming to the early Republican period (1600s–1900s); they actively collaborated with the government in militarization; and they tried to manipulate the government in controversies over water control projects. What our analysis shows is constant negotiation and competition between the *yuan* communities and the state over land and water resources in the late imperial and modern periods. The self-governing system of the *yuan* communities continued for centuries, though the state encroached on it to various degrees in the process, until the omnipotent regime under Mao Zedong reorganized the entire hydraulic and land system at the local level in the 1950s.

Although the fifth mode emphasizes the semiautonomous nature of those hydraulic communities, it does not reject the role of the state in resource management at the community level in the middle Yangzi region. As Perdue points out, "Studies of the Middle Yangzi must at least consider the role of the 'hydraulic state,' even if they ultimately reject its importance."[22] In his probe of global environmental history, Joachim Radkau discusses the prevalent initiatives at the community level in the middle reaches of the Yangzi between the sixteenth and nineteenth centuries, in which "the Chinese state was de facto not a real 'hydraulic despotism,' though it operated or let happen hydraulic projects that would have required a more effective centralized power in critical situations."[23] Perdue shows that more state-sponsored reclamation was required in the mid-Yangzi than in Zhejiang (in the lower Yangzi area), and most of all in the North China Plain, where the Yellow River and the capital were located. Military factors played a strong role. In the Southern Song dynasty (1127–1279), officials built a dike that was 100 miles long on the north bank of the Yangzi River, as a hydraulic *glacis* against the Jin, then the Mongols,[24] a defensive move that was the prelude to massive land reclamation. In the early Qing, during

22 Peter C. Perdue, "Lakes of Empire: Man and Water in Chinese History," review of *Xiang Lake: Nine Centuries of Chinese Life*, by R. Keith Schoppa, *Modern China* 16, no. 1 (1990): 124.

23 Joachim Radkau, *Nature and Power: A Global History of the Environment* (Cambridge: Cambridge University Press, 2008), 110. Radkau points out that the main problem in the mid-Yangzi region was that "landowners diked off some of the river meadows and thus exacerbated the flooding catastrophes" and that "the increasingly dense settlement of ecologically fragile mountain regions and the expansion of rice cultivation requiring water" were the two main factors to drive the hydraulic problem.

24 Pierre-Etienne Will, "State Intervention in the Administration of a Hydraulic Infrastructure: The Example of Hubei Province in Late Imperial Times," in *The Scope of State Power in China*, ed. Stuart R. Schram (Hong Kong: Chinese University Press, 1985), 300.

the Revolt of the Three Feudatories (1673–1681, also known as the Wu Sangui Revolt)[25], the Kangxi emperor (r. 1661–1722) set up a military base in the city of Jingzhou, thereby tightening the Qing state's control of the middle Yangzi region. From the end of the eighteenth century to the mid-nineteenth century, the middle Yangzi again became a major battlefield, where the Qing state army and various groups, including the White Lotus, Taiping, and Nian rebels, fought relentlessly. State military schemes in the middle Yangzi region inevitably put pressure on resource management. Official thinking on military logistics since the first millennium BCE had been preoccupied with the supply of food and its cheap transport by water at the expense of the issue of sustainability.[26] As Elvin says, "Short-term rewards from the over-exploitation of resources tended to reduce any inclination of the state to limit exploitation within sustainable limits at a time of crisis (at a given technological level)."[27]

Although most of these works provide structural analysis, Pierre-Etienne Will's study of the late-imperial water management of the Hubei Plain offers a temporal perspective. In his 1985 article, Will proposes a cyclical pattern of state intervention in the hydraulic system consisting of development—crisis—recession. He argued that the state could successfully mediate local hydraulic projects in the early Qing, but these interventionist approaches receded in the late Qing. However, "the state's efforts at developing large mechanisms for water control did not lead to a stricter control on water and land resources, but favored the hold of private interests over these resources and furthered the development of private ownership even at the expense of what was originally state-owned."[28] While challenging Wittfogel's permanent despotic social structure in a hydraulic society, Will's theory of a hydraulic cycle took a Wittfogelian approach by emphasizing the dialectics between hydraulics and politics and reducing the environment to merely a backdrop for political events. We need to develop new ways to analyze the role of water in shaping society and to

25 The Wu Sangui Revolt was a rebellion led by three warlords in Yunnan, Guangdong and Fujian against the Qing court during the early reign of the Kangxi emperor (also see Chapter 3 n 22). The White Lotus, Taiping, and Nian rebellions were three widespread peasant rebellions in nineteenth century China. See Chapter 4 for discussions on the rebellions and the environmental consequences of military events.

26 Mark Elvin, "The Environmental Legacy of Imperial China," *China Quarterly* 156 (1998): 755–756; idem, "Three Thousand Years of Unsustainable Growth: China's Environment from Archaic Times to the Present," *East Asian History* 6, no. 24 (1993). Elvin also mentions a famous case in Chen Shou, *Sanguo zhi* 三國志 [*Records of the Three Kingdoms*] (Beijing: Zhonghua shuju, 1969), 28: 775–776.

27 Elvin, "The Environmental Legacy of Imperial China," 755–756.

28 Will, "State Intervention," 298.

understand the complex and everchanging relationship between people and nature in Chinese history.

2 Revisiting the Relationship between Water and Society

As the Norwegian historian and geographer Terje Tvedt has written, "the dominant conceptual and theoretical traditions are still fundamentally water-blind in their analyses and understanding of society, history and climate."[29] Furthermore, although most scholars acknowledge the role of ecology in shaping human history, they do not always agree on what "ecology" means, nor do they agree on whether and how nonhuman elements behaved in the historical process.[30] In this book, I emphasize the materiality of water in the transformation of the Jianghan Plain. Water, with its flowing nature, was an inseparable part of local ecosystems and of a complex environmental network. Human and nonhuman agency were in constant interaction and discourse that ultimately transformed the social, political, economic, and environmental landscape in the plain.[31] I use the concept of a "water regime" in which all factors, including water, land, animals, plants, and pathogens, interacted and actively participated in the transformation of a plain; the water regime was a hydrosocial complex in which the materiality of water was interwoven with political, social, and cultural practices that controlled its flow. This book shows that the

29 Terje Tvedt, *Water and Society: Changing Perceptions of Societal and Historical Development* (London: I.B. Tauris, 2015), 1.

30 Philip C.C. Huang differentiates ecology from environment in his study on the peasant economy of the North China Plain. He argues that people were part of the ecosystem, and that "ecology" includes human-nature relationships, while "environment" refers to the natural environment. Although he analyzes agricultural production and its role in local peasant households' changes, his focus is predominantly on the social and economic transformation of the peasant economy and not on local environmental changes. See Philip C.C. Huang, *The Peasant Economy and Social Change in North China* (Stanford: Stanford University Press, 1985).

31 The emphasis on the non-human agency inevitably puts this argument in the actor-network-theory framework. Proposed by French scholars in science and technology studies, the actor-network-theory has sparked widespread discussion, especially on the agency of non-human factors. This book, however, dwells more on its proposition of the "network," though Bruno Latour clarified that this network had nothing to do with the social network theory (emphasis on institutions, social control, etc.) that has a solid foothold in sociology studies. See Bruno Latour, *Reassembling the Social: An Introduction to Actor-Network-Theory* (Oxford: Oxford University Press, 2007); idem, "On Actor-Network Theory: A Few Clarifications Plus More Than a Few Complications," *Soziale Welt* 47 (1996). http: //www.bruno-latour.fr/sites/default/files/P-67% 20ACTOR-NETWORK.pdf.

water regime in the plain had a rich cultural layer (i.e., local beliefs, cultural practices) that was derived from and acted upon the natural environment of the plain; it had a predominantly amphibious socioeconomic layer largely rooted in the particular topological and climatic conditions of the plain; and it had a material layer, embracing the historical role of physical factors ("things") in making the changes. The three layers constituted the water regime in the Jianghan Plain, constructing a contested domain for state politics, community management, and environmental transformation. In its political and social sense, the water regime here resembled "the second government" in Fujian hydraulic systems examined by Kenneth Dean or, to a lesser extent, the "cultural nexus" in the North China Plain studied by Prasenjit Duara.[32] The main difference is that the nonhuman factors in the water regime also acted as the "second government" and were part of the "cultural nexus" in between the state and the local communities.

I emphasize here the material aspect of the water regime and its significance in contextualizing social changes. Many scholars have acknowledged the role of local environments in contextualizing social events. For example, Elizabeth Perry points out that the uncertainty and restraints in the local environment contributed to the peasant uprisings in modern Huai Bei region, though she is careful not to assign a total role to the environment in shaping history.[33] Joseph Esherick argues that the ecological deterioration in northern China eventually led to the outbreak of the Boxer Uprising.[34] Their studies treat the local environment as only "the stage" on which politics take place. For the most part, nature has been typically depicted as passive and nonparticipatory.

In his important work on the peasant economy in the Jianghan Plain, Zhang Jiayan explores the central role of the interactive relationship between environmental changes and peasant responses to these changes in rural China, and he investigates how this relationship unfolded during the Qing and the Republican periods.[35] He argues that the local environment in the Jianghan

32 Dean and Zheng, *Ritual Alliances of the Putian Plain*, vol. 1 (2010); Prasenjit Duara, *Culture, Power, and the State: Rural North China, 1900–1942* (Stanford: Stanford University Press, 1988). In his book, Prasenjit Duara writes that the local powerful lineages served as brokers between the state and society in the Republican North China Plain and formed a "cultural nexus" among the local communities.

33 See Elizabeth J. Perry, *Rebels and Revolutionaries in North China, 1845–1945* (Stanford: Stanford University Press, 1980), 249.

34 See Joseph Esherick, *The Origins of the Boxer Uprising* (Berkeley: University of California Press, 1987).

35 Zhang Jiayan, *Coping with Calamity: Environmental Change and Peasant Response in Central China, 1736–1949* (Vancouver: University of British Columbia Press, 2014), 6.

Plain shaped peasant behaviors, especially their crop choices. In so doing, he argues against the classical economics approach in which the market is the driving force for "rational" peasants.[36] He tends to emphasize the social effects on the environment in a less simplistic way and proposes "an environmental approach that takes into account not only environmental change and population increase but also state politics, community action, market forces, and peasant behavior."[37] However, he uses environmental dynamics mainly to make an economic argument. A more in-depth analysis of the shaping role of the environment in the historical process of the Jianghan Plain is still needed.

Zhang Ling's book on the Yellow River and the Northern Song state is by far the most ambitious in China studies to call for an "all-encompassing approach that respects non-human environmental entities as fellow players in the historical making of a complex, fluid environmental world."[38] She analyzes the tendency of the Northern Song State to ignore the river's natural rhythms and to engineer the river course toward northern Hebei, which eventually led to catastrophic floods in the central plain. Zhang makes an important contribution by reorienting the theory of hydraulics and politics from a focus on the mode of production to a hydraulic mode of consumption. Zhang argues that, instead of building centralized power through water management, the Northern Song state vitiated its own power in expansive hydraulic commitments: to sustain its commitments to gigantic hydraulic projects, it had to devote a large labor force, provide monetary support, and transport a large amount of raw materials from other regions in the empire, thereby seriously affecting its financial and political capacity to run the state.[39] In stating this, Zhang reemphasized the validity of materialist explanations of state power and water management and effectively argued for a shaping role of water in politics and the transformation of a plain.

Firmly grounded in local sources and emphasizing the historical agency of grassroots movements in interacting with the state and local ecosystems, this book analyzes the materialist aspect of state power through its intervention in or, more precisely, "ordering" of nature. To modify the famous comment on war by the military theorist Carl von Clausewitz, "waging war on nature was the pursuit of politics by other means."[40] This book shows that the Chinese

36 This is in Chapter 4 of Zhang's book *Coping with Calamity*.

37 Zhang, *Coping with Calamity*, 6.

38 Zhang, *The River, the Plain, and the State*, 19.

39 Zhang, *The River, the Plain, and the State*, chap. 5.3.

40 David Blackbourn, *The Conquest of Nature: Water, Landscape, and the Making of Modern Germany* (New York: W. W. Norton, 2007), 45. For more on war and politics by Clausewitz, see Carl von Clausewitz, *On War*, translated by J.J. Graham (London: N. Trübner, 1873),

emperors had ideas about nature similar to those of the eighteenth-century Enlightenment absolutists. At the same time, we should realize that water is unpredictable and creates a counterforce to human intervention. Examining the transformative power of water over the 250 years of German history, the historian David Blackbourn points out that the nature of rivers is separate from human intervention: "Rivers flow and do their work whether or not people are present. That is to say, they do what we call 'flow' and 'work': the river has no name for these things, which are human constructs every bit as much as saying that the river has been 'conquered.' "[41]

As I show in this book, as with the German practice of "ordering" nature, the Chinese state viewed disorderly waters as dangerous and chaotic, just as it viewed wetlands, forests, fire, sand, and so on, as if they were something that needed to be eliminated or tamed. As the state coped with "disorder," it reclaimed lands, built dikes, straightened waterways, and constructed dams, which drastically transformed the landscape and waterscape of the plain. However, these "ordering" missions did not always have the expected results; the unpredictability of waters under human intervention had unintended consequences, such as worsening drainage problems, and the continuous sinking of the plain due to increased sedimentation in the rivers resulted from a variety of factors, including excessive land reclamation, deforestation, the state's geopolitical favoritism, and the hydrogeomorphological movements of the rivers.

This ordering was a form of violence, not only toward humans but even more so toward nature. This form of violence needs to be understood from a materialist perspective. As Chandra Mukerji argues, "the seventeenth-century French state located its power (even its capacity for violence) more in control of the material—in weapons systems, buildings, landmasses, and infrastructural objects such as roads, canals, and drainage systems. ... As a result, the power of the modern state began with intervention into nature through which a political material culture could be built."[42] By following her conception,

available at https://books.google.com/books?id=PQY4AQAAMAAJ&printsec=frontcover&source=gbs_ge_summary_r&cad=0#v=onepage&q&f=false/.

41 Blackbourn, *The Conquest of Nature*, 17. He also points out two different kinds of landscape culture in Germany: "looking closely at what happened when that flow and work were radically altered by human actions is still a very different enterprise from showing how Germans came to view a landscape as harmonious, or ordered, or quintessentially German."

42 Chandra Mukerji, "The Political Mobilization of Nature in Seventeenth-Century French Formal Gardens," *Theory and Society* 23, no. 5 (1994): 652.

I show here that the Chinese state effectively turned a hydraulic periphery, the Jianghan Plain, into a hydropower center, precisely through interacting with the water systems and altering the landscape and waterscape on the plain. In so doing, water was politicized, and politics was naturalized.

3 The *Yuan*

This book has its central focus on the *yuan*— an essential natural and human construction. Looking at the structural and functional changes in the *yuan*, I will reveal how the intricate complexity of three actors—the state, local communities, and the local environment—interacted and evolved in the domain as a hybrid structure. By hybrid hydraulic structure, I mean a structure that is neither completely human nor natural but a hybrid of nature and culture. Based on Richard White's concept of the organic machine in his 1996 book on the Columbia River, which he argues was hybridized into an essential part of the social infrastructure,[43] I emphasize the hybridity of the *yuan*, with its productivity and transient boundaries, in which human life intertwined with its natural systems and nature met culture at the local level of Chinese society.

3.1 *What Are* Yuan?

A *yuan*, an enclosed agricultural field, was an essential structure for managing the land and water in the Jianghan Plain (Figure 2).[44] In general, the major hydraulic solution attempted by those living in the plain was the prevention of damage to the farming zones in the river basin from seasonal floods, by building systems of dikes. The Jianghan Plain has three flood seasons every year: the

43 See Richard White, *The Organic Machine: The Remaking of the Columbia River* (New York: Hill and Wang, 1996). The most famous conceptualization of a "hybrid" is by Bruno Latour who defines it as some "thing" that represents the way social and cultural elements integrate in the modern world. "Hybrids" are central to Bruno Latour's theories and they illustrate Latour's efforts in reconnecting the social and the cultural aspects in understanding of the modern world. They represent a duality that paved the way for Latour's actor-network theory (ANT) that he is often associated with. See Bruno Latour, *We Have Never Been Modern*, trans. Catherine Porter (Cambridge: Harvard University Press, 1993).

44 *Yuan* was also referred as *weitian* 围田, *weitian* 圩田 or *weiyuan* 圩垸 in various records; though they might vary in sizes, they were similar in having fields enclosed by circular dikes.

peach blossom flooding from March to April, the summer flooding from May to August, and the autumn flooding from September to November. If the basin had been left unprotected, farming fields in the basin would have been flooded annually. At the same time, the outflow of waters from higher river streams was naturally delayed by the flatness of the plain and the very gentle incline of the river between the northwestern access point and its eastern outlet. The rapidly flowing floodwaters slowed and were retained for an extended time in the multitude of lakes, marshes, and floodplains scattered along the river basin.

Under these physiographical conditions, the most common way to enable agriculture was to create a land enclosure with dikes surrounding it. The purpose of the land enclosure was, on the one hand, to prevent flooding of the land and, on the other, to assist drainage. This region had two types of dike systems: official dikes (major river dikes along the Yangzi and Han Rivers), sponsored and supervised by the government, and the people's dikes (the majority of *yuan* dikes), managed mainly by local communities. *Yuan* were constructed as early as the Southern Song period, in the thirteenth century, as an official military *tuntian* scheme in the Jianghan Plain.[45] It was soon adopted by civilian peasants as a critical structure in agricultural irrigation and flood control. In the late sixteenth century, a huge influx of migrants moved to the Hunan-Hubei area of wetlands, lakes, and rivers; and *yuan* were constructed in massive numbers to aid in wet-paddy rice cultivation and to fend off floods. In the seventeenth and eighteenth centuries, as the population grew to an unprecedented level in the Jianghan Plain, local peasants constructed many more *yuan* to meet the need for food production.

Technically, a *yuan* included the surrounding dike (*yuandi* 垸堤), the sluice (*hanzha* 涵閘), and the aqueduct system (*paiguan xitong* 排灌系統). The dikes were usually made of earth and reinforced with stones in some important sections. By the mid-Qing period, a small *yuan* had an average area of 1,000 to 2,000 *mu*; a large *yuan* could include hundreds of small *yuan*; and a *yuan* zone

45 Shi Quan and Zhang Guoxiong, "Jianghan pingyuan de yuantian xingqiyu heshi 江漢平原的垸田興起於何時 [When Did *Yuan* Fields Start in the Jianghan Plain?]," *Zhongguo lishi dili luncong* 1 (1988). Brian Lander, based on findings of early texts written between 192 and 121 BCE, pushes back the time of agricultural colonization of the mid-Yangzi wetlands much earlier, to the early Han dynasty. He also points out the "North China bias" that led to an official focus on large-scale hydraulic projects in North China and neglected small-scale waterworks in the south. Brian Lander, "State Management of River Dikes in Early China: New Sources on the Environmental History of the Central Yangzi Region," *T'oung Pao* 100, nos. 4–5 (2014): 329.

(*yuanqu* 垸區) could include several large *yuan*.[46] The development of agriculture in this region initially required a substantial input of human labor; after continuous settlement by migrants and through natural population growth, population pressures became a strong motive for—and soon a burden on—the agricultural production in this region, which prompted intensive land reclamation and the construction of thousands of *yuan*. The ever-expanding *yuan* required a more efficient maintenance system, which led to changes in its organizational structure and its other functions.

Previous studies on *yuan* have mostly focused on economic considerations—on agricultural productivity per se—but have neglected the effects of those "self-contained geographical units of the enclosures."[47] To a large extent, this construction embodied the strategies of the local people to survive in a harsh environment and maximize their production of goods. *Yuan* were usually built in two ways: in an abandoned river tributary or silted river harbor or on land reclaimed from lakes.[48] The development of *yuan* agriculture was an essential part of the wet rice cultivation in this region. The local belief in water deities also showed the cultural resources that people mobilized in dealing with water disasters.

In addition, this book emphasizes the complex nature of the *yuan* structure, which was built to be between land and water. It was both transient and permanent: in a flood-prone environment, *yuan* were easily inundated, and they quickly disappeared. But in the meantime, people formed a bond associated with a certain community based on *yuan*, and this bond within a *yuan* was exclusive, supported by their rituals centered on water deities. A *yuan* had its own hydraulic interests and, at the same time, had to collaborate with other *yuan* in dike maintenance and flood control. Despite its precariousness, the *yuan* was the basis of a unique culture in the Jianghan Plain—spontaneous, dispersed, but, at the same, durable enough to negotiate with state authorities.

---

46 Zhang Jiayan, "Qingdai jianghan pingyuan yuantian nongye jingji texing fenxi 清代江漢平原垸田農業經濟特性分析 [The Agricultural and Economic Characteristics of the *Yuan* Fields in the Jianghan Plain during the Qing Dynasty]," *Zhongguoshi yanjiu* 1 (2001).

47 Perdue, *Exhausting the Earth*, 174.

48 For more details, see Mei Li, Zhang Guoxiong, and Yan Changgui, *Lianghu pingyuan kaifa tanyuan* 兩湖平原開發探源 [*The Origins of Opening the Hunan-Hubei Plain*] (Nanchang: Jiangxi jiaoyu chubanshe, 1995); Zhang Guoxiong, "Jianghan pingyuan yuantian de tezheng jiqi zai mingqing shiqi de fazhan yanbian 江漢平原垸田的特徵及其在明清時期的發展演變 [The Characteristics of Wet Paddy Rice Fields in the Jianghan Plain and Their Transformation in the Ming-Qing Period], *Nongye kaogu* 1–2 (1989); Zhang, "Qingdai jianghan pingyuan."

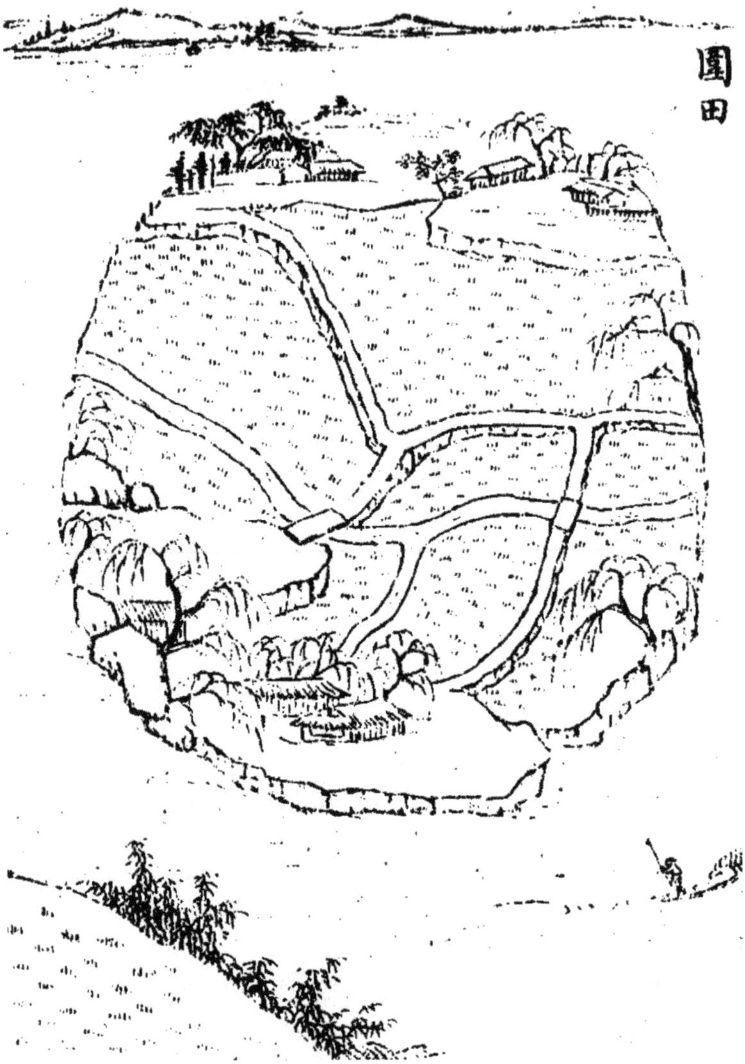

FIGURE 2 A *weitian* 圍田
SOURCE: [YUAN] *WANG ZHEN NONGSHU* 王禎農書 [*THE TREATISES OF AGRICULTURE BY WANG ZHEN*] 11: *NONGQI TUPU* 1*: WEITIAN* 農器圖譜 1: 圍田.

This book also has a spatial rationale. Previous scholarship on water control has revealed the existence of many different kinds of hydraulic systems: smaller-scale riverine systems in northern China, where water is often scarce; alluvial river systems, such as those in Putian, Fujian, where the seawater backs up into the system at high tide; and delta irrigation systems, such as that of the Pearl River Delta, where sand and silt deposited in the delta form new lands for reclamation. This book adds one more type of hydraulic system: a large-scale river valley, where wetlands, lakes, and rivers shaped people's everyday lives and were the main sources for land reclamation and economic gain. In this system, excessive water demanded flexibility and a subsistence level of agriculture, and flood control was of great importance for the river basin.

As the local people adapted to their water environment, different hydraulic organizations also developed. In northern and northwestern China, the basic unit of water management was the village (*cun* 村 or *she* /社),[49] a natural geographic unit, rather than administrative unit, through which people shared water resources. In the lower Yangzi region, the *wei* 圩 was the basic hydraulic unit—the activities involved in agricultural irrigation and rent resistance were organized on the basis of collaboration among *wei*.[50] In the Jianghan Plain, the *yuan* was an arena in which the state, society, and the environment encountered one another and interacted. These units differed in their construction, scale, and mechanism. For example, the *yuan* came in various sizes (which could include one or dozens of villages, and the length of its dikes could range from several *li* to tens of thousands of *li*), but the *wei* was confined to the village level, with more autonomous management (operating in mode four in Figure 1).

3.2 *A Long-term View of the* Yuan

Because this book covers the period from roughly the seventeenth century to the first part of the twentieth century, a time frame that might occasionally stretch farther back or forward at either end, I address the need for a long-term view of environmental history.[51] The main source used in this

49 A typical case is discussed by Dong Xiaoping and Christian Lamouroux, *Buguan er zhi—Shanxi sishe wucun shuili zuzhiguanli wenxianyuminsu* 不灌而治—山西四社五村水利組織管理文獻與民俗 [*Water Management without Irrigation—Hydraulic Organization "Four Communities and Five Villages" in Shanxi Province*] (Beijing: Zhonghua shuju, 2003).

50 Bai Shouyi, ed., *Zhongguo tongshi* 中國通史 [*A History of China*] (Shanghai: Shanghai renmin chubanshe, 1999), 10: 17, 顺成之岁，且图短少。稍涉旱涝，动辄连圩结甲，私议纳数.

51 It is true that, compared to social events or political regimes, environmental changes usually occur over a much longer time frame. Environmental historians often talk about the "risk spiral," which emphasizes the unpredictability of natural systems and indicates that the risks of managing nature become apparent only over the long term. Verena

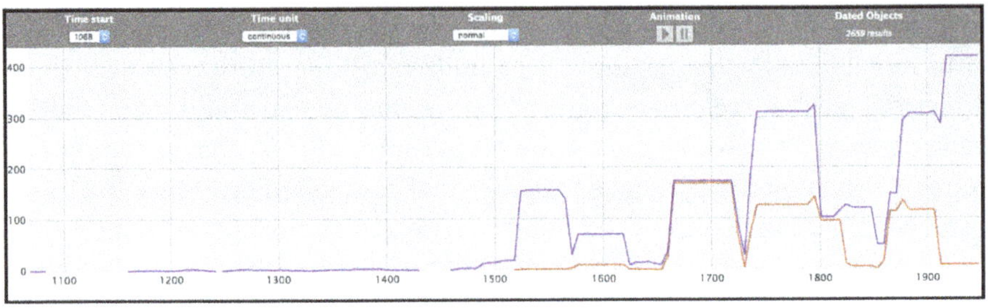

FIGURE 3 Changes in the frequency of *yuan* mentions in local gazetteers
Blue: number of local gazetteers
Red: number of times the word *yuan* is found in local gazetteers
SOURCE: LOGART, LOCAL GAZETTEER RESEARCH TOOLS, MAX PLANCK INSTITUTE FOR THE HISTORY OF SCIENCE, BERLIN, FEBRUARY 2017.

research—local gazetteers—has made it possible to study the changes in *yuan* and the Jianghan Plain over the long term. Reviewing the frequency of the word *yuan* in about four hundred local gazetteers (out of the two thousand gazetteers in the database) in the Hunan and Hubei regions from roughly the Ming dynasty to 1949, I found that the sociopolitical contexts and the construction of waterworks have an apparently positive correlation overall, as shown in Figure 3.

Based on the statistical results, I discern five distinct stages of *yuan* development, which correlate with well-known historical events:

1. Before the mid-1600s, *yuan* construction was the initial stage of development.

Winiwarter shows this by analyzing the Danube River basin from a long-term perspective. For example, the Danube Delta was once considered "one of the few landscapes in the [Danube] basin ... relatively unaffected by human influence"; but after examining the changing land use from circa 1000 CE onward, it is clear that the widespread clearing of forests for agriculture in the upper basin, which changed the sediment load of the river, markedly contributed to the delta in its current form. In addition, the interdisciplinary team at the Centre for Environmental History in Vienna reconstructed the long-term history of human interventions into the Danube in Vienna and showed that "serious attempts to redirect the river flow started as early as the fifteenth century." See Verena Winiwarter, "The Emerging Long-Term View: Challenges and Opportunities of Writing Environmental Histories in Central Europe," in *Man, Nature and Environment between the Northern Adriatic and the Eastern Alps in Premodern Times*, ed. Peter Štih and Žiga Zwitter (Ljubljana: Znanstvena založba Filozofske fakultete, 2014), 8–23.

2. From the mid-1600s to the mid-1700s, early Qing reconstruction prompted massive land reclamation, reaching the stage of "peak dike" (or peak *yuan*).[52]
3. From the mid-1700s to the mid-1800s, debates over the danger of excessive *yuan* construction escalated, but they were ineffective in checking the continuous efforts to build *yuan*, especially private *yuan* (*si yuan*).
4. Throughout the 1800s, the water systems were nearly paralyzed in the region because of extensive warfare and local militarization.
5. After the early 1900s, the minimal appearance of *yuan* in local records signaled a major shift in the water regime.

A closer look in the early to mid-1800s shows a sharp downturn in the frequency of the word *yuan* in local gazetteers, and the availability of local gazetteers also experienced a sudden decline. Not surprisingly, the same pattern existed in the war-torn era in the early to mid-1600s. In addition, the frequency of *yuan* mentions was almost the same in the second half of the 1800s as in the second half of the 1700s. However, the data seem to indicate a terminological or institutional change in the use of *yuan* in the early 1900s, because although more local gazetteers were available, the word *yuan* was nearly absent. This change might indicate a major breakdown in the *yuan* system in the early twentieth century or a major shift in *yuan* construction for technological, social, or institutional reasons. I believe that the premodern water regime centered on the tension between population growth and land usage was shifting to a newly defined water regime that revolved around issues of energy, hydroengineering, and watershed management. I discuss my findings on this trend in Chapter 6.

Looking at the *yuan* from a long-term perspective helps us better understand the relationship between water and society in the Jianghan Plain. Through the lens of the *yuan*, we not only can see the trend and pattern in the development of *yuan* over a long time frame but also extrapolate them to the political and social contexts of the plain.

52 The concept of "peak dike" was created by John McNeill at Georgetown University. He coined the term in his commentary on a panel of Central Yangzi water management at the annual meeting of the AAS in Washington, DC, 2018. Obviously, the conceptualization of this term derived from the concept of "peak oil," —a period of maximum rate of oil production is reached and followed by a terminal decline. See Chapter 2 for further discussion.

4 The Jianghan Plain

Lastly, a few words about the Jianghan Plain, which is located in the core area of Hubei Province at the confluence of the Yangzi and Han Rivers and encompasses vast wetlands, including rivers, lakes, and floodplains. According to the Qing administrative divisions, it consisted mostly of six large prefectures: Jingzhou, Anlu, Jingmen, Hanyang, Wuchang, and Huangzhou.[53] During the Qing era, the names of local administrative divisions underwent occasional minor changes, but these prefectural divisions remained the same. This book focuses mostly but not exclusively on the lower downstream area of the Jianghan Plain, comprising Jingzhou, Mianyang, Tianmen, Qianjiang, Jianli, Hanchuan, and Hanyang Counties. Their locations on the Jianghan Plain are shown in Figures 4 and 5. The names of all the counties and prefectures in this book are those used during the Qing dynasty and the Republic, though the names changed frequently after 1949.

A study of the Jianghan Plain provides an example of G. William Skinner's theory of physiographic macroregions. As Skinner points out, provincial boundaries rarely correspond to the limits of either natural or socioeconomic systems. Therefore, he proposes the watersheds of major rivers as an alternative basis for regionalization—natural resource flows through river systems, and social and economic exchanges across the transportation network (especially that of the waterways), reinforced regionalization.[54] These processes have produced eight (or nine) macroregions that conditioned the socioeconomic flows

53 Hubei shuilizhi bianzhuan weiyuanhui, ed., *Hubei shuili zhi* 湖北水利志 [*A History of Water Control in Hubei*] (Beijing: Zhongguo shuili shuidian chubanshe, 2000), 1–4. According to this book, Binhu Plain 濱湖平原 is just south of the Jianghan Plain. The Binhu Plain resembled the Jianghan Plain in its topology and hydrogeomorphology and has a blurred boundary with the Jianghan Plain. Usually, historical geographers consider the Binhu Plain to be part of the Jianghan Plain, together comprising what is called the Four-Lake Region. This book subscribes to this view and considers the Binhu Plain and the Jianghan Plain as a whole.

54 Skinner extensively discusses the logic and evidence for physiological macroregions, to analyze urbanization in late imperial China; G. William Skinner, ed., *The City in Late Imperial China* (Stanford: Stanford University Press, 1977). For an introductory essay on Skinner's work, see Mark Henderson, "Macroregions," *Oxford Bibliographies*, last modified April 22, 2013, DOI: 10.1093/obo/9780199920082-0055. Other discussions of the conceptualization and applications of the theory include Lloyd E. Eastman, *Family, Fields, and Ancestors: Constancy and Change in China's Social and Economic History, 1550–1949* (New York: Oxford University Press, 1988); Mark Henderson, G. William Skinner, and Lawrence W. Crissman, "A Hierarchical Regional Space Model for Contemporary China: Conceptualizing HRS and Constructing Tabular and Spatial Datafiles" (paper presented at the Geoinformatics conference, University of Michigan, Ann Arbor, MI, June 20, 1999); G. William Skinner, Mark Henderson, and Yuan Jianhua, "China's Fertility

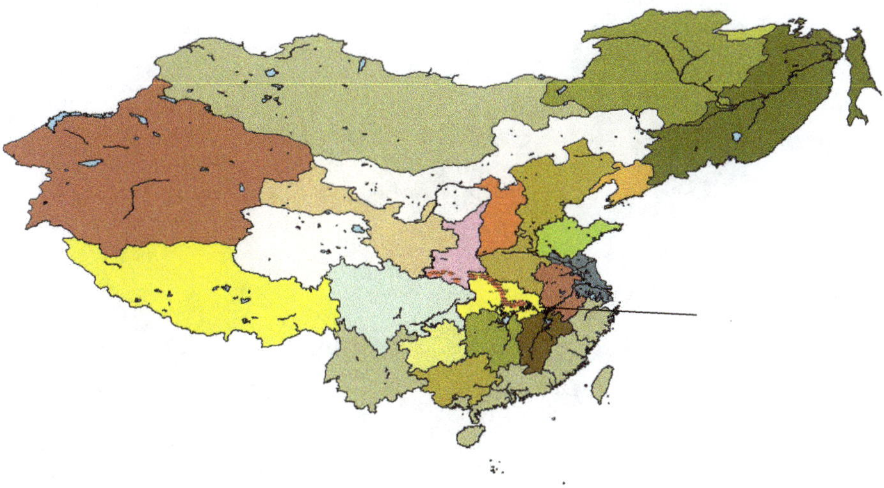

FIGURE 4 Location of Hubei, China, 1820
Note: Polygons in different colors represent different Chinese provinces in 1820. The arrow points to the yellow polygon in central China, Hubei Province. The red line roughly indicates the Han River.
SOURCE: CHINA HISTORICAL GEOGRAPHIC INFORMATION SYSTEM, VERSION 3.0 (CAMBRIDGE: HARVARD YENCHING INSTITUTE, APRIL 2005), HTTP: // WWW.FAS.HARVARD.EDU/~CHGIS

and urbanization in late imperial China.[55] The mid-Yangzi region, bounded by the Yangzi River and the mountain ranges north and northwest of the river valley, had been understudied for decades for various reasons, ranging from low political priority to scarce sources.[56] This book, by tracing the developmental trajectory of the Jianghan Plain, the core area of the mid-Yangzi macroregion, reinforces the historical significance of the central Yangzi watershed as a unit of analysis by providing an in-depth analysis of resource flows along the rivers and the transformation of the landscape in the watershed.

Transition through Regional Space: Using GIS and Census Data for a Spatial Analysis of Historical Demography," *Social Science History* 24 (2000): 613–652.

55 G. William Skinner, "Regional Urbanization in Nineteenth-Century China," in Skinner, *The City in Late Imperial China*, 211–252.

56 Brian Lander points out a "North China bias" in the previous understanding of the history of water works in early China. He asserts that, "Most texts that have survived from early times were edited and preserved in North China by central government officials, whose interest in water works was limited to large-scale flood control or irrigation projects in North China. These works rarely mention the south and do not discuss small-scale dikes and irrigation at all." Lander, "State Management of River Dikes in Early China," 329.

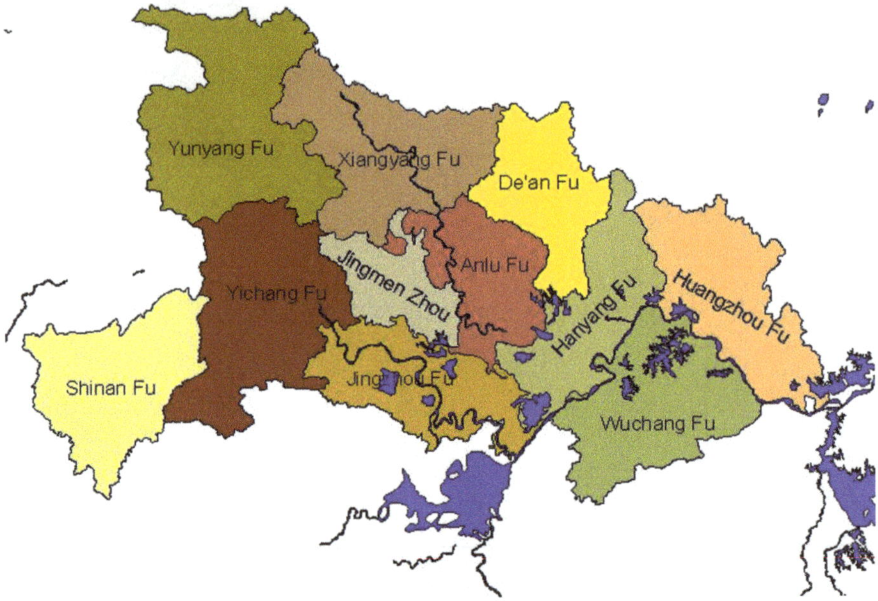

FIGURE 5 Human and water boundaries in Hubei, 1820
Note: If we overlap the GIS maps of 1820 and 1911, we see no significant difference in the administrative boundaries in the two years. I am grateful for assistance in GIS data application from my friend Pradhan Anura. The polygons with different colors are the prefectures (*fu*) in Hubei in 1820. In 1820 the Jianghan Plain encompassed Jingzhou Fu, Jingmen Zhou, Wuchang Fu, Hanyang Fu, and the lower portion of Anlu Fu.
SOURCE: CHINA HISTORICAL GEOGRAPHIC INFORMATION SYSTEM, VERSION 4.0 (CAMBRIDGE: HARVARD YENCHING INSTITUTE, APRIL 2007), HTTP://WWW.FAS.HARVARD.EDU/~CHGIS/.

I chose the Jianghan Plain as a focus of study for several reasons. First, it has a strikingly high frequency of disasters and a strikingly robust capacity for community resilience. The high frequency of disaster prompted the formation of cohesive hydraulic communities based on community residents' common experience with confronting natural disasters. Those communities demonstrated a great capacity for negotiating with the state concerning resource management. Second, state-society relations in this region showed an interesting pattern: in an era when the attention of rulers mostly concentrated on the Yellow-Huai River region and Jiangnan, the Jianghan Plain is an example of how the state managed the resources in the vast hinterland of central Yangzi region, which had a flexible local community. As shown here, the central Yangzi region was transformed from a hydraulic periphery in the early Qing period to a hydraulic center by the mid-twentieth century. A case study of the region reveals the historical driving forces in the social and environmental transformation of the plain. Finally, this region had a martial tradition, and the interaction between military practice and hydraulic practice was a major socioeconomic activity in the region. An examination of this region undoubtedly offers a kaleidoscopic view of the relationship between military and hydraulic systems in early and mid-nineteenth-century China.

Emphasizing the hydraulic functions of local communities, the historical geographer Lu Xiqi divides the Jianghan Plain into four zones: (1) the residential zone, the high ground in *yuan*, where people preferred to build their farmsteads; (2) the productive zone, where crops were cultivated; (3) the cooperative zone, where multiple *yuan* were linked; and (4) the survival zone, which was the nearest area encircled by major dikes.[57] As this shows, the agricultural activities, daily lives, and social connections of the people in Jianghan revolved around the *yuan* and its hydrosocial relations. A study of the Jianghan Plain offers a perfect case study of how social and ecological issues were entwined in transforming the plain.[58]

---

57 Lu Xiqi and Pan Sheng, *Hanshui zhongxiayou hedao bianqian yu difang* 漢水中下游河道變遷與堤防 [*The River Channel Changes and Dike Construction in the Middle and Lower Reaches of the Han River*] (Wuhan: Wuhan daxue chubanshe, 2004).

58 Some important works dealing with hydraulic issues of the Jianghan Plain include those of Morita Akira, Ts'ui-jung Liu, Pierre-Etienne Will, Zhang Jiayan, Shi Quan and Zhang Guoxiong, Zhang Jianmin, and Lu Xiqi. Morita Akira examines the dike systems in both Hunan and Hubei, especially in the management of the Wancheng dike in the Jingzhou section of the Yangzi River and the Han River section within Hubei territory. He argues that the late nineteenth-century Qing government turned control of hydraulic construction over to local gentry. Ts'ui-jung Liu conducts a thorough examination of the dike construction in Jingzhou in the late Qing and supports Morita's view on water control in the Jianghan Plain. Pierre-Etienne Will proposes a cyclic model to analyze the ebb and flow of power between the Qing state and local society in the Hubei region. Zhang Jiayan differentiates the dike management of the Yangzi River and that of the Han River, as well as the river dikes and the *yuan* dikes, and argues that although the Qing government officials had the intention of maintaining an orderly system of dike management, the innate structural institutional problems of relying on lower level informal officials (such as *yamen* runners) and of wide-spread corruption among officials precipitated the decline of the whole dike system. See Zhang, *Water Calamity*; Akira Morita, "Shindai Kokō ni okeru chisui kakai no tenkai [The Development of Water Control and Irrigation in Huguang under the Qing]," *Tōhōgaku* 20 (1960); Akira Morita, *Shindai suirishi kenkyu* [*Research on the History of Water Control in the Qing Dynasty*] (Tokyo: Aki shobo, 1974); Ts'ui-jung Liu, "Dike Construction in Ch'ing-chou: A Study Based on the 'Ti-fang chih' Section of the Ch'ing-chou fu-chih," *Papers on China* 23 (1970); Will, "State Intervention."

Studies by scholars at Wuhan University provided a firm foundation for my research, including Shi and Zhang, "Jianghan pingyuan." For a thorough introduction to Shi Quan's scholarship, see Lu Xiqi, "Shi Quan jiaoshou de daode wenzhang: 'Shi Quan Wenji' bianhou ganyan 石泉教授的道德文章—《石泉文集》編後感言 [The Morals and

In addition to an introduction and a conclusion, this book consists of six chapters. Chapter 1 discusses the natural environment of the Jianghan Plain and how it shaped people's community life and cultural understanding of disasters due to water. Chapter 2 traces the history of *yuan* construction, local management of *yuan*, and the apex of growth in *yuan* by the eighteenth century. Chapter 3 explores the Qing state's dilemma between preserving horse pasturelands and massive land reclamation in central China, deliberations over which led to a severe decrease in the number of horses in the plain by the mid-nineteenth century. Chapter 4 discusses the militarization in the mid-nineteenth century and how local militarization exacerbated the environmental crisis in the mid-Yangzi region. Chapter 5 analyzes the responses by

Research of Professor Shi Quan—Postscript to *A Collection of Shi Quan's Writings*]," July 4, 2005. Thanks to Dr. Lu Xiqi for sending me this article. It was also published at https: // site.douban.com/228138/widget/notes/15538304/note/565582902/. Peng Yuxin and Zhang Jianmin, *Mingqing changjiang liuyu nongtian shuili yanjiu* 明清長江流域農田水利研究 [*Agriculture and Water Conservation in the Yangzi Valley in Ming and Qing Dynasty*] (Wuhani: Wuhan daxue chubanshe, 1992). Zhang Jianmin's other works include *Hubei tongshi* 湖北通史 [*A General History of Hubei: Ming and Qing*] (Wuhan: Huazhong shifan daxue chubanshe, 1999); *Mingqing changjiang liuyu shanqu ziyuan kaifa yu huanjing yanbian: Yi qinling-daba shanqu wei zhongxin* 明清長江流域山區資源開發與環境演變：以秦嶺–大巴山區為中心 [*Resource Exploitation and Environmental Change in the Highlands of Yangzi Valley of the Ming and Qing Periods*] (Wuhan: Wuhan daxue chubanshe, 2007); Lu Xiqi, "Mingqing shiqi jianghan pingyuan de weiyuan: cong 'shuili gongcheng' dao 'shuili gongtongti' 明清時期江漢平原的圍垸：從"水利工程"到"水利共同體 [Yuan in the Jianghan Plain during the Ming and Qing Periods: From "Hydraulic Construction" to "Hydraulic Collectivity]," in *Lishi shiqi changjiang zhongyou diqu renlei huodong yu huanjing bianqian zhuanti yanjiu* 歷史時期長江中游人類活動與環境變遷專題研究 [*Human Activities and Environmental Change in Historical Middle Yangzi Region*], ed. Zhang Jianmin and Lu Xiqi (Wuhan: Wuhan daxue chubanshe, 2011), a collection of previously published articles; Chen Xi and Yang Guo, *Jingji kaifa yu huanjing bianqian yanjiu: Song, Yuan, Ming, Qing shiqi de Jianghan pingyuan* 經濟開發與環境變遷研究：宋元明清時期的江漢平原 [*Economic Development and Environmental Changes: The Jianghan Plain during the Song, Yuan, Ming and Qing Periods*] (Wuhan: Wuhan daxue chubanshe, 2008); Ren Fang, *Mingqing changjiang zhongyou shizhen jingji yanjiu* 明清長江中游市鎮經濟研究 [*The Cities and Townships in the Middle Yangzi Region in Ming-Qing Periods*] (Wuhan: Wuhan daxue chubanshe, 2003); Yang Guo'an, *Mingqing lianghu diqu jiceng zuzhi yu xiangcun shehui yanjiu* 明清兩湖地區基層組織與鄉村社會研究 [*The Local Social Structure and Rural Society of Hunan-Hubei Region during the Ming and Qing Periods*] (Wuhan: Wuhan daxue chubanshe, 2004); Xu Bin, *Mingqing e'dong zongzu yu difang shehui* 明清鄂東宗族與地方社會 [*The Lineages of Eastern Hubei and Local Society during the Ming and Qing Periods*] (Wuhan: Wuhan daxue chubanshe, 2010); Zhou Rong, *Mingqing shehui baozhang zhidu yu lianghu jiceng shehui* 明清社會保障制度與兩湖基層社會 [*Social Welfare System and the Local Society of Hunan-Hubei Region during the Ming and Qing Periods*] (Wuhan: Wuhan daxue chubanshe, 2006).

statecraft officials, local people, and rivers to the full-fledged environmental crisis at the end of the nineteenth century; it also shows how the landscape and waterscape of the plain were transformed after long-term deliberate government favoritism, continuous land reclamation, and the hydrogeomorphological movements of the rivers. Chapter 6 delineates the shift from decentralized water management to large-scale state watershed management projects, in particular the concept of a hydroenergy regime centered on the Yangzi in the early twentieth century.

CHAPTER 1

Water-based Disasters and a Cultured Nature

This chapter provides an overview of the landscape and waterscape of the Jianghan Plain and discusses the Jianghan people's hydroagricultural and cultural adaptations to their environment. It dwells on the concept of a "cultured nature" to understand the water regime in the Jianghan Plain in the late imperial period. The concept of this work was first formed by the historian David Bello, who used it to analyze the foraging practice of the Manchus in northern Manchuria in the Qing era. He argues that a distinct Manchu identity, which differed from that of the population in China proper, was shaped by the Manchus' interaction with the regional biodiversity of Manchuria north of the Great Wall, and that Manchurian biodiversity was shaped by the distinct Manchu foraging practice.[1] Similarly, the Jianghan Plain developed its unique amphibious culture from human activities on the Jianghan landscape and waterscape, and human interactions with the water, land, and natural disasters shaped the bonds within and among hydraulic communities. There was not only a cultured nature but also a natured culture. Specifically, the *yuan* emerged and developed from human practices of hydroagriculture and in dealing with disasters; in this sense, the *yuan* was the meeting point for humans and nonhumans and a key node in the environmental network in the plain.

1 The Amphibious Nature of the Jianghan Plain

The geological and climatic conditions of the Jianghan Plain largely shaped the materiality as well as the human activities in the plain. By the "amphibious nature" of the Jianghan Plain, I mean two characteristics of the Jianghan environment that had shaped and had been shaped by human activities: first, the plain was flood prone, largely because of its geological and climatic conditions; second, because the plain was a flood-prone region and it had always

1 David Bello, "The Cultured Nature of Imperial Foraging in Manchuria," *Late Imperial China* 31, no. 2 (2010).

© KONINKLIJKE BRILL NV, LEIDEN, 2022 | DOI:10.1163/9789004505285_003

suffered from excessive flooding and drainage issues, people lived in the balance between water and land and conducted hydroagricultural activities.[2]

1.1 *A Flood-prone Environment*

The Jianghan Plain was originally formed by the continuous sinking of the subcontinent since the Cretaceous period (145 to 66 million years ago). The plain is shaped like a diamond and is 300 kilometers (approx. 186 miles) from east to west and 400 kilometers (approx. 249 miles) from north to south. Mountains in the east, west, and north surround it. To the south, the dominant terrain consists of hills and wetlands. Therefore, the topological structure of the Jianghan Plain comprises three levels: at the center, the vast alluvial plain with an elevation of no more than 50 meters above sea level; in the outskirts of the plain, the mountainous regions in the east, west, and north, at an elevation between 1,000 and 2,000 meters above sea level; and between the alluvial plain and the mountainous regions, the hill areas at an elevation of 50-200 meters above sea level.[3] The alluvial plain is relatively high in the west and slightly inclining toward the south. The southern part of the plain is flat and low. When floodwaters run through the entire plain, it is difficult for the waters in the southern lowlands to be released in a timely fashion.[4] Therefore, the southern lowlands, where the drainage problem was the greatest, were colloquially called "water bags."

The formation of the Jianghan Plain is closely related to changes in the climatic patterns in distant antiquity—nearly eighteen thousand years ago, during the Quaternary Ice Age. Geologically, the plain stems from the lower Yangzi and Hunan-Hubei-Guizhou platform and the old Jianghan basin of the late Paleozoic Era; it was gradually enlarged by deposits from the Yangzi and Han Rivers, especially over the past several hundred years.[5] In a typical year, the amount of sunshine is around two thousand hours. The average annual rainfall is 1,100–1,300 millimeters. Almost 70 percent of the annual rainfall falls in April and September, when the Jianghan Plain is the inevitable path for cold

2 A portion of this section appears in a published article, see Gao Yan, "The Revolt of the Commons: Resilience and Conflicts in the Water Management of the Jianghan Plain in Late Imperial China," *Resilience: A Journal of Environmental Humanities* 3 (2016): 34–70.

3 Yang Huairen and Tang Richang, ed., *Changjiang zhongyou jingjiang bianqian yanjiu* 長江中游荊江變遷研究 [*A Study on the Changes of Middle Yangzi River*] (Beijing: Zhongguo shuili shuidian chubanshe, 1998), 45–46.

4 Will, "State Intervention," 298.

5 Fang Jingyun, Rao Sheng, and Zhao Shuqing, "Human-Induced Long-Term Changes in the Lakes of the Jianghan Plain, Central Yangtze," *Frontiers in Ecology and the Environment* 3, no. 4 (2005), 186–187.

air moving southward. If the monsoon season (usually from June to July) is long and the rainfall is excessive, the plain is easily subject to flooding in the summer and autumn. In drier years, the region suffers severe drought.

As shown in Figures 4 and 5, the Jianghan Plain is located in the downstream valley of the Han River, and the Yangzi River runs through the entire plain. In addition to the two major river systems, the area has numerous wetlands, lakes, and tributary rivers. This water-abundant environment is both a boon and a bane for people's livelihoods. The uneven distribution of monsoon rains and the problem of poor drainage lead to frequent water-based disaster in the region.

The mid-Ming records reveal that the Jianghan Plain experienced increasing frequency in natural disasters; therefore, some scholars consider this period a turning point in the relationship between people and nature there. As Pierre-Etienne Will states in his article, over the course of 276 years, in the Ming dynasty, floods occurred in 146 years and droughts in 95 years. Only 35 years in this period were agriculturally benign.[6] Based on sources from seventeen prefectures and counties in the Jianghan Plain, Zhang Guoxiong calculates the number of prefectures and counties affected by each natural disaster. A year would be considered a flood or drought year if a third to a quarter of the prefectures and counties were affected in a certain year. That year was a big flood or drought year if a third to half of the prefectures and counties were affected, and it was considered a catastrophic flood or drought year if more than half the prefectures and counties were affected. Based on this criterion, the Ming dynasty had forty-nine years with severe flooding and eighteen with severe drought. The number of forty-four disaster years in the 122-year period after the Jiajing reign (1521–1567) is almost double the number during the 154 year-period before the Jiajing reign, which totaled only twenty-three.[7]

More recent studies suggest an earlier turning point: the frequency of floods severely increased in the Song dynasty (or the Song-Yuan periods) and continued to rise in the Ming, Qing, and the Republican periods. To some extent, this increasing frequency was due to the initiation of massive land reclamation in the Jianghan region in the Southern Song, which is discussed in Chapter 2.

6 Will, "State Intervention," 298.

7 Zhang Guoxiong, "Mingdai jianghan pingyuan shuihan zaihai de bianhua yu yuantian jingji de guanxi 明代江漢平原水旱災害的變化與垸田經濟的關係 [Flood and Drought and the *Yuan* Economy in the Jianghan Plain during the Ming Dynasty]," *Zhongguo nongshi* 4 (1987): 28–34, 53.

Table 1 shows the changes in flood frequency from the Han dynasty to the Republican era.

Local gazetteers offer more records with testimony by Ming literatis about the increasing magnitude and severity of flooding on the plain.[8] In various gazetteers, local literati lamented that water disasters "started during the Chenghua reign (1465–1487), and culminated during the Zhengde reign (1506–1521) in Mianyang Prefecture [including today's Xiantao and Honghu cities]"[9] and that the biggest flood during the Zhengde reign was in 1516–1517 and it severely affected nine counties.[10] Forty-two years later, in the thirty-ninth year of the Jiajing reign (1560), another catastrophic flood affected twelve of the plain's prefectures and counties. Local literati asserted almost unanimously that 1560 commenced an age of water disasters: "Almost every year since the thirty-ninth year of the Jiajing reign, a considerable number of prefectures and counties were struck by water calamities, all dikes were breached, all *yuan* were flooded, and agricultural land was destroyed," especially in areas such as Jingzhou, Qianjiang, Mianyang, Hankou, and Hanchuan.[11]

In addition, the increasing number of water disasters created serious drainage problems on the Jianghan Plain. After a major flood, waterlogging might last in some places for three or four years. A long-popular saying in the Mianyang area was *Mianyang shahu zhou, shi'nian jiu bushou* 沔陽沙湖洲，十年九不收, meaning that in nine out of ten years, the area suffered from a poor harvest, evidence of the long-lasting problem with waterlogging in the region. Jianli, in the southern lowland of the plain, gained a reputation for being a "water bag" because of its frequent and severe drainage issues due to passing floods from upstream areas.

This analysis demonstrates that the Jianghan Plain was beset by water disasters, which placed tremendous pressure on the people in the region. The common perception of floods was that they were destructive and traumatic, as, indeed, they are; at the same time, the degree to which people suffered from floods varied significantly in relation to different ecosystems, social institutions,

8 The much more limited number of local gazetteers compiled during the Song dynasty probably played a part in the highlighting of the Ming turning point.

9 *Mianyang zhouzhi* 沔陽州志 [*Gazetteer of Mianyang Prefecture*] (1531), ed. Tong Chengxu, 8: 3, in *Zhongguo fangzhi congshu: huazhong difang* 中國方志叢書·華中地方 [*A Compilation of Chinese Local Gazetteers: Central China*] (Taipei: Chengwen chubanshe, 1975), 338: 186; *Huguang zongzhi* 萬曆《湖廣總志》 [*General Gazetteer of Huguang*] (1586), in *Siku quanshu* (History 195), 32: 195–233. In the following text, *xianzhi* is a county gazetteer, and *fuzhi* or *zhouzhi* is a prefecture gazetteer.

10 *Mianyang zhouzhi* (1531), 8: 3A–3B, in *Zhongguo fangzhi congshu*, 338: 186–187.

11 *Mianyang zhouzhi* (1531), 8: 3B; *Huguang zongzhi* (1586), 33: 138, 33: 143–144, 33: 147–148.

TABLE 1 Flood frequency in Hubei from the Eastern Han to the Republican period

Period	Eastern Han (202–220)	Age of Divisions (220–907)	Tang (618–907)	Northern Song (960–1127)	Southern Song (1127–1279)	Yuan (1279–1368)	Ming (1368–1644)	Qing (1644–1911)	Republican (1911–1949)
Flood frequency	8.43	8.71	7.96	5.68	4.20	1.93	1.63	1.10	1.06

Note: The numbers in the chart indicate the average gap years between two disasters. For example, in Eastern Han, a flood struck the region every 8.43 years, and in the Republican era, floods happened drastically more frequent, in every 1.06 years.
Most studies calculate the disaster frequency in dynastic periods, but an earlier study by Yao Shan-yu calculated the frequency based 100-year periods and found that the period 1501 to 1599 saw a doubling in the number of flood years from previous 100-year periods: 82 compared to 44 from 1301 to 1395 and 46 from 1404 to 1500. This is a similar conclusion to that of Zhang Guoxiong's. Yao Shan-yu, "The Chronological and Seasonal Distribution of Floods and Droughts in Chinese History, 206 B.C.E.–1911 C.E.," *Harvard Journal of Asiatic Studies* 6, nos. 3–4 (1942).

SOURCE: HUANG LIMIN AND LIU CHENGWU, "HUBEISHENG JINDAI HONGLAO ZAIHAI DE TEDIAN JIQI CHENGYIN FENXI 湖北省近代洪澇災害的特點及其成因分析 [THE CHARACTERISTICS AND REASONS OF FLOODS IN MODERN HUBEI]," *HUAZHONG SHIFAN DAXUE XUEBAO* 40, NO. 1 (2006): 115. HUANG AND LIU CALCULATED THE FREQUENCY BASED ON DATA FROM *HUBEI SHENG ZIRAN ZAIHAI LISHI ZILIAO* 湖北省自然災害歷史資料 (*HISTORICAL RECORDS OF NATURAL DISASTERS IN HUBEI PROVINCE*), COMPILED BY HUBEISHENG WENSHI YANJIU GUAN (WUHAN: HUBEISHENG WENSHI YANJIU GUAN, 1955), 5: 5.

and crisis management systems. As Andrea Janku argues, "One should understand disasters in the context of subjugation, chaos, and vulnerability of a potent political and social system."[12] To her statement, I would add consideration of ecosystems because a biodiverse and resilient ecosystem, as opposed to a monocultural one, obviously offers more protection to a disaster-ridden area. The following analysis shows that in the Jianghan people's adoption of hydroagricultural strategies in a flood-prone area, the primary adaptation was the construction and development of *yuan* as a major hydraulic strategy, used to a large extent because of its great flexibility in working between land and water in a way that maximized agricultural productivity.

1.2 *Wet-rice Cultivation and Its Significance*

The main crop grown in the flood-prone Jianghan Plain was rice. Growing rice and other semiaquatic plants in paddies on land subject to frequent flooding and water-drainage problems meant that the need for large amounts of water could be met by nearby sources, such as rivers, lakes, and other water channels. This method of maximizing agricultural production was almost intuitive for local peasants. As early as the Yuan dynasty (1271–1368), Wang Zhen discussed the importance of water in rice cultivation in southern China (the Jiangzhe region):

> To cultivate the rice, farmers shall build reservoirs to preserve and supply water, [and] shall build dikes and sluice gates to control water. ... After cultivating the land, farmers shall flood it, then seed the crops. ... When the crops are five or six *cun* tall, farmers shall trim the weeds. ... When the crops are seven or eight *cun* tall, farmers shall drain the water, till the soil,

12 Andrea Janku, "Towards a History of Natural Disasters in China: The Case of Linfen County," *Medieval History Journal* 10, nos. 1–2 (2007). Janku examines the great famine in Linfen County, Shanxi, in the late Qing and early Republican period. She argues that the conventional study of the history of natural disasters in China is oblivious to the great famine in the late 1800s in Shanxi Province and that this approach needs to be analyzed within the political and social context of the late Qing regime. She also examines the famine from the perspective of the nineteenth century state; see Andrea Janku, " 'Heaven-Sent Disasters' in Late Imperial China: The Scope of the State and Beyond," in *Natural Disasters, Cultural Responses: Case Studies Toward a Global Environmental History*, ed. Christof Mauch and Christian Pfister (Lanham: Lexington Books, 2009), 233–264. The revision of the history of disasters was first brought up by historian Greg Bankoff in his work examining the society of the Philippines. See Greg Bankoff, *Cultures of Disaster: Society and Natural Hazard in the Philippines* (London: Routledge Curzon Press, 2003), 3.

> then re-flood the fields. … When the crops are close to being harvested, farmers shall use water to soak the crops.[13]

Water is obviously inseparable from rice cultivation. The paddy fields cannot exist without water, but excessive river water can constantly flood them. The *yuan* system was constructed, therefore, as an optimal way to work between land and water. It could make use of water and provide sufficient irrigation for crops, and, if managed well, it could also fend off excessive waters from flooding the crops within it. The *yuan* system had several other advantages for crop cultivation: first, by making use of the fertile silt from floods; second, by cultivating multiple types of crops to maximize production; and, third, by allowing flexibility in cases of flooding.

A *yuan* could be constructed in two ways: first, by draining wetlands and building dikes around the drained area; second, by building dikes around abandoned or dry estuaries and turning them into an agricultural *yuan*.[14] When no more wetlands and dry estuaries remained, local farmers also targeted floodplains, lakes, and river courses. Furthermore, when sand and soil from upstream mountain regions formed sandbars and shoals in the riverbed, local farmers would quickly turn them into profitable crop fields. Thus, *yuan* agricultural fields consisted of alluvial soil rich in organic materials and mineral nutrients, such as nitrogen, phosphorus, and potassium,[15] and local farmers certainly appreciated the value of those lands. Chao-ting Chi has extensively discussed the supplementary system of floods and crop cultivation and has pointed out that the *yuan* was a construction designed to make the best use of flood siltation and that agricultural fields in the *yuan* had the most productivity.[16] Chi refers to a study by W.H. Mallory on flood control and agriculture in northern China to suggest the value of floods and siltation for improving agricultural production: "The silts brought by floods usually improve the fertility of soil. Therefore, the damage by floods to some degree was compensated by the fertile siltation."[17] In fact, this natural compensation system between the floods and agricultural production enabled the soil to obtain prolonged

13 Wang, *Wang Zhen nongshu*, 7: 1.

14 For the English equivalent of *yuan*, Pierre-Etienne Will suggests the term "enclosure"; it could also be defined as "caissons." See Will, "State's Interest," 298. See also Mei, Zhang, and Yan, *Lianghu pingyuan kaifa tanyuan*; Zhang, "Jianghan pingyuan."

15 Zhang, *Coping with Calamity*, 78.

16 Chi, *Key Economic Areas*, 21–22.

17 W.H. Mallory, *China: Land of Famine* (New York: American Geographic Society, 1926), 148, quoted in Chi, *Key Economic Areas*, 23.

fertility without additional fertilizers, a major source of which was biomass. Chi also mentions L.A. Wolfanger's research on soil to show the significance of floods in sustainable agriculture:

> The occurrence of a large part of densely populated China in the region of the redearths is of unusual interest in view of the natural low fertility of the group. These peoples make little or no use of their mature upland soils, however, but are crowded along the rivers. The floods are tragic; but the soils are young, fresh, and tillable and are periodically renewed. The natural productiveness is further increased by the extensive use of fertilizers.[18]

Local peasants knew well that flooding an area would sustain soil fertility, so they engaged in reclaiming land from floodplains, lake areas, wetlands, and river estuaries.

The *yuan* system had an important role in rice cultivation, as it did in the cultivation of various other crops. Zhang Jiayan extensively discusses peasants' strategies from an agricultural perspective—for example, cultivating water-resistant crops, such as deep-water rice and Chinese sorghum, and a secondary planting of various types of crops, such as buckwheat, beans, or millet, after high water had receded.[19] Cotton was one of the main cash crops grown in the Jianghan Plain. The cultivation of cotton requires dry, fertile soil and sufficient sunshine, so cotton is usually planted on land at a relatively high altitude and with good fertility that is not on hard-to-irrigate hillsides. The *yuan* land offered the fertile soil and drainage conditions that cotton cultivation requires, and they became the major location for cotton cultivation—of course, only when the *yuan* were not waterlogged. There were three general types of cottonseed: white, black, and green. The white type included golden seeds and "white fish seeds," with white fish seeds most often planted in the *yuan* fields, as only about a quarter of the mountainous fields were cotton friendly.[20] Around 40 to 60 percent of the land in the Jianghan Plain was planted to cotton, and in some areas the proportion was as high as 80 percent.

---

18 Louis A. Wolfanger, "Major World Soil Groups and Some of Their Geographic Implications," *Geographical Review* 19, no. 1 (1929): 106.

19 Zhang Jiayan, "Environment, Market, and Peasant Choice: The Ecological Relationship in the Jianghan Plain in the Qing and the Republic," *Modern China* 32, no. 1 (2006): 41.

20 *Hanchuan tuji zhengshi* 漢川圖記徵實 [*A Pictorial Record of Hanchuan County*] (1895), 5: 2.

Cotton might have become one of the major cash crops in the Jianghan Plain beginning in the Yuan dynasty; during the Ming dynasty, textile manufacturing became the most important industry for rural households in this region. During the Jiajing reign period (1522–1567), from autumn to winter, women in Luotian County were engaged in cotton textile manufacture.[21] The profit from cotton cultivation and cotton textile manufacturing was a critical component of the income of Jianghan residents. Cloth made in Xiaogan and Xianning Counties was of high quality and was sold in Jiangxi and other areas. During the Qing period, cotton cultivation was extensive, and cotton textiles were especially widespread in the rural communities of the mid-Yangzi.[22]

1.3 *Amphibious Living*

The *yuan* had a flexible, amphibious feature: it protected the land and controlled the water. The boundaries of the *yuan* were very transient and changeable. Unlike the official, and usually high, dikes along the main river course, the circular dikes around the *yuan* were narrow, low, and easily flooded. The *yuan* dikes varied in length, width, and height. The dike of the fifty-six *yuan* in Xiaogan County was about 5 *chi* wide and 10 *chi* tall as revealed in early Qing records, and the dike of the Diaocha *yuan* in Hanchuan County in the mid-eighteenth century was 2 to 5 *chi* wide and 3 to 6 *chi* tall.[23] Dikes with such a scale could collapse easily, especially under tremendous pressure from major floods. This feature of the *yuan* worked well with Jianghan people's amphibious way of living—it was convenient for local people to switch between agricultural cultivation and fishing. To this day, a saying in Jingzhou Prefecture goes: "when rice is cheap, fish are costly; when fish are cheap, rice is expensive." It shows the complementary nature of agriculture and fishing in the Jianghan Plain, which gave residents a degree of resilience. When floods struck this region, many agricultural households could switch to fishing as a source of income to compensate for their losses in property and agricultural production. In addition to fish, other aquatic resources, such as reeds (*wei di* 葦荻) and water chestnuts (*ling qian* 菱芡), became possible food resources during

21 Ren Fang, *Changjiang zhongyou shizhen de yanjiu* 長江中游市鎮的研究 [*A Study on Cities and Towns of the Mid-Yangzi Region*] (Wuhan: Wuhan daxue chubanshe, 2003), 71.

22 Ts'ui-jung Liu, "Trade on the Han River and Its Impact on Economic Development, c. 1800–1911" (PhD diss., Harvard University, 1974). It was published in Chinese by Academia Sinica in 1980. See also Zhang, "Environment, Market, and Peasant Choice," which discusses the cotton cultivation in the Jianghan Plain during the Qing and the Republican eras and argues that the peasants in the Jianghan Plain made crop choices based more on environmental pressure than the drive of the market.

23 Zhang, "Water Calamities and Dike Management." 1 *chi* is approximately 1.07 feet.

floods. Shen Menglan 沈夢蘭, an eighteenth-century provincial literatus, once commented that the lifestyle of the Mianyang people relied on aquatic products and turned the marshlands into a paradise.[24]

From the perspective of the state, the *yuan*'s flexible structure gave the local people a convenient way of evading state control. Normally, the premodern imperial state levied taxes on both agricultural cultivation and fishing; however, the constant switching between crop cultivation and fishing made it easy for people to escape their tax obligations. The agrarian state found it hard to tolerate the existence of a transient group that did not adhere to any definitive category. James Scott has extensively analyzed how wet rice cultivation played an important role in premodern Southeast Asian states and argued that, for states trying to incorporate as many resources as possible within the range of their authority, wet rice cultivation was one effective way of doing so.[25] The same argument applies to premodern China. This livelihood strategy of switching between fishing and cultivation was later rendered impractical by immense land reclamation efforts that encroached on large bodies of water.[26] In the eighteenth century, some officials even suggested adjusting the state's taxation policy: to maximize the production of a certain *yuan*, they levied taxes based on grain production in dry seasons and on fishing in wet seasons. This is further discussed in Chapter 2.

Because the *yuan* had an amphibious nature that connected water and land, and a flexible structure that accommodated people's lifestyle, it was an optimal choice for people to survive and maximize production on the Jianghan Plain. The *yuan*'s physical boundary was transient and changeable, so the definition and cohesion of a *yuan* community largely relied on its cultural dimension: the common experience of people dealing with crises and the collective management of a certain hydraulic system.

---

24 Shen Menglan, *Wusheng gouxu shuidao tushuo* 五省溝洫水道圖說 [*An Illustration of the Irrigation Aqueducts and Waterways of Five Provinces*] (1879), 62–63.

25 James C. Scott, *The Art of Not Being Governed: An Anarchist History of Upland Southeast Asia* (New Haven: Yale University Press, 2009), 51.

26 According to a study on fishery in late imperial China by Yin Lingling, taxes on fishery (魚課 *yu ke*) in the Huguang region provided a large portion of the statewide tax revenue during the Ming dynasty. However, fishery declined, to a large extent, due to the diminishing of bodies of water in the Qing dynasty. Yin Lingling, *Mingqing changjiang zhongxiayou yuye jingji yanjiu* 明清長江中下游漁業經濟研究 [*A Study on the Fishery Economy of the Mid- and Lower Yangzi Region in the Ming and Qing Dynasties*] (Jinan: Qilu shushe, 2004), 142–144.

2 Networks, Lineages, and the Creation of *Yuan*

In a flood-prone environment, the accrual of social capital was crucial for the survival of newly settled migrants from other regions. When migrants went to the Jianghan Plain, most resided on high ground because the vast wetlands in this region were not suitable for human habitation. Although early households were relatively scattered, most families did not live far apart. Early residents of what is now Tianmen County lived near each other; they celebrated festivals by drinking together, and households with an illness or death received collective donations and other forms of help from other households in the same village.[27] A community usually had two types of social networks—informal and formal, with both contributing to the management and consolidation of the community.

The construction and maintenance of hydraulic projects were especially important for people's livelihoods in this vast wetland; management of the hydraulic projects relied mostly on the collective efforts of the community, and most hydraulic projects required the collaboration of multiple families. Initially, this collaboration was loosely organized and based mainly on blood relations, proximity, and friendship. For example, building the foundation for a house depended on assistance from agnatic family members, neighbors, and friends. In this area, which often had floods and drainage problems, most houses were built on mounds of earth called *tai* 台. A group of houses built on such mounds formed a natural village. These mounds were usually man made, though they sometimes occurred naturally. People usually chose an area of high ground near their family's agricultural fields, moving earth from somewhere nearby to build a pile in the chosen area, and then built a house atop the mound. These mounds were usually 1.5 meters tall (in some cases, 2 or 3 meters tall) and covered more than 100 square meters. The construction of these mounds was seasonal; if they could not be completed in the winter and spring, the unfinished portion was most likely washed away by floodwaters in the summer and autumn. To finish a big project quickly enough, the family sought help from other people, including siblings, cousins, in-laws, neighbors, and friends.[28] Therefore, the speed of construction and the number of people

27 *Tianmen xianzhi* (1765), 1: 36–9, in *Zhongguo difangzhi jicheng*, 44: 383–384.

28 Chen Tao, "Hongshui yu cunluo kongjian jiegou de yanbian: Jianghan pingyuan yangmacun de taizi de shehuixue kaocha 洪水與村落空間結構的演變—江漢平原楊馬村的台子的社會學考察 [Floods and Transformations in the Spatial Pattern of Villages: A Sociological Analysis of *Tai* in Yangma Village of the Jianghan Plain]," *Gujin nongye* 2 (2007). Lu Xiqi also discussed the significance of social networks in building the houses in the Jianghan Plain based on his fieldwork in Hanchuan County

who participated in a project signified the strength of a family's social network and, hence, the power and prosperity of the family. Even today, the names of many natural villages combine a surname with *tai*, meaning the *tai* of a certain family—for example, the Yu family *tai* or the Huang family *tai*. In some cases, villages have names such as "the five-family *tai*" or the "six-family *tai*" meaning the *tai* of many families. The names indicate that the initial construction of the *tai* was due to collaboration among many families who may have shared the *tai* or merely participated in its construction.[29]

The local peasants relied on their social networks not only for building these mounds but also in agricultural cultivation. Stephen Lansing and John Miller found that Balinese farmers were willing to coordinate their simultaneous crop cultivation in order to mitigate potential damage from water scarcity, disease, and pests.[30] Such cooperation was especially valuable in the excessively wet ecological conditions in the Jianghan Plain as well. Considering the climate in this region—with three highwater seasons every year, in March and April, June and July, and late September—the most important task for a single agrarian household was planting on time. Planting late meant being caught in a heavy rain or floods and would yield a poor harvest in the fall. Likewise, a slow and unpunctual harvest could waste a year of cultivation efforts. Moreover, when floods threatened the fields, an intensive labor force was needed to save the crops; and when floods destroyed crops, a second round of planting would similarly require intensive and punctual labor to ensure the maximum agricultural output. In any case, if a crisis were not dealt with well, the peasants' efforts would be in vain, and they could face a year of starvation. Therefore, people in this region, bound by ties of blood, territory, and religion, shared an interlocking chain of mutual reciprocity. Families that received help from others were expected to return the favor in the future.

Informal and spontaneous help from family members, neighbors, and friends was very important to keep agrarian life running. Water further perpetuated these community bonds—households that shared water resources and were subject to flooding threats from the same body of water worked out

---

on May 29, 2008; see Lu Xiqi, "Tai, yuan, dadi: Jianghan pingyuan shehui jingji quyu de xingcheng, kuozhan yu zuhe 台、垸、大堤：江漢平原社會經濟區域的形成、擴展與組合 [Tai, Yuan, and Dikes: The Formation, Expansion and Combination of Socio-Economic Units in the Jianghan Plain]," *Shixue yuekan*, 4 (2004): 16–17.

29 Chen, "Hongshui yu cunluo," 11.

30 J. Stephen Lansing and John H. Miller, "Cooperation in Balinese Rice Farming," SFI Working Paper 2003-05-030, Santa Fe Institute, May 2003, https: //sfi-edu.s3.amazonaws.com/sfi-edu/production/uploads/sfi-com/dev/uploads/filer/69/b3/69b31b20-00af-4a55-947a-d47e32cd2276/03-05-030.pdf.

a more efficient way to improve their quality of life. Collective action was thus necessary to protect against or recover from water disasters. Scholars have observed this collective action in various contexts. For example, the Japanese scholar Akira Morita discussed the polder in Songjiang Prefecture, south of the Yangzi estuary, recorded in a mid-Qing gazetteer:

> An entire polder is interdependent. It is even so exceedingly hard to bring people's feelings into unison, since, if a polder contains a thousand *mu* of land, it will not have fewer than several tens of families. If, however, the "wall" [dike] of the polder for one family's holding has collapsed, then the wall in the sound condition of the rest of the polder is useless. Under these circumstances, the poor and rich will give each other mutual support.[31]

This description makes it clear that the households within the wall of the polder, whose security required a collective defense against floodwaters, had a well-defined sense of community. Although political scientists have questioned the ability of a traditional peasant society to overcome the internal problems inherent in trying to supply public goods, they have usually asserted that irrigation and flood control projects have large potential benefits for a village (through increased crop yield) and that these projects supply an indivisible public good (protection from flooding and waterlogging).[32]

Yuan on the Jianghan Plain assumed the same function in community bonding as in the polder in Guangdong Province mentioned above. What was also evident during the process of *yuan* construction was the social network in the agricultural Jianghan Plain—that is, the lineage connections and leadership. Whether voluntarily or formally, people on the Jianghan Plain relied on ties of lineage, neighborhood, and friendship to form a community bond. Furthermore, the locals' common experience with natural disasters consolidated their bond.

Local people also built numerous temples to worship various deities, some of whom were directly related to aspects of the region's waters. According to a study of Balinese farmers by Lansing and Miller, the building of water temples, which arose from the coordination of rice cultivation, was largely spontaneous and lacked the presence of a centralized power; those temples, in turn, facilitated coordinated activity. The water temples needed "no formal enforcement

---

31 Morita, *Shindai suirishi kenkyu*, 118–134, quoted in Elvin, *The Retreat of the Elephants*, 118.

32 Daniel Little, *Understanding Peasant China* (New Haven: Yale University Press, 1989), 34, 38.

power (such as the threat of force or ostracism), as each farmer has an incentive to seek, and follow, whatever advice is given."[33] Temple building on the Jianghan Plain followed a similar pattern—local people's common experience with frequent water disasters provided firm ground for them to cooperate and participate in water temple activities. In this sense, the nonhuman factor—water—helped shaped the culture in these communities.

The psychological burden from the menace posed by water was manifested in the notion of connecting the morality and virtue of people, particularly that of a leading member of the gentry or an official in the community, with people's livelihood. If a local magistrate was virtuous, the entire community would benefit from his virtue; otherwise, the heavens would send disasters to make people suffer. These ideas were evident in the prolific local records of prayers about rain. The following recounts a case in the late Ming.

> Jianli County is surrounded by water and is extremely prone to water calamities. As a result, people's lives and properties were closely related to the strength of river dikes. On the tenth day of the sixth lunar month of 1565 [during the Jiajing reign], a member of the gentry named Yin 殷 was appointed as the county magistrate of Jianli County. The next day, a tributary river of the Han River [Dongjing River] near the county seat flooded, and the floodwater attacked nearby communities. Very quickly, Chemu, Yinxing, and Waziwan dikes were breached. Thousands of people were drowned, to say nothing of the numerous houses and fields that were inundated. Facing this crisis, ... Yin therefore made very detailed plans to deal with it. Meanwhile, he went to the very front line of the floods to repair dikes in person. Even when his son was sick, he did not take time off to take care of him. People all respected him and followed him to defend the community against floods. After several months of hard work, the main dike was finally constructed and consolidated. ... It seemed that deities were protecting the people as well—the floods eventually receded. [In addition] Huangshi dike was once in a dangerous situation, but after gentry Yin prayed, an apparent omen revealing a white fish appeared, and the dike was safe too. People said, "It is all because of Yin's virtue."[34]

33 Lansing and Miller, "Cooperation in Balinese Rice Farming."

34 *Jianli xianzhi* 監利縣志 [*Gazetteer of Jianli County*] (1872), 11: 5–6, in *Zhongguo difangzhi jicheng*, 44: 277. Donald S. Sutton described a similar case of praying for rain in Yangzhou

This case demonstrates that virtuous leadership was equated with effective leadership. The traditional Chinese concept of disasters depicted them as being "heaven sent," meaning that people's morality was responsible for a disaster-free environment. This idea was firmly embedded in the notion of the "mandate of heaven," which regarded disasters as punishment from heaven for rulers who were immoral and had lost their divine legitimacy. In his analysis of the belief in a connection between weather and human virtues, especially as expressed by the Qing emperors, Mark Elvin labels this "moral meteorology."[35] This emphasis on virtue, in turn, reinforced the moral bond among people within the geographically water-bound community in the *yuan*.

Another record tells of a good local magistrate who defended a flood-threatened community and whose virtue sought assistance from the deity Guanyin, here known as Dashi, to defend against a flood.

> Liu Bingguo 劉禀國 became a provincial degree holder in 1642 (in the Chongzhen reign) and had been the county magistrate of Hejian County for years. When he retired, he returned to his hometown Yongfeng *yuan* in Qianjiang. Once, a big flood from the Han River almost broke the river dike. Liu Bingguo worked day and night organizing people to protect the dike. At midnight Liu was too tired and was dozing in his room. Suddenly he saw a woman standing in front of him who called herself Dashi 大士 and who said that her mission was to "save people from bitterness and disaster." Just in that moment, the river water stopped rising and the dikes were safe. Liu Bingguo then used his own money to build a temple with a Dashi statue to worship her. ... Thus, the temple was called Dashi Temple. Since Dashi was protecting the dike, the dike was firm and safe. People in the *yuan* all praised Liu's unshakable sincerity.[36]

In various contexts Dashi's association with the bodhisattva Guanyin appears to be associated with people's virtue and shows both officials' hard work and people's filial piety. The following story of Guanyin Dashi comes from the Shelin upper *yuan*:

---

in "Prefect Feng and the Yangzhou Drought of 1490: A Ming Social Crisis and the Rewards of Sincerity," *Min-su ch'u-i* 民俗曲藝 143 (2004).

35 Mark Elvin, "Who Was Responsible for the Weather? Moral Meteorology in Late Imperial China," *Osiris* 13 (1998): 213–214.

36 *Qianjiang xianzhi xu* 潛江縣志續 [*Gazetteer of Qianjiang County*] (1879), 7: 3.

> In the sixth year of the Tongzhi reign (1867), Liu Shixian's mother was very ill. Liu prayed to Guanyin Dashi continuously and cut off the flesh from his thigh to show his determination to bring his mother back to life. After several days, his mother miraculously recovered. People of the *yuan* all praised his great filial piety and reported his deed to the county magistrate so he might reward Liu. Liu later built a temple named Pudu Temple [普渡寺] to make offerings to Guanyin Dashi.[37]

Dashi followers believed that she could both cure disease and protect people from floods. Diverse beliefs about Guanyin were represented in various groups. For upper-class officials, Guanyin was a goddess of protection against disasters and a divine source of legitimizing power; for the local gentry and common people, Guanyin was a healer of disease and witness to filial piety. The two cases of Guanyin worship mentioned above signify that the *yuan* community was a moral community in which people stressed virtue and defined their interactions according to a system of moral standards.

Deity worship frequently had the pragmatic aspect of attempting to ensure survival during a crisis—many records show that some temples were initially built without being dedicated to a specific god or goddess but were intended to protect devotees from disasters. That is, the main goal of building temples was to defend themselves from a water threat, and it seemed not to matter which gods or goddesses were worshiped by the locals. In the face of a crisis, people needed to create cultural symbols to protect themselves. This pragmatic vision of worshiping in order to fend off water disasters was dominant in this region. In some cases, the temple was co-constructed by lineages within a certain *yuan*, and the records do not indicate which god or goddess the locals worshiped—this is true, for example, of the construction of the Long-Life Temple in Qianjiang County. In 1573, the Yecha dike along the Han River was breached, and the county magistrate Tu Binran asked two *yuan* communities to collaborate in repairing the dike. The elders in the two *yuan* said that it had to be done with divine assistance. Tu thus ordered a temple dedicated to the worship of the god Dongyue to be built at the point where the Yecha dike had been breached.[38] The next year, an official, Cao, constructed a gate to this temple, and many members of the gentry donated money for decorating the temple. After the temple was built, no flood, drought, or epidemics followed in

37 *Qianjiang xianzhi xu* (1879), 7: 3.

38 In Daoism, Dongyue is the god who dwells below Mount Tai, the place where all souls go after death. Mount Tai played an important part of the authority of Chinese emperors—they went to the mountain for enthronement and to worship heaven.

this area, enabling them to conclude that this was due to the god's blessings.[39] Interestingly, this temple was not listed in the temple survey of nineteenth-century gazetteers, but whether because it was destroyed by floods or riots or omitted because the people writing these accounts saw it as unimportant is unclear.

Many temples followed the pattern of the Long-Life Temple: they were built with the purpose of defending against a flood; they hosted a god or goddess chosen by the locals, who maintained them over a long period; and they were abandoned for known or unknown reasons. The choice of worshiping Dongyue is not explained in the available records, so it appears that this decision was spontaneous. It was certainly a critical time to have a god or goddess unite different communities to defend against floods. The building of temples enabled the consolidation of *yuan* communities.

In several cases, the presence of a god or goddess was not necessary for inspiring a decision to build a temple to defend against disasters—an object could also have a decisive divine power for avoiding a crisis. The Floating Bell (Liuzhong 流鐘) Temple in the Changsan 長三 lower *yuan* was one such case:

> The Changsan lower *yuan* was located in a muddy and easily inundated part of the lowlands. In the thirty-sixth year of the Qianlong reign [1752], the river waters rose up quickly during the flood season. People were worried that the river would soon overflow. Suddenly a huge bell floated from the upper stream of the river and stopped at the river section near the *yuan*. Soon river silt accumulated around the big bell and gradually created a piece of dry land along the river. This piece of dry land protected the *yuan* community from flooding. Therefore, local people built a temple made of grass on this dry land and served tea to passersby. In 1794, Wu Shidao renovated the temple with brick and stone. In 1865, Wu Dayang and Du Jiahuai rebuilt the temple and added more rooms to it.[40]

If we look closely at the symbolic meaning of the floating bell, *zhong* 鐘, the word for "bell," is homophonous with 終, the word that means "termination," signifying the "end" or "death" in Chinese culture. When a flood came, the floating bell signaled the horror that people felt about the impending destruction. However, the floating bell turned into dry land, thereby bringing survival and hope out of the crisis.

39 *Qianjiang xianzhi* 潛江縣志 [*Gazetteer of Qianjiang County*] (1694), 6: 8–11, in *Zhongguo difangzhi jicheng*, 46: 98–100.

40 *Qianjiang xianzhi xu* (1879), 7: 2.

Although the bond among people within certain *yuan* communities who shared an interest in the hydraulic system was strengthened in crises, the protection of these *yuan* communities was largely exclusive to them. The records show that a god or goddess was expected to protect the locals, not others, within a *yuan* where he or she was worshiped. The worship of General Nanmu 楠姆 is an interesting case in point (see Figure 6). During the reign of Kangxi (1661–1722), the Qianjiang County magistrate Huang Xuezhun 黃學準 described General Nanmu as follows:[41]

> People in some communities believe in General Nanmu, who can change forms swiftly, control the wind and waves, protect boats, and save people from water disasters. Therefore, a temple was built to worship General Nanmu. The Han River runs through Qianjiang County. … Dikes were built to defend fields from the flooding of the Han River. However, the soil of the riverbank was too soft to support the stone and wood materials needed to build the dike. Furthermore, the subterrestrial water eroded the base of the dike by hosting aquatic beings, which made dike construction even more difficult. During the Jiajing reign of the Ming dynasty, floodwaters threatened the downstream Han River communities in Qianjiang. The residents of those communities worshiped General Nanmu, promising to build a temple and a stone stele inscribed to Nanmu if he could save the communities from floods. … When the water level continued to increase, the upstream Renhe and Yifeng dikes were suddenly breached, relieving the flood pressure to the downstream communities. The elders all said it was because of the protection from General Nanmu.[42]

41 The locals told me about the origin story of Nanmu Temple: about two hundred years ago, there was a flood, and one day, a man who looked like a general arrived in this place. He rested under a *nanmu* tree for several nights. Afterward, he disappeared, and the flooding ceased, and the people realized that he was a deity and that he had appeared in the region to save people from the flood. In order to commemorate him, the people built Nanmu Temple and worshiped him as General Nanmu.

42 *Qianjiang xianzhi* (1694), 6: 17–18, in *Zhongguo difangzhi jicheng*, 46: 103–104. Even now, some still worship General Nanmu in some villages on the Jianghan Plain. During my fieldwork at the border area between Jianli County and Honghu County (part of Mianyang Prefecture during the Qing, Honghu was established as a county in 1951), I discovered a Nanmu Temple under reconstruction in October 2007 (see Figure 6). The main god in the temple was General Nanmu, who was accompanied by eighteen other gods and goddesses.

This record shows that the downstream *yuan* communities were only concerned about their own welfare; when the upstream *yuan* communities were flooded, the downstream ones thought it was General Nanmu who protected them from the flood. This exclusivity made collaboration among *yuan* communities difficult, creating the need for more-inclusive deities. When the *yuan* communities encountered conflicts over various water-related issues, people in each *yuan* also turned to divine powers for collective decision making. The story of the White Crane Temple on the border between Jingzhou and Qianjiang Counties depicts one such case:

> The Changyi *yuan* was located in the border area between Jingmen and Qianjiang Counties. One year the Han River flooded, threatening the people in Jingmen County who moved the dikes into the territory belonging to Qianjiang County in order to defend against the flood. The people in Qianjiang County sued the other *yuan* to the county magistrate to defend their possession of the piece of land. The boundary dispute did not cease even after several official investigations and negotiations. One day, people saw two white cranes hovering above the disputed area. They then followed the cranes to a place where the cranes stopped, and where people from both counties agreed to build a dike. This dike was located within the territory of Qianjiang County, but people from Jingmen County were responsible for the construction and maintenance. In commemoration of the help from the god of the white crane, people built the White Crane Temple on the dike a few years later.[43]

This record raises several issues. First, when a dispute was difficult to unwind, people relied on a sacred power external to the groups who were in conflict in order to find a solution; the white cranes, which were believed to be the incarnation of the god in animal form, became the decisive factor in resolving the dispute. Second, people in the same *yuan* strongly identified with the group to which they belonged. In this case, people in the Changyi *yuan* knew clearly which county they were in. The myth of the white cranes was thus used as a tool for collective decision making and reconciliation.

The construction of a *yuan* greatly inspired a sense of collectivity among the people within that *yuan*. The construction of a temple in a *yuan* was a manifestation of this collectivity, and the existence of a temple was vital for maintaining community morale. The following narrative about the reconstruction

43 *Qianjiang xianzhi xu* (1879), 7: 2.

of Guyi 古義 Temple in the South Lake *yuan* shows the significance of a temple for maintaining a local collective identity.

> Doubu was a very small market town, with no more than one hundred households. Occasionally schools were seen in this area, but rarely temples. Walking along the dike to the west, within several miles, there was a ferry called Nie'er Mouth. Taking this ferry, people could reach villages and towns in Tianmen County. Many passersby would take a break in this location before they took a boat to other places. There is a single temple, called Guyi Temple, standing on the dike. It was built in the renshen year of the Kangxi reign [1692], initiated and sponsored by Zhang and Li families. Over hundreds of years, the temple had been destroyed and reconstructed many times. During the renchen year of the Daoguang reign [1832], it was ruined by a flood, but it was rebuilt during the yisi year [1845]. In the jiayin year of the Xianfeng reign [1854], it was devastated by local riots, and after that it was deserted for about ten years. [Members of] the Lin lineage stated: "The maintenance of Guyi Temple meant much to the prosperity of our hometown. The ancestors had repaired it many times, and nowadays we have deserted it and do not even think about repairing it. Do we still consider ourselves virtuous people? Are we still preserving the *fengshui* [geomancy] of this place?" [Hearing this,] people thus all agreed to rebuild the temple.[44]

The temple symbolized community cohesion; the manual labor required to build a temple further promoted the collective efforts of the community. According to the records, the temple was originally built on the South Lake dike, with no other protection. If the upstream dike were breached, the floodwaters of the Han River would likely destroy the temple. If the people rebuilt the temple, it would be best to enable it to withstand the threat of flood. Because building a strong temple required substantial financial resources that a single gentry family could not afford, people mobilized, and donations were solicited while additional funds were granted by the government. The project

44 Lin Yijin, "Chongxiu guyi sibei 重修古義寺碑 [Reconstruction of the Guyi Temple Stele]," in *Hanchuan linshi wenzheng* 漢川林氏文徵 [*The Writings of Hanchuan Linshi*] (1863), vol. 5, quoted in Lu Xiqi, "Shuili shehui de xingcheng: yi mingqing shiqi jianghan pingyuan de weiyuan wei zhongxin 水利社會的形成：以明清時期江漢平原的圍垸為中心 [The Making of Water Community in the Traditional China: Discussion around the 'Enclosed Embankment' in Jianghan Plain during Ming-Qing Period]," *Zhongguo jingjishi yanjiu* 2 (2013).

started with a brick-and-earth base, allowing for only one room and no roof or eave decorations. This little temple showed the locals' thrifty life and shortage of money, yet its existence was important for the South Lake *yuan* community, because it gave them hope for revival of the community.

Although temples were frequently destroyed for a variety of reasons, ranging from natural disasters to riots, especially after the mid-eighteenth century, the reconstruction efforts by local communities confirmed that the existence of a wider social arena was crucial for a peasant community. For example, at the beginning of the Guangxu reign (1875–1908), the Huangzhang *yuan* was flooded; in response, the Xie, Li, and Tang families built a temple called the Xinzhou 新洲 Temple, to seek the protection of sacred powers (whose names were not mentioned in the text). Flooding damaged this temple several times, so members of the three lineages—Xie Shangxun, Tang Wenguang, and Li Bindao—launched a public drive to reconstruct the temple. The temple was repaired and enlarged by more than 70 *mu*. In 1854, rebels destroyed the temple. In 1857, people from the three lineages reconstructed it again.[45]

These examples show that the very water menace that threatened people's livelihoods became a mechanism for creating community collectivity. Deity worship and temple construction were strong indications of this collectivity. At the same time, the hydraulic interests of respective *yuan* communities were exclusive and required an external power to mediate conflicts; the external power was usually a god or goddess. These cases also indicate that a close temple-*yuan* relation appeared as early as the mid-Ming dynasty, but good evidence of a strong temple-*yuan* relation exists only in the mid-Qing. To further understand the relations between the waters and the shaping of human communities, it is helpful to analyze the spatial correspondence between the temples and *yuan* communities.

3 Temple-*Yuan* Relations: Seeing a Cultured Nature

Deity worship and temple construction were usually expressions of a community bond and provided a platform for people to make decisions collectively. One good example of this is the practice of rain prayers in the North China Plain, as studied by Prasenjit Duara.[46] Duara explored ritual hierarchies among irrigation communities and illustrated "how the authority of the Dragon God

45 *Qianjiang xianzhi xu* (1879), 7: 1.

46 Duara, *Culture, Power, and the State*, 26–38.

worked to maintain the overall stability of the system even as it permitted the pursuit of various sectional interests."[47] Regarding those hierarchies, Duara used the case of irrigation communities in Xingtai Prefecture, Hebei, to illustrate "the organizational levels all the way from the family to small groups to gate associations to alliances of gate associations and finally to the drainage basin of the river—the maximal unit."[48] He discovered not only that each village had a Longwang (Dragon God) temple but that each gate association also had a Longwang temple or its own Longwang deity at a Longwang temple, where the locals conducted rituals on several occasions—for example, the fifteenth day of the second lunar month.[49] Other regions had similar examples. For example, a group of French and Chinese scholars conducted extensive research in Shaanxi, where local communities suffered from a severe water shortage, and examined how people managed a water distribution system in which "water societies" administered water resources by sharing them among several communities.[50] Local people in this region also worshiped the Sacred Empress of the Yao Mountain (Yaoshan shengmu 尧山圣母), who was purported to provide sufficient water resources for local communities. People constructed a temple, made sacrifices to the empress, conducted rituals, and made collective decisions at the temple.[51] Kenneth Dean also examined the religious alliances in the irrigated alluvial plain of Putian, Fujian, including the early popular cults, the Ming lineages, the Qing multi-village alliances, and the late Qing spirit-medium associations. In his analysis, it is clear that these religious alliances sprang from the irrigation system developed in Putian; therefore, the boundary of a community's religious alliance and its irrigation system had substantial overlap.[52] These empirical studies confirmed Duara's observation that "this religious dimension of irrigation communities is perhaps one of their most nearly universal features in

47 Duara, *Culture, Power, and the State*, 25.

48 Duara, *Culture, Power, and the State*, 27.

49 Duara, *Culture, Power, and the State*, 31.

50 See *Shanshaan diqu shuiziyuan yu minjian shehui diaocha ziliaoji* 陕山地區水資源與民間社會調查資料集 [*A Compilation Record of Water Resources and Local Society in Shan-Shaan Region*], comp. Christian Lamouroux et al. (Beijing: Zhonghua shuju, 2003).

51 See Qin Jianming and Marianne Bujard, ed., *Yaoshan shengmumiao yu shenshe* 堯山聖母廟與神社 [*The Temple of Empress of the Yao Mountain and Shrine*] (Beijing: Zhonghua shuju, 2003). It is one of the four books in the compilation record *Shanshaan diqu shuiziyuan yu minjian shehui diaocha ziliaoji*.

52 Kenneth Dean, "Lineage and Territorial Cults: Transformations and Interactions in the Irrigated Putian Plains," in *Belief, Ritual, and Society: Papers from the Third International Conference on Sinology*, ed. Lin Meirong (Taipei: Institute of Ethnology, Academia Sinica, 2003).

China."[53] The few available studies on the religious dimension of communities on the Jianghan Plain examine the shamanistic belief and practice;[54] research on water god/goddess worship has been largely neglected.[55]

Traditionally, Jianghan people attributed floods to the trickery of water demons. As a defensive strategy, they built a variety of temples, towers, monuments, and statues of sacred animals. For example, people in the Lower Chewan *yuan* built the water-subduing tower; and residents of the Upper Chewan *yuan* worshiped the stone lion and the iron bull, which were viewed as sacred water-taming animals. The tower, the stone lion, and the iron bull, in particular, were usually built at critical locations (called *ji* 矶) on the river dikes. It is recorded that nine iron bulls were placed at Yangling *ji*, Guanyin *ji*, Heiyao *chang* 廠, and other critical locations, each of which had a length of one *zhang* (approx. 3.3 meters), a width of 6 *chi* (0.5 meters), and a height of 2 *chi* (0.67 meters).[56] In 1789, the iron bulls were made according to specific measurements, with the head and body hollow and the rest of the bull solid. Inscriptions were carved onto the backs of these iron bulls.[57]

The religious dimension of local communities in this area have been obscured for many reasons, involving both historical agents and researchers. However, a closer look at the sources shows many traces of temples dedicated to the worship of certain gods and goddesses and bits of descriptions of the mystic powers behind significant events, such as a successful dike construction, or flood defense. In fact, the diversity of the water deities in this region is stunning. A single gazetteer of Qianjiang County tells of numerous deities

53 Duara, *Culture, Power, and the State*, 31.

54 See more in Feng Tianyu, He Xiaoming, and Zhou Jiming, *Zhonghua wenhua shi* 中華文化史 [*The History of Chinese Culture*] (Shanghai: Shanghai renmin chubanshe, 2005).

55 In recent years, two scholars have made efforts in understanding the religious dimension of communities on the Jianghan Plain. Lu Xiqi explores the historical *yuan*-temple relationships in his 2016 book; Zhang Jiayang studies the popular beliefs on the contemporary Jianghan Plain. See Lu Xiqi, *Changjiang zhongyou de rendi guanxi yu diyu shehui* 長江中游的人地關係與地域社會 [*The Human-Land Relationship and Local Society in the Middle Yangzi Region*] (Xiamen: Xiamen daxue chubanshe, 2016), 319–326; Zhang Jiayan, "Water, Dike, and Temple: Water Deity Worship and Dike Management in the Jianghan Plain, 1788–2013," *Journal of Social History* 50, no. 1 (2016).

56 Stone lions and iron bulls were both considered sacred cultural symbols related to subduing water. Their symbolic power is associated not only with the choice of animals but also with the five-element theory, in which earth (stone) subdues water and iron (metal) subdues earth. The creation and practice of those water-subduing symbols still needs further study. Ni Wenwei, *Jingzhou wancheng dizhi* 荊州萬城堤志 [*A Record of the Jingzhou Wancheng Dike*] (Wuhan: Hubei jiaoyu chubanshe, 1876/2002), 3: 89–90.

57 Ni, *Jingzhou wancheng dizhi*, 3: 90.

TABLE 2 Temples in the *yuan* of Qianjiang County during the Ming-Qing period

Temple	*Yuan*	Time of construction
Guandi 關帝廟	Hongzhuang	Chenghua (1465–1487)
Fanjing 梵經寺	Hongzhuang	Chenghua (1465–1487)
Dongyu 東獄廟	Changting	Longqing (1567–1572)
Wanshou 萬壽寺	Changhu	Kangxi (1661–1722)
Tianqi 天啟寺	Zhuanqiao	Yongzheng (1723–1735)
Gubaolian 古寶蓮寺	Yongfeng	Qianlong (1736–1796)
Sanxian 三仙廟	Lilin	The twenty-ninth year of Daoguang (1850)
Fenglu 奉祿寺	Guanzhuang	Reconstructed in the fourth year of Xianfeng (1854)
Dadian 大殿廟	Yongfeng	Built during the Qianlong reign (1736–1796), destroyed in 1854, and reconstructed in 1855
Gushazushi 古剎祖師殿	Tuoyi	Xianfeng (1850–1861)
Dasheng 大聖廟	Changhu	Xianfeng (1850–1861)
Jiuyuan 九垸廟	Houwan	The eighth year of Xianfeng (1858)
Wenchang 文昌閣	Xiwan	Reconstructed in the ninth year of Xianfeng (1859)
Qingyun 青雲寺	Yonglin	The fourth year of Tongzhi (1865)

SOURCE: *QIANJIANG XIANZHI XU* (1879), 7: 1–9, IN *ZHONGGUO DIFANGZHI JICHENG*, 46: 411–415.

normally associated with temple construction.[58] Records on Qianjiang County also show that many of the temples were confined within the boundary of a *yuan*. Table 2 lists some of the temples in that period and the *yuan* where those temples were located.

58 *Qianjiang xianzhi xu* (1879), 7: 1–9, in *Zhongguo difangzhi jicheng*, 46: 411–415.

TABLE 3 Temples in Mianyang Prefecture during the Ming dynasty

Temple	Location	Construction year
Fuxi 伏羲廟	At the foot of Wuhua Mountain	unknown
Mahou 馬侯寺	5 *li* northwest of the prefectural seat	no record of its origin
Chenghuang 城隍廟 (City God)	In the southwest of the prefecture	
Guandi 關帝廟	east of City God Temple	1498
Baiqi 白起廟	At the Sancha outreach of Baiyun	
Shennong 神農廟	At the Linjin Gate of Wuhua Mountain	

SOURCE: *MIANYANG ZHOUZHI* 沔陽州志 [*GAZETTEER OF MIANYANG PREFECTURE*] (1530), 10: 1–6, IN *ZHONGGUO FANGZHI CONGSHU*, 338: 221–232.

The gazetteers of this area in different periods offer traces of the temporal changes in temple-*yuan* relations. During the Ming dynasty, temple locations were not recorded by *yuan* but by a signature landscape or building. Table 3 lists some examples in Mianyang Prefecture in the late Ming period. The *yuan* at the time were mostly associated with land, water control, and agricultural production, and no records show that temples were built within a *yuan,* for which several hypotheses have been proposed. One is that the recording system at temples may have changed from the Ming to the mid-Qing period, from a spatial system based on directions to one based on boundaries; another is that a *yuan* may not yet have been socially significant enough to justify discussion of temple construction in it. To these, another should be added: the social cohesion of the *yuan* had not reached a sufficient level for it to be acknowledged by the gazetteer compilers.

During the reign of Qianlong (1735–1796), as in the late Ming period, the locations of temples in Jingzhou Prefecture were indicated in terms of their distance from a signature building or landscape feature. For example, Fuxi Temple was located at the foot of Wuhua Mountain, and Guandi Temple was

TABLE 4 Temples in Jingzhou during and before the reign of the Qianlong emperor (1736–1796)

Temple	Location	Construction year
Dafo 大佛庵	on Small Corridor Street	
Doumu 痘母庵	on Cross Street	
Guanyin 觀音庵	inside the North Gate	
Baiyi 白衣庵	next to the Jinxia River	
Huosheng 火神廟	beside the Guandi Temple	
Magong 馬工廟	beyond the North Gate, formerly the Jingshan post station	Second year of the reign of Kangxi (1663)
Sansun 三孫祠	next to Dongshan Academy	

SOURCE: *JINGZHOU FUZHI* (1757), 81–86. ACCORDING TO THESE RECORDS, IN TOTAL THERE WERE AROUND 140 TEMPLES AND MONASTERIES IN JINGZHOU, EITHER EXTANT OR DESTROYED, BUILT MOSTLY DURING MING TIMES.

located east of the City God Temple.[59] Other examples of temples during the reign of Qianlong in Jingzhou Prefecture are listed in Table 4.

Most of the other counties on the Jianghan Plain, such as Tianmen County during the reign of Qianlong and Hanchuan County during the reign of Tongzhi (1861–1874), recorded temples not by the *yuan* in which they were located but by landmarks or by distances in a certain direction,[60] as with the temples mentioned above in Jingzhou Prefecture during the reign of Qianlong and Mianyang Prefecture during the reign of Jiajing.

Like villages, towns, and cities, the *yuan* was a concrete social unit, more than merely an agricultural unit. There are some indications that the *yuan* was regarded as a well-integrated community as early as the Kangxi period, although not to the same degree as in the Guangxu period. The records of temples in Qianjiang County during the Kangxi period are mostly based on landscapes and only sometimes based on *yuan*; roughly speaking, about ten of more than a hundred records of temples are based on *yuan*. This differs from

59 *Jingzhou fuzhi* 荊州府志 [*Gazetteer of Jingzhou Prefecture*] (1757), 81–86.

60 *Tianmen xianzhi* (1765), 2: 9–21, in *Zhongguo difangzhi jicheng*, 44: 395–400; *Hanchuan xianzhi* (1873), 8: 6–30, in *Zhongguo difangzhi jicheng*, 9: 201–213.

what we see in Table 2: an apparent temple-*yuan* relationship in Qianjiang during the Guangxu period. Table 5 lists temples in Qianjiang before and during the reign of Kangxi.

Table 5 shows that the connection between temples and *yuan* had appeared but was not a significant geographical feature in the knowledge system of gazetteer compilers. In only a few cases—for example, Wenchang Temple—was the location recorded as being in a *yuan* (Renhe *yuan*). Those listed in the table made up about half the total with a clear temple-*yuan* connection; the rest of the records refer to signature features in the landscape (in this case, Shuifu Temple was apparently one such landmark). Again, the reason might be that the concept of a *yuan* as a community was not yet well developed or simply that the *yuan* were not developed enough. The situation was similar during the reign of Tongzhi in Jianli County, where most of the temple locations were recorded with reference to directions and landmarks but a few temples with noted as being located in a *yuan*. For example, Zushi Temple 祖師殿 was in the Xinxing *yuan*, and Baoguo Temple 報國寺 was in the Baihu *yuan*.[61] Table 5 also shows that the local gentry played an important role in sponsoring the construction of temples. They were either local officials, such as Cao Yan and Huang Xueju, or prominent members of local lineages, such as Zhou Tingbin or Zhu Xiyan.

In Qianjiang during the reign of Kangxi, the locations of the tombs also referred to specific *yuan* in a significant number of cases. Table 6 lists some examples. Burial grounds have a significant meaning in Chinese culture; ancestral graves may have strengthened the sense of the *yuan* as a community and as a native place.[62] This analysis might make it logical to conclude that the initial concept of the *yuan* as a meaningful social unit and as a substitute for villages (one *yuan* usually included one or more villages) existed as early as the Kangxi period. Based on the discussion of the role of social capital in the creation of *yuan* at the beginning of this chapter, this concept might have originated much earlier, during the Ming dynasty. The population growth and rapid *yuan* expansion during the seventeenth and eighteenth centuries could support the speculation that people's daily lives were increasingly defined by *yuan*, which were increasingly treated as spaces for interaction between various social and natural actors.

---

61 *Jianli xianzhi* (1872), 2: 7–13, in *Zhongguo difangzhi jicheng*, 44: 61–64.

62 The same evidence is found in the genealogy of the Kuang lineage collected from Jianli County. Kuang Sihong, *Kuangshi tanyuan* 匡氏探源 [*Origins of the Kuang Lineage*] (2001), 132–135.

TABLE 5 Temples in Qianjiang County before and during the reign of the Kangxi emperor (1660–1722)

Temple	Location	Year of construction
Shuifu 水府廟	on Zhizheng Street	In 1470 county magistrate Wang Zhi moved it to the eastern bank of the river. In 1545 county magistrate Huang Xueju moved it to the river bank outside the North Gate. In 1581 county official Liu Ge remodeled it into a tower.
Nanmu 楠姆廟	left of the Shuifu Temple	Built by county magistrate Huang Xueju, but now collapsed and fallen into the river.
Sanyuan 三元閣	behind the Shuifu Temple	In 1596 built by county magistrate Cao Yan. In 1673 it collapsed into the river.
Wenchang 文昌閣	in the Renhe *yuan*	
Xiawang 夏王廟	in the city of Xinfeng	
Guanyin 觀音閣	in the Huanghan *yuan*	In 1600 built by county resident Liu Mingjian.
Zhongyi 忠義廟	in the Xiangling *yuan;* to its east is the ancestor hall of the Zhou lineage	Built by county resident Zhou Tingbin in 1658.
Zhenwu 真武廟	in the Xiangling *yuan*	Built by county person Zhou Tingbin in 1624.
Daizong 岱宗廟	in the Zhaoling *yuan*	Built by county person Zhu Xiyan in 1628. Remodeled by his grandson Zhu Guozhu in 1691.

SOURCE: *QIANJIANG XIANZHI* (1694), 6: 12–33, IN *ZHONGGUO DIFANGZHI JICHENG*, 46: 101–111.

TABLE 6 Locations of tombs in Qianjiang County before and during the reign of the Kangxi emperor (1660–1722)

Tomb	Location	Note
Tomb of Bi Jian 状元毕渐墓	80 *li* southwest of the county	Song dynasty
Tomb of She Long 都指挥佘隆墓	Lotus Lake	the eighth year of the reign of Hongwu (1375)
Tomb of Chu Gao 参政初杲墓	Cuijia *yuan*	
Tomb of Ouyang Dongfeng 太仆寺少卿欧阳东凤墓	Huanghan *yuan*	
Tomb of Ouyang Dongbai 德庆知州欧阳东白墓	Huanghan *yuan*	
Tomb of Liu Daolong 通政司刘道隆墓	Renhe *yuan*	
Tomb of Hu Lun 御史胡錀墓	Huanghanxia'er *yuan*	

SOURCE: *QIANJIANG XIANZHI* (1694), 8: 7–16, IN *ZHONGGUO DIFANGZHI JICHENG*, 46: 129–134.

Local gazetteers, stone inscriptions, and folk legends passed on for generations through oral transmission demonstrate that nearly every temple had a story behind it. Most of the stories were associated with a myth concerning the inherent danger in water, judging from the examples discussed earlier. Furthermore, as shown in this chapter, the records strongly suggest that deity worship was organized within the scope of a *yuan* and show that almost every *yuan* had its own god or goddess to worship. Because a *yuan* normally consisted of one or more villages, the worship of a certain god or goddess exceeded the scope of a village and promoted cultural cohesion at a supravillage level. The discussion here also indicates that the hydraulic unit, the *yuan*, was seen as a unit of social and cultural activities as early as the Ming dynasty and was further consolidated throughout the Qing.

Table 7 shows the diversity of gods and goddesses worshipped in this region, in an incomplete list of the temples in Qianjiang County for which we can find traces in historical records. It indicates that the local people relied on a vast number of divine powers in the form of objects, animals, gods, or goddesses to protect them from frequent disasters. Compared to other places, where a single water god or goddess dominated the belief system in surrounding communities, on the Jianghan Plain this social phenomenon was an important part of the culture concerning disasters. This culture is pragmatic and spontaneous, from the panic of facing the threat of disasters in general (mostly floods) to small-scale variety in community belief. Each *yuan* had its own main god or goddess whose protection was sought. Temples were constructed and maintained by the people in a particular *yuan*, and the temple worshippers were predominantly residents of a particular *yuan*. This pattern of folk beliefs not only represented the resilience of the people in dealing with the stress of disasters but also, to a large extent, contributed to and aggravated rifts, conflicts, and uprisings in this region. This is further discussed in Chapter 5.

Among the deities worshiped by local people, Guandi is the most noteworthy in the lower Han River region.[63] A *yuan* called Guanhu was in the Jianli-Honghu border area (part of Mianyang Prefecture during the Qing), located in the lower and southern Jianghan Plain. During my fieldwork, this was where I witnessed the Miaohui—the Moon Festival Celebration—in the courtyard beside the Great Buddha (Xiong Fo) Temple (see Figure 7). The main god of the temple is Guandi. In addition to this temple, three small temples are also in Guandi's domain. The people in the Jianli-Honghu border area expect Guandi to prevent floods from affecting their communities. This is evident from the inscription on the Great Buddha Temple:

63 The rainmaking Dragon God did not achieve prominence on the historical Jianghan Plain. There are records on the Dragon God Temple at critical sections of a dike, but few records specify the god's relative importance to Guandi, Guanyin, or the Great Yu. Chris Courtney examines the popular belief in the Dragon God in his analysis of the 1931 Wuhan flood and argues that "for a large proportion of the population, the experience of disaster continued to be influenced by cosmological and moral interpretations of the environment" in early twentieth-century China. See Chris Courtney, "The Dragon King and the 1931 Wuhan Flood: Religious Rumors and Environmental Disasters in Republican China," *Twentieth-Century China* 40, no. 2 (2015): 86. In his study on the popular beliefs on the contemporary Jianghan Plain, Zhang finds that the Dragon God was the third-most-worshiped god after Guandi and the water god (housed at Shuifu Temple) in the Jingzhou area. Zhang, "Water, Dike, and Temple," 123–125.

TABLE 7 Deities and associated temples in Qianjiang County in late Qing

Temple	Yuan	Deities	Legend
Sanxian 三仙廟	Lilin	Three unidentified deities	In 1849 the Xinfeng dike was breached. One deity told people in a dream to build a temple to prevent floods.
Hanqi King 韓蘄王廟	Nanhu	Hanqi King, Han Shizhong, the hero who protected the Han from the Jin attacks during the Southern Song (1089–1151)	Year of construction unknown. No associated legend.
Shi-tai 十台廟	Zhanghu Shang	Unidentified	During the reign of Shunzhi, the Shayang dike was breached; the five nearby counties cooperated in dike construction.
Zushi 祖師殿	Yongfeng	Zushi (Zhenwu Dadi or Zhang Sanfeng)	Year of construction unknown. No associated legend.
Dadian 大殿廟	Yongfeng	Unidentified	Was moved to the Yongfeng *yuan* when a flood occurred during the reign of Qianlong. In 1854, it was destroyed in the riots. In 1855, a member of the gentry, Zheng Renhong, organized the reconstruction.
Mafubo General 馬伏波將軍廟	Huanghan	Mafubo General, with Zhenwu Jun (Wave-Subduing General)[a]	Was built on the Gao dike. The general's name literally means "conquering waves."
Dongyue 東岳廟	Changting	Dongyue god	Year of construction unknown. No associated legend.

TABLE 7 Deities and associated temples in Qianjiang County in late Qing (*cont.*)

Temple	Yuan	Deities	Legend
Liuzhong 流鐘寺	Changsan lower	Bell	A bell turned into land during a flood.
Pudu 普渡廟	Yongfeng	Guanyin	Guanyin saved people from a flood.
Wenchang 文昌閣	Xiwan	Wenchang Jun	In 1859 it was reconstructed. Assumed destroyed during riots.
Hewang 何王廟	Peijia and Zhuhechang	He King	Ming dynasty. No associated legend.

a The worship of the Wave-Subduing General is most common in the Hunan and Hainan area, which can be seen as evidence of migration to the Jianghan region. For more detailed discussion see Donald S. Sutton, "A Case of Literati Piety: The Ma Yuan Cult from High-Tang to High-Qing," *Chinese Literature: Essays, Articles, Reviews* 11 (1989).

SOURCE: THIS TABLE IS MODIFIED FROM LU, "TAI, YUAN, AND DADI"; *QIANJIANG XIANZHI* (1694), 6: 1–34, IN *ZHONGGUO DIFANGZHI JICHENG*, 46: 95–112; *QIANJIANG XIANZHI XU* (1879), 7: 1–9, IN *ZHONGGUO DIFANGZHI JICHENG*, 46: 411–415; *PEISHI ZUPU* 裴氏族谱 [*THE GENEALOGY OF PEI LINEAGE*] (N.D., N.P.), 178–180.

> This place [the Jianli-Honghu area] was a place with good *fengshui*: in the north, there were evergreen plants and clouds with fortunate signs; in the east, three rivers—Hongpai, Neijing, and Hansha—surrounded this place, just like a living dragon embracing a precious token; in the south, flourishing villages and residents were busy with agricultural work, [and were] prosperous and peaceful; in the west, the plum and peach trees blossomed, and the scenes were beautiful. It was all because Guandi protected this place. In the twenty-fourth year of the Jiaqing reign [1820], a member of the local gentry, Chen Weizan 陳維贊, advocated and collected donations from locals to build the Xiong Fo Temple. Since then, the locals worshiped Guandi in this temple regularly, and Guandi's power brought peace and prosperity to this place. The temple was devastated by the great flood of 1954 but was reconstructed in 2004. Thus, it is recorded.[64]

64 Fieldwork observation, September 2007. The inscription hangs on the wall of the Xiong Fo Temple.

For the people of the Jianli-Honghu area, Guandi, then, was a guardian of the surrounding communities when they were threatened by various natural and sociopolitical events. In the flood-prone environment of the Jianghan Plain, Guandi's protective role was largely associated with floods. An essay by an early Qing literatus, Qianjiang Liu Changji 劉昌吉, noted, "People were living good lives because of Guandi's protection. ... It was Guandi's divine power to save Qianjiang people from floods and turn the fish and turtles' domain into crop land. ... Everyone should worship Guandi and appreciate his protective power."[65] In the fifty-third year of the reign of Qianlong (1788), the Yangzi River flooded the city of Jingzhou from the West and North Gates, and the city was inundated with three inches of water. Shen Shitao 沈世燾, a Jingnan official, prayed through his tears in the Guandi temple. That night, a red light started flashing in the temple, eventually flying through the southern gate of the city, at which point the waters in the city suddenly stopped rising.[66]

Duara analyzes the superscription of Guandi myth and emphasizes that various social groups in rural communities interpreted Guandi's role differently to suit their own particular circumstances.[67] He cites Li Jinghan's survey of Ding County, which indicated that the common rural folk worshiped Guan Yu to "seek fortune and avoid disaster"; that merchants worshiped Guan Yu as Caishen, the god of wealth; and that the rootless bandits and rebels in secret societies performed rites and ceremonies before the altars of Guan Yu and the founders of their secret society. Duara asserts that "ordinary villagers prayed to him for all kinds of benefits including rain and those from his healing powers."[68] This possession of a wider identity in the symbolism of a deity was also shared by Tian Hou, or the empress of heaven, in southeastern coastal China and by other widely popular gods in China.[69]

---

65 *Qianjiang xianzhi* (1694), 6: 13–5, in *Zhongguo difangzhi jicheng*, 46: 101–102.

66 Ni, *Jingzhou wancheng dizhi*, 10: 303.

67 Prasenjit Duara, "Superscribing Symbols: The Myth of Guandi, Chinese God of War," *Journal of Asian Studies* 47, no. 4 (1988). Duara argued that the Qing state successfully represented its authority in popular culture through the technique of "superscription," which means promoting desirable values, such as loyalty, through its sponsorship of the cult of Guandi—for example, through granting Guan Yu imperial status (with the title *di*) and through the Confucianization of Guandi. Duara concurred that what local people believed about Guandi did not really affect superscription of symbols from the state.

68 Duara, "Superscribing Symbols," 788.

69 Duara, "Superscribing Symbols," 786. In his 1985 article, James Watson analyzed the multiple interpretations of Tian Hou by various social groups in the southeastern coastal area—fishermen worshiped Tian Hou for protection of fishing on the sea, local gentry worshiped Tian Hou for protection of the community and legitimizing their local power, and women worshiped Tian Hou to have a male offspring. See James L. Watson,

FIGURE 6 The Nanmu Temple in the Zibeiyuan area
PHOTO BY THE AUTHOR IN 2007.

The construction of a temple required funding, and the donations came mostly from well-established lineages and gentry families. In the case of Xiong Fo Temple, the Chen lineage took the lead in organizing the donation drive and the construction of the temple. In addition to the Chen lineage, other families and lineages were also involved in the temple's construction and maintenance. A stone inscription (dated 1820) carved on the wall of the temple courtyard shows that the Wu lineage was also a major organizer of and donor to the temple. A comparison of the 1820 roster and the roster of those involved with temple reconstruction in 2004 indicates that the lineage-partnership has remained stable—the Chen and the Wu lineages have continued to maintain the temples, demonstrating the stability of the social structure and cultural cohesion of this community.

"Standardizing the Gods: The Promotion of T'ien Hou ('Empress of Heaven') along the South China Coast, 960–1960," in *Popular Culture in Late Imperial China*, ed. David Johnson, Andrew J. Nathan, and Evelyn S. Rawski (Berkeley: University of California Press, 1985), 292–324.

FIGURE 7 The Miaohui—the Moon Festival—in the Zibeiyuan area (the border area between Jianli and Honghu)
PHOTO BY THE AUTHOR IN 2007.

4 Conclusion

This chapter examines the amphibious nature of the Jianghan Plain and people's strategies for adaptation to the flood-prone environment. It shows that the *yuan* was the basic mechanism of resilience used by the Jianghan people. With a flexible and productive hydraulic structure, the *yuan* bound the communities through popular beliefs and the construction of temples. In so doing, this chapter goes beyond the dichotomy between culture and nature and argues that, although the Jianghan ecosystems were filled with human hydroagricultural practices and local beliefs that derived from floods and other disastrous events, the community practices and bonding were developed in the context of the local environment. It was hard to separate nature from culture and vice versa. The water regime on the Jianghan Plain was a "cultured nature" with a distinct "natured culture."

First, the *yuan* was a unique structure between land and water. It not only provided sufficient water and supplements to soil in the form of silt for agricultural cultivation, but also offered a convenient space for people to switch between cultivating crops and fishing. Physical boundaries did not define *yuan* communities; rather, the people's common experiences in crises, the social networks they formed for rice cultivation and water management, and the common belief practices and temple-building activities all created mechanisms for maintaining a cohesive *yuan* community.

Second, cultural adaptations to the frequent disasters on the Jianghan Plain fostered diversity, spontaneity, and pragmatism in *yuan* construction as well as in local religious beliefs. The accumulation of social capital was fundamentally important in a society forced to deal with water disasters, from which mutual interests emerged that strengthened the bonds among community members. Each individual *yuan* was inclusive based on shared experience with disasters, shared water resources, and shared gods and goddesses; but each *yuan* was exclusive with respect to other *yuan*, as shown in the records. At the same time, as we show in subsequent chapters, the diversity, flexibility, and pragmatism of the *yuan* formed a highly spontaneous and decentralized system; the dispersed, self-confined *yuan* communities presented great difficulty to a state that wished to intervene in local affairs. Although the Qing state implemented several policies to regulate *yuan* communities, those policies, in general, failed or had serious ecological consequences. At the same time, the *yuan* communities, due to the incorporative efforts by the state, slowly and with great resistance, ceded their regime to the government system and took up the social-control function.

Lastly, some evidence suggests that the *yuan* was a self-contained entity whose members developed distinct identities—they clearly knew to which *yuan* they belonged. In the late Qing, many people indicated their native place as a *yuan*.[70] In this respect, the *yuan* substituted for the village or other administrative unit and played a more significant role in defining people's locality.

70 *Qianjiang xianzhi xu* (1879), 19: 1–90, in *Zhongguo difangzhi jicheng* 46: 555–600.

CHAPTER 2

Disordering Nature

Wetlands and Empire Reconstruction (1600s–Early 1700s)

As discussed in Chapter 1, the unique topological, geographic, and climatic conditions in the Jianghan Plain shaped community residential patterns, hydroagricultural practices, and resilience mechanisms. The "amphibious nature" of the plain and the influence from how its disaster-prone environment shaped cultural practices in the communities were also considered. This chapter, tracing the early history of *yuan* construction on the plain and the dynamism of local management of dikes of the same period, argues that the hydrogeomophological conditions of the plain made it a governing frontier and a hydraulic periphery. By "hydraulic periphery," I mean that the early Qing empire applied its laissez-faire strategy to the Jianghan area: the early Qing rulers stimulated agricultural reconstruction in the region by intermediating community self-governance. The materiality of the plain played an active role in state governance and community management.

1 The Early History of the Wetlands in the Jianghan Plain

As early as the Song period (ca. twelfth century), the Jianghan Plain was largely uncultivated, with its "nonhumanness" noted by various contemporary poet-travelers. The famous poet Su Shi 蘇軾 (1037–1101), along with his father and brother, once traveled by boat through the Three Gorges to Jingzhou and then took the road northward to the capital. On his way north, Su Shi commented about the vast wetlands and withering agricultural cultivation on the Jianghan Plain:[1]

> How vast the Chu land is, endless with thousands of acres;
> Cattle never sweat, seeds never harvest;
> Who would persuade people to cultivate? People are all miserable;
> No work in normal years, not to mention times of disaster.

1 Su Dongpo, *Jingzhou shishou* 荊州十首 [*Ten Poems on Jingzhou*] (ca. 1060).

© KONINKLIJKE BRILL NV, LEIDEN, 2022 | DOI:10.1163/9789004505285_004

In the sixth year of the reign of Qiandao (1170), when the poet Lu You 陸游 (1125–1210) passed by the Jianghan Plain on his way to Sichuan, he witnessed the wildness of the land:

> On the first day of the ninth month of the year, I took the boat entering the Jianghan Plain. There were no people living in the plain, only reeds standing along the riverbanks, I called it the "one-hundred-*li* wildland." ... On the second day, I started to see about twenty families, all fishing in the lakes. ... On the third day, I saw some agricultural households, only a dozen of them, growing mulberry and willow trees. On the fourth day, I was told by a boatman that here there were only wetlands, and that tigers and wolves were everywhere, and if the boat people traveled before dawn, they would be attacked by them.[2]

Seven years later, another poet, Fan Chengda 範成大 (1126–1193), sailed downstream along the Yangzi River. When he arrived in Shishou County on the Jianghan Plain, he wrote,

> The Han River was really small, only a bit wider than a canal. ... Reeds were growing everywhere along the riverbank. ... Occasionally we saw families. ... The wetlands were indeed a "land of hidden bandits." ... When I passed through the so-called "one-hundred-*li* wildland," no traces of people were seen [and there was nothing] except for the water and reeds.[3]

In their poems, the poet-travelers emphasized the "nonhumanness," "unknowingness," and thus "wildness" of the Jianghan wetlands.

Eventually, however, the state intervened, initiating large land reclamation projects in the mid-Yangzi region to bolster its military endeavors. The origin of the practice of using *yuan* might be traceable to the Southern Song use of *tuntian,* the military colony system that accelerated land reclamation and increased agricultural production in the plain.[4] When the Mongols launched major attacks against the Southern Song (1127–1279), the Song government appointed General Meng Gong 孟珙 to establish the defense line in the mid-Yangzi region. Meng realized that the solidarity of the defense line depended not only on natural barriers such as the Yangzi River but also on a

2 Lu You, *Rushu ji* 入蜀記 [*Traveling to Shu*] (1170).

3 *Mianyang zhouzhi* (1530), 12: 5, in *Zhongguo fangzhi congshu,* 338: 265; Fan Chengda, *Wu chuan lu* 吳船录 [*A Record of Wuchuan*] (1177).

4 Shi and Zhang, "Jianghan pingyuan de yuantian xingqiyu heshi."

strong economic base to support the army.[5] With that in mind, he proposed the *tuntian*.

The *tuntian* originated in the Western Han dynasty (202 BCE–8 CE) and was widespread in the Three Kingdoms period (220–280) for providing military supplies. There were two types of *tun*: a military *tun* and a civilian *tun*. In a military *tun*, sixty soldiers formed a battalion unit, engaging in both combat and agricultural cultivation. In a civilian *tun*, fifty people formed a *tun*, equipped with state-sponsored agricultural equipment and draft animals, and each *tun* submitted a large proportion of agricultural products to the state. In wartime, the *tuntian* system was very effective in mobilizing civilians and soldiers to produce food and material supplies. To a large extent, the state impetus was necessary for economic construction at a regional level. In an area such as the Jianghan Plain—covered by extensive wetlands, ridden with disease, and constantly struck by natural disaster—without state sponsorship, large-scale agricultural production and hydraulic construction were almost impossible. In this sense, the Southern Song government played a positive role in opening the plain and gave a jump start to the transformation of the entire plain into a major agricultural region. In 1228, Meng Gong built a reservoir in northern Hubei that could irrigate 100,000 *qing* of land and produce 150,000 *shi* of grain. In 1239, Meng built several other embankments, allocated seeds and equipment to local households, and encouraged them to engage in agricultural production. The result of this massive *tuntian* project was the cultivation of 188,280 *qing* of land and the formation of over twenty *tun*.[6]

Meng's *tuntian* program was largely carried out in the Jingnan area, including the present-day Jiangling, Shishou, and Jianli, in the main part of the plain. This region had numerous rivers, lakes, floodplains, and wetlands that mostly remained uncultivated into the twelfth century. Its extensive river-lake system and its monsoon weather put it under threat of annual floods. Therefore, the best way of developing *tuntian* was to build dikes and reclaim the land from those waterlogged areas. *Tuntian* started with blocking several big outlets between lakes and the Yangzi River so that people could cultivate the land in the lowland plain with effective flood control and sufficient irrigation.

Tuntian were used at the preliminary stage of the proliferation of *yuan* in this region. After the Mongols ceased their attacks in the late thirteenth century, the public land of the military-agricultural colonies was gradually absorbed into the system of private land ownership. As Albert Feuerwerker

5 Shi and Zhang, "Jianghan pingyuan de yuantian xingqiyu heshi."

6 Will, "State Intervention," 301–302.

points out, public land turned largely private by the sixteenth century, "either through leases to civilian farmers or the transformation of military families into full-time farmers with permanent ownership rights in the land."[7] The construction of *yuan* soon turned into a civilian endeavor mainly undertaken by local people for their private gain. As discussed in Chapter 1, it was an optimal hydraulic structure for crop cultivation and the best strategy for the Jianghan peasants to develop agriculture in an area subject to flooding and drainage problems. When masses of people migrated to the Jianghan Plain in the early Ming (ca. fifteenth century), either being sponsored by the early Ming government or on their own initiative, *yuan* construction gained momentum from the extensive labor input, and they spread on a wide scale.

2 Crisis and Restoration

The Jianghan Plain became an integrated part of the empire's economy during the Ming period. However, wars and plagues during the Ming-Qing transition devastated the regional economy as well as the plain's infrastructure. The combination of warfare, natural disaster, and epidemics in the area was incredibly destructive.

Climate change might have contributed to the crisis during the Ming-Qing transition. An era of extreme cold in the seventeenth century, generally called the Little Ice Age, was during a prolonged period from at least the 1500s to the 1700s. The climatologist Zhu Kezhen 竺可楨 examined China's climatic cycle over the course of history and determined that the coldest era in Chinese history was the seventeenth century, followed by the nineteenth century. He points out several signs of the Little Ice Age (especially from 1650 to 1700) in the mid-Yangzi region—for example, Lake Tai, the Han River, and the Huai River froze four times, and Dongting Lake froze twice within this fifty-year period.[8] Zhu also showed some evidence that dates the emergence of the Little Ice Age to half a century earlier. For instance, Xu Xiake 徐霞客, a renowned Chinese geographer and traveler, experienced abnormally cold weather in 1616 during the

7 Albert Feuerwerker, "The State and the Economy in Late Imperial China," *Theory and Society* 13, no. 3 (1984). Pierre-Etienne Will's explanation of the demilitarization process of *tuntian* in the Jianghan Plain suggests that the *tuntian* area was encroached on by powerful local landlords who strived to protect their agricultural fields. Will, "State Intervention," 302.

8 Zhu Kezhen, "Zhongguo jin wuqiannian lai qihou bianqian de chubu yanjiu 中國近五千年來氣候變遷的初步研究 [Preliminary Study of the Changes in China's Climate in the Past 5,000 Years]," *Kaogu xuebao* 1(1972), 30.

reign of Wanli (1573–1620).[9] Yuan Xiaoxiu 袁小修, who lived in Shashi, Hubei, from 1608 to 1617, wrote diaries describing the local environment of his time. Based on Yuan's descriptions and contemporary climatic data, Zhu Kezhen concluded that the ripening of peaches, plums, cloves, and begonias occurred seven to ten days later in the Ming than in the 1970s.[10] The historian Young-tsu Wong 汪榮祖 concurred that in the early seventeenth century, peaches, plums, and *Osmanthus* ripened one to two weeks later than normal and that the average temperature was 1.5–2.0°C (34.7–35.6°F) lower than in preceding years.[11] In 1618, even subtropical areas such as Guangdong had a snowstorm that lasted for six to eight days.[12] The cold period lasted well into the second half of the seventeenth century, the early Qing period. The extremely cold weather inevitably affected agricultural production, which led to a widespread famine in the mid- seventeenth century. According to Geoffrey Parker, many prefectures and counties in the late Ming had a population loss of as much as 60 percent.[13]

Although historians generally agree that the Little Ice Age occurred around the 1600s, initiating an era that was rife with natural disasters, epidemics, and warfare, the accompanying severe population decline, plummeting agricultural production, and wide-ranging ecological collapse reduced the population pressure on the land and, as evidence suggests, enabled vegetation to regenerate by the early Qing. Scientists have detected a range of changes in geologic deposits worldwide that show the regeneration of vegetation beginning around 1600.[14] The resurgence of interactions between tigers and people

---

9 Xu Xiake, *Xu Xiake youji* 徐霞客遊記 [*The Travelogue of Xu Xiake*] (Taipei: Shijie shuju, 1999), 1: 12–16.

10 Zhu, "Zhongguo jin wuqiannian," 30–31. Zhu discussed climate change during the seventeenth century based on two records: one is *Yuan xiaoxiu riji* 袁小修日記, diaries written by Yuan when he lived in Shashi, Hubei, in 1608–1617 (from the 36th to the 45th year of the Wanli reign); the other is *Bei you lu* 北遊录 by Tan Qian 談遷, narrating his travel experiences in Beijing in 1653–1655.

11 Young-tsu Wong, "'Tiandi zhidao': Mingqing diguo shengtai weiji zongshuo 天地之盜：明清帝國生態危機綜說 ['Rob the Wealth of the Earth': The Ecological Crisis in Ming-Qing Empire]," *Zhongguo wenhua yanjiusuo xuebao*, no. 51 (2010): 104. https://www.cuhk.edu.hk/ics/journal/articles/v51p087.pdf.

12 Dongguanshi difangzhi bianzhuan weiyuanhui. ed., *Dongguan shizhi* 東莞市志 [*Gazetteer of Dongguan*] (Guangzhou: Guangdong renmin chubanshe, 1995), 9, cited in Wang, "'Tiandi zhidao.'"

13 Geoffrey Parker, "Crisis and Catastrophe: The Global Crisis of the Seventeenth Century Reconsidered," *American Historical Review* 113, no. 4 (2008): 1059.

14 Simon L. Lewis and Mark A. Maslin, "Defining the Anthropocene," *Nature* 519 (2015): 177. They discusses signs including the "charcoal reductions in deposits in the Americas and globally, decreases in atmospheric methane, enrichment of methane beta 13 C, and decreases in carbon monoxide in Antarctic ice cores; pollen in lacustrine sediments

on the Jianghan Plain might also suggest that the forests had regenerated in the region. From the late 1500s to the 1600s, local gazetteers recorded such tiger-contact incidents on the Jianghan Plain.[15] Considering that tigers require a large forest—between 20 and 100 square kilometers of forested habitat for a single adult tiger—to sustain itself, accounts of tigers' presence show that the forests had recovered enough for stabilization of the natural habitats for wildlife in the early Qing period.[16] Sounding a cautionary note, however, Wong argues that these tiger encounters were likely an indication of forestry exhaustion, rather than forestry abundance; because of the lack of natural habitat, tigers were frequently reported to roam through the towns and villages, harming people and animals.[17] Maybe in the late Ming and early Qing both versions were true: despite the level of regeneration in forests, it was still insufficient to sustain the tigers' natural habitat.[18]

3 Migration and Opening the Plain

Migrants went to the Jianghan Plain at the end of the Yuan and early Ming dynasties due to war, social unrest, and the state's interprovincial migration program. Because of extensive warfare between the Mongols and the *tuntian* soldier-peasants in central China, agricultural production on the Jianghan Plain was severely reduced: war had left a vast, deserted land with only a few people to cultivate it. In 1379, after the war had ended, the Wuling County

---

showing vegetation regeneration; ... changing beta 18 O derived from speleothems from caves in China and Peru and other studies noting changes coincident with 1600 and the coolest part of the Little Ice Age (1594–1677), a relatively synchronous global event noted in geologic deposits worldwide."

15 *Wuchang fuzhi* 武昌府志 [*Gazetteer of Wuchang Prefecture*] (1687), 3: 4, 3: 6, 3: 9, 3: 12; *Jingzhou fuzhi* (1757), 36: 2, 54: 16, 54: 17; *Wuchang xianzhi* 武昌縣志 [*Gazetteer of Wuchang County*] (1763), 1: 26, 1: 32; *Yunxi xianzhi* 鄖西縣志 [*Gazetteer of Yunxi County*] (1777), 1: 6.

16 Robert Marks studies the relationship among humans, tigers and forest coverage in late imperial Lingnan area, and he points out that the tiger attacks were highly correlated with the destruction of forest coverage, tigers' natural habitat. Robert Marks, *Tigers, Rice, Silk, and Silt: Environment and Economy in Late Imperial South China* (Cambridge: Cambridge University Press, 2004), 323–327. Mark Elvin also discusses in his book one case in which tigers attacked humans in Nanshi (present-day Enshi in Hubei) in late nineteenth century. Elvin, *The Retreat of the Elephants*, 34.

17 Wong, " 'Tiandi zhidao.' "

18 Marks wrote in his analysis of tiger habitat in Lingnan: "The record of tiger attacks in Lingnan, then, indicated not merely the destruction of tiger habitat, but also the existence of a forest reservoir from which more tigers emerged." Marks, *Tigers, Rice, Silk, and Silt*, 325.

government proposed a reconstruction plan to the Ming government that would relocate landless peasants from Jiangxi Province to Hubei, which had available lands. The Ming government immediately approved the proposal and initiated a prolonged wave of migration to the Jianghan Plain.[19]

In addition to the government-initiated migration, people also migrated on their own from outside the Jianghan Plain; the sparsely populated area, the naturally well-fertilized soil, and the loose government control were attractive to the migrants who risked going to a new environment. Most of the residents on the Jianghan Plain migrated from Jiangxi (also known as Jiang You 江右, literally, "to the right of the Yangzi River"). Much research has been done on the migration and demographic structure in this region, summed up in the expression *Jiangxi tian Huguang* (Jiangxi immigrants fill up the Huguang area). The historian Zhang Guoxiong examined 472 genealogies of the Hunan-Hubei area and found that 404 of the 530 lineages that had clear records were from Jiangxi Province.[20] In the genealogies I collected during my fieldwork, the prominent lineages, such as those of the Xiao and the Kuang families, migrated from Jiangxi to the Jianghan Plain during the Ming.[21] However, although most of the residents on the Jianghan Plain were migrants from Jiangxi, the demographic structure was not homogeneous. Some lineages were from other places, and the migrants from Jiangxi also had lineage divisions, all of which added to the social mosaic in the plain.

The large number of migrants—most of them war or economic refugees—to the Jianghan Plain made it a magnet for tax evaders, mainly because the early Ming government lacked an effective way of levying taxes on broad swaths of deserted and usually unmeasured land. The only comprehensive Ming-era land survey was completed during the reign of Wanli. Before this land survey, officials had been using outdated land records from hundreds of years earlier by the Song government (960–1279). A gazetteer compiler during the reign of Jiajing noted that large areas of land in Mianyang County were not recorded in the land registry, so the taxes paid on that land were very limited. And the migrants took advantage of it, cultivating land without paying any

19 "Preface" to *Sunshi zupu* 孫氏族譜 [*Genealogy of the Sun Lineage*]; "Preface" to *Hushi zongpu* 胡氏宗譜 [*Genealogy of the Hu Lineage*] (Tongzhi), Thanks to Dr. Lu Xiqi, who granted me the two genealogies.

20 Zhang Guoxiong, *Mingqing shiqi de lianghu yimin* 明清時期的兩湖移民 [*The Hunan-Hubei Immigration in Ming and Qing Times*] (Xi'an: Shanxi renmin jiaoyu chubanshe, 1995), 35, 257–286.

21 *Kuangshi tanyuan*; *Xiaoshi zupu* 蕭氏族譜 [*Genealogy of the Xiao Lineage*], from my field research.

tax.[22] After the Wanli land survey, many areas that were officially registered were left uncultivated because of the high casualties and subsequent flight of cultivators during the war in the mid-1600s, which created problems related to tax revenue in the early Qing.

The tension between those called "host" people (*tuhu* 土户) and those identified as "guest" people (*kemin* 客民) shows the complexity that migration added to land cultivation, dike management, and taxation in this region. The criterion used for designating a household as being composed of host or guest people was not the length of time that they had resided in the region but, rather, whether they were part of the *lijia* 里甲 system, the official taxation system throughout most of the Ming and Qing periods, for taxation purposes.[23] The tension between these host and guest people escalated as their economic interests collided. The earlier migrants often had the upper hand in power relations with the newcomers, but the newcomers were hardworking and shrewd; over time, the newcomers who accumulated wealth gradually gained advantages over their predecessors, the so-called host people. The Qing official Yan Ruyi 嚴如熤 (1759–1826) wrote about the landscape and the people in this region, noting, "Since the host people were few and arable lands were vast, the host people normally rent out their land to guest people ... and guest people sometimes hire other migrants to cultivate their land."[24] Because the guest people were mostly not on the tax registry, they easily evaded taxes and gained a higher net return on their cultivation. Records in the late Ming show new migrants and host people building circular dikes (rudimentary forms of the *yuan* dikes) to compete for available arable land. In many cases, the dikes built by the migrants, called guest dikes (*kedi* 客堤), exceeded those built by host people, called master dikes (*zhudi* 主堤), and the migrants were able to take control over the original residents' land.[25] Unable to compete with the

22 For example, in Mianyang Prefecture, wetland fields were not officially cataloged for taxation, so the taxes on registered land were meager, and the migrants took advantage of it. *Mianyang zhouzhi* (1530), 8: 5, in *Zhongguo fangzhi congshu*, 338: 190–191.

23 Yang Guo'an, *Mingqing lianghu diqu jiceng zuzhi yu xiangcun shehui yajiu* 明清兩湖地區基層組織與鄉村社會研究 [*The Local Social Structure and Rural Society of Hunan-Hubei Region during the Ming and Qing Periods*] (Wuhan: Wuhan daxue chubanshe, 2004), 113. The Ming government established the *lijia* system in the late fourteenth century for taxation and social control. Ten households constituted a *jia*; ten adjacent *jia* were combined into a *li*. Each *jia* had a "*jia* head" (*jiashou*), and each *li* had a "*li* head" (*lizhang*), and they were responsible for collecting and delivering taxes.

24 Yan Ruyi, *Sansheng bianfang beilan* 三省邊防備覽 [*A Survey of the Border Defenses of Three Provinces*] (1840), 11: 41–42.

25 *Mianyang zhouzhi* (1530), 8: 2, in *Zhongguo fangzhi congshu*, 338: 184–185.

new migrants, the host people often fell into poverty; in contrast, the guest people's lives improved.[26] The host-guest conflicts added further tension to the local resource management in this region.

4 Fluidity of the Jianghan Lifestyle

The Jianghan Plain had been part of the vast ancient Yunmeng Wetland, and much of this area "would have been swampy and inhospitable," with frequent floods.[27] However, in the process of settling into the Jianghan Plain, the migrants found the wetland environment an ideal place for survival. Because of the fluid nature of wetlands, people on the plain developed fluid ways of living, often shifting between land and water. In essence, it was an amphibious lifestyle that was not only a manifestation of local resilience in response to disaster but also a convenient way to avoid state interference. This lifestyle was especially salient in the period before the eighteenth century, when the population pressure stimulated massive land reclamation in the plain and when there were still plenty of bodies of water available for people to switch between agricultural cultivation and fishing.

The main method of land reclamation on the plain was draining the wetlands by building a series of long and circular dikes. However, because of the seasonal floods and the poor drainage of the plain, people lived a semi-farming and semi-fishing life. For example, in Hanchuan County, people cultivated crops in the spring and summer and switched to fishing in the fall and winter. In the spring, when the water rose, people moved to their original lands, which they would cultivate; and in the fall and winter, when the water receded, they moved closer to the lakes to fish.[28] This shows the complementary nature of agriculture and fishing in the Jianghan Plain. When floods struck the region, many agricultural households switched to fishing as their source of income, to compensate for their losses in property and agricultural production.

26 *Mianyang zhouzhi* (1530), 8: 2.

27 The Yunmeng Wetland was probably the largest in the second millennium BCE and remained a large swampland through the Han Dynasty (206 BCE–220 CE). Most of the wetland has now been turned into agricultural land. For more discussion on the Yunmeng Wetland in prehistory and the early historic periods, see Rowan K. Flad and Pochan Chen, *Ancient Central China: Case Studies in Early Societies* (Cambridge: Cambridge University Press, 2013), 27–30.

28 *Hanchuan xianzhi* 漢川縣志 [*The Gazetteer of Hanchuan County*] (1873), 6: 14, in *Zhongguo difangzhi jicheng*, 9: 174.

Jiaopai 茭簰 (see Figure 8), a floating house, was a creative way of living in wetlands and the best manifestation of the amphibious lifestyle of the Jianghan people. Because of the frequent floods and the excessive water retention on the plain, the houses there were either continually destroyed by floods or submerged for as long as three or four years. By building a *jiaopai*, essentially a houseboat, people's living spaces were no longer attached to the ground. After first tying lengths of bamboo together, they built a type of wattle-and-daub shelter of reeds and clay on bamboo rafts. The size of the bamboo boat could be easily adjusted by adding or eliminating bamboo sticks. People could move freely on the waters by boat, harvesting aquatic plants or fishing; when not in use, a *jiaopai* could be tied to a rock or a tree, so that it would not float away. The size of the boat was so adjustable that people could build shelters to engage in all sorts of family activities, including planting vegetables, raising pigs and chickens, opening a small school, celebrating weddings, and performing rituals to bury the dead. When the floodwaters receded, the boat people returned to their original houses to resume their crop cultivation.[29] But they identified as peasants more than fisher folk, so they returned to land when it was not inundated, though the seasonal flooding often drove them back to the water, especially when their plots of land remained underwater for years.

In addition to fish, aquatic resources such as reeds and water chestnuts became possible food sources during floods. Shen Menglan, an eighteenth-century provincial scholar, commented that people in Mianyang County made a living by harvesting aquatic products and they happily lived in their marshland.[30] Zhang Jiayan, examining the agricultural crops on the Jianghan Plain, concludes that the peasant economy there was driven by the environment, rather than the market.[31] His argument can best be understood in relation to the conditions before the eighteenth century, when Jianghan people's agricultural choices were much more limited by their living environment.

The early, agrarian Qing did not take a positive view of wetlands (often referred to as *shui ye*, literally, "water wilderness") or fisher folk, who were called *jianmin* 賤民 (literally, "debased people"), indicating that they had lower social status than agrarian households. This status was hereditary until the early eighteenth century, when the Yongzheng emperor abolished it. As Xu Bin points out, people looked at fisher folk in two ways: first, in terms of a romantic image of the fisher folk as hermits, and, second, based on the traditional

29 *Hanchuan xianzhi* (1873), 6: 15, in *Zhongguo difangzhi jicheng*, 9: 174.

30 Shen, *Wusheng gouxu shuidao tushuo*, 62–63.

31 Zhang, "Environment, Market, and Peasant Choice."

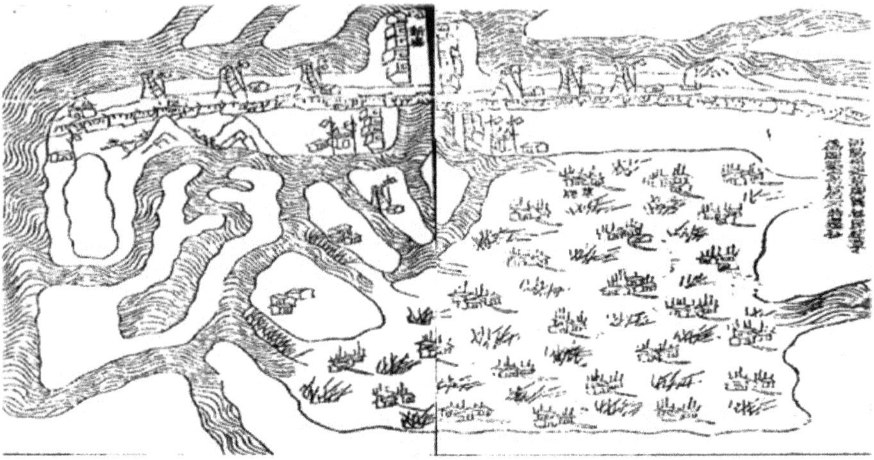

FIGURE 8 Jiaopai 茭簰 in Mianyang Prefecture in the eighteenth century
SOURCE: *HUBEI ANXIANG YUNDAO SHUILI JI'AN* 湖北安襄鄖道水利集案 [*LEADING CASES OF ANXIANGYUN DAO IN HUBEI*], COMPILED BY WANG GAI AND ZHANG ZHIYUN, 10B–11A, IN *ZHONGHUA SHANSHUI ZHI CONGKAN* 中華山水志叢刊 [*A COLLECTION OF GAZETTEERS OF MOUNTAINS AND WATERS OF CHINA*], ED. SHI GUANGMING, DONG GUANGHE AND YANG GUANGHUI (BEIJING: XIANZHUANG SHUJU, 2004), 17: 473–474.

Confucian criticism that fishing was an un-Confucian way of life, because women were heavily involved in both catching and selling fish in the market.[32]

In the early Ming, the state's taxation system, the *lijia* system, mainly covered reclaimed agricultural fields, as those *yuan* fields were an important source of tax revenue. But the two groups of people who reclaimed the lands in the Jianghan Plain—migrants and fisher folk—were mostly excluded from the system.[33] Therefore, they were not registered or taxed in the *lijia* system. Most of the fisher folk were in another system, the *yejia* 業甲 system, which was administered by the river bureaus (*he bo suo* 河泊所).[34] Fishing was an undesirable way of life because of its social denigration in comparison to farming;

32 Xu Bin, "Yishui wei benwei: Dui 'tudi shiguan' de fansi yu 'xin shuiyu shi' de tichu 以水為本位：對 "土地史觀" 的反思與 "新水域史" 的提出 [Rethinking Land and Water: A New Water History]," *Wuhan daxue xuebao* 1 (2017): 124.

33 Lu, *Changjiang zhongyou de rendi guanxi*, 239.

34 Separate from the *lijia* system, the regular taxation system that included households based on land, the *yejia* system organized the fishing households into *jia* for fishing taxes. "*Ye*" means occupation. One record shows that eight fishing households that fished in the same lake area were organized into one *jia*. People in the same *jia* were entitled to access the lake for fishing, harvesting aquatic plants, and sharing in fishing taxes. *Huanggang*

however, it offered a flexible way of life that compensated for losses from flooding. During flood season, people could switch from farming to fishing to make a living, and the government could still collect taxes from fishing in the lake. The amphibious lifestyle worked not only for people, but for the government which was eager to increase the tax revenue.

In a way, the government adopted a conservative policy, supervising the dikes as they existed so as to control floods and increase revenue at the same time. As mentioned earlier, *yuan* residents grew crops when waters were low and switched to fishing when waters were high. A *yuan* with a low dike worked well enough to sustain people's livelihoods. Therefore, the government forbade increasing the height of *yuan* dikes so that people could still rely on the traditional, cyclical alternation between farming and fishing to survive.

In addition to regulation of the height of the dikes, returning lands to lakes was another practice that helped achieve the dual goals of controlling floods and increasing revenue. A case in point is Diaocha Lake in Hanchuan County. Local peasants continually reclaimed Diaocha Lake for profit, turning the lake into a *yuan*. However, the Diaocha *yuan* was in a lowland area and was subject to serious drainage problems. During the Qianlong period, this *yuan* flooded three times. The cost of dike repairs and disaster relief exceeded 10,000 taels of silver, but the taxes collected from the *yuan* totaled only 1,200 taels and 80 *shi* of grain (approx. 12,000 kilograms). The financial burden of the *yuan* exceeded the taxes it generated, so officials decided to convert the *yuan* back into a lake.[35]

When the immense land reclamation encroached on large bodies of water, the strategy of switching between fishing and farming thus became impractical. Many fishing communities had to give up fishing and engage in farming. One example is the Liu lineage. The Liu family migrated to the Jianghan Plain in the late fourteenth century and settled on the Baigong Lake of Mianyang County. For generations, they lived on the lake by fishing and harvesting aquatic plants. The Baigong Lake was connected to the Yangzi and Han Rivers,

liushi zongpu 黄岡劉氏宗譜 [*Genealogy of Liu Family*] (1946), in Lu, *Changjing zhongyou de rendi guanxi*, 233.

35 Ma Huiyu, "Hutian zhanshui shu 湖田占水疏 [Opinions on Reclaimed Lands in Lakes Blocking Water]," in He Changling (ed.), *Huangchao jingshi wenbian* 皇朝經世文編 [*Collected Essays about Statecraft of the Qing*] 117, "Gongzheng"23, "Gesheng shuili" 4. 117 is the volume number, "Gongzheng" 23 is the title and number of the section, "Gesheng shuili" 4 is the title and number of the subsection. All citations from the series of *Huangchao jingshi wenbian* follow this format. All references to *Huangchao jingshi wenbian* come from Taiwan Academia Sinica online database 台灣漢籍電子文獻資料庫: https://hanji.sinica.edu.tw/.

thus loads of soil and sand from the rivers entered and stayed in the lake each year. The lake was gradually silted up and the shrinking lake surface could not sustain profitable fishing any longer. The Liu family, which had grown rich by the early sixteenth century, decided to reclaim the silted lake land and turned it to *yuan* for agricultural cultivation.[36] Yin Lingling compared tax collection between the Ming and Qing periods, finding that nearly 40 percent of the tax revenue in the Huguang region came from fishing (*yu ke* 魚課), the highest among all provinces, during the reign of Wanli in the Ming dynasty.[37] However, the bodies of water of the region diminished so much that fishing-related tax revenue decreased to around 20 percent in the last quarter of the nineteenth century, due not just to the smaller bodies of water but to the shrinking fish population elsewhere.[38] The agricultural settlement of the Qing state will be further discussed in the next chapter.

5 Complexities in Administration

In the eyes of most Ming-Qing state officials and scholars, this region was flood prone, poor, and peripheral. Wu Liangsi 吳亮嗣, a Ming scholar, describes the general conditions in the Chu region (roughly including Hunan and Hubei): "The Chu land was vast and fertile, but seven-tenths of the lands were wetlands. People were not business oriented—they only cultivated crops with no other profitable ventures. Therefore, most of the people had no savings and were vulnerable to disasters and hunger. It had been like this from early history on."[39] Wu probably did not have much experience living in the wetlands, but he was right in that the region had an unpredictable and flood prone environment. In the gazetteers of various counties, the Hanchuan people were

36 *Liushi zongpu* 劉氏宗譜 [*The Genealogy of the Liu Lineage*] (1948), vol. 64. The entire source is quoted by Yin Lingling in her book, *Mingqing lianghu pingyuan de huanjing bianqian yu shehui yingdui* 明清兩湖平原的環境變遷與社會應對 [*The Environmental Transformation and Social Response in the Hunan-Hubei Plain during the Ming and Qing Dynasties*] (Shanghai: Shanghai renmin chubanshe, 2008), 59–60. For more discussion on the case, see Xu Bin, "Mingqing shiqi lianghu diqu yuye shengchan yu guanli 明清時期兩湖地區漁業生產與管理 [The Fishery Production and Management of the Hunan-Hubei Region during the Ming and Qing Periods]" (MA thesis, Wuhan University, 2003), 50. Xu's thesis was later published as a book, *Zhidu, jingji yu shehui: Mingqing lianghu yuye, yumin yu shuiyu shehui* 制度、經濟與社會：明清兩湖漁業、漁民與水域社會 [*Institutions, Economy and Society: Fishery, Fishing Folks and Society in Ming and Qing Dynasties*] (Beijing: Kexue chubanshe, 2018).

37 Yin, *Mingqing lianghu pingyuan*, 35.

38 Yin, *Mingqing lianghu pingyuan*, 39–40, 51, 142–144.

39 Wu Liangsi, "Lun jingchu shuizai shu 論荊楚水災疏 [A Discussion on the Floods in the Jingchu Area]," in *Huangzhou fuzhi* (1884), 36: 32–33, in *Zhongguo difangzhi jicheng*, 15: 467. Wu Liangsi was a *jinshi* during the reign of Wanli.

described as "shrewd, precarious, and fierce," and the Macheng people were described as "cunning, pugnacious, and tough." Only a few counties, such as Qianjiang, Jianglin, and Jianli, were noted by the gazetteer compilers as "frugal, simple, and pure."

This perception by the state officials lasted from the Ming to the early Qing and was reflected in the categorization of the difficulty level of county management. To better manage the counties, the Yongzheng emperor (r. 1722–1735) divided counties into four categories based on their management: *chong* 冲 (strategic), *fan* 繁 (onerous), *pi* 疲 (tiresome), and *nan* 难 (difficult). *Chong* means "strategic in transportation"; *fan* means "excessive petty administration"; *pi* means "ineffectiveness in levying taxes"; and *nan* means "high frequency of crime." Counties could be labeled with one or more of these terms, and many of the county administrations on the Jianghan Plain were branded as *pi* and *nan*. For example, Jiangxi County in Wuchang Prefecture was considered "extremely *chong fan pi nan*";[40] Puqi County, in the same prefecture, was called *chong fan*;[41] and Hanyang County was branded as *chong fan pi*.[42] Normally, an official post in places called *pi nan* had midlevel importance but managing it entailed considerable difficulty. The court's perception of this region, and its categorization method, certainly contributed to the hands-off governing strategy of the early Qing government.

The hydrogeomorphological conditions of the Jianghan region added to the complexity and difficulty of managing local water resources—a better way of governing the region was to let the locals govern themselves. Normally, success at water control was an important criterion in the evaluation of local officials, but one of Yongzheng's rescripts noted that it was very hard to evaluate the accomplishment of local officials, especially in areas with constant flooding and drainage problems, such as the Jianghan Plain.[43] The court's labels for county administration, which branded many counties in the mid-Yangzi region as *fan* and *nan*. The complexity of water control undoubtedly contributed to the Yongzheng emperor's categorization. Obviously, a region like this could not compete with the wealth of the Jiangnan region or with the great political significance of the north and northeast regions. To intervene directly from the

---

40 Zhang Zhi, ed., *Huayi fengtu zhi* 華夷風土志 [*A History of Customs in China*] (Yangzhou: Guangling shushe, 2003), 331.

41 Zhang, *Huayi fengtu zhi*, 332.

42 Zhang, *Huayi fengtu zhi*, 335.

43 *Daqing shizong xian (Yongzheng) huangdi shilu* 大清世宗憲（雍正）皇帝實錄 [*A Veritable Record of the Yongzheng Emperor*] (Taipei: Hualian chubanshe, 1964), 54: 1727. It is shortened as *Qing shizong shilu* in the following text.

top down in this region would require substantial resources and effort. When the early Qing state set up the statewide control system, environmental factors certainly weighed in the rulers' decision making.

Disease played a large role in the early Qing state's approach to the Jianghan Plain. The area had large wetlands, rivers, and lakes and was humid and rainy in the summer; this made it an ideal place for disease to thrive. Common diseases in the area included schistosomiasis, malaria, dengue fever, influenza, and plague. The pastoral people of the steppe, who lived by hunting and gathering, were generally healthier and had less exposure to diseases that were common in sedentary agrarian societies, with their subsequent crowding.[44] The Manchus and Mongols had not developed immunity to many of those diseases and thus were vulnerable to infection. Not surprisingly, they were reluctant to travel far into the North China Plain. The effects of these diseases were even seen in the imperial court: the Kangxi emperor was chosen as the successor in part because as a child he had survived smallpox and had developed immunity to it, unlike his father, the Shunzhi emperor (r. 1644–1661), who had died of it. Manchus' interactions with Han people employed many methods to prevent infection with smallpox. For instance, many Manchu officials who had not been exposed to the disease were excused from posts in Han-populated areas.[45] Manchus adopted the Chinese practice of inoculation against smallpox at the end of the seventeenth century, but it remained a privilege of the royal family, and, even at the end of the eighteenth century, those outside that circle were still largely vulnerable to the disease.[46] It was not difficult to sense Manchus' fear of penetrating the densely populated Han areas in the early eighteenth century. When Dr. John Dudgeon went to Beijing in 1869–1871 and witnessed smallpox epidemics in 1869–1870 and 1870–1871, he wrote in his report on the health of people there that "this loathsome disease in Peking is supposed to have come from the South."[47]

Leprosy (now more commonly called Hansen's disease) was a disease that Western doctors closely associated with the "miasmatic condition" (in which a poisonous vapor was produced in a stagnant, contaminated locale) of the Jianghan Plain. During his two years of residence in Hankou (also written as

44 Jared Diamond has discussed this in depth in his book *Guns, Germs, and Steel: The Fates of Human Societies* (New York: W. W. Norton, 1997).

45 Peter C. Perdue, *China Marches West: The Qing Conquest of Central Eurasia* (Cambridge: Harvard University Press, 2005), 47.

46 Perdue, *China Marches West*, 47–48.

47 "Dr. John Dudgeon's Report on the Health of Peking for the Half-Year Ended 31st March 1871," *Customs Gazette*, no. 10 (September 11, 1871): 7.

"Hankow") from 1869 to 1871, Dr. George Shearer observed 73 cases of leprosy. After carefully describing each case, he concluded that most of the leprosy had been imported to Hankou from "malarious localities, i.e., where there is no natural drainage."[48] He commented that "the stiff, tenacious clay of the outlying and surrounding districts retains the water on the surface in impermeable ponds and pools, in which both animal and vegetable life abounds, until the solar evaporation has converted the whole into a semi-fluid, festering mass of decay, the very hot-bed of malaria."[49] He also suggested that "the most important part of the [treatment] system ... consists in the removal of the patients from the neighborhood of marshes."[50] The notion that leprosy was caused by miasma was replaced by the germ theory towards the end of the 19th century (G.H. Armauer Hansen discovered the causative agent of leprosy, *M. leprae*, in 1873),[51] but Dr. Shearer's report on leprosy in Hankou clearly indicated the marshy nature of the Jianghan Plain, though with an urban-rural difference. Hankou and other urban centers did not fully develop until the late eighteenth century, so the extent of wetlands in the Jianghan Plain before the eighteenth century is unquestionable.

6 The Early Qing State and Its Laissez-faire Policy in Central China

After the destruction caused by warfare and natural disasters during the Ming-Qing transition, the early Qing state engaged in extensive economic reconstruction of the empire, and its political agenda for the reconstruction was as important as its economic agenda. The basic goal of economic reconstruction was to use extensive wet-rice cultivation to increase agricultural production, increase tax revenue, and strengthen state governance. The importance to the state of rice cultivation was embedded in the concept of a "paddy state," in which the ruling class used rice cultivation as a way of incorporating peasants under state rule, and when successful, it created "a uniform agroecological landscape based on irrigated wet rice."[52] Coined by Richard O'Connor, this

48 "Dr. George Shearer's Report on Leprosy at Hankow," 27.

49 "Dr. George Shearer's Report on Leprosy at Hankow," 27.

50 "Dr. George Shearer's Report on Leprosy at Hankow," 29.

51 For a compelling analysis of leprosy in Chinese history and the relationship among disease, race, Western imperialism, and medicine, see Angela Ki Che Leung, *Leprosy in China: A History* (New York: Columbia University Press, 2009).

52 Richard A. O'Connor, "Agricultural Change and Ethnic Succession in Southeast Asian States: A Case for Regional Anthropology," *Journal of Asian Studies* 54 (1995): 988n11.

concept was used by James Scott to emphasize the significance of rice in governance in premodern South and Southeast Asian states. Scott quoted John Furnivall on the popular diet and its relationship to a state's fiscal revenue to make his point:

> What rice is to the mild Hindoo, and to the anything but mild Burman, what macaroni is to the Italian, beef and beer to the Englishman, all that and more than that, is land revenue to *Leviathan Indicus*, the species of Leviathan that inhabits India; it is his victuals, his sustenance. Income tax, customs duties, excise receipts and so on. … he could in a pinch do without them, but without land revenue he would starve to death.[53]

For the early Qing state, having as many people as possible engaged in agricultural production was likewise related to state consolidation.

As discussed earlier, the early Qing rulers perceived the Jianghan Plain as a hard-to-access peripheral region with tax complications and tough-to-govern people. However, another perception was also true: it was an area with plenty of arable land and a rich source of labor, which, if used properly, could become a source of increased agricultural production and tax revenues. Incorporating the Jianghan region into, to use Scott's term, a "legible state space" for the control of resources made perfect sense for the early Qing state. Instead of the strong interventionist approach that was manifest in the North China Plain, the early Qing state employed a noninterventionist approach that allowed maximum self-government by the local communities on the Jianghan Plain.

The early Qing state took this approach for several reasons. First, the Qing state perceived the Jianghan Plain as impoverished, full of people who originated in various places, and difficult to administer. Second, because of the hydrogeomorphology of the Jianghan region, the early Qing rulers realized the complexity of managing local water resources. The third reason may have to do with the Kangxi emperor, who, during his reign, strongly advocated nongovernance, which allowed for more active community-level management by minimizing intervention at the local level. William T. Rowe stated that the late-stage empire skillfully used "self-regulatory groups within the

James Scott discussed the term to elaborate the significance of rice cultivation in the state rule and its changes to the landscape. Scott, *The Art of Not Being Governed*, 74.

53 John S. Furnivall, *The Fashioning of Leviathan: The Beginnings of British Rule in Burma*, ed. Gehan Wijeyewardene (1939; Canberra: Department of Anthropology, Research School of Pacific Studies, Australian National University, 1991), 116. Scott, *The Art of Not Being Governed*, 75–76.

society itself—kinship organizations, agrarian villages, water conservancy communities, and merchant and artisanal guilds—to achieve the state's goals of maintaining order, providing welfare services, and so on."[54] The minimal intervention by the Qing state, according to Rowe, was a good plan":

> "Benevolent governance"—governance by a few good men rather than by proliferating, interventionist institutions—was a positive Confucian value self-consciously trumpeted by the regime itself. For much of the Qing, it worked tolerably well and might even have been the best way to rule China's expansive domain, given the available technology.[55]

In the early Qing, when resources were poor and many areas were devastated by wars and disasters, implementing minimal administration of a place that needed substantial resources made perfect sense.

The main part of the early Qing reconstruction was land reclamation for agricultural production. In the twelfth year of his reign (1673), Kangxi instructed the Board of Revenue as follows:

> The foremost task for a state's long-term prosperity is to fulfill the needs of people. You shall have lands cultivated and have people equipped with extra food storage. … However, at the beginning of the land reclamation, people might encounter difficulties due to shortages in material supplies; if taxes were [to be] enforced on them immediately, they would lose work again. … Therefore, taxes are exempted for ten years on the newly cultivated lands.[56]

At the end of the decree, Kangxi emphasized that any newly appointed officials who wished to gain credits toward promotion by intervening in the affairs of the people and using force would be harshly penalized.[57] In 1674, the Board of Revenue started to improve the condition of hydraulic works nationwide. Many counties in the Jianghan Plain, including Hanyang, Jingzhou, and Anlu, launched large-scale dike construction and built polders of various sizes.[58]

---

54 William T. Rowe, *China's Last Empire: The Great Qing* (Cambridge: Belknap Press, 2012), 33.

55 Rowe, *China's Last Empire*, 33.

56 *Daqing shengzu ren (Kangxi) huangdi shilu* 清聖祖仁（康熙）皇帝實錄 [*A Veritable Record of the Kangxi Emperor*] (Taipei: Hualian chubanshe, 1964), December 1673. It is shortened as *Qing shengzu shilu* in the following text.

57 *Qing shengzu shilu*.

58 *Daqing huidian shili* (1899) 大清會典事例 (光緒朝) [*Cases on Qing Collected Statues*] (Beijing: Zhonghua shuju, 1991), 931: 688.

In addition, the Qing government distributed seeds and agricultural tools to local peasants and encouraged them to take part in agricultural cultivation.[59] Several decades later, in 1716, Kangxi further allotted sixty thousand taels of silver to Hunan and Hubei for dike construction and repairs along major rivers.[60]

Kangxi did not show much interest in the Jianghan area. In the early years of his rule, he built a banner military garrison system in strategic locations to ensure Manchu conquest over the majority of the Han population, but he did not initially approve of the establishment of a banner garrison in Jingzhou. Not until after the suppression of the Wu San'gui rebellion in the Yunnan region, for which Jingzhou served as the key military base for banner armies and for the highly scattered infantry green standard forces,[61] did Kangxi finally approve the establishment of a banner garrison in Jingzhou.[62]

In 1705, Huguang governor Liu Dianheng 劉殿衡 delivered a "sincere petition" from local gentry to the Kangxi emperor and invited him to inspect the Huguang area. In his petition, Liu said,

> Your majesty inspected Jiangzhe quite a few times, and had investigated the Shaanxi/Henan region, too, but left the Chu area unvisited. Since your majesty inspected the water projects in the Jiangnan area, the Jianghan people are expecting the honorable visit of your majesty. The local gentry asked me to send their humble request and I did so after we finished the due water [management] construction. If your majesty could come to the Jianghan area, we would feel great honor and good fortune.[63]

After reading the petition, Kangxi responded only "understood" (*zhi dao le* 知道了). A month later, he gifted Liu Dianheng with deer meat and other luxury foods in appreciation of his sincere invitation.[64] No evidence shows that Kangxi ever made a trip to the Huguang area.

Kangxi's attitude toward rainfall and the harvest in various regions also showed his particular attention to the Jiangnan area, Manchuria, and northern China. A review of memorials submitted during the reign of Kangxi creates the

59 *Daqing huidian shili.*

60 *Qing shizong shilu*, the sixth year of the Yongzheng emperor (1728), vol. 66.

61 In various accounts of *Qing shengzu shilu*, especially in the accounts of the 1680s.

62 *Qing shengzu shilu*, December 1881.

63 *Kangxichao hanwen zhupi zouzhe huibian* 康熙朝漢文硃批奏摺汇编 [*Chinese Annotated Memorials of the Kangxi Reign*], comp., First Historical Archives of China. (Beijing: Dang'an chubanshe, 1985) 1, no. 123: 229–231.

64 *Kangxichao hanwen* 1, no. 129: 240–242.

impression that fewer reports were from the Huguang area than from Jiangnan, southeastern coastal areas, northern China, and northwestern China, except for the period during Wu San'gui's rebellion. It is not surprising, though, that Kangxi's focus was political stability and territorial security.

The memorials reporting rainfall and harvest data in a certain region also demonstrate the differences in Kangxi's attitude. In the seventh month of 1693, Kangxi responded to a memorial by Li Xu, his official in Jiangnan, "In the two months since I heard that there was no rainfall in Jiangnan, I could not sleep well at night, could not eat well, and I worried about the harvests in Jiangnan all the time. If there was anyone coming from Jiangnan, I would go question them about the drought. … Now, it is good that rainfall has come and the harvest has been secured."[65] In 1701, after reading a report on the good harvest in Jiangnan by Cao Yin, who was another representative of Kangxi in Jiangnan, Kangxi wrote, "Knowing that Jiangnan has good harvests and the price of rice is low, I am very delighted."[66] In contrast to these enthusiastic comments, the interest displayed by Kangxi regarding the Huguang region was more subdued. Among the memorials sent from Huguang that I reviewed, I saw only one comment: "understood."

The intensity of disaster relief also shows the extent of the state's efforts in the economic reconstruction of any given region. During the sixty-year reign of the Kangxi emperor, the Jianghan Plain received disaster relief only twice, but over twenty natural disasters were recorded over that period. The first recorded disaster relief effort was in 1671 and 1673 to deal with the drought of 1670–1671, in which thirty-three counties and prefectures were exempted from taxation.[67] The second round of relief was granted in 1681 to help people in the region who had suffered losses from extreme flooding in 1680–1681; four counties and prefectures were exempted from taxation.[68] No other disaster relief was recorded, even for the great flooding in 1663 and 1676 and extreme drought in 1674, 1689, and 1690.[69]

A comparison of disaster relief offered by different rulers in the Qing dynasty gives a clearer picture of the treatment the Jianghan Plain received from the Kangxi government, based on Zhang Guoxiong's research results (see Table 8).

---

65 *Kangxichao hanwen* 1, no. 3: 6.

66 *Kangxichao hanwen* 1, no. 63: 101.

67 *Qing shengzu shilu*, 37: 1671; 44: 1673.

68 *Qing shengzu shilu*, 48: 1681.

69 *Hubeisheng jin wubai nian lai lishi qihou ziliao* 湖北省近五百年來歷史氣候資料 [*Historical Climates of Hubei in the Most Recent Five Hundred Years*], ed. Wuhan zhongxin qixiangtai (Wuhan: Wuhan zhongxin qixiangtai, 1978), 58–86. For more discussion, see Chapter 4, 160n72.

TABLE 8 Comparison of disaster years and related disaster relief during the Qing dynasty

Emperor	Recorded disasters	Counties covered	Frequency of disasters[a]	Disaster relief efforts	Counties given relief
Shunzhi (1644–1660)	8	7.1	2.3	2	7.5
Kangxi (1661–1723)	27	6.8	2.3	2	18
Yongzheng (1722–1736)	4	7.7	3.3	2	5.5
Qianlong (1736–1796)	25	7.4	2.4	21	8.4
Jiaqing (1796–1820)	4	6.5	6.3	12	8.6
Daoguang (1820–1850)	23	7.8	1.3	27	14.8
Xianfeng (1851–1861)	8	11.1	1.3	6	16.3
Tongzhi (1862–1889)	12	7	1	12	16
Guangxu (1889–1907)	20	No data	1.7	27	16
Xuantong (1908–1911)	2	No data	1.5	2	16

Note: Zhang's definition of "disaster" was a flood or drought that affected five or more counties. The compilation of historical meteorological records used by both Zhang and me indicated the intensity level of each disaster. During the Kangxi reign, there were at least nine disaster years classified as "extreme disaster" years, including floods and droughts.

a Measured in disasters per year.

SOURCE: ADAPTED FROM ZHANG GUOXIONG, "JIANGHAN PINGYUAN DE HANLAO ZAIHAI YU YUANTIAN SHENGCHAN 江漢平原的旱澇災害與垸田生產 [THE DROUGHTS AND FLOODS OF THE JIANGHAN PLAIN AND THE AGRICULTURAL PRODUCTION IN THE YUAN]," *ZHONGGUO NONGSHI* 1 (1990), CHART 7. I MODIFIED THE DATA FROM ZHANG'S ORIGINAL CHART, PARTICULARLY THAT OF THE KANGXI AND YONGZHENG REIGNS, BASED ON SOURCES OF DISASTERS IN *HUBEI JIN WUBAI NIAN LAI LISHI QIHOU ZILIAO*.

Based on Table 8, it would be hard to say that the early Qing state paid more attention to hydraulic construction and disaster relief in the Huguang region during the reign of Kangxi than afterward. Under his reign, twenty-seven disasters were recorded, but as mentioned above, the Kangxi government granted disaster relief only twice. In contrast, the Yongzheng government granted disaster relief twice though only four disasters had occurred, and the Qianlong government granted disaster relief twenty-one times for the twenty-five recorded disasters. Starting with Yongzheng, disaster relief to counties and prefectures was given much more frequently, covering at least half the years with a disaster, as seen in the table—which seems likely to be due to the increasing financial strength of the Qing state from the reign of Kangxi to that of Yongzheng and Qianlong.

Among the signs of strong state intervention into water management in this region in the early Qing are changes in water-conservancy bureaucratic appointments. For example, since 1674, most local officials, including those at the county and prefectural levels, had been given clear responsibility for water management in their own areas.[70] But those changes only strengthened the negotiating power of the locals. The additional lower-level officials represented territorial hydraulic interests and added to the intensity of conflicts over territoriality. This, combined with the self-protective characteristic of *yuan* communities, created additional difficulties for water management in the region.

In his article, Will discusses an edict in 1715 that portrays the contrast between the Yellow and Yangzi Rivers in an interesting way. The edict asserts that

> … dykes [dikes] of the Yangzi and the dykes of the Yellow River are not the same thing. The course of the Yellow River is not fixed and changes constantly, and this is why "river officials" [*heguan*] have been appointed to keep watch on it. The waters of the Yangzi never change course, and for this reason it is enough to entrust their control to the field administration.[71]

The Yongzheng emperor realized the differences between the Yellow and Yangzi Rivers, though he made fallible assumptions on the hydrography of the Yangzi. As Will pointed out in his discussion, "the Hubei basin, when considered as a whole, offered an extremely unstable hydrography … and would most

70 Will, "State Intervention," 314–316.

71 Will, "State Intervention," 317–318n51.

certainly have justified the institution of an autonomous administrative hierarchy for river conservancy."[72]

The Yongzheng emperor's approach to the water control project was very different from Kangxi's. Over the course of Yongzheng's short reign, he employed a strong interventionist approach to local water management. In one of Yongzheng's decrees, he carefully examined the crops in different areas, emphasizing that agriculture was the foundation of the empire (Figure 9). As irrigation and flood control were essential to agricultural prosperity, Yongzheng's efforts in managing water were evident. Significant increases occurred in the presence of high officials overseeing the Huguang region and their related reports on this region. In 1726, the Yongzheng emperor asked Huguang governor Li Chenglong 李成龍 and Hubei governor Zheng Renyue 鄭任钥 to pay special attention to maintenance of the dike on the Yangzi River. Yongzheng also noted that the long dikes along the Yangzi River were usually managed by counties and prefectures but that negligence was unavoidable because of the distance from the mid-Yangzi region to the capital; thus it was of the utmost importance that those high officials closely inspect the dikes and report accordingly.[73] Later that year, Yongzheng sent detailed instructions on the dams that needed repair, the number of laborers who should be committed to the project, the local officials who were appointed to supervise the projects, and the specific issues of dike maintenance.[74] His meticulous approach was unmatched by other Qing rulers. In 1727, Yongzheng again urged former governors of Hunan and Hubei to work with the newly appointed Huguang governor Maiju 迈柱 to inspect and strengthen the dikes in the Huguang area.[75] However, this interventionist approach should not be overstated, as the state was willing to cede some of its own interest to address the local interest. The state vacillated in making decisions on local hydraulic construction.[76] Even Yongzheng realized that it would be unrealistic to evaluate officials based on their local water management in areas with constant flooding (*ju ru zhi di* 沮洳之地), such as Jiangling and Mianyang.[77] Therefore, keeping people motivated and working was an important task for the Qing rulers. Hence, the Yongzheng emperor rejected a proposal to turn these local dikes into those that the state would have to manage. He knew well that once a dike

---

72 Will, "State Intervention," 317–318n51.

73 *Qing shizong shilu*, 46: 1726.

74 *Qing shizong shilu*, 54: 1727.

75 *Qing shizong shilu*, 54: 1727.

76 Will, "State Intervention," 307.

77 *Qing shizong shilu*, 54: 1727.

FIGURE 9 Yongzheng emperor's decree on agricultural production, 1727
COURTESY OF FIRST HISTORICAL ARCHIVES OF CHINA.

was designated as "official," the state would have to be responsible for its maintenance, and local people would shirk all responsibility for it.[78]

In subsequent periods, during the reign of Qianlong, Jiaqing, Daoguang, and Xianfeng, some evidence showed that higher officials became increasingly involved in the hydraulic investigations, dike maintenance, and conflict mediation. The hands-off approach of the early Qing state in the Jianghan Plain left a great deal of room for self-governing institutional development and rapid intensification of the use of *yuan*.

7 Hydraulic Communities: Official and People's *Yuan*

Yuan came in two types: official *yuan* (*guan yuan* 官垸) and people's *yuan* (*min yuan* 民垸). The official *yuan* reported to the government and were recorded in the land registry. The people's *yuan* were not registered with the government, and the people decided whether to repair *yuan* or abandon them.[79] Most of the *yuan* in the Jianghan Plain were people's *yuan*. The annual maintenance of the official *yuan* in this region usually had to be reported to the Board of Public Works of the central government. These annual projects followed a model in which officials supervised and the people managed the *yuan*" (*guandu minxiu* 官督民修). The official *yuan* were not owned by the government; rather, they were mostly owned or co-owned by various lineages. The government was not even the main source of finance for an official *yuan*; that came from the people

78 *Zhupi yuzhi* 4.1.56 (vol. 19), cited in Perdue, *Exhausting the Earth*, 230.

79 *Hanchuan tuji zhengshi*, 3: 26, "其垸有二： 告请于上者为官垸，民自筑者为民垸。官垸岁修达部，听考覆，必计工程；民垸则修废自由， 档册不备载。" See also Ni, *Jingzhou wancheng dizhi*, 322–323: "报部有名者曰官垸，又曰部垸，例应官督民修；民私筑者曰私垸，讳称'私'则自号曰'民垸'。"

who lived there. Funds for dike maintenance were allocated among lineages and households based on the lands they owned.[80] Occasionally, the government allocated funds for dike repairs, but mostly for disaster relief. People's *yuan* were on their own. Both official *yuan* and people's *yuan* were managed by the people. The state performed only a supervisory role in *yuan* management, with no direct official assignments from the government to the *yuan*. A third type of *yuan* also existed: private *yuan*, usually built without consent from officials, which evaded taxes and blocked water flows. In practical terms, however, it was hard to distinguish them from people's *yuan*; people did not want to call them "*si*" *yuan* (private *yuan*), so they used the term "*min*" *yuan* (people's *yuan*) instead.[81]

The government had three main roles in *yuan* management. First, the local government determined the types of projects to be undertaken and when those projects were carried out. Regular maintenance and repairs were usually performed in the winter. Second, the local government sent officials to examine the progress of the work and quality of construction while the projects were going on and when they were completed. Lastly, the officials supervised the entire hydraulic management system, which effectively existed only between the 1560s and the 1640s.[82] The best example was the implementation of "*dijia* legislation" 堤甲法 on the long dikes of both the Yangzi and Han Rivers. The *dijia* legislation was issued by Jingzhou prefectural magistrate Zhao Xian 趙賢 in 1568. It regulated the river dike management system as follows: one dike elder (*dilao* 堤老) for every 1,000-*zhang* dike, one dike head (*dizhang* 堤長) for every 500-*zhang* dike, one dike lead (*dijia* 堤甲) and ten dike workers(*difu* 堤夫) for every 100-*zhang* dike.[83] Although these people were elected by the locals and from among the locals, they reported to the local government. The system did not last very long and was dismantled because of conflicts among counties over dike responsibilities, as well as the chaotic politics of the late Ming, and the devastating warfare in the 1640s.

80 Peng and Zhang, *Mingqing changjiang liuyu*, 208–210.

81 Ni, *Jingzhou wancheng dizhi*, 322–323. Also see Will's discussion on *yuan* for more distinctions. Will, "State Intervention," 332.

82 Perrier-Etienne Will, "Zhonghua diguo wanqi guojia dui shuili de guanli 中華帝國晚期國家對水利的管理 [The Late Imperial Empire's Water Management]," in *Mingqing yilai changjiang liuyu shehui fazhan shilun* 明清以來長江流域社會發展史論 [*The Social Development in the Yangzi Valley in Ming and Qing Periods*], ed. Chen Feng (Wuhan: Wuhan daxue chubanshe, 2006), 796–810.

83 *Huguang zongzhi* (1586), 33: 6–7.

The model in which "officials supervise and people manage" had its positive effects in providing some financial security for the long and crucial dikes along the Yangzi and Han Rivers, because the construction and maintenance of those dikes were obviously beyond the financial capacity of local governments and communities. But many provincial officials expected that even the "official dikes" should be completely managed by the local government and financed by local taxes.[84] However, the state's involvement was very limited in the water management of the mid-Yangzi region. As Will states, the Qing rulers were hesitant to manage the Yangzi River system in the same way as the Yellow River, the Huai River, and the Grand Canal. Furthermore, no evidence indicates that Qing rulers and statesmen ever considered the establishment of a Yangzi River Commission.[85]

Various historical records show evidence of private *yuan*, but the descriptions in those records do not indicate any fundamental differences between people's *yuan* and private *yuan*. In a strict sense, the people's *yuan* and the private *yuan* were both illegal.[86] The spread of private *yuan* was especially problematic when population growth created a burden on the capacity of agricultural production, which is discussed in Chapter 3. Numerous private *yuan*, to a large extent, narrowed the river and slowed the speed of runoff, which often led to floods; at the same time, they competed for resources previously available only to official *yuan*.[87] Figure 10 illustrates the distribution of official *yuan* and people's *yuan* in Hanchuan County in the nineteenth century.

Official *yuan* and people's *yuan* were both managed by the local people through a local system, consisting of a loosely organized community hierarchy for resource management in accordance with rules and regulations. The lineages and social networks of leading figures of those lineages played a significant role in the construction of the South Lake *yuan*. This network was usually formed to create a managerial hierarchy in the *yuan* communities. For example, in the South Lake *yuan*, a hierarchy of *shoushi* 首士, *zongli* 總理, and *baizhang* 百長, the titles of those in charge of sections of dikes, was established to manage the construction of *yuan* dikes. Local scholar Lin Dayou also drafted

84 Will, "Zhonghua diguo."

85 Will, "Zhonghua diguo."

86 Ni, *Jingzhou wancheng dizhi*, 322–323. Zhang Jiayan distinguished the people's *yuan* from private *yuan*; but his analysis states that they were both created by people themselves and were not registered with the government. There seems to be no fundamental difference between the two. Zhang, "Water Calamities and Dike Management," 73, 89.

87 *Jingzhou fuzhi* (1880), 20: 4.

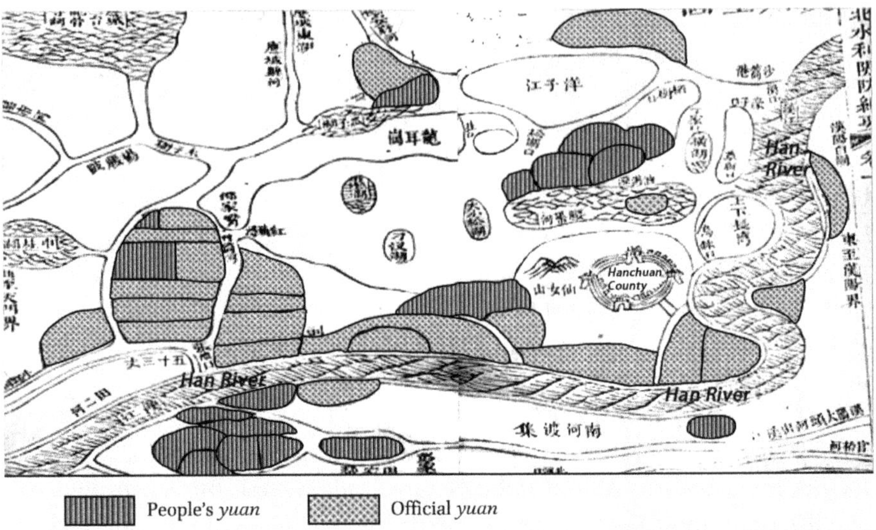

FIGURE 10 The official *yuan* and people's *yuan* in Hanchuan County
SOURCE: ADAPTED FROM "*YUAN* IN HANCHUAN COUNTY," IN YU CHANGLIE, *CHUBEI SHUILI DIFANG JIYAO* 楚北水利堤防紀要 [*DIKE MANAGEMENT IN HUBEI*] (HUBEI: HUBEI FANSHU KEBEN, 1865), 1: 51–52.

rules for dike management in the South Lake *yuan* that were adopted by other *yuan*, such as the Gaojia *yuan* constructed later. In the historical records, it is not clear precisely when *yuan* became institutionalized, but this process was an integral part of the process of constructing and expanding a *yuan*. When a *yuan* was constructed, its management was put on the agenda, and inevitably its institutionalization began. Based on most of the available records on the management of *yuan*, this institutionalization began no later than the mid-Ming era, which was synchronized with a surge in the frequency of disasters.[88] This might indicate that the high frequency of disasters prompted the process of institutionalization. By the mid-Qing, most of the *yuan* had a *yuan* chief or head to administer affairs, and the hierarchy was usually created in two ways: public elections or lineage rotation. Sometimes, the two were complementary and not mutually exclusive.

88 Perdue discussed the increasing crisis in private polder construction that posed a threat to the Dongting Lake area during the mid- and late Ming periods; see Perdue, *Exhausting the Earth*, 178–185. See Chapter 1 of this book for discussion on the frequency of disasters during the mid-Ming era.

These public elections were held in the South Lake *yuan* as well as in other regions of prerevolutionary rural China. For example, Mark Elvin stated that the Sanyuan polderland in Guangdong Province held "regular annual meetings of publicly selected representatives and systematic public selection of hydraulic managers."[89] In Shanghai County in eastern China, the county magistrate summoned an assembly of local nobles for advice and legitimacy in making dredging decisions.[90] Elvin concluded that it might be "a sort of proto-democracy"[91] and that it was a counterexample to Karl Wittfogel's assertion of a "despotic" society in China.

In most cases, *yuan* heads were dominated by big clans and lineages. For example, in the Bailü 白莒 *yuan* in Jiangling County, heads of the five *zong* 總 (head unit) were alternately chosen by elders in five big lineages: Liu, Chen, Peng, Ma, and Zhang.[92] In some places, "the post of *yuanzong* (polder chieftain), unlike the *dilao* (dike elder) and *yujia* (polder tithe head) along the river, who are rotated yearly, is held by one surname, and it has been this way for generations."[93] Perdue considered this as an illustration of consolidated local power in Huguang in the late Ming era. The *yuan* heads were responsible for inspecting dikes, making plans for dike repairs, and supervising construction projects. They also worked as intermediaries between a higher hierarchy (usually the leader of a bigger *yuan*) and people in the *yuan*. In a big *yuan*, a hierarchy was set up to ensure that the hydraulic responsibility was allocated and delegated properly. For example, the Bailü *yuan* was surrounded by a dike longer than 16,500 *gong*[94] and enclosed more than 19,890 *mu* of farmland. It was divided into thirteen small *yuan*. Five head units were established to administer the *yuan*, with two dike elders for each head unit. Each head unit administered several small *yuan*. A *yuan* head was also appointed to each small *yuan*. Each small *yuan* also included several *wei* 圩, whose leader was called a *weijia* 圩甲. Each *wei* had several households under its control. Therefore, from top to bottom, a distinct hydraulic hierarchy was established in the *yuan*. Each

---

89 Mark Elvin, "Market Towns and Waterways: The County of Shang-hai from 1480 to 1910," in Skinner, *The City in Late Imperial China*, 466–467. Elvin also noted that the "public election" indicates a form of informal election without quantified balloting; Elvin, *The Retreat of the Elephants*, 117.

90 Elvin, *The Retreat of the Elephants*, 117.

91 Elvin, *The Retreat of the Elephants*, 117.

92 *Jiangling Bailü yuan yuanshou zongyince* 江陵白莒垸首总印冊 [*A Catalog of the Chiefs of the Bailü Yuan in Jiangling*], cited in Peng and Zhang, *Mingqing changjiang liuyu*, 207.

93 Perdue, *Exhausting the Earth*, 184.

94 One *gong* equals 1.65 meters, so the *Bailü yuan* was surrounded by a dike about 2,712.5 meters long.

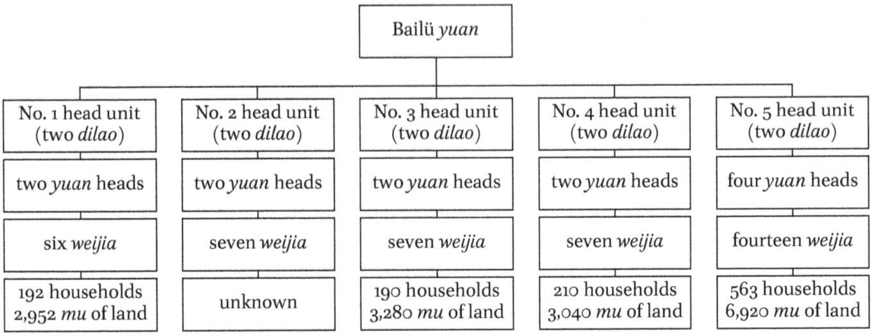

FIGURE 11 Hydraulic hierarchy in Bailü *yuan* in Jiangling County in Ming-Qing times
SOURCE: "JIANGLING BAILÜ YUAN YUAN SHOU ZONG YING CE," CITED IN PENG AND ZHANG, *MINGQING CHANGJIANG LIUYU NONGYESHUILI YANJIU*, 207. THE SOURCE IS NOT CLEAR ABOUT THE PRECISE PERIOD OF THE DATA, BUT IT IS LIKELY FROM THE LATE MING AND EARLY QING (AROUND 1600S).

layer in the hierarchy could be held liable for the irresponsibility of those affiliated with them.[95] Elvin called this type of system a "consultative oligarchy under central legitimation."[96]

Figure 11 illustrates the hydraulic hierarchy in a straightforward way.[97] The systematic approach to local institutions was a strong and effective check on the noncooperative nature of the *yuan* communities. It became an integral part of local water management that enforced collaboration and mediated conflict.

8 Enforcement on Collaboration: The Formation of *Yuan* Zones

By the late Ming systematic and detailed local rules already existed. In local gazetteers, particular chapters were devoted to technological tips on the construction of dikes, the procedures for dike repairs, and ecological strategies for dike maintenance.[98] But until the mid-eighteenth century, no clear

95 Perdue, *Exhausting the Earth*, 184.
96 Elvin, *The Retreat of the Elephants*, 117.
97 The number in parenthesis indicates the number of units in one level, but the direct correlation between levels is not clear due to a dearth of sources. For example, we know that thirteen small *yuan* were less than five head units, but we do not know how many small *yuan* were included in each head unit.
98 *Huguang zongzhi* (1586), vols. 32 and 33.

legislation was issued by the state to govern the hydraulic communities in this region—the local hydraulic order was maintained through tacit rules mutually agreed on by inhabitants of certain communities. For example, no houses could be built on the dike, no working factories could be set up on the dike, no tombs could be dug on the dike, no soil could be transported from the dike, and water-tolerant plants (e.g., reeds or willow) could be planted.[99] The Qing state had general guidelines regarding water management, however. For example, the dikes had to be examined and repaired annually, with dikes subject to a major inspection and repair every ten years.[100] But, as our previous analysis shows, the actual implementation of those rules was in local hands.

As discussed in Chapter 1, *yuan* communities were self-contained and paradoxical by nature: they needed to collaborate in water management with communities that were connected by dikes, but they were also self-protective and sometimes refused cooperation. During the reign of Kangxi, Zhou Tingbin 周廷彬, a local scholar who lived in Qianjiang, wrote the following, which suggests collaboration among various communities on dike construction and maintenance: "Qianjiang and Mianyang County need to collaborate to manage the Han River dikes. If the dikes are breached, the people would become the fishes and turtles in the water. ... One zone should watch for its zone. If people all take good care of their own dikes, their homes will be protected."[101]

The paradoxical nature of the *yuan* communities, to a large extent, determined the rule of cooperation among those communities, especially in the absence of clear rules enforced by the state. Basically, cooperation in public dike construction followed a rule in which dike maintenance should be paid for by those who benefited from it. This rule was mentioned in many historical documents and was practiced by different administrative units. For example, for centuries the Shayang dike was managed cooperatively by five counties: Qianjiang, Tianmen, Mianyang, Jiangling, and Jianli;[102] construction of

99 *Huguang zongzhi* (1586), 33: 29–30.

100 *Daqing huidian shili* (1899), vol. 929.

101 Zhou Tingbin, "Shuishang cheng you huamingfu 水上呈幼華明府," *Qianjiang xianzhi* (1694), 19: 15–17, in *Zhongguo difangzhi jicheng*, 46: 321–322. Zhou became a *juren* during the reign of Tianqi in the Ming and worked in Fengxiang Prefecture during the reign of Shunzhi in the Qing. *Qianjiang xianzhi* (1694), 16: 18–9, in *Zhongguo difangzhi jicheng*, 46: 280.

102 Li Zanyuan, "Qing Jing'an ge shu ticheng bici xiexiu shu 请荆安各属堤塍彼此协修疏 [Memorial Asking That the Counties of Jingzhou and Anlu Give Each Other Mutual Aid

the Wanfu Dam was undertaken by Tianmen and Mianyang Counties;[103] and the Zhongxiang dike was maintained through cooperation among four counties: Zhongxiang, Jingshan, Tianmen, and Qianjiang.

In the late Ming and early Qing, this rule started to be neglected. On top of conflicts between the interests of various *yuan* communities, the existing boundaries, both administrative and natural, created tensions in the once-smooth cooperation in dike management. Many communities adopted pragmatic rules to protect their own hydraulic interests. The responsibility for the collective work of flood control thus changed from the communities that benefited from dike collaboration to each community taking charge of its own dike.

The Shayang dike, which was administratively in downstream Jingmen Prefecture but was important to upstream Anlu Prefecture, was an example of this change in responsibility for flood control and dike maintenance by various communities. For centuries, five counties (Jiangling and Jianli in Jingmen Prefecture and Qianjiang, Tianmen, and Mianyang in Anlu Prefecture) had maintained a local custom of providing mutual aid. However, in 1547, the inhabitants of Jingzhou blamed residents of Anlu for the collapse of the dike and objected to helping Anlu to repair it. Anlu retaliated and stopped cooperating with Jingzhou. The result was that Anlu had to take sole responsibility for the dike. After 1680, downstream counties Qianjiang and Mianyang both ended their help with the dike by claiming that it was not part of their territory.[104]

Conflicts in the river basin greatly increased: between upstream and downstream communities, between left-bank and right-bank communities, between fisher folk and merchants, between households that shared an irrigation canal, and between officials and local people. As the number of *yuan* grew and the frequency of conflict increased, a new practice was adopted to enforce collaboration. Several *yuan* were grouped into zones, and *yuan* in the same zone had to cooperate on dike construction and maintenance, allocating labor based on the acreage of land owned by each *yuan*. Cooperation with other zones was forever forbidden.[105] This practice was initiated in the twenty-ninth year of the reign of the Kangxi emperor (1690) by Qianjiang County magistrate Liu Huan 劉焕, who grouped the *yuan* in Qianjiang into eleven zones (see Table 9). Around thirty *yuan* were not grouped into zones and stayed as

in Dike Works]," in *Xia jingnan dao zhi* 下荊南道志 [*The Gazetteer of the Lower Jingnan Circuit*], ed. Jing Daomo and Lu Zhiyu (1816) 24: 22B–25B.

103 Chen Guangwen and Hu Zixiu, comp., *Xiangdi cheng'an* 襄堤成案 [*Leading Cases on the Xiang Dike*] (Taipei: Wenhai chubanshe, 1894/1969), vol. 4.

104 Li, "Qing Jing'an ge shu ticheng bici xiexiu shu."

105 *Qianjiang xianzhi* (1694), 10: 59, in *Zhongguo difangzhi jicheng*, 46: 202.

TABLE 9 *Yuan* zones in Qianjiang in the early Qing dynasty

Yuan zone	*Number of yuan* included
Tuobu	15
Mutou	7
Hongshui	8
Yifeng	4
Hexi (upper)	17
Hexi (lower)	13
Hebei (upper)	16
Hebei (lower)	12
Xiangling	3
Yuanwan	13
Hedong Huanghan	6

SOURCE: *QIANJIANG XIANZHI* (1694), 10: 60.

single-unit *yuan*,[106] perhaps because they were not geographically connected to each other, making it hard to organize collective responsibility for dike maintenance.

During the reign of Kangxi, the *yuan* zone system was not implemented only in Qianjiang County. Similar cross-*yuan* collaborations took place in Tianmen County during the reign of Qianlong, though records do not indicate when they started in Tianmen; it is possible that they followed the practice of *yuan* zones, as in Qianjiang, in the late seventeenth and the early eighteenth centuries. The records do show that four *yuan* zones were formed on the southern bank of the Niuti branch river 牛蹄支河, including the Shangtaolin *yuan* zone, and thirteen *yuan* zones were on the northern bank of the Niuti branch river, including the Tanjia *yuan* zone.[107]

Although the *yuan* zone system was enforced, prevalent hydraulic rivalries between *yuan* persisted in post-Kangxi periods, as with conflict between the Bianhe and Wenjia *yuan* in Tianmen County from the Kangxi to Qianlong eras. The Bianhe and the Wenjia *yuan* were once in the same zone, and their respective communities were supposed to collaborate on *yuan* dike maintenance.

106 *Qianjiang xianzhi* (1694), 10: 60.
107 *Tianmen xianzhi* (1765), 6: 14–15.

However, the Wenjia community did not want to cooperate (for reasons unspecified in the text) and built a separation dike between its own *yuan* and the Bianhe *yuan* in 1701. Afterward, the Wenjia community did not maintain the dike that surrounded the Bianhe *yuan*, and the Bianhe community was too small to maintain the dike itself. In 1702, the Bianhe *yuan* was abandoned, though its *yuan* dikes were not. The maintenance of the dikes was the subject of a lawsuit that began in 1759 and lasted about seventy years, when it was ultimately investigated and settled by the magistrate Hu Yi.[108] How it was settled was not indicated in the records, but this case shows that even small-scale collaboration among the *yuan* communities was sometimes problematic in the face of the self-interest of people in an individual *yuan*.

9 Customs in Common: Various Solutions for Collaboration

Other cases indicated hydraulic rivalries among the *yuan*, such as conflicts between the Gongxin and Shihe *yuan* in Tianmen County. When one part of the dike in Tianmen territory was breached, the seventy-two *yuan* in the county were accused of shirking their responsibilities and refusing to cooperate.[109] Many other management systems were developed to coordinate different *yuan*.

The proportional allocation of dike work according to landholdings or tax-grain production was widely practiced. For different administrative units (prefectures and counties), for example, the Chedun *yuan* was maintained by Qianjiang and Tianmen based on a customary 6:4 division of the dikes.[110] In the case of the Wangfu dam project during the reign of Qianlong, 6/4, 7/3, 8/2, and 7.5/2.5 divisions of funding and labor were negotiated between Tianmen and Mianyang. After measuring the land in both counties, they agreed on a division of 7.675:2.325![111] As for the allocation among different *yuan*, project funds were collected according to the area of land in each *yuan*—for example, in Qianjiang County, when thirty-eight *yuan* cooperated in the construction of the Qima dike in the Shawo *yuan* 沙窩垸, 12 *wen* were levied for each *mu*.[112] In addition to the fundraising, allocating labor based on area was also common, as seen in the case of the Mutou *yuan* in Qianjiang. During the reign of

108 *Tianmen xianzhi* (1765), 6: 12–13.
109 *Xiangdi cheng'an*, 1: 23.
110 *Xiangdi cheng'an*, 1: 121–127.
111 *Xinagdi cheng'an*, 4: 1259–1264.
112 *Qianjiang xianzhi xu* (1879), 10: 61–62.

Tongzhi (1862–1874), the dike, which was 2,702 *gong* in length, was divided into three portions and allocated to different lineages based on the land owned by each lineage. The Zhu lineage owned 9,402 *mu* (1,567 acres) of land and therefore had to construct a dike 554 *gong* long; the Huang lineage owned 15,312 *mu* (2,552 acres) of land and accordingly took responsibility for a 903 *gong* length of the dike; mixed-surname lineages had a total of 21,096 *mu* (3,516 acres) of land, so they were allocated 1,244 *gong* of the dike to maintain.[113] Because land and dike work allocation were so closely related, dike work obligations were also clearly specified in some contracts for land and property transactions.[114]

Because of the development of commercialization and privatization, the land and water transactions became an effective way of solving water conflicts among parties. For example, in the late nineteenth century, in conflicts involving Qianjiang, Tianmen, and Mianyang concerning the flood drainage in the Huangzhongshanger *yuan*, the problem was solved upstream by Qianjiang buying the downstream lands from Tianmen and Mianyang for use as a floodplain.[115] Cases like this suggested an incipient private property regime, and if not well addressed, could be a big obstacle to collective decision making on flood control.

10 Turn Sea to Land: Population Growth and Dike Proliferation

For the Jianghan Plain, the late seventeenth to the early eighteenth century was a productive period, as the region became a major source of rice for Jiangnan. The early Qing rulers understood the significance of rice cultivation in the Huguang region, and the Jianghan Plain was a major area of cultivation. The Kangxi emperor was aware that people in the Jiangzhe area relied on rice from Huguang. If the price of Huguang rice was high, ordinary people would not be able to afford it. Therefore, Kangxi banned rice-wine production to ensure that rice would be available for purchase.[116] An important indication of the economic impact of Huguang rice in the early Qing period was fluctuation in its price in Jiangnan. In 1699, the Kangxi emperor inquired about the outrageously high price of rice and was told that it was due to a shortage of Huguang rice.[117] When reporting to the emperor about the rice market

113 *Qianjiang xianzhi xu* (1879), 10: 61–62.
114 See Peng and Zhang, *Mingqing changjiang liuyu*, 212.
115 Peng and Zhang, *Mingqing changjiang liuyu*.
116 *Qianjiang xianzhi xu* (1879), 6: 458.
117 *Kangxichao hanwen zhupi zouzhe huibian* 1, no. 31, no. 33: 42, 44.

in a given region, local officials referred to whether and how much Huguang rice had been imported to that region. In 1704, Cao Yin reported to the Kangxi emperor that the Jiangnan area had bought 15,800 *dan* (790,000 kilograms) of rice from Huguang to relieve its grain shortage.[118] In 1712, Li Xu 李煦 reported that grain was being transported through Yangzhou via 214 boats from Jiangxi and 403 boats thought to be from Huguang.[119] In 1716, Li Xu reported that the price of rice remained low in Suzhou and Yangzhou because there were sufficient rice imports from Huguang.[120] Apparently, the early Qing emperors saw the Huguang area as a key source of grain for almost all of China. In 1719, the Kangxi emperor wrote the following on a memorial from Huguang governor Zhang Liandeng 張連登 about the rice price of Hubei: "It is well known that the realm would be in [a state of] rice sufficiency when there are good harvests in the Huguang area."[121] The status of Huguang rice in the national market remained high until the early Qianlong period. In 1747, Zhao Qingli 趙青藜, a censor (*yushi* 御史), wrote a memorial about improvement in hydraulic projects, especially in the Jingzhou rice-production area, so that more rice could be exported to Jiangnan and the price of rice in Jiangnan would decrease.[122]

Population growth on the Jianghan Plain reached its climax during the eighteenth century, which strongly drove agricultural production. The extensive use of *yuan* was closely associated with the rapid population growth. According to a population study by the economic historian Wu Chengming, in the eighteenth century, the population increase in Hubei was 19.9 births per thousand, much higher than 11.5 per thousand in Guangdong and 8.9 per thousand in Hunan.[123] The main area of Hubei, the Jianghan Plain, accounted for the majority of the population growth. Tables 2.3 shows population growth in

118 *Kangxichao hanwen zhupi zouzhe huibian* 1, no. 83: 124.

119 *Lixu zouzhe* 李煦奏摺 [*Memorials of Lixu*], ed. Gugong bowuyuan mingqing dang'an bu (Beijing: Zhonghua shuju, 1976), 109–110.

120 *Lixu zouzhe*, 123.

121 俗語雲: 湖廣熟，天下足。湖北如是，湖南亦可知矣 ... 頗為好年. This is a well-known phrase to indicate the abundant rice production in the Huguang area. It appeared in early Ming times. *Gongzhongdang kangxichao zouzhe* 宮中檔康熙朝奏摺 [*Memorials of the Kangxi Reign*] (Taipei: Guoli gugong bowuyuan, 1719/1976), 551–552.

122 Zhao Qingli, "Qingjian gujia xingshuili shu 請減谷價興水利疏 [A Pledge to Decrease the Grain Price and to Resurrect the Hydraulic Systems]," in He, *Huangchao jingshi wenbian* 38, "Huzheng" 13.

123 Wu Chengming, "18 yu 19 shiji shangye de zhongguo shichang 18 與 19 世紀上葉的中國市場 [China's Market during the Eighteenth and the First Half of the Nineteenth Centuries]," *Zhongguo jingjishi luntan* (2004).

Hubei compared to Hunan and China as a whole, from the end of the seventeenth century to the early nineteenth century (from the Kangxi to the Jiaqing periods).

If we compare the population in different regions during the Qing dynasty, as Table 10 shows, from 1684 to 1749, both Hubei and Hunan experienced rapid population growth, which was mainly triggered by economic reconstruction in the early Qing; but after the mid-eighteenth century, population growth was much more rapid in Hubei than in Hunan. In the early nineteenth century, the population density in Hubei was almost double that of Hunan and almost triple that of all of China.[124] This rapidly expanding population exerted great pressure on the limited arable land in Hubei. After people exhausted the available agricultural land, they started to reclaim the lakes, floodplains, and river courses, building thousands of *yuan* for agricultural production. Table 11 shows the number of *yuan* built in different counties and prefectures during various reigns.

Table 11 shows that in counties and prefectures such as Qianjiang, Mianyang, Tianmen, and Hanchuan, the construction of *yuan* increased significantly in the early Qing period, from the seventeenth to the eighteenth centuries. In Mianyang Prefecture, the number of *yuan* was thirteen times higher in the eighteenth century than in the sixteenth century. And in Hanchuan, the number of *yuan* increased from 44 in the late seventeenth century to 308 in the eighteenth century. All the statistics show that land reclamation was at full magnitude by the mid-eighteenth century, reaching the phase of "peak dike" (or peak *yuan*), a period when the maximum number of *yuan* was mentioned in local gazetteers (as shown in Figure 2). They also indicate that after this period, the *yuan* proliferation began to wane—it experienced several waves of increase and decrease, but it never regained its peak in the mid-eighteenth century. One of the important reasons for this change was the official check on excessive land reclamation, which decreased the number of *yuan* to some extent, even though the overall trend was still toward massive land reclamation. This is discussed in Chapter 3.

By the end of the eighteenth century, many wetlands had been converted into agricultural land. Reporting on the issue of land reclamation, Hunan governor Jiang Pu 蔣溥 wrote to the Qianlong emperor in 1744:

124 Historian Ping-ti Ho studied households and population of fourteen provinces in 1812 (Table 13) and found that Hubei had an average of 6.74 persons per family, the highest among all fourteen provinces that he studied. The national average was 5.33 persons per household. Ping-ti Ho, *Studies on the Population of China, 1368–1953* (Cambridge: Harvard University Press, 1959), 56.

TABLE 10 Population growth from the reign of the Kangxi emperor to the reign of the Jiaqing emperor

	24th year of Kangxi (1684)		14th year of Qianlong (1749)		End of Qianlong (1790s)		17th year of Jiaqing (1814)	
	People[a]	Density	People	Density	People	Density	People	Density
Hubei	1,772,160	9.76	7,527,486	41.1	19,711,667	108.64	27,370,098	150.85
Hunan	1,215,248	5.44	8,672,033	38.8	16,308,167	79.95	18,652,507	84.43
China	93,699,792	21.92	177,495,039	33.15	296,991,000	55.49	361,693,379	67.57

Note: Population density is determined by the population (*kou*) per square kilometer. The early Qing population data is recorded as *ding*. Normally, one *ding* was equal to five *kou*. Considering that *ding* was a unit of taxation, not of population, it is hard to calculate the real population in the early Qing, and it varied across areas. For example, 1 *ding* equaled 9.5 *kou* in Shengjing, 4.5 *kou* in Jiling, and 3.5 *kou* in the hinterland. Here we use 1 *ding* as equal to 5 *kou* as the base. Zhang, however, used 1 *ding* as equal to 4 *kou*.

SOURCE: ADAPTED FROM ZHANG JIANMIN, "QINGDAI JIANGHAN-DONGTING HUQU DIYUAN NONGTIAN DE FAZHAN JIQI ZONGHE KAOCHA 清代江漢—洞庭湖區堤垸農田的發展及其綜合考察 [THE DEVELOPMENT OF JIANGHAN-DONGTING LAKE *YUAN* FIELDS OF THE QING DYNASTY]," *ZHONGGUO NONGSHI* 2 (1987), TABLE 4.

TABLE 11 The number of *yuan* in counties/prefectures during the Ming-Qing periods

County/prefecture	Number of *yuan*	Period
Jianli	360+	Xianfeng reign (1850–1861)
Qianjiang	48	Chenghua and Zhengde (late 15th to early 16th centuries)
	126	10th year of Kangxi (1670)
	160+	Qianlong reign (1736–1796)
Mianyang Prefecture	167+	Jiajing reign (1521–1567)
	1,368	Qianlong reign (1736–96)
Jingzhou	953+	Guangxu reign (1875–1908)
Tianmen	87	Qianlong reign (1736–1796)
	200+	Guangxu reign (1875–1908)
Hanchuan	44 (36 official *yuan*, 8 people's *yuan*)[a]	Kangxi reign (1661–1722)
	43 official *yuan*, 265 people's *yuan*	Qianlong reign (1736–1796)

a The records indicate a total of forty-four *yuan*, of which thirty-six were official *yuan*. It is also stated that the lengths of the people's *yuan* dikes were not recorded. On Tongzhi, *Hanchuan xianzhi*, 9: 7.

SOURCE: *JIANLI XIANZHI* (1872), 11: 18, 20; *QIANJIANG XIANZHI* (1694), 10: 60; *QIANJIANG XIANZHI XU* (1879), 3: 11–30; *MIANYANG ZHOUZHI* (1530), 8: 4, IN *ZHONGGUO FANGZHI CONGSHU*, 338: 188; *MIANYANG ZHOUZHI* (1894), 3: 34–35; *JINGZHOU FUZHI* (1757), 12: 1–14; *JINGZHOU FUZHI* (1880), 20: 2–21; *TIANMEN XIANZHI* (1765), 6: 6–13, *HANCHUAN XIANZHI* (1873), 9: 7, 34.

> The wetlands of the southern Chu area [including the Jianghan Plain and Dongting Lake area] used to be neglected. … After decades of land reclamation since the thirty-sixth year of the Kangxi emperor (1697), prompted by population growth, the wetlands all became *yuan* agricultural lands. … We shall also build a main dike to protect the *yuan* fields from floods and the *yuan* fields will be more than 10,000 *mu*.[125]

Because land was limited, many peasants started to look for alternative crops with higher yields and a more flexible way of growing them. Hubei governor Chen Hongmou 陳宏謀 (1696–1771) reported to the Qianlong emperor in June 1748:

> The Jinghan Plain was mainly cultivated with rice … however, because of the rapidly increasing population and because the available arable lands were very limited, people could hardly make ends meet. Therefore, I proposed cultivating wheat in rice fields. Peasants could still seed rice after harvesting the wheat. If the timing is too late people could cultivate late-seeding rice. I remember that I passed through the Chu area (Hunan and Hubei) twenty years ago, there were no wheat fields at all, but now there are fields cultivated with wheat in such density that it was like the wheat cultivation in northern and northwestern China.[126]

These comparisons described by Chen Hongmou demonstrate that by the mid-eighteenth century, land reclamation had reached an unprecedented level. The shortage of land prompted people to look for new areas, pushing the limits of river-lake systems, and going so far as the mountains, which all created new complexities in various sociopolitical contexts, which are further analyzed in subsequent chapters.

11 Conclusion

The wetlands of the Jianghan Plain enjoyed a fair amount of autonomy in the early Qing period. They were not the "wastelands" perceived by the earlier poets and bureaucrats of the Song; rather, they were a region of great

125 Zhongguo kexueyuan dili kexu yu ziyuan yanjiusuo and zhongguo diyi lishi dang'an guan, *Qingdai zouzhe huibian—nongye, huanjing* 清代奏摺匯編—農業、環境 [*A Collection of Memorials of the Qing Dynasty—On Agriculture and Environment*] (Beijing: Shangwu yinshu guan, 2005), 84.

126 *Qingdai zouzhe huibian*, 100.

biodiversity that people could use to make a living. The frequent floods were not much of a threat to people, nor were the people vulnerable to constant water disasters. Instead, people constructed a landscape of the plain, whether *yuan*, houseboats, or temples; those spaces were the medium in which people could survive, live, and connect with one another. As the wetlands were drained amid large-scale land reclamation projects, local communities gradually lost their flexible way of life, which is evident in the people's conversion from fishing to farming.

Water management in the Jianghan Plain remained in the hands of the *yuan* communities. The early Qing state always tried to minimize its expense of human and financial resources to attain the best effects possible with local management. That was especially true of a "hydraulic frontier" such as the Jianghan Plain that had a complicated local environment. The local rules regulating collaboration among *yuan* communities loosely oversaw the chaotic development of the *yuan*. The central authorities had to work with strong local elites who actively participated in official decision making and shaped final decisions.

The water problem in the Jianghan Plain remained a local issue in the late seventeenth and early eighteenth centuries under a laissez-faire approach by the state and self-governing local communities. However, this autonomous management could be effective only when society and the environment were kept in balance. As the population grew and *yuan* construction reached an unprecedented level, which greatly harmed the river-water system, the state had to step in. In the eighteenth century, the water issue in the Jianghan area became a national issue, rather than a local one, triggering a broad discussion among Qing officials about water management in the context of Manchu-Han tensions.

CHAPTER 3

The Retreat of the Horse

The Manchus, Pasturelands, and Water Management on the Jianghan Plain (ca. 1700s–mid-1800s)

In 1761, the Jingzhou garrison general Demin 德敏 investigated the Jingzhou horse pasturelands to ensure that no Han Chinese peasants had trespassed onto and cultivated crops within the pasturelands. To his dismay, some had reclaimed over 100 *mu* of land around Crescent Lake at the center of the Yellow Banner pasturelands in the area of Jianli County. The reclaimed lands were not only a violation of the "exclusion policy" that forbade Han Chinese peasants and fisher folk from having access to the pasturelands; they also restricted the movement of the horses of the bannermen. Demin immediately reported this to the Huguang governor general Aibida 愛必達, who ordered all agricultural lands within the Yellow Banner pasturelands returned to the banner and stressed again that Han peasants were not allowed into the pasturelands.[*,1] In addition, the Yellow Banner built an earthen wall to mark the boundary of the banner pasturelands.[2] After this incident and the subsequent closure of the pasturelands, Aibida also ordered other officials, especially the interior administration official (*lishi tongzhi* 理事同知) to investigate whether Han Chinese peasants had reclaimed other banner pasturelands in the Jingzhou area.

While enforcing the exclusion policy, Aibida demonstrated that he was not completely unaware of the peasants' urgent need for more agricultural land in this region. The Han Chinese peasants were not allowed to cultivate horse pasturelands, but he suggested that they could farm the wastelands on the outskirts of the pasturelands, as long as a distance of at least half a *li* (about 250 meters) separated the pasturelands and the newly converted agricultural land.[3] The incident ended with an interesting twist: the garrison officials eventually decided to open up the pasturelands to local peasants. Starting in 1761,

* An early version of this chapter appears as an article in *Environmental History in East Asia: Interdisciplinary Perspectives*, ed. Ts'ui-jung Liu (New York: Routledge, 2014), 100–125.

1 *Daqing gaozong chun (Qianlong) huangdi shilu* 大清高宗純（乾隆）皇帝實錄 [*A Veritable Record of the Qianlong Emperor*] (Taipei: Hualian chubanshe, 1964), 9514. It is shortened as *Qing gaozong shilu* in the following text.

2 *Qing gaozong shilu.*

3 *Qing gaozong shilu.*

© KONINKLIJKE BRILL NV, LEIDEN, 2022 | DOI:10.1163/9789004505285_005

the Jingzhou horse pasturelands were used for pasturing horses from the seventh to the third or fourth month of the following year; the rest of the year they were open to peasants.[4]

This event shows the competing interests of the banner garrison of Jingzhou and the Han peasants in this region—the Han Chinese peasants reclaimed lands from floodplains, lake areas, and riverbanks that were also used by the banner garrisons for horse pasturelands. The floodplains, lakefronts, and riverbanks functioned here as a "strategic space,"[5] a contested space that could be used either for settling Han peasants or preserving Manchu privileges in an era of "land hunger." By analyzing the situation of the horse pasturelands of the Jingzhou garrison, this chapter probes the ambivalent acts of the Qing state in central China in terms of land reclamation, water management, and managing Manchu-Han tensions in the eighteenth-century Jianghan Plain as well as how its decision-making interacted with the local environment on the plain. I show here that the large bodies of water and the local environment on the Jianghan Plain played an important role in shaping Qing state's decisions on governing the region, and that the Qing state's political agenda of settling the Han peasants overrode its concern for the river-lake system. Adaptation to the wet, humid environment of the Jianghan Plain was a challenge for the Inner Asians and their horses. This, in turn, contributed to a decrease in the horse population in the Jingzhou garrison, from over 13,000 during the reign of Kangxi (1661–1722) to around 2,000 during the reign of Guangxu (1875–1908).[6] By the early nineteenth century, as the horse population fell, the vast pasturelands were converted to agricultural lands.

4 *Daqing huidian shili* (1818) 大清會典事例 (嘉慶) [*Cases on Qing Collected Statues*] (Taipei: Wenhai chubanshe, 1991), 647: 113, says "from the seventh month of the lunar calendar to the next fourth month of the lunar calendar"; in *Qing gaozong shilu*, 9514, it says "from the seventh month of the lunar calendar to the next third month of the lunar calendar."

5 Nicholas K. Menzies, "Strategic Space: Exclusion and Inclusion in Wildlands Policies in Late Imperial China," *Modern Asian Studies* 26, no. 4 (1992). Menzies poses the concept of "wildlands" and argues that "wildlands" were a source of disorder and that the Qing state tried to bring those wildlands under control by settlement.

6 According to the records of *Daqing huidian shili* (1899), the number of horses during the reign of Guangxu was around 2,600, but according to the records of the Jingzhou Garrison, only around 1,000 horses were left at the garrison during the reign of Xianfeng (1850–1861). The numbers might be manipulated or recorded in error, or there might have been fluctuations in the number of horses because the horse population was replenished by horses from other regions. Nevertheless, the huge decrease in the horse population is clear.

1 Manchus and Horses

To understand the Qing state's decision-making regarding horses, we start with the symbiosis between them and Manchus. Horses were first domesticated in the western part of the Eurasian Steppe and reached China in the late Neolithic period. Initially they were not domesticated for use as studs, which was a complicated invention by agriculturalists in the Inner Asian steppes.[7] Training horses for riding was difficult and so was training them for warfare, as they reacts nervously and violently to even the slightest danger.[8] However, a combination of factors enabled horseback riding to become an integral part of the lives of people in Inner Asia, including the Mongols, Manchus, Jurchens, Uighurs, Zunghars, and Russians: the limitations of the steppe environment, the development of horse-handling techniques, the successful breeding of bigger horses, and the need to train cavalry.[9] In this sense, horseback riding shaped the Inner Asian nomadic identity to a large extent. Three additional aspects of Manchu tradition demonstrate the specific significance of the horse in their lifestyle.

First, in their homeland on the northeastern frontier of China proper (*kou nei* 口内), the Manchus developed military organizations that revolved around cavalry; handling horses was deeply ingrained in the Manchu martial tradition. "Being good at riding horses and accurately shooting arrows" were important criteria to be considered a capable Manchu soldier. Portraits of the Qing emperors and Manchu/Mongol soldiers showed them riding on horseback and equipped with arrows. When the Qing state established military garrisons in various places in China proper, the cavalry was an important component of the banner troops, although its military significance was declining. During the reign of Kangxi, the Xi'an garrison had 700 infantry soldiers and 6,700 cavalry (90 percent of the military force), whereas the Jingzhou garrison had 700 infantry soldiers and 4,700 cavalry (85 percent of the troops).[10] This large cavalry required a substantial number of horses.

Second, horseback riding was an essential part of the Manchu identity, "a package of virtues expected of the complete bannerman" and an "identifying code for everyone in the banners, particularly males."[11] Other elements included

7 James F. Downs, "The Origin and Spread of Riding in the Near East and Central Asia," *American Anthropologist* 63, no. 6 (1961): 1193–1194.

8 Downs, "The Origin and Spread of Riding."

9 Downs, "The Origin and Spread of Riding."

10 *Daqing huidian* (1690) 大清會典 (康熙朝) [*Qing Collected Statues in the Kangxi Reign*] (Taipei: wenhai chubanshe, 1992), 82: 4114.

11 Mark C. Elliott, *The Manchu Way: The Eight Banners and Ethnic Identity in Late Imperial China* (Stanford: Stanford University Press, 2001), 8–9.

mastery of the Manchu language, archery skills, and frugality. The Kangxi emperor once noted that, to be considered a man, a ten-year-old boy had to be able to handle horses properly.[12] The Yongzheng emperor (r. 1722–1735) also emphasized that since the founding of the empire, the key to Manchu success had been arrows and horses.[13] Likewise, the Qianlong emperor (r. 1735–1796) acknowledged the significance of training in shooting and horseback riding for the banner army's military vitality: the Manchus, whether soldiers or ordinary people, were expected to become proficient in horsemanship and archery.[14]

Horses were also the subject of elaborate Qing court arts and rituals. Giuseppe Castiglione (1688–1766), a well-trained Italian Jesuit painter, painted numerous paintings with horses in them, including a portrait of the Qianlong emperor in armor on horseback (Figure 12) and a portrait of a steppe solider (Kalmouk Ayusi) on horseback (Figure 13). Castiglione's masterpiece, "One Hundred Horses," has a naturalistic style showing horses in various sizes and poses, with no two of them identical; it portrays a harmonious relationship among people, horses, and nature (Figure 14).[15] Castiglione's work was largely produced under the patronage of the Qing court, a sign of its special interest in horses.

Shamanistic rituals practiced by the Qing court also showed great concern for horses. The Kangxi emperor once vividly described the ritual of praying for horses:

> We have the shamans pray aloud in our presence before five pair of white horses who stand with heads turned toward the west, near the holy tree where twenty-seven paper offerings hang: "Oh Lord of Heaven, Oh Mongol leaders, Manchu princes, we pray to you for our swift horses. Through your power may their legs lift high, their manes toss; may they

12 Jonathan D. Spence, *Emperor of China: Self-Portrait of Kang-Hsi* (New York: Vintage Books, 1998), 12.

13 *Jingzhou zhufang zhi* 荊州駐防志 [*Gazetteer of the Jingzhou Garrison*], comp. Xiyuan (Wuhan: Hubei jiaoyu chubanshe, 1879/2002), 2: 20, 21, 25.

14 *Jingzhou zhufang zhi*, 2: 27.

15 Giuseppe Castiglione worked as a muralist in Europe and helped to create a new, hybrid style that combined Western realism with traditional Chinese conventions of composition and brushwork. According to an introduction to a collection of Castiglione's paintings, the preparatory drawing for "One Hundred Horses" was "executed almost exclusively in the European manner: the landscape is represented using Western-style perspective, figures are often shown in dramatically foreshortened views, and vegetation is depicted with spontaneous arabesques and cross-hatching." Metropolitan Museum of Art (http://www.metmuseum.org/art/collection/search/44632/).

FIGURE 12 Portrait of the Qianlong emperor in ceremonial armor on horseback, 1739 or 1758, by Giuseppe Castiglione
SOURCE: PAMELA KYLE CROSSLEY, *A TRANSLUCENT MIRROR: HISTORY AND IDENTITY IN QING IMPERIAL IDEOLOGY* (UNIVERSITY OF CALIFORNIA PRESS, 1999), 272–276, HTTPS://UPLOAD.WIKIMEDIA.ORG/WIKIPEDIA/COMMONS/D/D4/THE_QIANLONG_EMPEROR_IN_CEREMONIAL_ARMOUR_ON_HORSEBACK.JPG.

FIGURE 13 Ayusi on Horseback (in the eighteenth century) 阿玉錫持矛蕩寇圖 (detail), by Giuseppe Castiglione
Note: Ayusi, a chieftain of the Zunghars, in a powerful image of the steppe warrior. After Ayusi submitted to the Qing court, the Qianlong emperor appointed him to the Imperial Guard. In 1775, Ayusi won a critical victory at Kedeng'ela 格登鄂拉 during the Qing campaign in Ili, Xinjiang. Qianlong was very impressed by his bravery, wrote a song, and ordered Castiglione to paint his portrait.
SOURCE: HTTP: //COMMONS.WIKIMEDIA.ORG/WIKI/FILE:LANGSHIMING_MAO.JPG.

> swallow the winds as they race, and grow ever sleeker as they drink in the mists; may they have fodder to eat, and be healthy and strong; may they have roots to nibble, and reach a great age. Guard them from ditches, from the precipices over which they might fall; keep them far from thieves. Oh gods, guard them; oh spirits, help them![16]

In this prayer, it is clear that healthy horses were believed to be essential for a bannerman's life as well as the military vitality of the cavalry.

Raising horses and managing horse pasturelands, therefore, were inseparable from Qing domestic affairs. Horses could be raised in two ways: collectively 圈馬 (*quanma*, raising horses in fields), and individually 栓馬 (*shuanma*, allocating horses to individual officials and soldiers). Qing law allowed 200 horses

16 Spence, *Emperor of China*, 12.

FIGURE 14 One Hundred Horses 百駿圖 (detail), dated to 1728, by Giuseppe Castiglione
SOURCE: METROPOLITAN MUSEUM OF ART (HTTP://WWW.METMUSEUM.ORG/ART/COLLECTION/SEARCH/44632).

to be raised collectively by each Manchu banner, 100 horses for each Mongol banner, and no horses for Han banners.[17] Each Manchu banner official could raise forty-five horses, each Mongol banner official twenty-two, and each Han banner official only seven.[18] The total number of horses held by the Qing was 75,304 in the reign of Kangxi, 95,305 in the reign of Yongzheng, and 79,542 in the reign of Guangxu.[19] The total number of horses remained more or less constant during the reign of Kangxi and Guangxu, but increased during the reign

17 *Daqing huidian* (1899) 大清會典(光緒朝) [*Qing Collected Statues in the Guangxu Reign*], vol. 50, in *Xuxiu siku quanshu* 續修四庫全書 [*Complete Collection in Four Treasures*] (Shanghai: Shanghai guji chubanshe, 1994), 794: 475.

18 *Daqing huidian* (1899), vol. 50.

19 The calculation was done by Niu Guanjie, "Qingdai mazheng chutan 清代馬政初探 [A Study of Horse Administration in the Qing Dynasty]," *Yanshan daxue xuebao* 2 (2006). I verified all the data from original sources: *Daqing huidian* (1690), 82: 4114–4115; *Daqing huidian* (1732) 大清會典(雍正朝) [*Qing Collected Statues in the Yongzheng Reign*] (Taipei: Taiwan wenhai chubanshe, 1990), 114: 7451–7453; *Daqing huidian* (1899), vol. 50, in *Xuxiu siku quanshu*, 794: 475.

of Yongzheng. In contrast, the number of horses decreased significantly with the Jingzhou Garrison, from over 13,000 in the reign of Kangxi to only about 2,000 in the reign of Guangxu. The total number of horses remained somewhat stable across the empire, therefore, some horses were transferred from this region and transferred to other regions. During the eighteenth and early nineteenth centuries, horses retreated to the northern, northwestern, and northeastern parts of China.

The Qing state used large pasturelands to meet the needs of the cavalry. The choice of a location for pasturelands was usually based on the quality and availability of grass and water; a sufficient water supply helped grow rich grass, which was an important food source for horses. In addition to grass, legumes and root plants that normally grew in a watery environment were an important dietary supplement to the rations allocated by the Qing government. Wetlands, including floodplains and lakes, were thus ideal. For example, the horse pasturelands for the Xi'an garrison were near the Wei River, and the Hangzhou garrison pasturelands were on the south bank of the Qiantang River. For the Jingzhou garrison, the area of confluence between the Yangzi and Han Rivers was the ideal place for the horse pasturelands.[20] When the land became pastures, the Qing state forbade access to local peasants and fisher folk. This exclusion policy became a problem for the Qing state, because it led to a loss of tax revenue, and for the local people, because it hindered their search for more land for agricultural cultivation. The Jingzhou garrison horse pastureland is a prime example of the ambivalence of the Qing state, which was torn between the demands of competing interests: encouraging land reclamation versus preserving the local ecology, and promoting agriculture versus preserving the banner privilege.

2 The Jingzhou Garrison

The Jingzhou garrison[21] was one of the few large banner garrisons in the early Qing. It was in the center of the Huguang region, a key location for controlling the vast area of Hubei and a gateway to Hunan (see Figure 15).

20 *Daqing huidian shili* (1818), 647: 111–113.

21 Few studies have been conducted on the Jingzhou garrison. Some important works include: Wan Qian, "Wanqing jingzhou mancheng jiating jiegou fenxi yu dianxing juzhu moshi tuice 晚清荊州滿城家庭結構分析與典型居住模式推測 [Analysis of the Family Structure and Inhabitancy Pattern of Jingzhou "Man"-district of Late Qing Dynasty]," *Xin jianzhu* 1 (2006); Chen Yue, "Qingdai jingzhou mancheng chutan 清代荊州滿城初探 [An Analysis of the Manchu City of Jingzhou in Qing Dynasty]," *Sanmenxia*

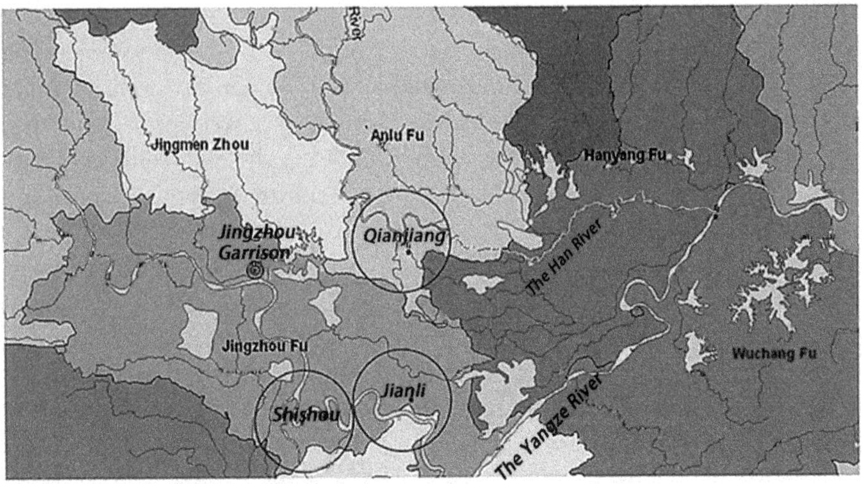

FIGURE 15 Jingzhou garrison and its horse pasturelands
Double circle: Jingzhou garrison
Single circle: main Banner Horse pasturelands (the circles do not indicate the sizes of the pasturelands)
SOURCE: 1820 HISTORICAL DATA, "CHGIS, VERSION 3.0" (CAMBRIDGE: HARVARD YENCHING INSTITUTE, APRIL 2007), HTTP://WWW.FAS.HARVARD.EDU/~CHGIS/.

The early Qing rulers were reluctant to set up a garrison in Jingzhou, largely because they did not consider the Huguang area important enough to justify doing so. But the Revolt of the Three Feudatories (1667–1681) demonstrated the strategic military importance of Jingzhou.[22] When Wu Sangui (1612–1678)

zhiye jishu xueyuan xuebao 8, no. 1 (2009); Pan Honggang, "Qingdai zhufang baqi de minzu guanxi wenti yanjiu—cong jingzhou qi/min de jici dou'ou shijian rushou de tantao 清代駐防八旗的民族關係問題研究—從荊州旗、民的幾次鬥毆事件入手的探討 [A Study on the Ethnic Relations of the Jingzhou Garrison in the Qing Dynasty–with Case Studies on the Banner and Han Conflicts of Jingzhou]," *Jianghan luntan* 2 (2005).

22 Wu Sangui was a Ming general who had been in the crucial position of defending the northern frontier of China proper. In 1644, Wu helped the Manchu army cross the critical military defense line of the Ming court and directly contributed to the military success of the Manchu army over the Ming. To reward Wu for his contribution, the early Qing rulers granted substantial power to Wu and two other local warlords in south and southwest China. When the Kangxi emperor realized that the power of these three warlords was so great that they might be a threat to the Qing court, he tried to eliminate their power. This led to an uprising by the three warlords; the subsequent war lasted about a decade and severely damaged the foundation of the early Qing state. But the Qing army, led by the Kangxi emperor, was eventually victorious.

and two other local warlords declared war on the Qing court and marched into Hunan, the Qing court dispatched a significant number of banner troops to defend Jingzhou and used it as the main military base to put down the rebellion. However, the Kangxi emperor did not fully acknowledge the military significance of Jingzhou until after Wu's troops were defeated.[23] In 1683, the Jingzhou garrison was established. The major military resources of Jingzhou were reallocated from Jingshi, Xi'an, and Jiangning.

Many officials, high and low, attested to the significance of the Jingzhou garrison. Mark Elliott quotes a statement by the editors of the history of the Jingzhou garrison on the role of the banner garrisons in maintaining order in the provinces by inspiring fear of their strength:

> When things are calm, [the garrisons are there to] provide protection and keep control, secretly, like a tiger or panther on the mountain. When things are stirred up, then they are to match the enemy's hostility and give everything in the defense of the city that depends on them.[24]

Although this was a general statement, the officials writing the history were clearly aware that the Jingzhou garrison was crucial for the Qing to maintain its rule in central China.

The Jingzhou garrison was unique because, unlike the other major garrisons stationed at Xi'an, Jiangning, and Hangzhou, it had only Manchu and Mongol soldiers and no Han banner soldiers.[25] The city was divided in two: the Manchu city, inhabited by the banner people, and the Chinese city, inhabited by the Han (Figure 16). The Han population was much larger than the Manchu and Mongol population. This made Jingzhou a banner city within a vast landscape that was largely Han.

---

23 E'ertai, *Baqi tongzhi chuji* 八旗通志初集 [*A Collective Record of the Eight Banners*] (Changchun: Dongbei shifan daxue chubanshe, 1739/1985), 536; *Qing shengzu shilu*, 1482.

24 Elliott, *The Manchu Way*, 129.

25 In the twenty-third year of the reign of Kangxi (1684), it was decided that the garrison banner officials, soldiers, and their families, from garrisons including Jiangning, Hangzhou, Jingzhou, and Xi'an, had to relocate to the capital when they were old, sick, retired, or dead. Their families had to accompany them to the capital; any family members who were in the army had to quit it and return to the capital. *Daqing huidian* (1690), 4130. This regulation changed during the reign of Qianlong. In 1756, the Qianlong emperor stopped the practice of having the remains of all banner officials and soldiers returned to the capital after their death, and the banner officials and soldiers were allowed to settle outside the capital. The garrison even helped poor banner soldiers with procuring a burial location in Jingzhou. *Jingzhou zhufang zhi*, 28.

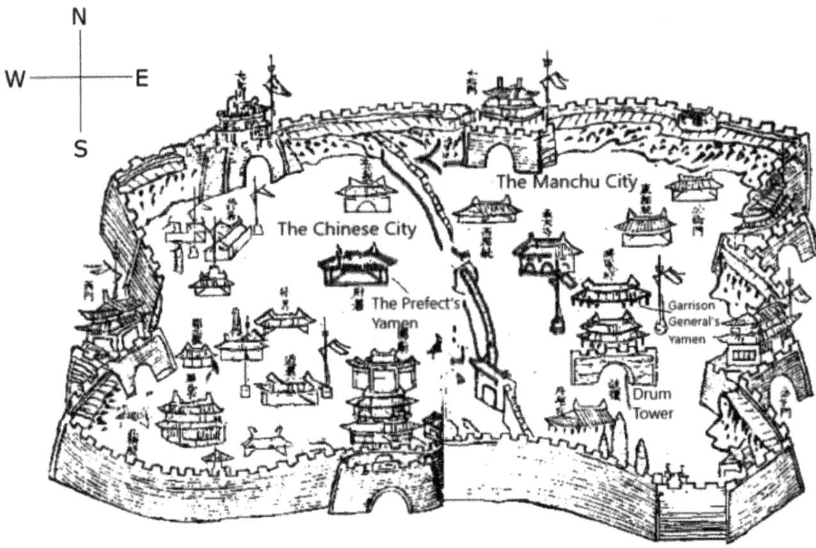

FIGURE 16 Jingzhou garrison
Note: This is a contemporary rendering of an image of the Jingzhou garrison. According to Elliott, "Chinese living in the 'wrong' part of town were moved over to the western side in 1683 when thirty-six hundred bannermen … were settled here permanently with their families, servants, and horses." Elliott, *The Manchu Way*, 112.
SOURCE: *JINGZHOU FUZHI* (1880), FIGURE 2.

In the early Qing period, the Jingzhou garrison successfully maintained its traditional banner features, but after the second half of the eighteenth century, it gradually lost its military vitality. During the reign of Kangxi, the garrison had 4,000 cavalry, 700 battalions, and 13,300 horses (including 1,114 horses for officers and 12,186 horses for soldiers).[26] In the reign of Yongzheng, the number of soldiers in the Jingzhou garrison remained stable (4,690 in all), as did the number of horses (13,233 horses, including 1,065 for officers and 12,168 for soldiers).[27] But the records show that in the reign of Guangxu, only 2,600 horses (including 874 horses for officers and 1,726 horses for soldiers) were left in the Jingzhou garrison.[28] Within decades, the number of horses in the Jingzhou garrison had fallen by over 80 percent.

26 *Daqing huidian* (1690), 4114, 4115.
27 *Daqing huidian* (1732), 7448, 7452.
28 *Daqing huidian* (1899), vol. 50, in *Xuxiu siku quanshu*, 479.

TABLE 12 The horse pasturelands of the Jingzhou garrison

Banner pasturelands	Location of the horse pasturelands (with Jingzhou garrison at the center)	County where the horse pasturelands were located
Bordered Yellow Banner	240 *li* east of the city	Jianli
White Banner	220 *li* east of the city	
Yellow Banner	210 *li* east of the city	
Red Banner	200 *li* east of the city	
Bordered Red Banner	180 *li* east of the city	
Bordered White Banner	140 *li* east of the city	
Blue Banner	240 *li* northeast of the city	Qianjiang
Bordered Blue Banner	90 *li* southwest of the city	Shishou

SOURCE: *DAQING SHILI HUIDIAN* (1818), 647:113.

To raise the horses, the banner garrison established pasturelands in nearby areas, especially in Jianli, Qianjiang, and Shishou—all located in downstream areas of the Han River and along the main part of the Yangzi River (see Figure 15). The total area of the pasturelands was more than 200,000 *mu*,[29] including eight pasturelands for collective horse raising, one for each banner. Table 12 lists the approximate location of each pastureland and shows their relative position on the Jianghan Plain.

Based on this description, Figure 17 shows the organization of horse pasturelands on the Jianghan Plain.

The use of the pasturelands was seasonal: during the autumn, winter, and spring, they were open for horses; in the summer monsoon season, the water level usually rose and inundated the floodplain, so they were closed.[30] When horse pasturelands were closed, they helped relieve the excessive water flow of the summer's monsoon; when the floodwaters receded, the pasturelands were left with nutrients that were beneficial for grasses and, hence, horses.

29 *Jingzhou zhufang zhi*, 108.

30 *Daqing huidian shili* (1818), 647: 113.

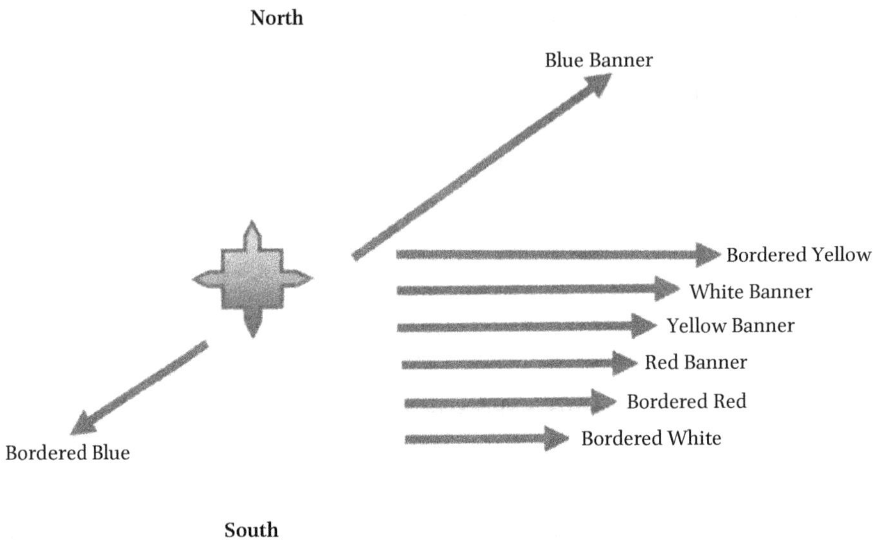

FIGURE 17 The eight Banner horse pasturelands of the Jingzhou garrison
SOURCE: DRAWN BY AUTHOR BASED ON TABLE 12

However, Manchu-Han tensions were usually heightened by the barring of Han Chinese peasants from the pasturelands, as discussed at the beginning of this chapter. The pasturelands were opened up to the peasants for many reasons. The veritable records of the Qing do not enumerate them, but one key reason for this compromise, elaborated in the next section, was the increasing population pressure and insufficient arable land for agricultural production.

3 Population Growth and Land Reclamation in the Eighteenth-century Jianghan Plain

The history of land reclamation in China proper has an ethnic dimension. The banner garrison wanted to have the best available resources for their horses, but they had to deal with the heightened day-to-day pressure of population growth and limited arable land. In the Shengjing area (from which the Manchus originated), the challenge of protecting the pasturelands was addressed by excluding Han people from all of Manchuria. However, in China proper this was not possible because the majority of the population was Han, and they sought more land for agricultural settlement. The reclamation of land on the Jianghan Plain in the eighteenth and early nineteenth centuries needs to be viewed in a broader context.

The eighteenth century was an era of rapid population growth in nearly all of China, especially in China proper,[31] and the Jianghan Plain and the Jingzhou garrison were no exception. The Jingzhou garrison grew from 3,534 soldiers and officers at the time of its founding (late 1600s) to 5,180 in 1776, and his increase was unmatched by other garrisons, except Xi'an, according to Elliott.[32] As early as 1722, the Qing court relocated 1,500 Manchu and Mongol officials and soldiers from Jingzhou to the Chengdu garrison (in southwest China) to relieve the pressure in the Jingzhou garrison. More than 5,000 people relocated, including family members of the officers and soldiers.[33] In 1871, the Jingzhou garrison relocated another 500 households, totaling 2,638 people, to the Jiangning garrison. In 1875, 300 households, or 1,933 people, left the Jingzhou garrison for the Hangzhou garrison. The following year (1876), the Jingzhou garrison relocated another 300 households, a total of 1,421 people, to the Jiangning garrison.[34]

Meanwhile, the Jianghan Plain also experienced rapid population growth, including both a natural increase in the local population and an increase in migrants from other regions. It grew from around 1 million in the early seventeenth century to over 10 million in the mid-eighteenth century.[35] By the late Qing, the plain had become the most populated area in the mid-Yangzi region. As a result, land became scarce, even though farmers were continually reclaiming land to meet the needs of the food supply. In Hubei, the average agricultural land per capita was 3.03 *mu* in 1786, which decreased to 2.12 *mu* in 1820 and to 1.75 *mu* in 1849.[36] Because population growth was not accompanied by major improvements in agricultural technology that would have increased the crop yield, 2.5 *mu* per capita was hardly adequate for producing enough food.[37]

---

31 China's population more than doubled during the eighteenth century, from around 150 million to over 300 million. In the period from 1779 to 1850 alone, it increased 56 percent, so on the eve of the Taiping rebellion the population was around 430 million. Ho, *Studies on the Population of China*, 64, 278, 282. For more discussion on the population increase on the Jianghan Plain, see Chapter 2.

32 Elliott, "Appendix C: Foundation and expansion of provincial garrisons," in *The Manchu Way*, 369–370; figures include all soldiers as well as officers below the rank of lieutenant.

33 Elliott, *The Manchu Way*.

34 Elliott, *The Manchu Way*.

35 Zhang, "Qingdai Jianghan pingyuan."

36 Mei, Zhang, and Yan, *Lianghu pingyuan kaifa tanyuan*, 165.

37 Philip C.C. Huang has discussed the "agricultural involution" in late imperial China in *The Peasant Economy* and in *The Peasant Family and Rural Development in the Yangzi Delta, 1350–1988* (Stanford: Stanford University Press, 1990). Mark Elvin makes a similar argument using the term "high equilibrium trap," in *The Pattern of the Chinese Past* (Stanford: Stanford University Press, 1973).

Thus, in the mid-eighteenth century, competition for agricultural land reached an unprecedented level.

As a consequence, land reclamation on the Jianghan Plain also reached new heights in the eighteenth century. From the reign of Kangxi and Yongzheng to the early Qianlong period, the Qing state engaged in economic reconstruction and encouraged people to reclaim land for agricultural production. The newly reclaimed lands were exempted from taxation for a certain period, from three to five years, and the local peasants obtained the most benefit from this policy. By the mid-eighteenth century, local peasants had built hundreds, if not thousands, of *yuan* to reclaim land in the vast lowlands of the Jianghan Plain. Initially encouraged by the Qing government, local peasants now carried out the reclamation spontaneously and on a large scale (see Chapter 2 for a discussion on the rapid increase of *yuan* construction in this region from the late Ming to mid-Qing period). Many of those private *yuan* were built in floodplains and near lakes, and at outlets from rivers to lakes. During the flood seasons, the floodwaters rushed through the narrowed river course and could not easily escape because many waterways were blocked and the lakes were not able to drain their floodwaters into the rivers. The result was usually the breakdown of river dikes and flooding of large areas of communities.

4 The Debate over Land versus Water

By the mid-1740s, a debate had arisen between officials who supported waterway conservation and those who continued to encourage agricultural settlement. In the early years of the reign of Qianlong, Wang Gai 王概, the Anxiangyun circuit official, and Tu Jiazheng 屠嘉正, the Jingyishi circuit official, suggested forbidding the construction of any private *yuan* and not repairing those that had been destroyed to prevent blockage of the waterways.[38] In 1744, Jiang Pu, the governor of Hunan, proposed prohibiting the reclamation of land from the lakes and floodplains in his jurisdiction.[39]

38 Peng Shukui, "Chajin siyuan tandi shu 查禁私垸灘地疏 [Forbidding Private *yuan* and Encroachments on Wetlands]" (1748), in He, *Huangchao jingshi wenbian* 117 "Gongzheng" 23, "Gesheng shuili" 4.

39 Yang Xifu, "Qing yan chitang gaitian zhi jinshu 請嚴池塘改田之禁疏 [A Plea to Forbid Converting Lakes to Fields]," in He, *Huangchao jingshi wenbian* 38, "Huzheng" 13, "Nongzheng xia"; He Xiling, "Qing cha pinhu siyuan yongjing sizhu shu 請查瀕湖私垸永禁私築疏 [A Plea to Investigate Private yuan and Forbid Them Forever]" (1824), in Rao Yucheng, ed., *Huangchao jingshiwen xubian* 皇朝經世文續編 [*A Sequel to Collected Essays about Statecraft of the Qing*] 117, "Gongzheng" 23. All references to *Huangchao*

In 1745, the new Hunan governor, Yang Xifu 楊錫紱 (1700–1768), submitted a memorial stressing the importance of forbidding land reclamation in the Dongting area:

> People are reclaiming land from those areas relentlessly. They cut river courses and cultivate rice in the middle of a river, and they reclaim the official lakes for land too. ... The local people cannot take a long-term perspective on this matter, and local officials care more about the tax revenue than the waterways. When there is excessive water, the upper land has flooding issues and the lower land has drainage problems.[40]

Therefore, he suggested the imposition of strict measures: land that had already been reclaimed had to be examined and recorded in the land registry; land reclamation was forbidden in areas with critical water outlets and water storage. If local peasants converted the ponds to agricultural land without reporting it to the government, they should be heavily penalized. If local officials were not serious about tamping down excessive land reclamation and just wanted to levy more taxes and gain a reputation for "being diligent in reclamation," they should be punished severely.[41]

Yang pointed out that this was a serious problem not only in Hunan, but in other areas in south and southeast China.[42] In 1744, Pan Si 潘思, the Zhejiang provincial civil commissioner, petitioned to forbid encroachment on lakes.[43] In 1764, Zhao Zhenye 趙振業, a county magistrate in Suzhou, also lamented encroachment by people on Lake Tai to profit from aquatic plants, such as lotus. He noted that water had no outlet for overflow during the flood season because aquatic plants covered the lake. He thus suggested that anyone who had land could not reclaim any water surface, and those who did not could claim no more than a few acres.[44]

In 1748, a memorial from Hubei governor Peng Shukui 彭樹葵 started a campaign to restrict massive land reclamation on the Jianghan Plain. In his

---

jingshiwen xubian come from the Taiwan Academia Sinica online database (http://hanji.sinica.edu.tw/index.html).

40 Yang, "Qing yan chitang gaitian zhi jinshu"; *Tianmen xianzhi* (1765), vol. 6, in *Zhongguo difangzhi jicheng*, 44: 455.

41 Yang, "Qing yan chitang gaitian zhi jinshu."

42 Yang, "Qing yan chitang gaitian zhi jinshu."

43 Yang, "Qing yan chitang gaitian zhi jinshu."

44 Zhao Zhenye, "Wujiang zhanshui siyi 吳江占水私議 [Encroachments on Wujiang]," in He, *Huangchao jingshi wenbian* 38, "Huzheng" 13, "Nongzheng."

memorial, he used the metaphor of a healthy human body to demonstrate the importance of a functioning water system:

> The water system is like a human body. The lakes along the Yangzi River, such as Chang Lake, Sang Lake, Hongma Lake, and Bailu Lake are like the respiratory system of the human body. The lakes in Qianjiang, Jianli, and Mianyang county are like the continuation of the waste-disposal system of the lower human body. The tributaries of the Yangzi River are like the blood vessels of human limbs. The upper body should be broad, the waste system should be blockage-free, and the blood flow should be unrestricted. Otherwise, a human body would deteriorate and be unable to function. The *yuan* construction is like a blockage and a constraint on the human body. In addition, the river waters in this region contain a large amount of silt that is easily deposited in downstream areas. Now, people in the Jianghan Plain are building illegal dikes and benefiting from their private gains; they do not know that if people compete with water for land in order to gain a profit, water must compete with people for land and cause disasters.[45]

In his report, the private *yuan* were considered a public nuisance: they interrupted the normal function of a river-lake system, like diseases blocking a human body, and they should be treated accordingly. The river-lake system was portrayed here as an organic system in which damage in one part would lead to problems in the others.

Realizing the damage caused by extensive private *yuan*, in 1763 the Qianlong emperor issued a series of orders forbidding excessive private *yuan* around lakes, river courses, and floodplains and at critical outlets from lakes to rivers. Local officials were also asked to survey the agricultural land and record it in the official land registry.[46] If any illegally constructed *yuan* blocked the waterways, they were to be destroyed. Since 1763, Hunan governor Qiao Guanglie 喬光烈 had been examining the land every year and reporting *yuan* construction to a higher department every other year.[47] In 1803, Hunan governor Ma Huiyu 馬惠裕 followed up with policy implementation, inspected the Changsha area

45 Peng, "Chajin siyuan tandi shu."

46 Peng, "Chajin siyuan tandi shu."

47 Qiao Guanglie, "Tongzhoufu huangdi ququan yi 同州府荒地渠泉議 [Opinions on Wastelands and Trenches in Tongzhou]," in He, *Huangchao jingshi wenbian* 38, "Huzheng" 13, "Nongzheng"; He Xiling, "Qingcha binhu siyuan yongjin sizhu shu 請查濱湖私垸永禁私築書," in Rao, *Huangchao jingshiwen xubian* 117, "Gongzheng" 23, "Geshengshuili" 4.

for private *yuan* construction, and reported his findings to the central government.[48] On the Jianghan Plain, actions were taken immediately after the policy was issued. In 1764, when Dongxi Lake in Tianmen County was encroached on by local peasants for private gain, the county magistrate Hu Yi issued an order forbidding excessive cultivation in the lake.[49]

However, the policy could be implemented in ways that were more flexible and acknowledged people's need to make a living; for example, limiting the height of the *yuan* dikes instead of banning them outright. Many private *yuan* in the Jianghan-Dongting area were built before 1763, when the official prohibition was issued, so they were not on the list of *yuan* to be destroyed.[50] The *yuan* dikes were normally very low, from 1–2 *chi* to 6–7 *chi* (approx. 0.3–2.3 meters). In this way, local residents could switch to fishing when waters were high and pay their taxes from fishing, so these *yuan* helped to sustain people's livelihoods. Therefore, the government issued the policy forbidding an increase in the height of *yuan* dikes so that people could still rely on this traditional alternation between farming and fishing to survive.[51]

Sometimes, *yuan* land was turned back into lakes, for example, Diaocha Lake in Hanchuan County, a case that I discussed briefly in Chapter 2. Local peasants continually reclaimed Diaocha Lake for use in agriculture or for harvesting aquatic plants; consequently, the lake became a giant *yuan* with a dike more than 7,500 *zhang* long. However, the Diaocha *yuan* was in a lowland area and was subject to serious drainage problems. During the Qianlong period, this *yuan* flooded three times—in 1762, 1765, and 1776. The cost of dike repairs and disaster relief exceeded 10,000 taels, but the taxes collected from the *yuan* totaled only 1,200 taels and 80 *shi* of grain.[52] The financial burden from the *yuan* exceeded the taxes it could generate, so it was better to convert the *yuan* back to a lake. People could switch back to fishing, the government would receive taxes, and the presence of more lakes to relieve the pressure of flooding allowed the drainage system to be more effective. In addition, the shrinking of regional bodies of water led many who had relied on fishing to farm instead. For example, during the reign of Qianlong, one part of the Liu lineage, which used to make a living through fishing, had to switch completely

48 Ma Huiyu, "Hutian zhanshui shu 湖田占水疏 [Opinions on Reclaimed Lands in Lakes Blocking Water]," in He, *Huangchao jingshi wenbian* 117, "Gongzheng"23, "Gesheng shuili" 4.

49 *Tianmen xianzhi* (1765), vol. 6 "Shuili," in *Zhongguo difangzhi jicheng*, 44: 455.

50 Ma, "Hutian zhanshui shu."

51 Ma, "Hutian zhanshui shu."

52 1 *tael* is equivalent to 37.3 grams and 1 *shi* is equivalent to a little over a hectoliter.

to agricultural cultivation.[53] Returning land to lakes was a better option for both government revenue and people's livelihoods. In 1767, officials had the Diaocha *yuan* destroyed and converted to a lake,[54] and many other *yuan* in Hanchuan County were also converted to lakes, such as the Shibali *yuan* and Shangxiaxiyangsanguan *yuan*. Literati and officials both considered this policy "beneficial for both the state and the people."[55]

In 1788, Jingzhou had a flood that was one of the most catastrophic in the mid-Yangzi region in the eighteenth century; many sections of the main Yangzi River dike were breached, and the floodwaters submerged the entire city. The Qianlong emperor was furious when he heard that the flood had mainly been caused by a sandbar blocking the river water and that a local peasant in the Xiao lineage had reclaimed this sandbar to profit from aquatic plants. Huguang governor general Agui 阿桂 investigated and found that the peasant had been cultivating the silted lands in the middle of the riverbed and earning income from selling aquatic plants every year from the Yongzheng period to the twenty-seventh year of the Qianlong emperor (1762). The sandbar grew larger and larger and eventually blocked the discharge of floodwater. Ultimately, the property of the Xiao lineage was confiscated, the peasant was punished according to Qing criminal law, and dozens of officials who had ignored the growth of the sandbar over the years were stripped of their official titles and years of stipends.[56] The Qianlong emperor was angry indeed, complaining in one of his edicts that the local peasants were pursuing private interests and disregarding the public order and that the officials were only interested in levying more taxes on all possible land to advance their careers. He ordered anyone who had committed the same crime as the peasant to be penalized without any leniency.[57] The Qianlong emperor clearly understood the hydrology of the river-lake system and was determined to ban land reclamation of bodies of water that might harm the empire's economy and environment.

53 Xu, "Mingqing shiqi lianghu," 50.

54 *Hanchuan tuji zhengshi*, 3: 5; *Hanchuan xianzhi* (1873), 9: 17–18.

55 Dingchang, "Qing zhuogai yuanliang shu 請酌改垸糧疏 [Suggestions on Modifying the Grain Taxation of *yuan*]," in Renhe qinchuan jushi 仁和琴川居士, ed., *Huangqing zouyi* 皇清奏議 [*Memorials of the Qing Dynasty*], vol. 56 (Taipei: Wenhai chubanshe, 1768/1968), 4685–4696.

56 This case was discussed in detail by Peter C. Perdue in "Official Goals and Local Interest: Water Control in the Dongting Lake Region during the Ming and Qing Periods," *Journal of Asian Studies* 41, no. 4 (1982). Six edicts from Qianlong discuss this case exclusively in *Jingzhou zhufang zhi*, 3: 53–58.

57 *Jingzhou zhufang zhi*, 3: 53–58.

However, proto-conservationist attempts did not last long; many private *yuan* were not destroyed, and many others were restored after a while and again blocked the waterways. In his 1803 inspection, Ma Huiyu discovered that among the ninety-four private *yuan* reported, only three were destroyed, while the remaining ninety-one were preserved. The government had ordered those ninety-one private *yuan* to be left unrepaired, but local peasants in search of profit had repaired them anyway. Local officials could be easily bribed by local clients to overlook these cases.[58] In 1824, He Xiling 賀熙齡 found that many private *yuan,* such as Lianpeng and Yangjia, both of which should have been destroyed in the mid-Qianlong period, were simply renamed and were restored by local peasants.[59] In the 1850s and 1860s, Diaocha and Shibali Lake, which had been converted from *yuan* back to lakes, were again reclaimed as *yuan*.[60] Many lakes disappeared because of the massive land reclamation during this period.

The statecraft officials continued to be concerned. For example, in 1821, He Changling emphasized that maintenance of hydraulic works was of fundamental importance for agricultural production and that "people should not seek immediate profit and forget about the long-term damage."[61] Wei Yuan 魏源 (1794–1857) stated in his account, "Irrigation in Huguang," that the spread of illegal dikes had led to deterioration in the water control network, which caused severe environmental damage; therefore, he proposed the destruction of dikes that blocked vital water routes. However, their efforts failed to stop the massive land reclamation. A description by Wang Huixian 汪慧先, written in the Republican period (1912–1949), shows that the land reclamation continued and became even worse later:

> The construction of polders in the lowland plain was completely chaotic. They were all built for private profits. ... Sometimes one polder was built first and other polders were attached to the first one; sometimes one patch of silted lands stood out in the lake and were reclaimed as agricultural fields. The shapes of polders were many—round, square, rectangular, and irregular. ... All were based on the topography of the land. There were also many types of sluices between polders and rivers and lakes:

58 He, "Qingcha binhu siyuan."

59 He, "Qingcha binhu siyuan."

60 *Hanchuan tuji zhengshi,* 3: 5.

61 He Changling, "Quanmin kaigou chuliao shi 勸民開溝出糧示 [Asking People to Dig Trenches and Engage in Cultivation] (1821)," in He, *Huangchao jingshi wenbian* 38, "Huzheng" 13, "Nongzheng."

some of them were stone dams, some were wood sluices, some used tubes, and some were the cut-outs on the earth dam.[62]

5 The Dilemma for Statecraft Officials

The Qing government was aware of the damage from excessive land reclamation, so why did it not implement stronger measures to conserve the water system, instead of allowing the reclamation to continue at various scales? One important reason was that in the mind of the Qing rulers, having people engaged in land cultivation was an essential strategy for maintaining social stability. Various arguments have been made regarding the acculturation of the Manchus and the Han during the Qing period,[63] but one thing is very clear: the Manchus were always sensitive about ethnic tension with the Han. They put a high priority on maintaining stability and extinguishing any possibility of social uprising. In a prosperous age, the Manchu rulers and bureaucrats were fully aware of the dangers of a highly competitive society in which one ethnic group (Manchus) was favored over another (Han). The Qing era had a large number of vagrants, beggars, migrants, and "shack people" (*pengmin* 棚民), who were mostly Han, and the Qing rulers and officials worried that if there was not enough land for those rootless people to settle, grow crops, and provide

62 Zhang Jianmin, *Hubei tongshi* 湖北通史 [*A General History of Hubei: Ming and Qing*] (Wuhan: Huazhong shifan daxue chubanshe, 1999), 81, citing *Yuanjiang xian shuili zhigao* 沅江縣水利志稿 [*A History of Water Control in Yuanjiang County*] (1985).

63 Ping-ti Ho and Evelyn Rawski had an extensive debate on the theme of "sinicization." While Ho emphasized the significance of sinicization on Qing rule, Rawski favored an empire-building model in which the "Chinese empire's cultural links with the non-Han peoples of Inner Asia" were more important. Ping-ti Ho, "The Significance of the Ch'ing Period in Chinese History," *Journal of Asian Studies* 26, no. 2 (1967); idem, "In Defense of Sinicization: A Rebuttal of Evelyn Rawski's 'Reenvisioning the Qing,'" *Journal of Asian Studies* 57, no. 1 (1998); Evelyn Rawski, "Reenvisioning the Qing," *Journal of Asian Studies* 55, no. 4 (1996). Pamela Crossley also re-envisioned the history of Manchu rule, especially that of Hongli [Qianlong], and argued that the ethnic categories that had been solidified during the eighteenth century became a source of nationalism in the early twentieth century. Pamela Kyle Crossley, *A Translucent Mirror: History and Identity in Qing Imperial Ideology* (Berkeley: University of California Press, 1999). Mark Elliott further developed the revisionist view of ethnic identity in his detailed examination of the banners and argued that the Manchu remained differentiated from the Han throughout Qing rule and that this was an important strategy for the Manchus to maintain ethnic sovereignty and the rule of the empire, in *The Manchu Way*. For a comprehensive discussion of arguments and important works on new Qing history, see Joanna Waley-Cohen, "The New Qing History," *Radical History Review* 88 (Winter 2004): 193–206.

for themselves, they would become dangerous elements that could destabilize local society.

Many statecraft officials argued that reclaiming land was a good strategy for stabilizing the population. In the early Qing economic reconstruction, Huang Liuhong 黃六鴻, magistrate of Tancheng County in Shandong, urged the exploitation of land in every possible way. In addition to discussing the labor shortage and regulating land tenure, he commented on settling young people as follows: "young males who are over sixteen years old, … if they cannot do well in study, should engage in agricultural work. How can we let them wander around and not do anything?"[64] Huang even suggested that a sixteen-year-old be considered a *ding* (丁), an adult male who was subject to taxation, which was two to four years younger than normal.[65] Of course, his main purpose was to increase tax revenue by urging more people to farm, but he was also concerned about people being lazy and rootless.

As the governor of Shanxi province, Chen Hongmou 陳宏謀 (1696–1771) recognized the importance of having sufficient arable land for maintaining social stability, writing:

> Shanxi province is vast and the villages are sparse. … Local people are not well civilized—they are ignorant and narrow-minded, bound to old customs, and are easily confused by various mistaken views. When they are not able to make a living, they easily commit crimes. Local officials should investigate villages and educate local people. They should teach people to engage in agricultural production, water control construction, and sericulture.[66]

He was subsequently appointed governor of Hubei and governor general of Hunan-Hubei.

---

64 Huang Liuhong, "Yangmin sizheng 養民四政 [Four Ways of Nourishing People]," in He, *Huangchao jingshi wenbian* 28, "Huzheng" 3.

65 Liu Xiusheng, "Qingdai xianzheng guanli de baike quanshu–ping Huang Liuhong <Fuhui quanshu> jiqi weiguan zhidao 清代縣政管理的百科全書—評黃六鴻《福惠全書》及其為官之道 [An Encyclopedia of the Qing County Administration: Evaluating *Fuhui quanshu* and Huang's Way of Being an Official]," In *Zhongguo shehui jingjishi luncong: Wu Chengming jiaoshou jiushi huadan jinian wenji* 中國社會經濟史論叢：吳承明教授九十華誕紀念文集 [*An Anthology on Chinese Social and Economic History: In Celebration of the Ninetieth Birthday of Professor Wu Chengming*], ed. Fang Xing. Beijing: Zhongguo shehui kexue chubanshe. 762–769.

66 Chen Hongmou, "Xunlixiangchun xingchu shiyi xi 巡歷鄉村興除事宜檄 [Inspecting Villages and Issues that Need to Be Dealt With]," in He, *Huangchao jingshi wenbian* 28, "Huzheng" 3. William T. Rowe extensively discusses the *jingshi* ideology of Chen Hongmou in *Saving the World: Chen Hongmou and Elite Consciousness in Eighteenth-Century China* (Stanford: Stanford University Press, 2002).

Manchu officials had the same concerns as their Han counterparts. In 1732, the Guangdong provincial governor Emida 鄂彌達 sent a memorial to emphasize the importance of reclaiming land in Guangdong Province, arguing that:

> The local people of Guangdong are poor and uncivilized; therefore, they fight for even a small profit. For an instance, they steal ore from forbidden mine sites and smuggle it for profit. They do not care in the least about the law of the state. It is all because those people have no land to cultivate, and have no work to do, that they gradually turn to vagrants and rebels. … To settle those rootless and restless people, a good way is to lead them and give them ways of living. … So, officials should engage poor people in land reclamation and agricultural production. …Within a few years, most of the land in Guangdong province shall be cultivated and the people shall have sufficient livelihoods. If there are no vagrants and beggars, the local order will be secured.[67]

Throughout Chinese imperial history, the ruling class prioritized the prevention of disorder in the regime over many other issues. Apparently, the belief that people would commit crimes and become rebels if they did not have enough land to cultivate was so prevalent among both Han and Manchu officials that they prioritized the economy and stability over the sustainability of the local environment, even though they recognized that the chance of floods and drainage problems was increased by the blockage of the waterways due to land reclamation.[68]

Many state officials believed that the existence of uncultivated land not only hindered the economic recovery and the settling of local people but also posed a serious threat to their careers. If land were left uncultivated, and officials could not collect enough taxes in the form of grain from local peasants, the officials would be penalized for their underperformance. Therefore, they would investigate the available but uncultivated lands and encourage people to settle and cultivate it.[69]

---

67 Emida, "Kaiken huangdi shu 開墾荒地疏 [A Discussion on Land Reclamation]," in He, *Huangchao jingshi wenbian* 34, "Huzheng" 9.

68 Philip Kuhn discussed the soulstealers case of 1768, which also showed the deep worry held by Manchu rulers about vagrants, beggars, monks, and other rootless people, in *Soulstealers: The Chinese Sorcery of 1768* (Cambridge: Harvard University Press, 1990).

69 Chu Fangqing, "Huangtianyi 荒田議 [Discussing the Wildlands]," in He, *Huangchao jingshi wenbian* 34, "Huzheng" 9.

Furthermore, officials considered land reclamation an effective way of establishing firm control over the local people. When people were granted land to cultivate, they were also recorded in the official registry and considered assigned to the place. As Chu Fangqing 儲方慶 emphasized in a memorial:

> People who cultivate land in the east were not allowed to move to the west; people who cultivate land in the north were not allowed to move to the south. After several years of tax exemption, they will be enrolled into the *lijia* system making them officially registered, localized tax-paying people.[70]

The contradictory goals of economic development and water management increased the difficulty of maintaining a functional river-lake system. As Anne Osborne has commented, "[the state's] efforts to restrict reclamation, control or prevent interregional migration, and control of lands use must be judged to have failed."[71] In addition to the Qing rulers' need to navigate between two incompatible agendas, the Manchus had many challenges to deal with in settling an alien environment such as the Jianghan Plain.

6 The Manchus and the Local Ecology of Central China

As officials were vacillating between restricting land reclamation for water conservation purposes and advocating land reclamation for the sake of the economy and stability, the Manchus in the Jingzhou garrison were confronted by a choice between raising horses in accordance with their Manchu identity and converting the horse pasturelands to agricultural land to meet the increasing needs of Han peasants. Ultimately, the environmental limitations and the pressure for more food production proved to have greater weight in the Qing state's resource management.

The encounter between the northern banner soldiers and the local ecology on the Jianghan Plain was not pleasant. The soldiers in the Jingzhou garrison were mostly from the North China Plain and Manchuria, where the climate was much drier and colder. By contrast, the climate on the Jianghan Plain was humid and hot in the summer. Therefore, although the Jingzhou garrison was designed

---

70 Chu, "Huangtian yi."

71 Anne Osborne, "Property, Taxes, and State Protection of Rights," in *Contract and Property in Early Modern China*, ed. Madeleine Zelin, Jonathan Ocko, and Robert Gardella (Stanford: Stanford University Press, 2004), 126.

in a Manchu style,[72] many parts of the city dwellings were adjusted to suit the needs of the banner people. For example, the soldiers' dorms were constructed so as to repel the heat and humidity; at the same time, many features of the northern houses, such as a fire-warmed bed (*kang* 炕), had been eliminated to improve ventilation and cooling.[73] Another factor that played an important role in the slow migration of the northern people of China to the south, according to William McNeill, was parasites: the Jianghan Plain's wetland environment incubated many diseases to which the northern banner soldiers were vulnerable, such as malaria, schistosomiasis, and influenza.[74] Disease undoubtedly threatened the soldiers' survival during the wet warm summers. Elliott's analysis of the impacts of the change in environment for the ordinary banner soldiers summarizes the Manchus' experience in the military garrisons in China proper:

> For ordinary banner soldiers and their households, life in China was a fundamentally different proposition from life in Manchuria. Over the course of two generations, people found themselves moved from a mainly village-based existence into a crowded and tightly controlled urban environment ... the life in China brought immense changes in their life choices and expectations. It is hardly surprising that this dislocation also meant major changes for the banners themselves.[75]

The environment of the Jianghan Plain was challenging not only for the banner soldiers but also for their horses. For horses, the wetlands of the Jianghan Plain were both a blessing and a curse—they were a source of abundant grass and water, but the horses, especially those brought by the Manchus from north and northeast China, found it difficult to tolerate the high humidity; many fell ill, lost their ability to reproduce and were unfit for battle.

Another reason that horses struggled to thrive in central China was dietary. A horse requires sufficient calcium intake from its diet to maintain its bone

72 When Dzengseo returned from Yunnan and reached Jingzhou, it was almost like coming home: "There were our soldiers' homes and our soldiers' camp, with doors and windows just like Manchu houses"—an indication that the distinctive architecture of Manchu cities was reproduced throughout the empire; quoted by Elliott, *The Manchu Way*, 190.

73 Wan, "Jingzhou mancheng jiating jiegou fenxi."

74 William H. McNeill, *Plagues and Peoples* (New York: Anchor, 1976), chap. 3. He distinguishes two concepts: microparasites and macroparasites. Microparasites refer to contagious diseases, and macroparasites refer to social institutions in which the ruling class lived upon the production of the large peasantry in a society.

75 Elliott, *The Manchu Way*, 131–132.

health. Under normal conditions, a horse can absorb as much as 50–70 percent of the calcium from its food.[76] Although the floodplains provided abundant grasses for the horses, they had a low calcium content and could pose growth problems for horses. One study has indicated that "the horse cannot be bred successfully in China due to the calcium deficiency in all organic matter including water."[77] Susan Whitfield also pointed out that "the lands and water in central China contain too little calcium for successful horse-breeding."[78] Several memorials feature complaints from horse officials that "the soil in this region is too wet" to support high-quality horses.[79] The horse at the top left of Figure 14 looks malnourished, which could be related to the shortage of calcium in the watery environment.

The inability of the horses from north and northeast China to adapt to other regions was also reported in south China. In 1724, Yunnan governor Gao Qizhuo 高其倬 (1676–1738) stated that "the grass of the Yunnan pasturelands seemed 'toxic'," so the grass-fed horses mostly fell ill and died.[80] Not only the officials but also the Yongzheng emperor recognized the problems with horses in central and south China. In 1731, he commented:

> There are fewer horses in the south than in the north. However, the military budget may be too tight to buy more horses for the south. In addition, it would be harder to raise horses in the south than in the north, since it was difficult for horses to survive in the south. Therefore, officials of the south should raise fewer horses for now and wait for the horses reallocated from the north, so that the horses needed for business and on the battlefield can be fulfilled.[81]

Despite the difficulties with their adaptation, the Qing government still tried to sustain the horse population in the Jingzhou garrison to enable them to maintain a banner army and military control of this region.

---

76 http: //www.understanding-horse-nutrition.com/calcium.html.

77 Frances Wood, *The Silk Road: Two Thousand Years in the Heart of Asia* (Berkeley: University of California Press, 2002), 54. Wood also mentions that the horses the Chinese imported from Mongolia were "small, shaggy, furry little creatures, looking as much like dogs or bears as horses" (in n17).

78 Susan Whitfield, *Life along the Silk Road* (Berkeley: University of California Press, 1999), 85.

79 *Jingzhou zhufang zhi*, 6: 108.

80 Gao Qizhuo, "Qing ken machang dimu shu 請墾馬場地畝疏 [A Plea to Convert the Horse Pasturelands to Agricultural Lands]," in He, *Huangchao jingshi wenbian* 34, "Huzheng" 9.

81 *Jingzhou zhufang zhi*, 2: 22.

The unsuitability of horses for the wetland environment also became evident on the battlefield, as expressed in the Chinese saying "southerners take boats, and northerners ride horses." After several battles with rebels, many officials realized the inefficiency of battlefield cavalry in this region. They pointed out that a watery environment hindered the swift movement of troops and that reliance on cavalry was therefore largely responsible for the military failure of the Qing banner army in the mid-Yangzi region.[82] This led directly to official consideration of reducing the banner cavalry in the Jingzhou garrison.

The official horse population began to drop in the late Qianlong period because banner soldiers used them less, though the Qianlong emperor, worried that the banners might lose their Manchu identity, tried hard to revive the glory of Manchu traditions.[83] For example, in 1752, the Qianlong emperor sent an edict to ensure that the banner people practiced riding and archery.

7 Efforts to Reinforce Manchu Cultural Identity

Despite the efforts of maintaining a distinct Manchu identity, the Manchus became more acculturated to the dominant Han environment, and there were increasing signs of the weakening of Manchu power in local garrisons. In 1816, the Jiaqing emperor emphasized riding and archery in the military civil service examination. In 1827, the Daoguang emperor complained that among the 5,000 soldiers in Guangzhou garrison, no banner people knew the Manchu language and stressed again that they had to practice riding, archery, and the Manchu language.[84]

The problem of controlling the Jianghan Plain was made worse by badly structured garrison institutions. The garrisons were established mainly as a military means of putting down large rebellions and waging large-scale warfare; however, they were restricted in their military duties by their separation from other institutions. For example, the banner soldiers only participated in wars against other ethnic groups, whereas maintaining local order and combating crime and religious cults was the responsibility of the Green Standard Army.[85] In addition, garrison generals normally did not have access to the

82 *Qianjiang xianzhi* (1879), 3: 1, in *Zhongguo difangzhi jicheng*, 46: 353.

83 Elliott points out that this fear of being acculturated by the Han reached its height in the Qianlong period, in *The Manchu Way*, 8–9.

84 *Jingzhou zhufang zhi*, 61, 62, 68, 71.

85 Ding Yizhuang, *Qingdai baqi zhufang yanjiu* 清代八旗駐防研究 [*A Study of the Qing Banner Garrison System*] (Shenyang: Liaoning minzu chubanshe, 2003), 129–136.

provincial treasury, which was controlled by provincial governors and household administration officials.[86] Separating the Jingzhou garrison from civilians unavoidably weakened Qing control over the Jianghan Plain.

A conflict in Jingzhou in the mid-nineteenth century demonstrated the tendency of Manchu rulers to compromise banner privileges in order to pacify Han commoners. In 1846, a group of Manchu banner soldiers went to watch the dragon boat contest, normally held on the fifth day of the fifth lunar month, outside the Jingzhou garrison. During the contest, the banner soldiers shouted too loudly, and some people in the Han crowd complained and asked the banner soldiers to be quiet. The banner soldiers became irritated and destroyed sixty-one Han-owned shops. The next day, a group of banner soldiers again gathered and destroyed another eighty-eight shops in the Han part of the city. In addition, they threw away the shops' inventories and set the Xianning and Wuchang guildhalls on fire. The next day, Changyuan 長元, a Manchu bannerman who had already been stripped of the title of military degree-holder, attempted to evict some Han people from their houses and killed one of them. The incident was reported to the Daoguang emperor two months later, and he asked the Huguang governor-general, Yutai 裕泰, to investigate and punish the culprits. He also sent an edict to Jingzhou general Hengtong 恆通, scolding him for not reporting the incident until two months after it happened. Hengtong replied that he did not report it because the culprits had not yet been found, leading Daoguang to rebuke Hengtong for "being most stupid and incapable."[87]

The Manchu emperor could not ignore the possibility of a Han rebellion if the situation were not resolved. According to Qing legislation under the early emperors regarding the military garrisons, any banner official who assaulted a member of the local community would be demoted one official grade and lose a year's worth of stipend; any banner soldier who assaulted a member of the local community would receive a beating of eighty strikes. Other offenses were penalized according to Qing law, but the punishments enforced in this case were much heavier than the nominal legal practice: the leader of the banner culprits was decapitated, the bannerman who killed a Han resident was strangled, and the rest were exiled to border regions.[88] Hengtong was demoted from

86 Wei Yuan, "Kangxi zhanding sanfanji 康熙戡定三藩記 [Record of Suppressing the Sanfan Rebellion by Kangxi Emperor]," in Wei Yuan, *Shengwu ji* 聖武記 [*A Military History of the Qing Period*] (Beijing: Zhonghua shuju, 1842/1984), 80–81.

87 *Daqing xuanzong cheng (Daoguang) huangdi shilu* 大清宣宗成（道光）皇帝實錄 [*A Veritable Record of the Daoguang Emperor*], vol. 432, in the twenty-sixth year of the Daoguang reign (1846). It is shortened as *Qing xuanzong shilu* in the following text. The entire case was recorded briefly in *Jingzhou zhufang zhi*, 136–137.

88 *Daqing huidian* (1690), 4122–4123.

a seventh-rank official to a third-rank official, and Tieling 鐵麟 was transferred from Chaha'er to become the Jingzhou general.[89] The severe penalties showed Daoguang's determination to stress stability over banner privileges.

This episode had a theme similar to that of the soul stealers, discussed by Philip Kuhn.[90] The Qianlong emperor was aware of ethnic tensions between Manchus and Han and worried about stability; therefore, he constantly pressed officials to investigate rumors of soul-stealing sorcery reported in various provinces, even though little concrete evidence was found to prove the existence of such sorcery. Ultimately, the Qianlong emperor's fear that petty soul-stealing sorcery might foment Han rebellion, and his attempt to eliminate any sources of insecurity through constant interrogation, can be understood as having the same impetus as decisions made by other Manchu emperors to compromise horse pasturelands in favor of agricultural cultivation. They all valued stability.

8 The Retreat of Horses in the Jianghan Plain in the Eighteenth and Nineteenth Centuries

Manchu rulers had many concerns, including maintaining local military control, reviving the economy, managing the river-lake system, reinforcing their ethnic identity, and keeping an eye on Han rebels. Many of these concerns were in conflict with each other; the rulers accepted that there were tradeoffs and chose to compromise the river-lake systems.

The number of horses was gradually reduced in the Jingzhou garrison. When the Qing court established the Jingzhou garrison in the 1680s, it had 4,000 Manchu and Mongol cavalry and around 12,000 horses.[91] In 1742, Guntai 衮泰, a former garrison general, reported to the Qianlong emperor that the garrison was short of funds as a result of sustaining a large number of horses and asked to decrease that number so that the money could be saved for banner soldiers' stipends. The request was approved by the Qianlong emperor, and 8,000 horses were removed from the garrison; each banner soldier was equipped with only one horse, instead of three.[92]

The reduction was but the start of a continuous process of using an increasing amount of land for purposes other than pasturing horses—chiefly for

89 *Qing xuanzong shilu*, vol. 438, in the twenty-seventh year of the reign of Daoguang (1847).

90 See Kuhn, *Soulstealers*.

91 *Jingzhou zhufang zhi*, 127.

92 *Jingzhou zhufang zhi*, 127. Guntai, a bordered yellow Manchu bannerman, was appointed Jingzhou general in 1732; *Jingzhou zhufang zhi*, 129, 136; *Qing huidian shili* (1899), 113.

agricultural cultivation. Within a few years, the population in the Jingzhou garrison surged, with an embarrassing shortage of funds to support banner people's livelihoods. In the late Qianlong and early Jiaqing periods (roughly in the 1790s), the Jingzhou garrison generals Xingzhao 興肇 and Hongfeng 弘豐 each proposed reducing the number of horses by another 2,000, but their proposals were not granted.[93]

In 1833, the Jingzhou garrison general Sulefang'a 蘇樂芳阿 sent a memorial saying that "the Jingzhou area is filled with wetlands, and horses easily die in this humid environment." Therefore, he insisted that 2,000 of the remaining 4,000 horses should be removed from the Jingzhou garrison,[94] and his proposal was approved.[95] Again, in 1852, the Jingzhou garrison general Taiyong 台湧 repeatedly asked for an additional 1,000 horses to be removed from the garrison to save money, and his suggestion was also accepted. So, by the early Xianfeng period, the Jingzhou garrison had only 1,000 horses left.[96]

Because of the large decrease in the number of horses, less pastureland was needed; many floodplains and silted areas that had previously been used as pasturelands were gradually converted to agricultural land. The decrease in pastureland was part of the story of massive land reclamation during this period, including the disappearance of the newly silted wetlands (*xinyu zhou* 新淤洲) on the Jianghan Plain.

The Xinyu wetlands in Jiangling County, extending about 7 *li* (approx. 3.5 kilometers), were originally claimed by the Jingzhou garrison as horse pasturelands, where 440 horses grazed every summer and autumn.[97] However, garrison officials complained that the wetlands were mainly silted floodplains and were too humid for horses.[98] At the same time, there were fewer horses to feed, so a memorial to the Xianfeng emperor proposed that they "convert the horse

93 *Jingzhou zhufang zhi*, 127. Xingzhao, a member of the royal household, who held the title Feng'en Fuguogong 奉恩輔國公, was appointed Jingzhou general in 1774, 1793, and 1809, respectively. Hongfeng 弘豐, a member of the royal household, and a blue bannerman, was appointed Jingzhou general in 1798. See *Jingzhou zhufang zhi*, 130.

94 *Jingzhou zhufang zhi*, 128. Sulefanga, a Manchu bannerman stationed in Chengdu, was appointed Jingzhou general in 1832; *Jingzhou zhufang zhi*, 130.

95 *Qing shili huidian* (1818), 647: 113.

96 *Qing shili huidian* (1899). Tai Yong, a Manchu white bannerman, was appointed Jingzhou general in 1849; he was promoted to Huguang governor later; *Jingzhou zhufang zhi*, 131.

97 *Qing shili huidian* (1899).

98 *Jingzhou zhufang zhi*, 108–109. Fusen, a Manchu yellow bannerman in Beijing, was appointed the Jingzhou right-wing deputy general 荊州右翼副都統 in 1855; *Jingzhou zhufang zhi*, 134.

pasturelands into agricultural land, so that people could produce more food."[99] The pastureland was soon converted and yielded annual rent of more than 1,800 *chuan* (1 *chuan* equaled 1,000 copper coins). Hubei governor Hu Linyi 胡林翼 (1812–1861) designated these funds for maintaining banner academies and other schools within the garrison, including stipends and allowances for schoolteachers and to pay for paper and ink.[100]

Small pasturelands such as the Xinyu wetlands were not the only target of land reclamation; so were the original banner pasturelands that had belonged to the Jingzhou garrison. In 1761, as discussed earlier, the garrison's pasturelands began to be opened between the fourth and seventh months of the year for local Han peasants to farm.[101] In the mid-nineteenth century, the repurposing of the pasturelands became more substantial. In 1861, Bayang'a 巴揚阿, the deputy general of the garrison, proposed to Huguang governor-general Guanwen that they reduce the horses by 1,000, rent the pasturelands to local peasants, and use the rent to relieve the shortfall in funding for the soldiers' stipends.[102] In the same year, Guanwen 官文 and the former deputy garrison general, Fusen, proposed to the Xianfeng emperor that they "remove 1,000 horses, all the horse pasturelands shall be rented out to peasants for crop cultivation, most of the tax revenue from that land should go to the military supplies for the Green Standard Army, and the rest should be saved in case of famine years."[103] In 1862, Bayang'a was promoted to Jingzhou garrison general and again sent a memorial to the Xianfeng emperor stating the necessity of converting pastureland to agricultural land.[104]

The main goal of converting the pastureland was to increase agricultural production as well as to generate tax revenue. Bayang'a's proposal asked the Qing government to send a delegate to work with garrison officials in order to measure existing pasturelands every five years and to record the acreage properly. According to an investigation after the proposal, it had over 170,000 *mu* of pastureland (down from over 200,000 *mu*, indicating that it had been

99 Zhao Er'xun, ed., *Qingshigao* 清史稿 [*A Draft History of Qing*] 126, "lands" (12), in *Xuxiu siku quanshu* 續修四庫全書 [*Complete Books of the Four Repositories*] (Shanghai: Shanghai guji chubanshe, 1998), 425–426.

100 *Jingzhou zhufang zhi*, 108–109.

101 *Qing shili huidian* (1818), 647: 113.

102 *Jingzhou zhufang zhi*, 137. Bayang'a, a Manchu yellow bannerman in Heilongjiang, was appointed Jingzhou right-wing general in 1861. Guanwen, a Manchu white bannerman, was appointed Jingzhou general in 1854 and promoted to Huguang governor later; *Jingzhou zhufang zhi*, 134.

103 *Jingzhou zhufang zhi*, 108.

104 *Jingzhou zhufang zhi*, 108.

decreasing over time), all of which was converted to agricultural land. More than 7,000 *chuan* in rent was collected on that converted land, but even this was not enough for the banner soldiers to support themselves.[105] By the time of the reign of Guangxu, the Jianghan Plain had neither enough horses nor pastureland left.

Fifteen years after Bayang'a sent his memorial to the Tongzhi emperor, in the seventh month of 1877 he sent another memorial to the Guangxu emperor, in which he proposed an increase in the tax levied on the peasants farming this land. The rent on the different grades of land was adjusted accordingly: the top-quality land was taxed from 1.85 to 3.7 *qian* 錢 (copper coins), the medium-quality land from 0.88 to 2.58 *qian*, and the low-quality land from 0.02 to 1.35 *qian*.[106] The rent paid by the peasants was used as stipends for eight banner soldiers and the Green Standard battalions of the Jingzhou garrison, as well as for the schools in the area.[107]

The rental of the Jingzhou pasturelands was just one case of the garrisons responding to the thirst for land that was becoming more and more widespread through the last few decades of the Qing dynasty. As early as 1856, Weng Tongshu 翁同書 (1810–1865) complained in a memorial that many officials manipulated the number of horses in their reports, and the actual number was less than half the number reported. This situation was especially severe in Gansu Province, one of the largest sources of horses, where many banner people rented out pastureland as a source of income. For example, in 1908 half the 210,000 *mu* of pastureland that belonged to the Ningxia garrison was converted to agricultural production. In 1911, more than 82,700 *mu* of pastureland in Anhui Province was rented to local peasants and vagrants for farming, and the proceeds were used to support the livelihoods of the banner people.[108]

105 *Jingzhou zhufang zhi*; Zhao, *Qingshi gao* 126, "lands" (12), in *Xuxiu siku quanshu*, 425–426. It says that over 200,000 *mu* of banner horse pasturelands in Jianli and Shishou County had been converted to agricultural land during the reign of Guangxu, because the horse pastureland was extremely underused. The period of this source is different from *Jingzhou zhufang zhi*.

106 *Jingzhou zhufang zhi*, 108; Grand Council Memorial, Bayang'a, "Huikan jingzhou machang dimu biantong zengjian kezu 會勘荊州馬廠地畝變通增減課租 [Changes in Acreages of Jingzhou Horse Pastureland and Increase in Land Taxation]," Harvard Yenching Database.

107 Zhao, *Qingshi gao*, vol. 126, "lands" (12), in *Xuxiu siku quanshu*, 425–426.

108 Weng Tongshu, "Tiaochen mazheng shu 條陳馬政疏 [Analyzing the Horse Administration]" (1855), in Sheng Kang, ed., *Huangchao jingshiwen xubian* 皇朝經世文續編 [*A Continued Collection of Statecraft Writings*] 79. All references to *Huangchao*

The disappearance of the pastureland was a sign of the decline of the banner army in the mid-Yangzi region. At this time, the Qing court relied almost completely on the Green Standard Army, made up of Han soldiers but under the command of Manchu generals, to maintain control over the local population. However, this composition of the Green Standard Army also proved to be inefficient and ineffective in eliminating local rebels, especially those in the White Lotus and Taiping Rebellions. The weakness of Manchu military power in this region paved the way for the development of the locally financed and managed regional army (*tuanlian*) system, which became the major force defending the region against the Nian and Taiping armies in mid- and late nineteenth-century China.

Though severely weakened and no longer the primary military force, the banner army continued to participate in warfare. Ironically, the shortage of horses became a big obstacle to warfare against the rebels in Hubei and Hunan. The reduced horse population in the Jingzhou area is reflected in the records of the mid-nineteenth century reporting horse shortages on the Hunan-Hubei battlefield and requests for horses to be transferred from Shandong or Chaha'er.[109] In 1854, a report from the Board of the Military indicated that the horses in Chaha'er had been frequently transferred to other regions, so it had fewer horses than it was supposed to have.[110] During a battle in May 1861, the troops led by Yuan Jia 袁甲, who had only three hundred cavalry soldiers, requested more horses to fight against the Nian rebels. However, difficulties apparently arose in allocating horses to Yuan Jia's troops because only a small number of horses were available in Manchuria due to excessive reallocation of horses to other regions; only five hundred horses were available in Chaha'er, but they had been underfed in the summer and were not fit for long-distance travel and subsequent battle. Therefore, Yuan Jia had to buy horses nearby for use in battle.[111]

In 1859, Zeng Guofan 曾國藩 (1811–1872) sent a memorial to the Xianfeng emperor asking for more cavalry for the Xiang Army so that it could fight more effectively against the Taiping rebels. He was surprised that the rebels had

---

jingshiwen xubian come from Taiwan Academia Sinica online database 台灣漢籍電子文獻資料庫: https://hanji.sinica.edu.tw/.

109 See *Daqing wenzong xian (Xianfeng) huangdi shilu* 大清文宗顯（咸豐）皇帝實錄 [*A Veritable Record of the Xianfeng Emperor*], vol. 354 (1860, 1861). It is shortened as *Qing wenzong shilu* in the following text.

110 Board of Military Affairs, "Tiaoni zhengdun mazheng zhangcheng shu 條擬整頓馬政章程疏 [Suggestions on Clarifying the Horse Administration]" (1862), in Sheng, *Huangchao jingshiwen xubian*.

111 *Qing wenzong shilu*, 354: 5708.

been able to use cavalry with horses captured from the Qing army as frontline attackers and that the Nian rebels had more cavalry than the Qing army. To press his point, he mentioned several times that the rebels had defeated the Qing army: Li Xubin's troops were defeated in Sanhezhen, Jiangxi, because "the Xiang Army had never seen the Taiping rebels with cavalry"; and Wu Guozuo's troops were defeated in Jingdezhen, and this was again "because of the fierce cavalry of the Taiping rebels." He concluded that the Xiang Army needed to increase its cavalry to defeat the rebels. However, Manchuria was the base of the Manchus' military, so no cavalry could be taken from there. Therefore, Zeng Guofan worked with Guanwen to transfer 3,000 horses from Chaha'er to the Hunan-Hubei battlefield. At the same time, he also suggested recruiting 2,000 local horse-riding braves, called *mayong*, to join the Xiang Army.[112] Transferring 3,000 horses from north China to central China in a short time was an ambitious and risky venture—the horses had to travel about 1,000 kilometers to reach Hubei from Chaha'er, requiring about ten days of constant travel. When the horses reached battlefields in central China, they were feeble, tired, and ineffective in battle. This was one reason for the constant defeats by the Manchu banner army in battling the Taiping and Nian rebels.

9 Conclusion

The dramatic decrease in the number of horses in the Jingzhou garrison demonstrates the Qing state's shifting policies regarding water management, agricultural settlement, and state stability, as well as the impotency of the Qing state's military control over the Jianghan region.[113] Riding horses, the symbol of Manchu identity and military vigor, was a burden on state military finances and a barrier to expanding agricultural production. The Chinese character for "banners" (*qi* 旗) is a homophonous with that for "riding" (*qi* 騎). In the early twentieth century, a local saying in the Jingzhou region showed the shift in the relative social status of Manchu and Han Chinese by playing on the word

112 Zeng Guofan, "Tongchou quanju rengqing tianlian madui shu 通籌全局仍請添練馬隊疏 [A Pledge to Increase the Number of Cavalry]" (1859), in Ge Shirui, ed., *Huangchao jingshiwen xubian* 皇朝經世文續編 [*A Sequel to Collected Essays about Statecraft of the Qing*]. All references to *Huangchao jingshiwen xubian* come from Taiwan Academia Sinica online database 台灣漢籍電子文獻資料庫: https://hanji.sinica.edu.tw/.

113 The decline in state power in the late eighteenth century is a major topic for many historians of Qing China; see in particular Ch'ü T'ung-tsu, *Local Government in China under the Ch'ing* (Stanford: Stanford University Press, 1962); Philip A. Kuhn, *Rebellion and Its Enemies in Late Imperial China* (Cambridge: Harvard University Press, 1970).

qi: "Now you [the Manchus] are no longer riding horses [*qiren* 騎 (旗)人], we masters [the Hans] are riding horses; if you are riding [horses] again [*zaiqi* 在旗], we masters are going to beat you up."[114] Interestingly, the riding of horses and being a bannerman were connected here in a single Chinese word, which also shows that the decrease in the number of horses and horse pastureland was symbolic of the decline of Manchu military control over central China.

This decrease was also a sign of the Manchu (and Mongol) failure to adapt to the environment in central China. The horse pastureland and the Jingzhou garrison were still more evidence of an ideal that was ill suited to an inhospitable environment. However, Manchu identity should be understood as having been shaped and reshaped by Manchus' interactions with the environment in which they lived; therefore, Manchu identity was not completely dependent on the garrisons or the ecology in China proper.[115] In this case, Manchu identity did not depend solely on the number of their horses, the structure of the garrison, or the land they lost to Han peasants, but those elements combined to signify their declining banner military control in central China.

The state had tried to preserve land for horses but, in practice, the need for reclamation to accommodate the surging needs of a growing population and to increase tax revenue mattered more. This was by no means unique to the Qing, but the intricate relationship among the economy, the ecology, and ethnic tension in the story of the horses and horse pastureland on the Jianghan Plain offers a new perspective on land reclamation and state resource management in late imperial China. Although Qing statecraft officials intended to restore the river-lake system, they instead compromised with the local Han population in the interest of social and political stability. The decrease of pastureland in Jianli and Shishou led to an increase in the number of *yuan*, legal and illegal, and inevitably disrupted the river-lake system. This disruption contributed directly to the catastrophic flood in 1788, one of the most devastating incidents of flooding of the Yangzi River. More than thirty counties and prefectures in Hubei were affected by the flood, and tens of thousands of people lost their lives. It is ironic that even as the Qing rulers were desperately settling Han

114 This is in Pan, "Qingdai zhufang baqi." He cites "Neimenggu zizhiqu manzu shehuilishi diaocha 内蒙古自治區滿族社會歷史調查 [A Social and Historical Survey of the Manchus in the Inner Mongolia Autonomous Region]," in *Manzu shehui lishi diaocha* 滿族社會歷史調查 [*A Historical Survey of Manchu Society*] (Shenyang: Liaoning renmin chubanshe, 1985), 151: "今天是我們的天下，你們的天下被我們推翻了，現在你們騎（旗）人，老爺騎馬，你們要再騎（在旗），老爺就再打。"（Now you [the Manchus] are no longer riding horses [*qiren* 騎 (旗)人], we masters [the Hans] are riding horses; if you are riding [horses] again [*zaiqi* 在旗], we masters are going to beat you up.).

115 I am grateful to Prof. David Bello for pointing this out.

populations, at a high cost to the river-lake system, the seeds of disorder sown by the Qing government were starting to germinate: the 1788 flood created large groups of refugees who soon became sources of uprising (*luan* 亂): the outbreak of the White Lotus rebellion was just a few years away, ushering in an era of crisis in the mid-nineteenth century.

CHAPTER 4

Militarizing Water

Forts, Polders, and Landscape in an Era of Crisis (1796–1860s)

From the late eighteenth century to the mid-nineteenth century, a series of mass uprisings occurred: first, the White Lotus Rebellion in the 1790s and then, the Taiping and Nian Rebellions starting in the 1850s. The mid-Yangzi region was one of the main regions heavily affected by warfare, violence, disasters, and profound militarization amid insurgencies and counterinsurgencies. The Qing government implemented a policy of "strengthening the walls and clearing the fields" (*jianbi qingye* 堅壁清野) to exterminate the rebels. The policy initiated large-scale fort building in the mountainous regions that exacerbated soil erosion in the upstream river valley; meanwhile, a local militia was organized in the lowlands of the Jianghan Plain, which further deteriorated the hydraulic system. In this case, both the forts and the polder militias were militarized spaces in which intertwined human-nature relationships unfolded during the successive crises. Although these militarized strategies were temporary, their impacts on the environment were by no means trivial or short lived; on the contrary, this half-century of conflicts and resource depletion led to a catastrophic rural famine in central China in the late 1860s. The nineteenth-century Jianghan Plain had reached its environmental tipping point.

1 The Rebels and the Jianghan Plain

The earlier history of the Jianghan Plain reveals that riots, banditry, and warfare frequently besieged this region because of its strategic location and bountiful resources. The most famous battle was between the Wei kingdom and the Shu kingdom during the Three Kingdoms period (roughly 220–280 CE), in which Shu lost the critical city of Jingzhou to Wei.[1] In his book *Crimson Rain*, William Rowe observes a culture of violence in this region, the natural outcomes of which were the popular practice of martial arts, frequent group fights, and failed insurgencies. He argues that the long tradition of violence in Macheng

1 Chu Dawen, "Jingzhou lun 荊州論 [A Discussion on Jingzhou]," in He, *Huangchao jingshi wenbian* 89, "Bingzheng" 20, "Jiaofei."

© KONINKLIJKE BRILL NV, LEIDEN, 2022 | DOI:10.1163/9789004505285_006

was fertile ground for the seeds of fierce group fights and rebellions to grow during the eighteenth century.[2]

Although the government was wary of "rootless people" (some of whom were vagrants who had arrived as part of waves of migration) and considered them potential troublemakers and the main instigators of various rebellions, the border area among Hubei, Henan, and Shaanxi, as well as the upstream highlands of the Han River, was especially appealing to migrants, given its steep mountains, forest cover, and biodiversity. The migration into the highlands came in two major waves: in the sixteenth century and, then in even greater numbers, in the eighteenth century. Many of these migrants were "shack people" from adjacent Jiangxi Province; they clustered in the mountainous regions, lived in simple shelters, and plowed hillside slopes.[3] From the perspective of officials, the highland landscape at the provincial borders was full of unharnessed energy and a potential staging ground for insurgency. As Hubei governor Hu Linyi commented, "Those areas have complicated landscape and heavy contrary energy (*niqi* 逆氣), so it is better to clear them."[4]

The White Lotus Rebellion broke out in 1796 in western Hubei highland areas, particularly in Yunyang, Junzhou, Gucheng, Xiangyang, and Nanzhang, in the Han River upstream region (county seats are marked in Figure 18). It later spread westward and northward into Sichuan and Shaanxi. The White Lotus Rebellion was unique for its decentralized organization, made up of bandits, vagrants, refugees, and sectarians, without a unified leadership. At the same time, their activity was thoroughgoing, as the rebels even had connections within the county-level bureaucracy. Until 1799, the Qing state's pacification strategy of deploying large military forces to pursue the rebels had been largely unsuccessful. When the Qing realized that it was futile to rely on the banner army to eliminate the rebels, they resorted to mass militarization at the local level. Under these circumstances, the *jianbi qingye* policy was initiated in 1799. It ended after the White Lotus Rebellion was put down around 1804–1805, but many practices resulting from the policy, especially building forts and organizing local militia (*tuanlian*), remained and were reinforced during the Taiping Rebellion in the mid-nineteenth century.

---

2 See William T. Rowe, *Crimson Rain: Seven Centuries of Violence* (Stanford: Stanford University Press, 2008).

3 Yan Ruyi, "Pingding jiaofei zonglun 平定剿匪總論 [A General Discussion on Exterminating the White Lotus Rebels]," in He, *Huangchao jingshi wenbian* 89, "Bingzheng"20, "Jiaofei."

4 Wang Shiduo, ed., *Hu wenzhong gong fu'e ji* 胡文忠公撫鄂記 [*Hu Linyi Pacifying Hubei*] (Changsha: Yuelu shushe, 1988), 79.

FIGURE 18 The administration of Hubei during the Taiping Rebellion
SOURCE: MODIFIED FROM HUA QIANG, *TAIPING TIANGUO DILI ZHI* 太平天國地理志 [*A GEOGRAPHICAL CATALOG OF THE TAIPING REBELLION*] (NANNING: GUANGXI RENMIN CHUBANSHE, 1991), 68.

The Taiping Rebellion began in 1852 in the village of Jinping, Guangxi, spreading northward to Hunan and Hubei and then eastward to Nanjing. In January 1853, the rebels occupied Wuchang and launched extensive warfare against the Qing army. Between 1853 and 1860, the rebels spread across the area, occupying most of Hubei.[5] The main part of the Jianghan Plain was devastated by the fighting between the Qing army and the rebels, in addition to damage caused by numerous other small battles between the pro-Qing local militia groups and the rebels.

5 Wang Fang, *Dunbi suiwen lu* 盾鼻隨聞录 [*Wang Fang's Observations on the Taiping Wars*], vol. 7, quoted in Hua Qiang, *Taiping tianguo dili zhi* 太平天國地理志 [*A Geographical Catalog of the Taiping Rebellion*] (Nanning: Guangxi renmin chubanshe, 1991), 69n1. Wang Fang recorded that the Taiping troops occupied thirty-eight counties and prefectures in Hubei, most of them on the Jianghan Plain.

2 *Jianbi Qingye*: The Qing State's Counterinsurgency Agenda

The *jianbi qingye* policy was the main military strategy employed by Qing statecraft officials to exterminate the rebels. *Jianbi* means "strengthening the walls" by building forts and organizing local defense forces, whereas *qingye* means "clearing the fields" so as to cut off resource supplies for rebels. *Ye,* often translated into English as "wilderness," has a connotation of unruliness, uncertainty, and threat to the existing order. As discussed in previous chapters, the state was very uncomfortable with the notion of *ye*, seeing locations such as "mountain wilderness" (*shan ye*), "water wilderness" (*shui ye*), and "land wilderness" (*tian ye*) as launching pads for insurgencies.[6] Therefore, *jianbi qingye* was essentially a policy to eliminate the "wildness" in people and the "wilderness" in nature.

Building earthen forts and digging trenches were the main ways of defending against the White Lotus rebels and thus were strongly advocated by officials in central China. In 1796, the rebels marched from Xiangyang to Xiaogan, and the Huguang governor-general Woshibu 倭什布 (d. 1810) and Henan governor Wu Xiongguang 吳雄光 (1750–1833) were surprised by the fact that the only place left relatively untouched between them was Suizhou 隨州. Suizhou and surrounding villages had been protected by the deep trenches and earthen forts built around them by the local people, prevented the rebels from entering the area. They were later defeated by the Qing army. The two officials described the success of this strategy in Suizhou to the Qing court and proposed its use elsewhere as an effective way of defending against the rebels,[7] inspiring subsequent future counterinsurgency policies. In 1797, Mingliang 明亮 (1735–1822), a Manchu general, joined by Delengtai 德楞泰 (1749–1809), strongly suggested the use of this policy, declaring: "with rebels walled out, and people and food walled in, the White Lotus rebels would be starved, isolated and easily defeated."[8]

Mingliang's successor, Lebao 勒保 (1740–1819), and Lebao's adviser, Gong Jinghan 龔景瀚 (1747–1819), argued in 1804 that "the reason the suppression of the White Lotus rebels was not as effective as expected was that local officials had not carried out an aggressive policy of torching all surrounding farmlands

6 I am grateful to Professor Robert Marks for pointing out the ambiguous meaning of *ye*.

7 Wei, *Shengwu ji*, 9: 400.

8 Delengtai, "Chou ling min zhubao yuzei shu 筹令民筑堡御贼疏 [A Proposal of Ordering People to Build Forts and Defend against Rebels]," in He, *Huangchao jingshi wenbian* 89, "Bingzheng" 20, "Jiaofei."

so as to starve out the rebels."[9] Gong Jinghan in particular called for a combination of methods—"fort building, crop destruction, fortress-head nomination, militia organization, and financing via countrywide supplementary tax assessments"—in counterinsurgency policies.[10] Another critical contributor to local militarization was Yan Ruyi, who was enthusiastic about "clearing the fields." In his view, this strategy was "absolutely essential" for wiping out any traces of the rebels.[11] In 1842, Wei Yuan also praised the spontaneous efforts by the people in the Han River valley to build forts and dig trenches to defend against the White Lotus rebels.[12]

The attitude toward the policy was hardly unanimous among officials. Many of them considered the policy detrimental to the daily life of rural communities, though they agreed that it was effective in defending against the rebels. Some officials referred to this policy as absolutely "the last resort" for exterminating the rebels.[13] Nevertheless, the policy was implemented first in eastern and northern Sichuan by Lebao 樂保, then in Shaanxi and Gansu by Nayancheng 那彥成 (1764–1833) and his colleagues, and in Hubei by Shulin 書麟 (d. 1801) and Wu Xiongguang 吳雄光. Within three to four years of its implementation, numerous forts were built there, which strongly assisted the Qing army in defeating the White Lotus rebels.[14]

3 Fort Building in the Hubei Highlands

The highlands in the border areas of Hubei, Sichuan, and Shaanxi were once covered with vast forests, but they were extensively farmed by *pengmin*, the "shack people," who had migrated to the area in large numbers in the sixteenth century and in even greater numbers in the eighteenth century. Considering a river as an organic entity, upstream ecology undoubtedly has critical impacts on downstream ecology, and the repercussions extend to how local communities cope with those effects.

9 Gong Jinghan, "Jianbi qingye yi 堅壁清野議 [A Discussion on Strengthening the Walls and Clearing the Fields]" (1799), in He, *Huangchao jingshi wenbian* 89, "Bingzheng" 20, "Jiaofei."

10 Gong, "Jianbi qingye yi."

11 Yan Ruyi, "Sansheng shannei bianfang lun 三省陕内邊防論 [Three Provinces Shaanxi Inner Border Defense Theory]," no. 4, "Baozhai," and no. 5, "Tuanlian," in He, *Huangchao jingshi wenbian* 82, "Bingzheng"13, "Shanfang."

12 Wei, *Shengwu ji*, 9: 400.

13 Zheng Qinghua, introduction to "Great Military Events," quoted in Rowe, *Crimson Rain*, 209, 365n58.

14 Wei, *Shengwu ji*, 9: 400.

First, we discuss how the highland river ecology changed in upstream regions prior to the nineteenth-century militarization. Many scholars have studied these "shack people" in northern Hubei and southern Shaanxi from the perspective of migration and state control over vagrants.[15] But here we view them in terms of their effects on the highland ecology. They mostly employed slash-and-burn farming methods, burning the forest and turning the cleared fields, with the ash from the burned trees, into agricultural land.[16] This did not require much fertilizer or technology, so people could grow crops at a low cost. But the soil was soon depleted and became unproductive, leading them to abandon it for another area with virgin forests and start the cycle again. For a while, they were able to sustain themselves in this way in the mountainous regions, but as their population density rose, this slash-and-burn agriculture became unsustainable.[17]

After migrants went to the mountains in large numbers, they similarly turned the hillsides into agricultural fields and grew nutritious crops that could flourish in the highland environment. But the excessive and unskillful cultivation of these crops depleted the topsoil in the mountains. For example, maize, a New World crop, was introduced in China in the sixteenth century and spread quickly throughout the country by the eighteenth century. Maize was mostly cultivated in the sandy soil of hillsides, and its strong and long

15 Anne Osborne, "The Local Politics of Land Reclamation in the Lower Yangzi Highlands," *Late Imperial China* 15, no. 1 (1994); Ho, *Studies on the Population of China*, 143–148; Zhang Xiaohong 張曉虹, Man Zhimin 滿志敏, and Ge Quansheng 葛全勝, "Qingdai Shannan tudi liyong bianqian qudongli yanjiu 清代陝南土地利用變遷驅動力研究 [A Study on Changes in Land Use in Shannan during the Qing Dynasty]," *Zhongguo lishi dili luncong* 17, no. 4 (2002); Zhao Gang 趙岡, "Qingdai de kenzhi zhengce yu pengmin huodong 清代的墾殖政策與棚民活動 [Land Reclamation and the Shack People the Qing Dynasty]," *Zhongguo lishi dili luncong*, no. 3 (1995); Zhao Zhui 趙贅, "Qiangshi yu huayu: Qingdai pengmin lishidiwei zhi fansi 強勢與話語：清代棚民歷史地位之反思 [Power and Dialogues: A Reflection on the Historical Significance of the Shack People during the Qing]," *Zhongguo nongshi*, 3 (2007).

16 The slash-and-burn agricultural practice is usually associated with tropical rain forests. We found a similar practice in the subtropical evergreen broad-leaf forest vegetation, as in the mountainous region of the Jianghan Plain, known as fire-fallow agriculture.

17 Wang Shufen, "Qingdai zhishan fanghong huanbao celue zhi tantao: Yi changjiang liuyu wei zhongxin 清代治山防洪環保策略之探討：以長江流域為中心 [A Study on the Mountain Management and Flood Control during the Qing: A Case Study of the Yangzi River]," *Guoli Taipei jiaoyu daxue xuebao* 19, no. 1 (1995). Gong Shengsheng also points out that the main reason for extensive maize cultivation in the mountains of the Huguang region was the rapid increase of population. See Gong Shengsheng, *Qingdai lianghu nongye dili* 清代兩湖農業地理 [*Agricultural Geography in Hunan-Hubei during the Qing Dynasty*] (Wuhan: Huazhong shifan daxue chubanshe, 1996), 132.

roots easily loosened the topsoil. Maize also needed twice as much water as other crops, and, without it, the topsoil became dry and sandy. Thus maize cultivation loosened the topsoil and contributed to erosion. In some northern Hubei counties, soil erosion was so severe that the land had to lie fallow for decades to regain its fertility.[18]

In addition to growing crops, the shack people also cut down trees for sale in the market, which was very profitable. According to Evelyn Rawski, timber felling was so extensive in the Qing dynasty that even the most remote forests in the highlands of the Han River valley did not escape deforestation.[19] The shack people in Jiangxi also "dominated the trade in 'wood ears,' an edible tree fungus. … They cut down the withered trees on which the fungus grew and in the winter opened shops to sell the wood ears they had harvested."[20] Paper making, salt making, and coal mining also flourished in the highlands.[21]

By the end of the eighteenth century, many highland regions had been deforested for conversion into agricultural fields or cleared to make way for factories and mining operations. Yan Ruyi observed that the highlands in southern Shaanxi "were loaded with villages … only left with the bare mountain ranges."[22] He also recognized the problem of excessive highland exploitation:

> Within the past few decades, the mountains covered with forests were all opened up and became agricultural lands and villages; the soil became so loose that each summer and autumn flood season the rainfall running through mountains easily took a large quantity of topsoil away to the rivers, leading to a quick rise in the riverbed downstream. The flood

18 Ho, *Studies on the Population of China*, 149–150; Zhang Xiangwen and Hui Fuping, "Qingdai zhongwanqi shandi zhongzhi yumi yinfa de shuitu liushi jiqi e'zhi cuoshi 清代中晚期山地種植玉米引發的水土流失及其遏止措施 [The Soil Erosion Caused by Maize Cultivation in the Highlands and Its Prevention Measures in the Mid- and Late Qing]," *Zhongguo nongshi* 25, no. 3 (2006).

19 Evelyn S. Rawski, "Agricultural Development in the Han River Highland," *Ching shih wen-t'i* 3, no. 4 (1975).

20 Anne Osborne, "Highlands and Lowlands: Economic and Ecological Interactions in the Lower Yangzi Region under the Qing," in *Sediments of Time: Environment and Society in Chinese History*, ed. Mark Elvin and Liu Ts'ui-jung (Cambridge: Cambridge University Press, 1998), 203–234. See also Robert Marks, *China: Its Environment and History* (Lanham: Rowman & Littlefield, 2012), 212.

21 Zhuo Bingtian, "Chuanshanchu laolin qingxing zhengyiquchu 川陝楚老林情形亟宜區處 [The Situation of the Chuanshanchu Forests]," in Yan, *Sansheng bianfang beilan* (1843), 14: 17.

22 Yan, *Sansheng bianfang beilan*, 14: 76–77.

> torrents, filled with sand and soil, either destroyed numerous dikes or silted up outlets of rivers and lakes or the sluice gates.[23]

Scholars have acknowledged the soil erosion problem in the Yangzi watershed. Ping-ti Ho wrote that the intensive farming in the hinterlands of the Yangzi valley had two effects. On the one hand, total agricultural production rose; on the other hand, extensive land reclamation and deforestation caused severe erosion and, therefore, diminishing marginal returns in agricultural production.[24] Awareness of these effects of highland exploitation was reflected in the nineteenth-century writings of an official, Mei Zengliang 梅曾亮, which discussed the costs and benefits of shack people's activities. Mei pointed out that having shack people grow crops in the mountain highlands was helpful in supplementing the insufficient rice supply and settling people but these exploitative activities placed great pressure on the ecosystem in those highlands.[25] Mei discussed the opposition by local people to allowing migrant settlement in the mountains:

> [Previously,] when the mountaintops were not tilled by the shack people, the mountain rocks were solidly grounded, and grass and trees provided thick vegetation. Rotten leaves had accumulated for years to a depth of two to three *cun* [1 *cun* equals approximately 3.3 cm] above the ground. When it rained, water fell from the trees to the thick layer of rotten leaves, from the rotten leaves to the mountain rocks, and it trickled down from cracks in the rocks. The slow trickling of water could not take away the topsoil from the mountains and neither did it flood the lowland fields. However, shack people destroyed the mountain vegetation, loosened topsoil, and rocks flew down to the lowlands, leading to siltation downstream. This was harmful to the lowland fields where taxable grain was grown and created infertile land in the mountains.[26]

Mei was concerned about both social control and tax revenue and demonstrated a clear awareness of the correlation between highland exploitation and lowland cultivation. As Anne Osborne showed in her work on land reclamation

---

23 Yan, *Sansheng bianfang beilan*, 8: 4.

24 Ho, *Studies on the Population of China*, 150.

25 Mei Zengliang, "Ji pengmin shi 記棚民事 [The Story of *Pengmin*]," in Mei Zengliang, *Bojian shanfang wenji* 柏梘山房文集 [*The Anthology of Mei Zengliang*] (Taipei: Huawen shuju, 1968), 5.

26 Mei, "Ji pengmin shi."

in the Jianghan highlands in the eighteenth and nineteenth centuries, the large highland economy generated short-term profits but was unsustainable in the long term.[27]

By the time of the massive militarization of the late eighteenth and early nineteenth centuries, the highlands in the Han River valley were already fragile. The numerous forts built during extensive militarization would only cause further deterioration in the highland ecology, and their number increased exponentially from the end of the eighteenth century to the mid-nineteenth century. Writing about southern Shaanxi when the *jianbi qingye* policy was first implemented, Wei Yuan recorded that 541 forts were built in Lantian, Shangzhou, Wulang, and seven other counties, of which 80 percent were sponsored by the local people, and the remaining 20 percent were financed by the government.[28] However, we should not assume that only the pro-Qing forces engaged in fort building; in fact, the Taiping rebels also did so. For example, within a month of taking control in 1857, the rebels built fifty-eight forts surrounding the Macheng County seat to defend against the Qing troops.[29] The scale of the fort building was astonishing, as shown in Figure 19, which illustrates the increase in forts in Zhushan County, and Table 13, which lists the estimated numbers of forts in northern and western Hubei, comprising the upper- and midstream area of the Han River.

The fort size varied; most forts were 5.4–6 meters tall, 4.5 meters wide at the bottom, and 1.33 meters wide at the top. On top of the fort was an observation platform (*duo* 垛) that was 1.67 meters tall.[30] Forts were usually protected with a circular trench (*hao* 濠) that was 9 meters wide and 6–9 meters deep.[31] Inside the trench, people laid down numerous iron nails, bamboo sticks with sharpened tips, and iron nets.[32]

The density of forts was very high, as seen in Zhushan County and elsewhere. In Liangshan 梁山, Sichuan, forts were densely placed in an area of just a couple of hundred *li* (1 *li* equals 0.3 miles). Some forts were responsible for an area of 30 to 40 *li*; others for over 10 *li*; and still others for only 7 to 8 *li*.

27 Osborne, "Highlands and Lowlands," 229–230; see also Osborne, "The Local Politics"; Ramon H. Myers and Yeh-Chien Wang, "Economic Developments, 1644–1800," in *The Cambridge History of China*, ed. Willard J. Peterson, vol. 9, part 1, *The Ch'ing Empire to 1800* (Cambridge: Cambridge University Press, 2002), 638–639.

28 Wei, *Shengwu ji*, 9: 434.

29 Wang, *Hu wenzhong gong fu'e ji*, 141.

30 Wang, *Hu wenzhong gong fu'e ji*, 58.

31 Wang, *Hu wenzhong gong fu'e ji*, 114.

32 Wang, *Hu wenzhong gong fu'e ji*, 26–27, 46.

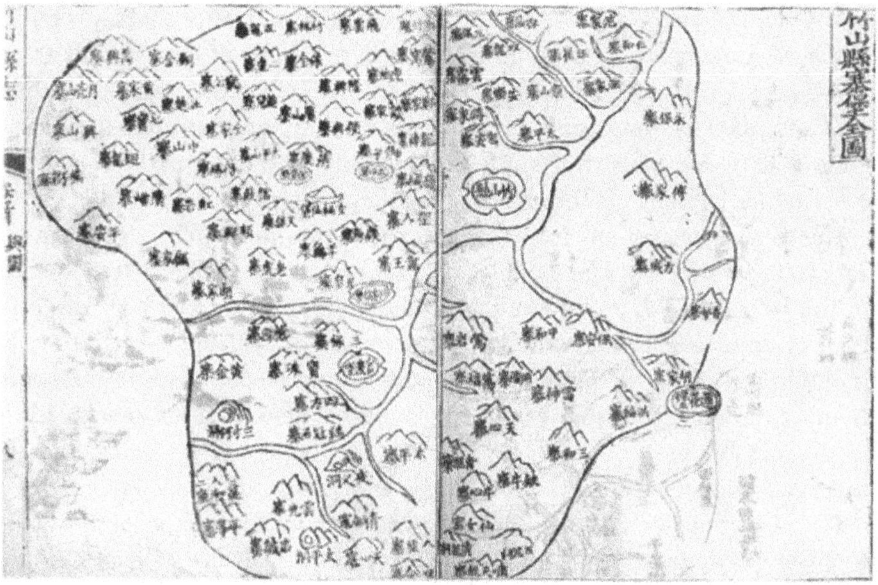

FIGURE 19 Forts in Zhushan County 竹山縣寨堡全圖 (Jiaqing reign)
SOURCE: *ZHUSHAN XIANZHI* 竹山縣志 [*GAZETTEER OF ZHUSHAN COUNTY*] (1807), 1: 58.

TABLE 13 Forts in Hubei counties in the early nineteenth century

Xiaogan	Macheng	Qizhou	Luotian	Jingshan	Zhushan	Xiangyang	Zhuxi
127	101	82	49	138	156	95	60

SOURCE: MODIFIED FROM YANG GUO'AN, "SHEHUI DONGDANG YU QINGDAI HUBEI XIANGCUN ZHONG DE ZHAIBAO 社會動盪與清代湖北鄉村中的寨堡 [SOCIAL TURMOIL AND *ZHAI/BAO* IN RURAL HUBEI OF QING]," *WUHAN DAXUE XUEBAO* 54, NO. 5 (2001): 576.

Forts were usually built on cliffs with only one narrow path to the outside.[33] The distance from one fort to another ranged from a few *li* to more than a few dozen *li*. Designed in this way, the forts facilitated observation and enabled

33 "Liangshan lingfanggong choulianbing xiuzhai sishi 梁山令方公籌練兵修寨四事 [Four matters on organizing local militia and building forts]," in *Kanjing jiaofei shubian* 堪靖教匪述編 [*Chronicles of Exterminating the Rebels*], ed. Shixiangcun jushi, 12: 321.

mutual assistance for defense among the inhabitants.[34] After a fort was built, people residing nearby moved into the fort. The houses of local people were torn down if they were simple shelters; houses with solid stone structures were left intact so that people could occasionally return to resume their agricultural activities. Forts were stuffed with grain and other provisions, as well as numerous logs and giant rocks to be used as weapons to protect the forts.[35]

The construction of one fort normally took a month. To build a fort, an area was cleared to construct the foundation; then stone was transported to the site for use in building it. Stone was the primary building material because forts made of stone were much sturdier than those made of earth.[36] It was also easy to obtain stones in the mountains, and they could be cut down to transport them more easily.[37] In the wave of fort building, deforestation intensified to make room for the forts as well as to provide the numerous logs for use in warfare; in addition, collecting the stones exacerbated the erosion.

The numerous forts in the highlands were effective defense structures, but they were extremely vulnerable to fire. The forts, normally built in clusters that formed a condensed space to accommodate people, could easily catch fire, risking the people and materials inside.[38] The records show that both the Qing army and the rebels often used fire in battles. In December 1855, the Qing troops used fire to attack the rebels in Wuchang, and "not a single Taiping soldier escaped their forts."[39] The Qing army took over four forts in and around the city, and over three thousand Taiping soldiers died. In 1856, the Qing troops contemplated taking over Nanzhang County, in northwestern Hubei, which

34 "Hezhou gongcishi jianbiqingye bing zhaofu yi 合州龔刺史堅壁清野並招撫議 [Official Gong of Hezhou on strengthening the walls and clearing the fields]," in *Kanjing jiaofei shubian*, 12: 294.

35 "Liangshan lingfanggong choulianbing xiuzhai sishi," in *Kanjing jiaofei shubian*, 12: 322.

36 The forts in the nineteenth-century Philippines were made of wood. In his article, Greg Bankoff traces the construction of forts in an attempt to subjugate the Cordilleras region of Luzon during the nineteenth century, analyzing the vast amount of timber used for fort building, which led to a scarcity of "valuable trees of large dimensions" and their place being taken by "juvenile ones," which resulted in the "impoverishment" of the forest. According to Bankoff, each pueblo or township in Isabela was assigned a quota of timber for delivery, and that number could be as high as 5,658 beams. See Greg Bankoff, "Wood for War: The Legacy of Human Conflict on the Forests of the Philippines, 1565–1946," in *War and the Environment: Military Destruction in the Modern Age*, ed. Charles E. Closmann (College Station: Texas A&M University Press, 2009), 32–48.

37 Yan, "Sansheng shannei bianfang lun 三省山內邊防論," no. 4, *zhaibao*, in He, *Huangchao jingshi wenbian*, vol. 82, "Bingzheng" 13.

38 Wang, *Hu Wenzhong gong fu'e ji*, 81; Wei, *Shengwu ji*, 9: 434.

39 Wang, *Hu Wenzhong gong fu'e ji*, 26–27.

was then under rebel control. After careful investigation, they discovered that it was extremely difficult to attack the rebels in the mountains of Nanzhang: the rainfall from the fifth to the seventh month of the year washed away mountain soil, which made marching extremely difficult; forts were built all over the mountains; and the rebels had ample food provisions previously stored by villagers in the forts. Therefore, they concluded, the best way to attack them was to lay down burning materials and wait for the right time and the right wind direction for starting a fire attack. The rebels had used this strategy to attack this area in 1800 and take it over from the villagers.[40] Precisely how many fire attacks were used in warfare is unknown, but even a single fire attack could have disastrous consequences for the mountain forest and vegetation, as well as to the people living there.

The cost of building forts was staggering. In August 1856, Hu Linyi ordered the building of fifty forts on the border of Hubei and Anhui, with each fort costing around two hundred thousand taels.[41] During the battles with the Taiping rebels, the cost of building forts contributed significantly to the large military expenses of the Hubei government. According to a memorial by Hu Linyi, from 1855 to 1856, Hubei's military expenses, including provisions for officials and soldiers, horses, uniforms, weapons, transportation workers, ships, fort building and trench digging, and other miscellaneous expenses, added up to 1.3 million taels.[42] These military expenses, accompanied by declining tax revenue, created financial difficulties for Hubei; this was one of the main reasons that Hu implemented tax grain reform in Hubei in the 1850s.[43] In addition to government funds, local funds were also an important source of revenue for fort building. Yang Guo'an described three ways of financing the forts: donations from gentry and officials, public funds collected from local residents, and corvée labor based on land acreage.[44] In two villages (*xiang* 鄉, a subdivision of a prefecture) in Qi Prefecture, 121 members of the gentry donated 1,019 *shi* in tax grain as the forts' annual maintenance fee.[45]

40 Wang, *Hu Wenzhong gong fu'e ji*, 81.

41 Wang, *Hu wenzhong gong fu'e ji*, 114.

42 Wang, *Hu Wenzhong gong fu'e ji*, 131.

43 For an in-depth analysis of Hu's tax grain reform, see William T. Rowe's article, "Hu Lin-i's Reform of the Grain Tribute System in Hupeh, 1855–1858," *Ch'ing-shih wen-t'i* 10, no. 4 (1983).

44 Yang Guo'an, "Shehui dongdang yu qingdai hubei xiangcun zhong de zhaibao 社會動盪與清代湖北鄉村中的寨堡 [Social Turmoil and *zhai/bao* in Rural Hubei of Qing]," *Wuhan daxue xuebao* 54, no. 5 (2001): 576.

45 *Qizhou zhi* (1882), 4: 31–38, in *Zhongguo difangzhi jicheng*, 23: 88–91.

Local militarization in the highlands of Hubei, Shaanxi, and Sichuan facilitated fort-building activities on a massive scale, which stressed the already vulnerable highland ecology. Deforestation for building the forts, activities carried out by people living in the forts, the removal of logs and rocks to be used as weapons to defend the forts, and the use of fire to attack enemy troops all played a role in further deterioration of the highland ecology. Mountains were denuded by the loss of forest cover, and topsoil became looser because of extensive agricultural activity and continual fires. When the loosened topsoil was washed away by rainfall and carried downstream to the lowlands, the rivers and lakes experienced severe siltation. The ecological deterioration was no longer a local problem; it had started to affect the entire ecological system in the Yangzi-Han watershed.

4 Local Militarization and the Lowland Communities

Forts were built in both highland and lowland areas. Forts in the highlands were called *zhai* 寨, and forts in the lowlands were called *bao* 堡. Whereas *zhai* were detrimental to the highland ecology, *bao* in the lowlands were an essential feature of the local militia used in the first half of the nineteenth century. They were essentially similar though different names were used in the literature, and they were both environmentally damaging. The defining boundary of the local militia system, as Philip Kuhn pointed out, was a perplexing one: "There was a non-congruence between the *tuan* boundaries and standard administrative boundaries. As a matter of fact, in many cases, the natural and administrative divisions were combined as a way of organizing *tuanlian*."[46] The bonds of kinship, and of customary association, were more important than administrative boundaries in organizing local militia groups.[47]

In central China, the official attitude toward establishing a local militia was extremely flexible, too. For example, Kuilian 魁聯, the magistrate of Baoqing Prefecture, Hunan, in the early 1850s, discussed the principles of establishing a local militia system: "Either a *tu* [a *lijia* unit], or a village, or a *jia* [a *baojia* unit], or a *xiang* [an administrative division], or a lineage could all be used as

46 Philip Kuhn discussed the case of extended multiplex *tuan* in Yulin 玉林, Guangxi, organized with scant regard for local administrative divisions. Kuhn also discussed how the case of the *lang* league, in which the *lang* headmen were not appointed by the magistrate, was an example of using "natural units to take over the functions of bureaucratic units at the corresponding scale of organization." Kuhn, *Rebellion and Its Enemies*, 128, 101n70.

47 Kuhn, *Rebellion and Its Enemies*, 101–102.

the unit of organizing the local militia system. A small *tuan* could include several *li* [of a *lijia* unit], and a big *tuan* could include dozens of *li*. The principle is to 'accord with the place.' "[48] This flexible organizing principle reflected the urgency of militarization and a strong emphasis on localization and made it reasonable to use existing units of cohesion in a particular locale.

Officials often considered the hydraulic units a convenient and effective way to organize the local militia. In his book on water control, Shen Menglan, an eighteenth-century scholar-official, discussed fourteen advantages of establishing the system of trenches for drainage. These advantages included making the fields fertile by supplying proper irrigation, serving as a barrier to prevent the easy passage of military horses and carts, serving as transportation paths for trade, providing deep trenches for catching locusts and limiting locust plagues in any one area, helping to control floods and increasing the capacity of fields to catch floodwaters, and facilitating the system and land reclamation required for military provisions. In this system, villagers also shared the same trench and water resources, so they were more likely to help and protect one another, were more easily organized in the *baojia* system, and were more effective in comanaging the community granary.[49] *Yuan* served all of these purposes. Morally bound as a community, they had their own administrative hierarchy (see Chapter 1). In addition, the *yuan* had irrigation channels and dikes as natural defense lines. It was intuitive for the local militia organizers to start with the hydraulic units of the lowlands.

A few other officials and scholars also argued in favor of organizing defenses based on water boundaries. In the defense against the Nian rebels, Ge Shida 葛士达, a Henan government official, suggested the organization of local defenses based on hydraulic units, called *wei* 圩, in the lower Yangzi area, stressing that it would be effective to connect all the people in a *wei* to facilitate their defense. Furthermore, he asserted, people in the same *wei* or *yuan* normally had common life experience, including facing disasters, and thus could be easily organized into militia.[50] According to research by Bai Shouyi,

48 Kuilian, "Yu tuanlian shi 諭團練示 [On *tuanlian*]," in Ge, *Huangchao jingshiwen xubian* 81, "Bingshi"20, "Jiaofei." See Chapter 2 for discussions on the *lijia* system. The *baojia* system was a community-based system of civil control and self-defense starting in the 11th century. During the Ming dynasty, ten households made a *jia*, and ten *jia* made a *bao*.

49 Shen, *Wusheng gouxu*, 6–8.

50 Ge Shida, "Lian minwei 聯民圩 [Connecting People's Polders]," in Shao Zhitang, ed., *Huangchao jingshiwen tongbian* 皇朝經世文統編 [*A Comprehensive Collection of Statecraft Writings*] 77, "Jingwubu" 8, "Bingfa." This is the third piece of a series of essays on exterminating the rebels. All references to *Huangchao jingshiwen tongbian* come

rent-resistance activities against powerful landlords in the Jiangnan area were organized based on *wei*.[51]

As discussed in Chapter 1, the *yuan* community was, in fact, a moral community based on an extensive social network that included families, lineages, relatives, friends, and neighbors. People shared common cultural practices within the community-oriented hydraulic unit. This loosely organized but firmly consolidated network provided an effective platform for local militia. In Xiangyin County in the Dongting region of Hunan, the militia bureaus established in the late nineteenth century were mostly organized around *yuan*.[52] As illustrated in the case study below, the cooperation of *yuan* in Qianjiang County resulted in a regional quasi-military administration for local defense. This administration based on the *yuan* was especially evident in Qianjiang County; however, Lu Xiqi argues, it can be seen as a common trend throughout the Jianghan Plain, considering the strong ties of those communities derived from water-control practices.[53]

5 *Yuan* and *Tuanlian*: Qianjiang County as a Case Study

The conditions in Qianjiang County show that the *yuan* communities were the basis of local militarization in the mid-nineteenth century. The establishment of the local militia system in this region was a combined effort by the government and local gentry. The county-level government initiated the local militia system, and the elite activism organized the local militia unit.

In 1853, the Taiping rebels swept the mid-Yangzi region, and Dong Xiguo 董熺國, a member of the gentry in the Zhanghu *yuan*, was elected the leader of the local defense and afterward he organized the local militia.[54] The militia group was divided into *qi* 旗 and *tuan* 團: several people constituted a *qi* or *tuan*, with a leader for each subgroup. The number of people in a *qi* or *tuan* were not indicated in the records. Qianjiang County had six big *tuan*. Dong Xiguo led one *tuan* that operated at the central headquarters, in the Changyi *yuan*; and other elites led *tuan* in various strategic locations, coordinating with the *tuan* at the center. Strict rules were set up for the local militia system with clear

from Taiwan Academia Sinica online database 台灣漢籍電子文獻資料庫: https://hanji.sinica.edu.tw/.

51 Bai, *Zhongguo tongshi*, 10: 8.

52 Perdue, "Official Goals and Local Interests," 763.

53 Lu, *Changjiang zhongyou de rendi guanxi yu diyu shehui*, 338–339.

54 *Qianjiang xianzhi xu* (1879), 15: 1–5, in *Zhongguo difangzhi jicheng*, 46: 476–478.

rewards and punishment.[55] When the Nian army went through Qianjiang in the 1860s, county magistrate Xiang Shiming led a few members of the gentry to organize local militia for defense. The local militia used the Han River as a natural defense in their fight against the Nian rebels. Within the 100-*li* length of the river dike, the military camps were "as dense as a line of shacks."[56] The examples show that the initiation of the county officials was important and sometimes decisive in the establishment of local militias but the organization and management of the local militia system were basically in the hands of local gentry.

Local gentry unquestionably played an important role in operating the local militia system, and Dong Xiguo was clearly a critical figure in mobilizing the local militia groups in Qianjiang County. As a lower gentry the Changyi *yuan*, Dong was ambitious and talented, and he used his political acumen to establish a social network among the lower gentry in the communities. His career in organizing local defense started during the White Lotus Rebellion. When the White Lotus rebels besieged the region of Qianjiang, people from six *tuan*, including fifteen *yuan*, all recommended him as the leader of the local militia to fight against the rebels. Thereafter, in the critical Yufanhong battle against the Taiping rebels in 1855, Dong's local militia was the main military force that defeated them.[57] After the battle, the county government rewarded all the *tuan* heads and local soldiers. The gentry leaders—including Dong Xiguo, Tang Tingjian, Dai Zipei, and Dong Ranguo, who were the key initiators and organizers of the local militia system—were posthumously given official rank after they died in the battle. Gong Huanzhi, the Qianjiang County magistrate, also held a public ceremony to commemorate those who had died in the battle, praising their great bravery, their commitment to the state, and their efforts to protect the people. He especially praised the important role played by the six *tuan* and decided to build a temple beside the Han River to commemorate the martyrs.[58]

The government was responsible for initiating the local militia system, with the local gentry managing it, for two main reasons. First, the local gentry, in general, were still weak in power and unable to effectively mobilize the locals. Therefore, during the mid-nineteenth century the local gentry collaborated

---

55 *Qianjiang xianzhi xu* (1879), 15: 1–5, in *Zhongguo difangzhi jicheng*, 46: 476–478.

56 Gan Pengyun, *Qianjiang jiuwen lu* 潛江舊聞錄 [*Old Stories of Qianjiang*], vol. 7: *Qianjiang xiangtuan fangyu nianfei ji* 潛江鄉團防禦捻匪記 [*Qianjiang Xiang and Tuan Defending against the Nian Rebels*], 157–158.

57 *Qianjiang xianzhi xu* (1879), 18: 3, in *Zhongguo difangzhi jicheng*, 46: 540.

58 *Qianjiang xianzhi xu* (1879), 15: 5, in *Zhongguo difangzhi jicheng*, 46: 478.

closely with the local government, working in the interest of both the government and the local residents. Second, during this period the Hubei government was strongly interventionist. In particular, Hubei governor Hu Linyi's military plans in Hubei tended to curb local power. The conditions in this region also show that the decentralization and the retreat of state power did not occur to the same degree as in many other regions during the same period, as seen in the increase in power of the local elites in Zhejiang Province, analyzed by Keith Schoppa.[59]

A record on the martyrs of the Yufanhong battle demonstrates the relationship between the militia system and the hydraulic unit. It shows that the local militia system comprised fifteen *yuan* and the *tuan* leaders' names were listed based on the *yuan*. In all, there were fifty-two *tuan* leaders from nine different *yuan*, with the Dong lineage the most represented. This lineage was the dominant lineage in the Changyi *yuan* (sixteen out of twenty-four *tuan* leaders were from the Dong lineage), and a few members of the Dong family spread to other *yuan*, including the Chang'er, Changsan, Changsi, and the Guangze *yuan*. The Dong lineage certainly played a significant leadership role in the local militia system, further indicating that big lineages and powerful families took the lead in the local militia system.

The same record also lists the number of *tuan* soldiers who were martyred based on the *yuan* unit for the same battles. For example, 632 *tuan* soldiers from Changyi *yuan* died, 439 *tuan ding* from Chang'er *yuan* died, and 366 *tuan ding* from Changsan *yuan* died.[60] This is further evidence that *yuan* were actively mobilized and incorporated in the course of local militarization.

6 Disruptions in the Hydraulic System with Local Militarization

Unfortunately, in an era of massive local militarization, many hydraulic construction projects were neglected or manipulated for military purposes. First, as discussed earlier, peasants were engaged in local militarization for various reasons, ranging from the benefits of tax exemption to the receipt of a food quota from the local militia system. Thus, a massive number of workers were diverted from agricultural production and hydraulic maintenance. Second, the

59 R. Keith Schoppa especially discusses this process in his book *Chinese Elites and Political Change: Zhejiang Province in the Early Twentieth Century* (Cambridge: Harvard University Press, 1982). Mary Rankin has also documented an expansion of elite control in post-Taiping Zhejiang in *Elite Activism and Political Transformation in China: Zhejiang Province, 1865–1911* (Stanford: Stanford University Press, 1986).

60 *Qianjiang xianzhi xu* (1879), vols. 15 and 16, in *Zhongguo difangzhi jicheng*, 46: 481–514.

government often diverted funds for dike construction to military needs. In the summer of 1850, when a dike collapsed in Qianjiang County, the county magistrate Gong Huanzhi 龔煥枝 allocated two thousand *taels* from government funds for dike repairs, funds that should have been returned to the government within two years by the *yuan* communities that benefited from those repairs. However, when the Taiping rebels ravaged the region in 1853, the county government decided to have the *yuan* recruit local people for the militia, and the funds for dike repair were used to finance local militarization.[61] In addition, a significant portion of the hydraulic funds also went into the pockets of local officials. Hubei governor Hu Linyi commented,

> To organize the local militia is good and necessary, but in recent years many counties have not realized the significance of [government] finances and the grain tax and have constantly asked for exemptions, not because they cannot pay, but because they are interested in private gain. … Therefore, local officials shall report any money [earmarked] for local militia accordingly and shall not divert funds from other projects.[62]

In other cases, war with the Taiping rebels disrupted dike repairs. The opening and closing of the Zekou outlet is one example. When the dikes of the Zekou outlet were breached by floods in 1853, the surrounding counties—Qianjiang, Jianli, and Mianyang—were slated to corepair the dikes at the outlet. However, the repair work had to stop because of fighting with the rebels. The repairs were delayed for almost six years and were finally completed in 1860, yet the dikes were breached again soon afterward. In 1861, a local scholar, Yao Yinan 姚以南, led the building of an earthen embankment to block the river waters at the Zekou outlet, but the project was interrupted again by the Taiping rebels and did not resume until the following year.[63] The constant interruption of dike repairs by warfare in this period led to the eventual breach of the Zekou outlet; the roaring river waters passing through the broken outlet created a new river path that swept through several densely populated *yuan* communities, causing extensive damage. This case is further discussed in Chapter 5.

Dismayed by the government's ineptitude in maintaining the water system, local people repeatedly petitioned it to take action. In July 1857, a provincial degree candidate, Yu Fengci 余鳳慈, collaborated with some fifty people to petition the local government over its failure to provide funding for repairing

61 *Qianjiang xianzhi xu* (1879), 10: 18, in *Zhongguo difangzhi jicheng*, 46: 438.

62 Wang, *Huwenzhong gong fu'e ji*, 25.

63 *Qianjiang xianzhi xu* (1879), 10: 23–24, in *Zhongguo difangzhi jicheng*, 46: 441.

dikes; because of this failure, a large area of the downstream section of the Han River was severely flooded. Two representatives—Zhang Xueqing and Yang Tizhang—went to the capital to sue the county government. According to their statement, the Zhongxiang dike was breached during flooding, but the Zhongxiang County government lacked sufficient funds to repair it. At the same time, all levels of magistrates and prefects were preoccupied with ending the Taiping Rebellion and did not pay attention to dike repairs and disaster relief. Zhang and Yang petitioned higher local officials a few times but received no reply. After receiving the complaints, officials at the Censorate carried out investigations and reported their findings to the Xianfeng emperor. Only at this point were officials appointed to examine the dike condition thoroughly and to supervise the repair work closely.[64] However, the records reveal no evidence that the dike was actually repaired. Considering the situation in 1857—flooding, rebel movements, financial shortfall, and mass militarization, not to mention the immediate threat of war with the British army, which had assembled outside Tianjin and Beijing—the Xianfeng government was at a moment of crisis, so it is unsurprising that it put off dike repairs.

In addition to the delays in hydraulic repairs due to warfare, these structures were also sometimes used to defeat enemies in battle. In April 1854, the Taiping rebels attacked Jingmen and marched to a river nearby. To defend their homes, local peasants opened a sluice gate and let the riverwater flush the rebel troops away.[65] Then, in December 1855, the rebels, who were battling the Qing army in Wuchang, dug a bank at the Sha Lake to flood the city and the Qing army.[66] In 1856, as the rebels approached Liuhouji 劉侯集 in eastern Hubei, the Qing army opened the sluice gate to the nearby Juzhang River to allow its waters to hinder the rebel troops.[67] Four years later, when the rebels reached Yiyang, in Hunan, the local people destroyed the dikes around Lan'ni Lake so that its water would stop them.[68] The constant digging and destruction of river and lake banks, and the frequent flooding caused by these military strategies, undoubtedly had disastrous consequences for the lowlands of the Jianghan Plain.

By the mid-Qing, water control in the downstream Jianghan Plain had become an extremely grave issue. Extensive deforestation and land reclamation in the upstream mountains had led to severe soil erosion and contributed to deterioration in downstream flood control. The riverbed level had risen, the

64 Hu and Chen, *Leading Cases on the Xiang Dike*, 608–610.
65 Wang, *Hu Wenzhong gong fu'e ji*, 81.
66 Wang, *Hu Wenzhong gong fu'e ji*, 28.
67 Wang, *Hu Wenzhong gong fu'e ji*, 81.
68 Wang, *Hu Wenzhong gong fu'e ji*, 82.

river course had narrowed, and an increasing number of river-lake outlets had become silted with sand and soil washed down from the rivers upstream. The water system's capacity for controlling floods had reached its limit. According to Ping-ti Ho, the average interval between inundations of the Han River increased from 4.17 years in the period of 1796–1820 to 1.43 years in 1851–1861.[69] The statistics suggest that the flood incidence increased drastically in the mid-Yangzi region in the first half of the eighteenth century. The late Qing official Wei Yuan discussed the ecological condition of Huguang in an article:

> After more than two hundred years of peace and prosperity, people are everywhere and almost all available lands have been converted to agricultural lands. The flood-relieving areas, including the floodplains, lakes, and wetlands have all been enclosed and turned into fields and villages. So, there are no resources left in the lowlands. Moreover, many jobless people migrated into the [highland] border areas of Sichuan, Shanxi, Hubei, Guizhou, and Guangdong, conducting slash-and-burn cultivation. So, resources in the highlands are also exhausted. The lowlands are losing their capacity to relieve floodwaters ... the highlands are full of floating sand, loosened soil, and exposed plant roots. When it rains, the sand and soil are all washed off and taken away by the rainfall, from mountains to streams, from streams to rivers, from rivers to lakes. The sand stays in the lowlands when the waters slow down. And 70 to 80 percent of the flood-relieving areas are now missing in the lowlands because of *yuan* construction. ... In the lowlands, the river courses and lakes are shrinking; in the highlands, more and more sand and soil are washed off. How could the floods not come? How could the dikes not be broken?[70]

Wei Yuan's analysis captured the ecological conditions of the mid-Yangzi region in the early and mid-nineteenth century. What he had seen was the effect of population pressure and extensive land reclamation on the ecological system, but he did not realize that state policy had played a role in causing the deterioration of the ecological system. Massive militarization, in the form of fort building, had exerted further pressure on the ecosystem, with a severe effect on the river system. The problems of downstream water control increasingly became the problems of the entire river system—from the upstream

69 Ho, *Studies on the Population of China*, 230.

70 Wei Yuan, "Huguang shuili lun 湖廣水利論 [A Discussion of the Water Control of Huguang]," in Sheng, *Huangchao jingshiwen xubian* 17, "Gongshi" 14, "Gesheng shuili."

highlands to the downstream lowlands, the hydraulic system was on the brink of collapse.

7 The Rural Famine in the Jianghan Plain from the Late 1850s to the 1860s

The *jianbi qingye* policy (along with the local militia system) was implemented for almost sixty years, from the end of the eighteenth century to the mid-nineteenth century. When the policy was first implemented, the statecraft officials prioritized state security, and very few of them could anticipate what was to come. As mentioned earlier, some officials worried about the extremely detrimental effects the policy might have and warned that it should be used only as an absolutely last resort.[71] The policy's destructive power was gradually revealed after it had been in force for several decades. In addition to deforestation, soil erosion, river siltation, dike disrepair, and water-control negligence, the policy exhausted the natural resources and paralyzed the hydraulic system at the local level. To a large degree, it contributed to the famine in the Jianghan Plain from the late 1850s to the 1860s.

"Natural" disasters (which might not be caused by nature alone) were inseparable factors that led to the famine. A severe drought affected the Hubei region from 1856 to early 1857. Most counties experienced harvest failures and therefore food shortages, which led to rocketing food prices. Because they could not afford these high prices, many local people were reduced to eating tree bark, leaves, and even dirt.[72] It did not take long for the tree bark and leaves to be exhausted. In addition, trees were dying because of the drought.

The locust attack, culminating in 1857 in the Jianghan Plain, undoubtedly had a devastating impact on the remaining food production in this region. The geographical reach of the locust swarm during the reign of Xianfeng was so large and lasted so long that it was called "seven years of flying

71 Zheng Qinghua, introduction to "Great Military Events," quoted in Rowe, *Crimson Rain*, 209, 365n58.

72 *Hubeisheng jin wubai nian qihou lishi ziliao*, 168–169. This is a collection of statistics on the regional distribution of flood and drought over the past five centuries, constructed on the basis of information taken mainly from local gazetteers, along with other sources such as official memorials and private diaries. The Hubei Meteorological Bureau organized researchers to collect materials based on county and prefecture and divided the natural disasters of each location into five categories as follows: (1) extreme flood, (2) flood, (3) normal, (4) drought, (5) extreme drought. Each county and prefecture was assigned a grade, where information was available.

locusts."[73] Its impacts on the local economy were severe. Hu Linyi, the Hubei provincial governor, stated that wiping out the locusts was the top issue for Donghu County to address in 1857.[74]

Beginning in 1858 and throughout the 1860s, the Jianghan Plain experienced frequent flooding, severely and consecutively, from 1862 to 1864 and from 1866 to 1870.[75] Extremes of both dry and wet weather in this region from the late 1850s and into the 1860s might be the result of an El Niño weather pattern, according to several scholars. Mike Davis discussed concurrent droughts caused by El Niño in three countries—India, China, and Brazil—and emphasized that it was not merely the weather but imperialism, free trade ideology, and unfair entitlement to food that led to large-scale famines.[76] Xia Mingfang observes that from the 1860s to the 1890s, China experienced extreme weather conditions and frequent natural disasters.[77] In the Jianghan Plain, in addition to El Niño, the famine might be attributable to two significant factors: the dysfunctional water system and the disabled granary system,[78] both of which were consequences of local militarization.

---

73 Locust swarms also occurred in Jiangsu, Zhejiang, and Anhui during the same period (in 1856 mostly). Min Zongdian discussed the frequency and measures taken to exterminate the locusts in these three provinces; see Min Zongdian, "Qingdai suzhewan huangzai yanjiu 清代蘇浙皖蝗災研究 [A Study on the Locust Disaster in Jiangsu, Zhejiang and Anhui Provinces during the Qing Dynasty]," *Zhongguo nongshi* 2 (2004).

74 Wang, *Hu wenzhong gong fu'e ji*, 149.

75 *Hubeisheng jin wubai nian qihou lishi ziliao*, 173–189.

76 See Mike Davis, *Late Victorian Holocausts: El Niño Famines and the Making of the Third World* (London: Verso, 2002).

77 Xia Mingfang, "Cong qingmo zaihai qunfaqi kan Zhongguo zaoqi xiandaihua de lishi tiaojian—Zaihuang yu yangwu yundong yanjiu zhiyi 從清末災害群發期看中國早期現代化的歷史條件—災荒與洋務運動研究之議 [A Study on the Historical Condition of Early Modernization during the Disaster Cluster of the Late Qing]," *Qingshi yanjiu* 1 (1998).

78 The granary system of the Qing was initiated by the Kangxi emperor based on precedents from previous dynasties. There were three types of civilian granaries: ever-normal granaries (changping cang), operated by the imperial government; community granaries (yicang), managed by lineages at a community level; and voluntary granaries (shecang), containing grain donated by local people. Community and voluntary granaries were relatively small compared to the ever-normal granaries. In the 1750s annual civilian stocks averaged about 1.5 billion liters of husked rice, equivalent to about 7.5 liters of rice per person, or roughly 3 percent of the consumption of an adult per year. Carol H. Shiue, "Local Granaries and Central Government Disaster Relief: Moral Hazard and Intergovernmental Finance in Eighteenth and Nineteenth-Century China," *Journal of Economic History* 64, no. 1 (2004): 104–105. For a comprehensive discussion of the granary system in Chinese history, see Pierre-Etienne Will, R. Bin Wong et al., *Nourish the People: The State Civilian Granary System in China, 1650–1850* (Ann Arbor: University of Michigan Press, 1991). On food riots, see R. Bin Wong, "Food Riots in the Qing Dynasty," *Journal of Asian Studies* 41,

Of all the factors that led to famine, the most destructive might be the dysfunction in the regional water system. As discussed in the previous section, in the course of local militarization the hydraulic system had been devastated by the diversion of funds, negligence in dike maintenance, lack of government input, and destruction in warfare. Deforestation and erosion in the upstream area of the Han River led to increased sedimentation, a rise in the riverbed level, siltation, and the blocking of river outlets in the downstream area of the Jianghan Plain. The water system thus could not function well during droughts, and it became more vulnerable to floods after those droughts. In the drought of 1856, every body of water—aqueducts, ponds, springs, and reservoirs—ran dry. Lakes silted up, trenches became blocked, and there was no harvest at all.[79] Memorials penned by Hubei governor Hu Linyi detail the extensive areas struck by flooding or drought in 1856 and 1858 (see Table 14).

Hu reports the severity of the floods and droughts from 1856 to 1858, and all the areas that were affected. The areas damaged reflected the ineffectiveness of the water system, which failed to protect the region from either flooding or drought.

Nor could the paralyzed water system handle the flood sequence from 1859 to the late 1860s, when numerous dikes were breached, and polders were flooded. In the flood of 1859, the dikes of Shenhetan and Huanghan *yuan* in Qianjiang County collapsed. In 1860, the Zhanglin *yuan* in Qianjiang was flooded, accompanied by breaches in the dikes in many other places, such as Mianyang, Shishou, Jiangling, and Songzi. In 1861, the dikes at the Sigang outlet of Qianjiang collapsed. In 1862, the Yanglingguan and Mutou *yuan* in Qianjiang were flooded. In 1864, 1865, and 1866, the Yongfeng *yuan* in Qianjiang was flooded three times.[80] The constant breakdown of dikes in Qianjiang clearly revealed the area's dysfunctional hydraulic system. In another county, Jianli, 134 *yuan* were flooded in 1866, 148 *yuan* were heavily inundated in the flood of 1869, and 158 *yuan* were flooded in 1870.[81] The excessively wet weather in those years may have contributed to the floods, but the frequent flooding of a large area of *yuan* was due to the water system.

The granary system, which played a critical role in disaster relief in imperial China, was also altered by local militarization. According to Zhao Gang, the productivity of marginal land declined after the mid-Qing period. Zhao

no. 4 (1982); see also R. Bin Wong and Peter C. Perdue, "Review: Famine's Foes in Ch'ing China," *Harvard Journal of Asiatic Studies* 43, no. 1 (1983).

79 *Hubeisheng jin wubai nian qihou lishi ziliao*, 169.

80 Bingdaodunjun, "Nongcun shehui yanjiu biji," 173–83.

81 Bingdaodunjun, "Nongcun shehui," 183–189.

TABLE 14 Areas of flood and drought in 1856 and 1858 mentioned in Hu Linyi's memorials

County	Flooded areas in 1856	Areas of flood or drought in 1858
Hanchuan	32 *yuan*	33 *yuan*
Jiangling	34 *yuan*	29 *yuan* (heavy), 92 *yuan* (light)
Tianmen	111 *yuan*	47 *yuan* (110 *jia*) (heavy), 5 *yuan* (36 *jia*) (light)
Yingcheng	9 *tu*	No record
Jiayu	8 *li*, 37 *jia*	8 *li*, 36 *jia*
Songzi	2 *du* 28 *jia*	9 *du* (heavy)
Hanyang	8 *li*	8 *qu*
Mianyang	72 *yuan*	48 *yuan*
Jingshan	37 *tu*	No record
Huangpi	223 *she*	223 *she*[a]
Jianli	121 *yuan*	51 *yuan*
Shishou	Meizhao *yuan*, Yidu *yuan*, including 21 *jia*	16 *yuan*, 1 *du*, 14 *yuan*, including 31 *jia*
Jingmen	13 *tu*	1 *tu*, 28 *qu*
Xiaogan	19 *hui* (heavy), 138 *hui* (light)	202 *she*

Note: *tu, li, jia, she, qu, du and hui* were all the units of local taxation and administration. The presence of *yuan* here could indicate that *yuan* had been used as a taxation unit. The core areas of the Jianghan Plain, such as Hanchuan, Jiangling, Jianli, Mianyang and Tianmen, all adopted the *yuan* as the basic taxation unit. Other areas, such as Jiayu, Jingshan, Hanyang, and Jingmen maintained the traditional *lijia* system, using *tu, li* and *jia* unit. Xiaogan used *hui* as the taxation unit, and Huangpi used *she* as the taxation unit. All these units, be it *tu, li, hui*, or *she*, might or might not overlap with *yuan*. But the *yuan* apparently included *jia* in Shishou County. This chart shows that some counties of the Jianghan Plain had adopted the *yuan* as a basic taxation unit, while other areas of Hubei used a mixed system of the traditional *lijia* system and the hydraulic unit.

[a] The taxation based on the unit of *yuan* was most evident in Qianjiang County in the late nineteenth and early twentieth centuries. I collected two tax documents from the Archives of Qianjiang County—the tax catalogs of the Liutanzi *yuan* and Zhuantanwai *yuan* of Qianjiang County. Both catalogs were created in 1889. They clearly recorded the number of households, lineages, head of each household, social status, tax quota for each household, and changes of tax quota for each household up until 1946. From the record, we know that the Liutanzi *yuan* had 275 households and 37 lineages, and that people in the *yuan* were classified as either gentry or commoners. The Zhuantanwai *yuan* had more than 300 households and 37 lineages. The two tax catalogs had the same recording style, which may indicate that the *yuan-xiang* taxation system was standardized and routinized. See *Qianjiangxian taihexiang shizheng dice: Liutanzi yuan* 潛江縣太和鄉實證底冊: 流灘子垸 (1889) and *Qianjiangxian taihexiang shizheng dice: zhuantangwai yuan* 潛江縣太和鄉實證底冊: 磚淌外垸 (1889).

TABLE 14 Areas of flood and drought in 1856 and 1858 mentioned in Hu Linyi's memorials (*cont.*)

[a] For discussions on *she*, see Bingdaodunjun, "Nongcun shehui yanjiu biji 農村社會研究筆記 [Notes on the Study of Rural Society]," in *Jingdai zhongguo de xiangcun shehui* 近代中國的鄉村社會 [*Rural Society of Modern China*], ed. History Department of Fudan University (Shanghai: Shanghai guji shushe, 2005), 179–255.

SOURCE: HU LINYI, "KANMING GEZHOUXIANWEI BEIYAN QINGXING QI FENBIE HUANZHENG SHU 堪明各州縣衛被淹情形乞分別徵疏 [A MEMORIAL OF FLOODS AND RELIEF IN PREFECTURES AND COUNTIES]," DECEMBER 15, 1856, IN *HU WENZHONGGONG YIJI* 胡文忠公遺集 [*A COMPILATION OF HU LINYI'S WRITINGS*] (1864), 26: 3–5; HU LINYI, "KANMING GEZHOUXIAN YANHAN QINGXING FENBIE HUANZHENG SHU 堪明各州縣淹旱情形分別緩徵疏 [A PLEDGE FOR FLOOD RELIEF]," DECEMBER 18, 1858, IN *HU WENZHONGGONG YIJI*, 33: 1–3.

argued that the serious deterioration in the local ecology affected agricultural production and reduced agricultural productivity.[82] Not only did the declining agricultural output adversely affect food production but the *jianbi qingye* policy also disrupted the community granary system on the Jianghan Plain.[83] Both factors contributed to the severe famine in the late 1850s and early 1860s. One local militia regulation stated that peasants who had plenty of grain had to transport their grain to the fort and store it in the fort granary. Peasants who had little grain had to transport their share to the fort if rebels were more than about 150 *li* (45 miles) away; but if rebels were within 100 *li* (30 miles), they had to destroy their crops and enter the fort. Anyone who did not do so would be regarded as a rebel.[84] Deliberately destroying the crops, evidently more common in summer than in winter, became a common practice to cut off the rebels' food supply. Resources were normally more abundant in the summer than in winter, so destroying crops at that time of the year would be less problematic for the local community. Because rebels frequently went into villages and demanded food from villagers, those fighting the rebels preferred to burn their harvest down to ashes before the rebels could get their hands on it. Ts'ui-jung Liu and John Fei studied the adequacy of early nineteenth-century granaries in Sichuan and found that the combined stocks of the

82 Zhao, "Qingzhongqi yilai liangshi chanliang zhi biandong"; Wang, "Qingdai zhishan fanghong huanbao celue zhi tantao."

83 On the historical Jianghan Plain, the granaries were community granaries. The Jianghan communities had very few ever-normal granaries.

84 "Zhifu Fang dati tuanlian tiaogui 知府方大堤團練條規 [County Magistrate Fang Dati's Tuanlian Regulations]," in *Xiangyang xianzhi* 襄陽縣志 [*Gazetteer of Xiangyang County*], 4: 67–72, in *Zhangguo difangzhi jicheng*, 64: 147–150.

ever-normal granaries and the community granaries could sustain an adult population for only twenty-three days.[85] In the nineteenth-century, Hubei was one of the provinces with the least local granary storage, partly a result of frequent disaster reliefs from the center and a better market integration,[86] so it is not surprising that Hubei had only a small grain inventory during the droughts, given declining agricultural production, warfare, and grain destruction. Severe material shortages were an inevitable outcome.

The local militia system was also destructive for the food supply. One official commented:

> The local peasant households were normally poor—nine out of ten households could barely sustain themselves, and only one out of twenty households had extra food provisions. After those households were organized into the local militia system, they became increasingly engaged in training for the militia, fighting with rebels, defending strategic locations, and marching through different counties and prefectures once ordered to do so. Food provisions from the central government could hardly reach this area; meanwhile local granaries that could have supplemented the food supply were mostly burned or robbed by the rebels. Therefore, [when the drought hit], thousands of people died of hunger; not to mention the fact that many *tuanzhai* [forts] were already on the brink of collapse [due to the lack of maintenance and shortage of food] even before the rebels' attacks.[87]

This comment, made during the reign of Jiaqing (1796–1820), describes the social and environmental consequences of the earliest local militia system. After decades of local militia organization and destructive warfare, it is no surprise that the food supply was devastated.

85 The study was done by Ts'ui-jung Liu and John C.H. Fei, "The Public Granary Institutions of the Ch'ing Dynasty, 1644–1911," Center Discussion Paper, No. 299, Economic Growth Center, Yale University (1978), 18.

86 Shiue, "Local Granaries and Central Government Disaster Relief," 117, 119–120. Shiue studied the correlation among local granary storage, central government's disaster relief, and the market access and integration of provinces in her article. She found that provinces that received less relief stored more than their targets and that a better market access could offset low local granary storage; she also pointed out that "if central relief led to reductions in local civilian storage, …, then the overall outcome for potential beneficiaries of the granaries in those areas could be worse than what would have occurred without the government's tax relief."

87 Shixiangcun jushi, *Kanjing jiaofei shubian*, 11: 225.

Furthermore, government policies were not aimed at flood relief. For example, Hu Linyi once sent an order to a county magistrate, insisting that "the rent in kind [that is] due to residents of the county seat [should] not be forcibly diverted to relieve rural food shortages,"[88] because doing so would not only jeopardize the security of the city but also risk alienating the elites, who were the major initiators and contributors to local militarization. Also, in 1855, the prefect of Wuchang Prefecture asked the provincial government for relief, but it rejected his request: "It is not because we do not care about people's hunger, but if people have food, the rebels would take advantage of it, too. People's hunger can be solved by migration, but it is a crime to have rebels fed."[89]

As a result of extensive warfare, government malfunction, and plummeting agricultural production, the granaries were severely damaged, and the food supply for the local people deteriorated further. According to the records, the granary system has at its height under the reign of Yongzheng and Qianlong (the eighteenth century). Beginning in the late eighteenth century, the community granaries in many counties—such as Tianmen, Jiangling, Gong'an, Shishou, Jianli, Songzi, Macheng, and Huanggang—gradually became less and less filled. Not until the reign of Tongzhi and Guangxu (late nineteenth century) did granaries have more grain storage again. As noted, during the reign of Xianfeng, the Qing army and the Taiping rebels fought a series of battles in the main part of the Jianghan Plain, including Wuchang, Hanyang, Jingzhou, De'an, and Huangzhou Prefectures. Many of the community granaries were destroyed in the fighting. In this turbulent period, the granary system was also affected in various ways by corruption and natural disasters (see Table 15).[90]

Table 15 shows that warfare was the main reason for the failure of the granary system in a number of counties in this region. In addition, a lack of granary maintenance in wartime also led to abandonment of the granary system. The state's shift of attention from civilian livelihood to militarization was a major cause of the food shortage and eventual famine in the late 1850s and early 1860s.

---

88 Hu Linyi, "Macheng xian bingchen difang qingxing pi 麻城縣稟陳地方情形批 [Endorsement on Report on Local Conditions by the Macheng Magistrate]," in *Hu Linyi ji* 胡林翼集 [*The Collection of Hu Linyi's Writings*] (Changsha: Yuelu shushe, 1999), 2:1008–1009.

89 Wang, *Hu wenzhonggong fu'eji*, 52.

90 Hu Linyi, "Daofu binni guangrencang getiaopi 道府稟拟廣仁倉各條批 [Government on Granaries]," in Sheng, *Huangchao jingshiwen xubian* 43. In the late 1850s Hu complained about official corruption in managing the ever-normal granaries and decided to wipe it out and preserve the grain in the granaries in a better way. In so doing, he hoped to decrease the surging price of food in order to improve Hubei's fiscal situation.

TABLE 15 The condition of community granaries on the Jianghan Plain during the reign of Jiaqing (r. 1796–1820), Daoguang (r. 1820–1850), and Xianfeng (r. 1851–1861)

Condition	Causes	Counties/prefectures affected
Destroyed	Warfare	Macheng, Jingmen, Hanchuan, Jinzhou, Zhongxiang, Huanggang, Wuchang, Hanyang
Destroyed	Natural disasters	Gong'an, Shishou
Deserted	Administrative corruption	Yunmeng, Jiayu, Jiangling
Deserted	Unknown	Xiaogan, Daye, Jiangxia, Jianli, Songzi, Zhijiang, Qianjiang, Mianyang, Tianmen, Huangpi

Note: Adapted from Bai Liping, "Qingdai lianghu pingyuan de shecang yu nongcun shehui 清代兩湖平原的社倉與農村社會 [The Community Granary and Rural Society in the Lianghu Plain during the Qing Times]," in *Mingqing yilai changjiang liuyu shehui fazhan shilun* 明清以來長江流域社會發展史論 [*Studies on the Social Development of the Yangzi Valley since the Ming and Qing Times*], ed. Chen Feng (Wuhan: Wuhan daxue chubanshe, 2006), table 3. For more discussion on the granaries in Lianghu area, see Bai Liping, "Qingdai lianghu pingyuan de shecang jianshe 清代兩湖平原的社倉建設 [The Granaries in the Lianghu Plain during the Qing Dynasty]," *Wuhan daxue xuebao* 59, no. 1 (2006): 75–81.

SOURCE: *HUBEI TONGZHI* 湖北通志 [*A GENERAL GAZETTEER OF HUBEI*] (REPUBLIC OF CHINA), 48: 6.

The mass consumption of resources made the food shortages even worse. War requires resources. The large mobilization of these resources is evident in many records. In March 1856, a report by the Jingzhou subbureau on munitions production indicated that at times of intensive battles, the Hubei navy needed at least 15,000 kilograms a day of potassium nitrate (saltpeter, an essential component in gunpowder). From February to December 1855, the Hubei government transported nearly 14,000 kilograms of potassium nitrate from Hunan Province to fight the battles in Hubei. Sichuan Province was too far away from Hubei to be practical for obtaining gunpowder, and Henan Province was too preoccupied with the Nian rebels. The Jingzhou subbureau produced as much munitions as needed.[91] In June 1856, a report to Commander of the Xiang Army

91 Wang, *Hu Wenzhong gong fu'e ji*, 39.

Zuo Zongtang 左宗棠 showed that officials such as Zhang Liangji 張亮吉, Luo Bingzhang 羅秉章, and Zeng Guofan were very efficient at mobilizing resources for warfare. They managed a considerable amount of materials for Hubei munitions, including 21,500 kilograms of gunpowder, 37,500 kilograms of lead bombs, over 15,000 kilograms of wax, 16,000 fire arrows 火箭, 100,000 pieces of incense sticks, 300,000 pieces of parchment, 4,000 each of bamboo helmets and knives, and 600 tents.[92] This large-scale production unavoidably exhausted the resources in many areas of Hubei Province. As mentioned earlier with regard to gunpowder, many materials used in warfare in Hubei had to be transported from other provinces, such as Hunan. The demand for potassium nitrate also triggered extensive mining in the mountain areas, which further exhausted highland resources.

The shortage of resources was evident for both the military and civilians. Warfare drained Hubei's coffers, and having smaller financial resources paralyzed the Qing army,[93] which in turn drove more extensive militarization at the local level, derailing regular agricultural activities and further draining material resources—creating a vicious cycle. Witnessing the depletion of the region's resources, Hu Linyi wrote in a memorial in 1857,

> There was a big financial shortage everywhere in Hubei—[with] insufficient funds for military support, and the prices of rice and salt skyrocketing. It was not surprising that rice was not available even when people were willing to pay a higher price. The Qing soldiers could not get enough food and even relied on congee [rice porridge]. During some battles with the Taiping army, the Qing soldiers were easily defeated because of hunger.[94]

The Qing soldiers continued to receive at least partial stipends from the government, but the food shortage for the common people was no doubt much more severe.

---

92 Wang, *Hu Wenzhong gong fu'e ji*, 49.

93 Peter C. Perdue commented on the connection between war and tax reform in his book *Exhausting the Earth* (pp. 75–76), in which he argued that Qing officials completely relied on the last reliable Ming land survey done by Zhang Juzheng from 1576 to 1580 because of a lack of military pressure. He also argued that "the demands of war were the primary force driving European states to create new forms of taxation," which was similar to the situation in nineteenth-century Hunan.

94 Hu Linyi, "Qing chicui gesheng yingjie Hubei yuexiang pian 請饬催各省應解湖北月餉片 [A Plea to Ask Provinces to Assist Hubei]" (1856), in Hu, *Hu Linyi ji*, 1: 243.

Not until the mid-1860s did the Tongzhi government begin to pay great attention to minimizing famines, which might have helped avoid a series of famines following the El Niño–linked droughts and floods.[95] The state famine-relief policies included vast shipments of food, requiring the rich to open their storehouses to the poor, and price regulation.[96]

8 Conclusion

The functioning of the state-society-environment complex on the Jianghan Plain was severely challenged in the wartime of the mid-nineteenth century. The case for local militarization (e.g., building forts, organizing local militia, mass mobilization for warfare, and altering the food storage system) in the highlands and lowlands in Hubei was based on the state's critical needs at that moment. From the perspective of the state, the local military buildup helped it defending the community and the region. But by employing large-scale militarization to wipe out the rebels, the state altered the regional landscape. The local ecology was altered by the meticulous, large-scale planning for military purposes. The extensive fort building succeeded in protecting the local community and enabling it to defeat the rebels, but the way in which it was implemented, on top of hillside-farming activities by shack people, was the last straw, damaging the local ecology in the highlands beyond its ability to cope. Although, based on currently available sources, the direct environmental effects of the fort construction are hard to assess, the combined destructive effects on the highland ecology from various factors—the preexisting unsustainable agriculture, the large-scale fort building, and the use of fire to battle enemies—cannot be denied. In the lowlands, the militarization pulled farmers away from cultivation, engaged them in military training and warfare, exhausted funds for the upkeep of irrigation works, and even destroyed waterworks to prevent their enemies from using them. The highland and lowland ecologies were both manipulated by the state for the purpose of warfare—they were made into powerful weapons that were amenable to human command.

After the warfare in the mid-nineteenth century, many forts were abandoned, left to deteriorate and collapse, and can no longer be located. Poor maintenance led to the breakdown of 60 to 70 percent of them, and the rest collapsed because of structural defects in their construction. A massive

95 See Davis, *Late Victorian Holocausts*, chap. 2.

96 See Pierre-Etienne Will, *Bureaucracy and Famine in Eighteenth-Century China* (Stanford: Stanford University Press, 1990).

number of forts, which accommodated tens of thousands of people for a time, were built on the loose mountain soil, but in bad weather (i.e., excessive rainfall), they easily fell apart.[97] The forts constructed in the lowlands were even less sturdy and collapsed over time.[98] A few signs of these forts can be found in the highland areas, and some became popular tourist sites, such as the Lying Bull Fort, the biggest fort remaining in Hubei today.

The *yuan*, which were extensively mobilized in local militarization, did not perform military functions any more after the Taiping Rebellion or during the Republican period. However, *tuan* continued to be a part of the *baojia* system of this region. According to a Hu family genealogy of Tianmen County, the households were organized under the *tuan* unit, which in terms of function was identical to the *baojia* system.[99] The Nationalist government implemented the *baojia* system nationwide from the 1920s to the 1940s. However, the *yuan* were never explicitly integrated into the *baojia* system of the Nationalist government.[100]

Although the militarization of landscapes and waterscapes was a wartime strategy, the environmental consequences were by no means temporary. Decades of militarization derailed the local ecological systems. Soil erosion intensified, and siltation in the rivers increased. The riverbeds narrowed, and outlets silted up, which together led to extensive controversy over opening and blocking waterways in the late nineteenth and early twentieth centuries. More importantly, the catastrophic rural famine from the late 1850s to the early 1860s signified the drain on material resources. Because the granaries were bare, the government was facing a financial shortage that decreased disaster relief, and food stored by agricultural households contracted to the vanishing point, the rural Jianghan Plain faced periodic devastating famines.

97 Yan, "Sansheng shannei bianfang lun," no. 4, in He, *Huangchao jingshi wenbian* 82, "Bingzheng" 13, "Shanfang."

98 Yan, "Sansheng shannei bianfang lun."

99 *Hushi zongpu*, 2: 80–81. The Hu lineage was a big lineage of Tianmen County.

100 The information about the *baojia* system of the Nationalist Government can be found in *Hubei xianzheng gaikuang* 湖北县政概况 [*The Basic Situation of Hubei Administration*], ed. Hubeisheng minzhengting, vol. 1, 1934.

CHAPTER 5

Coping with Environmental Crisis in the Post-Taiping Era

The summer of 1852 seemed to be a summer of no significance. The water level of the Yangzi during flood season showed no drastic fluctuation from previous years. However, this seemingly uneventful summer turned out to be the turning point of the Yangzi River–Dongting Lake system. In midsummer, the Malingong dike, a section in Shishou County on the south bank of the Yangzi River, suddenly collapsed, and the water gushed out of the Yangzi River at Ouchi Township. However, because of a shortage of funds and labor, the local government did not repair the dike immediately. This breach was worsened by flooding in subsequent years and remained unrepaired. In 1860, flood torrents from the Yangzi escaped via the Ouchi breach and formed a tributary that became the origin of the present-day Ouchi River. In 1870, another large flood affected the Yangzi and its midstream valley. The rushing waters from the Yangzi damaged the Huangjiabu dike section on the south bank, about 150 kilometers upstream from the newly formed Ouchi outlet. After three years of futile attempts to repair the dike breach, Songzi County eventually let the outlet remain open, and the Songzi River, a new branch of the Yangzi, took shape. Until then, the two new outlets, Ouchi and Songzi, along with two previously extant outlets—Hudu and Tiaoxuan—had served as the main relief for floodwaters from the Yangzi to Dongting Lake and to the south of the Yangzi. The formation of the four-outlet diversion system (*sikou fenliu* 四口分流) signified a major shift in the Yangzi–Han–Dongting Lake system and prompted a wide range of flood-control ideas among officials, various stakeholders' claims of interest in the river-lake system, and different responses and strategies by social groups coping with an impending environmental crisis. The nineteenth-century environmental crisis witnessed changes and dysfunction in the river-lake systems on the Jianghan Plain, and in turn, the changes in landscape and waterscape stimulated violence and claims of a "moral hydraulic order" among the social groups at the grassroots of Jianghan society.[1]

1 In my 2016 article "The Revolt of the Commons," I use the concept of "panarchy" and "adaptive cycle" to analyze the Jianghan Plain. I suggest that the late nineteenth-century Jianghan society reaches a point where "the resilience is low and the level is particularly vulnerable" and a point "where fast and small events overwhelm slow and large ones, and can cascade to

© KONINKLIJKE BRILL NV, LEIDEN, 2022 | DOI:10.1163/9789004505285_007

After the Taiping Rebellion, the Jianghan Plain was devastated—the landscape was destroyed, the socioeconomic system disrupted, and the lifestyle of local people changed. The draconian military projects on the Jianghan Plain had altered the landscape and had serious ecological consequences. In addition to large-scale deforestation, Chinese officials also saw other severe problems: irrigation structures were unattended and thus collapsed, agricultural fields were abandoned and full of weeds, and masses of people migrated from the war-torn region, leaving the area short of labor power. Officials realized that the central problem after the Taiping Rebellion ended was the restoration of social and economic order. One key task was reconstruction of the water-control system.

The intellectual debates driving the reconstruction of water control were, in fact, diverse, drawing in various social groups, including ordinary people, local gentry, and high-ranking government officials. The debates covered a wide spectrum of ideas about how to manage the environment, from destroying the dikes (both long and *yuan* dikes) for the sake of water flow, which was the dominant view of the provincial and central governments, to the strongly anthropocentric method of using dikes to constrain water flow so as to reclaim the land for agricultural cultivation, which was the main focus of some local communities. Furthermore, communities on the southern and northern banks of the Yangzi and those on the western and eastern banks of the Han engaged in escalating levels of conflict, fighting for their own hydrogeographical interests. This chapter examines several water-control controversies from the late Qing to early Republican periods, demonstrating that the post-Taiping environmental crisis stimulated responses at all levels—government officials, gentry, and ordinary people. As shown by this wide spectrum of social responses, the forces from below played a major role in thwarting official geopolitical interests in managing the hydraulic system between the Yangzi and the Han Rivers.

---

higher, slower levels." Gao, "The Revolt of the Commons," 36–37. Lance Gunderson and C.S. Holling coined the term "panarchy" as an antithesis to the word hierarchy. They propose a four-phase adaptive cycle of exploitation, conservation, release, or creative destruction, and reorganization to understand the resilience of human and natural systems. For more discussion, see Lance Gunderson and C.S. Holling, *Panarchy: Understanding Transformations in Human and Natural Systems* (Washington, D.C.: Island Press, 2002), 21, 32.

1 Post-Taiping Social Distress and Environmental Crisis

It is difficult to reconstruct the population data in the Jianghan Plain during and after the Taiping Rebellion because Hubei compiled its population figures arbitrarily after 1851, so comments of population reduction for certain prefectures often contradict the official figures.[2] During the first five years and some of later years, the population loss in Hubei was considerable; in 1853 somewhere between 300,000 and 500,000 people were captured by Taipings, and after the war some counties testified to the abundance of land and shortage of labor.[3] After carefully examining the population and land data from the fourteenth to the twentieth centuries, Ping-ti Ho concluded that, although the population declined because of intense warfare during the Taiping Rebellion and the subsequent famine, the conditions for the large population and the limited available arable land per capita remained unchanged.[4] The growing population continued to reclaim land to feed their hunger for it. According to Zhang Jiayan, from 1875 to 1908, Jingzhou Prefecture had 802 *yuan* (i.e., 4,010,000 *mu* of land), comprising almost 70 percent of the agricultural acreage in the prefecture.[5] In Jianli County alone, the *yuan* fields made up about 77.6 percent of the total agricultural fields over the same period.[6] He thus concluded that, by the end of the Qing, the *yuan* fields covered at least two-thirds of the total agricultural fields on the Jianghan Plain.[7] This great increase in land reflected not only the promotion of agricultural cultivation but also the reduction in flood-relief areas and the subsequent risk of flooding.

The region experienced a widespread environmental crisis from the mid-nineteenth century to the post-Taiping era. From a long-term perspective, this period was at the tail end of the Little Ice Age and was in an El Niño cycle.[8] In the last few decades of the nineteenth century, the entire plain

2 Ho, *Studies on the Population of China*, 244–245.

3 Ho, *Studies on the Population of China*, 245.

4 Ho, *Studies on the Population of China*, 278.

5 Zhang, "Qingdai jianghan pingyuan."

6 Zhang, "Qingdai jianghan pingyuan."

7 Zhang, "Qingdai jianghan pingyuan."

8 For a study on the late nineteenth-century famine on a global scale, see Davis, *Late Victorian Holocausts*. For an analysis of the 1870s famine in northern and northwestern China, see Kathryn Edgerton-Tarpley, *Tears from Iron: Cultural Responses to Famine in Nineteenth-Century China* (Berkeley: University of California Press, 2008); Lilian M. Li, *Fighting Famine in North China: State, Market, and Environmental Decline, 1690s–1990s* (Stanford: Stanford University Press, 2007); Andrea Janku, "'Heaven-Sent Disasters'"; idem, "Drought and Famine in Northwest China: A Late Victorian Tragedy?" *Journal of Chinese History* 2: 373–391. https://doi.org/10.1017/jch.2018.4.

became more vulnerable to flooding and drainage problems. Statistics show that, between 1368 and 1464, big floods occurred, on average, every 12.1 years, but, by the end of the nineteenth century, their frequency increased to every 1.5 years.[9] Over the course of a few decades, the region suffered multiple large disasters. The Xianfeng earthquake in 1856 was followed by a series of large floods of the Yangzi River, especially in 1860 and 1870. The 1860 flood was caused by excessive rainfall and simultaneous flood seasons of the Yangzi and the Han Rivers. The floodwaters from Sichuan upstream to the midstream of the Yangzi were supplemented by water from the Han River, which exerted additional pressure on the two rivers and flooded large areas between them, including Yichang, Jiangling, Gong'an, and Pinshan.[10] Within ten years, the same area was visited by another flood. According to existing hydrological records, the flood in 1870 was the largest in the Yangzi valley in eight hundred years. The water rose to as much as 81.16 meters above ground. Most areas in five provinces in the central Yangzi valley were submerged. At the peak of the flood, 105,000 cubic meters of floodwater per second flowed through Yichang, four times more than the average flood flow of the Yangzi through the same section, and seventy times more than the peak flow of the Yellow River.[11] The flood left historic high watermarks on the two poles inside the Huangling Temple on the banks of the Yangzi (see Figure 20), which provided reference marks for the construction of Three Gorges Dam in the late twentieth century.

2 Managing the Waters

The continuous expansion of *yuan* and the opening of the mountains under constant population pressure exacerbated problems in water control that led to many controversies over water outlets. By the late Qing, excessively reclaimed lands often blocked the outlets from one river to another and from river to

9 Zhang, "Mingdai jianghan pingyuan shuihan." For more discussion on the frequency of historical water disasters on the Jianghan Plain, see Chapter 1.

10 Changjiang liuyu guihua bangongshi, *Changjiang shuili shilue* 长江水利史略 [*A Brief History of the Yangzi River*] (Beijing: Shuili shuidian chubanshe, 1978), 130–131.

11 The peak flow number is based on a description of the 1870 flood at the Huangling Temple. *Changjiang shuili shilue* (1978, 130) claims 110,000 cubic meters per second; Luo Chengzheng, ed., *Zhongguo lishi dahongshui diaocha ziliao huibian* 中國歷史大洪水調查資料彙編 [*A Collection of Surveys on Historical Floods in China*] (Beijing: Zhongguo shudian chubanshe, 2006), 287–294.

FIGURE 20
Historical watermarks from the 1870 Yangzi flood on the two poles in the Huangling Temple
Note: Each pole is 17.4 meters tall and has a diameter of 0.783 meters.
PHOTO BY THE AUTHOR IN 2015.

lake. As a result, many areas in the Jianghan Plain suffered from flooding and drainage problems. To address those problems, various stakeholders competed to block or open key water outlets of this region, discussed later in this chapter. Controversies over how to control the water focused on two main issues: flood control and coping with increased sedimentation. In addition, undergirding the official hydraulic decisions was the state's favoritism toward the north bank of the Yangzi and left bank of the Han.

2.1 *Flood Control: Restoring, Diking, or Diverting*

Officials were divided into three main streams of thought regarding flood control in the late nineteenth century. The first supported digging trenches and canals so as to restore the previous "nine reservoirs and thirteen outlets" from the Yangzi to its branch rivers and lakes. The second favored building high dikes to restrict the floodwaters and confine the river course; this was the dominant view among officials, because until the 1870s no major floods had occurred since 1788, and they attributed this hydraulic stability to solid dike construction and maintenance. And the third advocated diverting water to both the north and south of the Yangzi, though that would have benefited the north and harmed the south. This third view was enthusiastically promoted by the scholar official Wang Boxin 王柏心 (1799–1873) and gradually gained the support of the top echelons of statecraft officials in the late Qing.

Wang Boxin was a firm believer in diverting the rivers. Wang grew up in Jianli County on the Yangzi River and thus had childhood memories about flood damage as well as deep compassion for the people living along the river. He became a provincial degree holder in 1844, and was appointed to the head of the Board of Punishments. However, he was not interested in the official post and retired to his home in Hubei. In 1852, when the Taiping rebels passed through Hubei, Wang organized the local militia in Jianli County to fight them. Subsequently, during the Taiping and post-Taiping era, Wang befriended the leaders and top officials of the Xiang Army, including Zeng Guofan, Hu Linyi, Zuo Zongtang, and Li Mengqun. Wang's investigation and analysis of the hydraulic problems in the region were mostly completed before the Taiping uprising, but his ideas had a profound influence on post-Taiping hydraulic reconstruction and revealed the reasons for the discrepancy between policies from above and actions from below.

Wang was very knowledgeable about the hydrology and geomorphology of the Jing River, the Jingzhou section of the Yangzi. Based on his experience with the Jing River floods, he maintained that it was insufficient to build long dikes along the river—outlets needed to be opened along it to relieve water pressure and to allow excessive water to be diverted to Dongting Lake. He firmly opposed building long dikes to constrain the Jing River; in his view, it was too risky to constrain the river between the long dikes in the absence of outlets to relieve the water pressure.[12] He also observed the Yangzi's worsening sedimentation problem: "The riverbed rose suddenly in the recent decade, sand bars accumulated in the river, and minuscule river course changes happened frequently."[13] He then stated that "flood waters, sandbars, and wind and rain were all working against the dikes. Strengthening the left bank would hurt the right bank; strengthening both banks would inevitably hurt the downstream dikes. ... The more we build dikes to restrain the river waters, the less we can gain from the waters."[14] Thus he suggested opening the Hudu outlet and giving

12 Wang Boxin, "Jun hudukou daojiang liuru dongting yi 浚虎渡口導江流入洞庭議 [Opening the Hudu Outlet and Diverting the Yangzi River Wates into the Dongting Lake]," in Ni, *Jingzhou wancheng dizhi*, 258–264.

13 Wang, "Jun hudukou daojiang."

14 Wang, "Jun hudukou daojiang."

up the areas along the Hudu River (including Gong'an, Songzi, in Hubei, and Lizhou, Anxiang, in Hunan) to guarantee the safety of a bigger area around the Jing River.[15]

In 1848, a series of dikes collapsed in Gong'an, Songzi, Shishou, and Jiangli, on the southern bank of the Jing River. Wang immediately went to the south bank to inspect the collapsed dike. After the inspection, he wrote *Following a Discussion of Diverting the River* (*Daojiang xuyi*), advocating that the river course not be blocked. He proposed leaving it open where the dikes had collapsed, so that the floodwaters could be diverted to Dongting and Hong Lakes.[16]

Wang wrote the second part of the work in 1849, after the Jing River dike experienced another series of major breaks. In it, he detailed a range of water-control issues, including agricultural irrigation, drainage, floods, and damage resulting from blocking outlets, and the advantages of diverting the river. He debated these issues in the form of dialogues with a hypothetical person:

> Someone asked, "Did the danger of the river become more serious?"
>
> Wang answered, "No, it was not because of the river itself, but because of the dikes. ... Big rivers shall not be diked. ... Instead, natural water paths shall be preserved and river waters diverted."[17]

Wang's hydraulic ideas clearly showed his understanding of natural laws: respect natural water flows and refrain from human intervention. His ideas heavily influenced the official flood-control policy in the region, which led to the formation of two branch rivers—the Songzi River and the Ouchi River—which originated at the dike breaches that were simply left open.

These outlets newly formed from 1852 to 1873 fundamentally reorganized the Yangzi-Dongting hydraulic system—the Yangzi River was diverted to Dongting Lake through four key outlets, three of which were located on the south bank of the Yangzi. The same period was also the turning point for Dongting Lake, as the Yangzi waters carried a large amount of sediment to the lake through these outlets and led to its siltation and shrinkage. Furthermore, peasants continuously reclaimed land from the lake's silted sandbars, which created fertile land suitable for agriculture. According to hydrogeomorphological records, around 16 billion cubic meters of sand and mud traveled every year from the Yangzi

15 Wang, "Jun hudukou daojiang."

16 Wang Boxin, "Daojiang xuyi 導江續議 [Following a Discussion of Diverting the River]," part 1 (1848), in Ni, *Jingzhou wancheng dizhi*, 264–265.

17 Wang Boxin, "Daojiang xuyi 導江續議 [Following a Discussion of Diverting the River]," part 2 (1849), in Ni, *Jingzhou wancheng dizhi*, 266–267.

to Dongting through the four outlets. Within three or four decades, a sandbar had grown so big that the Qing government formally established Nanzhou Prefecture in 1894.[18] Conversely, the silted and shrunken Dongting Lake could not relieve as much flood pressure from the Yangzi as it should have. This compromised river-lake system could not survive flooding of any large scale. In the twentieth century, three big central Yangzi floods—in 1931, 1954, and 1998—were partly attributed to the Jianghan river-lake system's low capacity for flood relief.

2.2 *Sedimentation: Ban the Reclamation on Mountains*

Another growing environmental problem was the sedimentation of the Yangzi and Han Rivers. As discussed in Chapter 4, in the mid-nineteenth century, the further destruction of mountainous vegetation coverage increased sedimentation in the downstream area, and Qing officials widely acknowledged the issue of sedimentation in the Yangzi and Han Rivers, trying to understand the origins of the problem and offer solutions.

Officials had written extensively about the problem of sedimentation since the late eighteenth century. For example, Zhao Renji 趙仁基 (1789–1841), who served as a Hubei surveillance commissioner, had an analysis of the physiodynamics of increased sedimentation and its damage to the downstream river ecology. He wrote,

> The water overflowed because of increased sedimentation; the increased sedimentation was due to land reclamation on the upstream mountains. ... Before reclaiming the mountains, [the movement of] sand and soil from upstream mountains was limited and the river flow velocity was strong enough to carry it away. After the mountain lands were reclaimed, more and more sand and soil were loosened and washed downstream, which slowed the water flow, accumulated sediments in the riverbed—from inches to several feet—and thus sandbars grew larger and larger in the riverways, blocking the river flows. ... Furthermore, with accumulated sediments, the riverbed became higher and higher, while the riverways broadened. ... The waterways used to be narrow, and the fast-flowing waters could scour away the sediments to [a location] further downstream. Now the large amount of sediment has broadened the waterways, and the riverbed has become shallower due to the accumulation of sand and soil in the riverbed. As a result, water thus cannot flow at a high

18 *Changjiang shuili shilue*, 140.

> velocity and sand stays in the riverbed. [The amount of] sand and soil accumulated on the riverbed in one year equals the amount accumulated in the past ten years.[19]

His son Zhao Liewen 趙烈文 (1832–1894) inherited his hydraulic ideas and was a key figure in the network of late Qing statecraft officials.

Lin Zexu 林則徐 (1785–1850), who served as the governor of Huguang from 1837 to 1838, conducted a thorough investigation of the Yangzi and Han River systems and analyzed the origins of the sandy river waters. He wrote,

> The jobless people of Hubei and Hunan mostly moved to the border areas of Sichuan and Shaanxi, Guizhou, and Guangzhou. They were engaged in slash-and-burn [cultivation] and turned the vastly forested hills into agricultural lands. All mountainous areas were thus exhausted … sand, mud, rotten leaves and roots, loosened due to lack of vegetation, were all washed off by the heavy rainfall, from the upstream mountains to the creeks, from creeks to the Han River, and to the Yangzi, and then from the Yangzi and Han to all satellite lakes. When the water ran off, the sand and soil stayed in the riverbed, gradually growing into shoals … the downstream lake surface and riverbed became narrower and narrower, and more and more sand from upstream accumulated in the riverbeds.[20]

Tao Shu 陶澍 (1779–1839), who had overseen the salt administration and river conservancy in the Huainan, Huaibei, and Jiangsu areas, stated that

> the proliferation of shoals on the riverbed is because of the excessive reclamation in the upstream border areas of Sichuan, Shaanxi, Guizhou, and Yunnan. Vagrants felled the trees, turned the forests to fields, and cultivated [new world] crops on the hillsides. The topsoil loosened and was carried away by rainfall … the more the mountain lands were reclaimed, the more shoals appeared downstream.[21]

19 Zhao Renji, "Lun jiangshui shi'er pian 論江水十二篇 [Twelve Theses on the Yangzi Waters]," in *Zai xu xingshui jinjian (Changjiang)* 再續行水金鑑 (長江卷) [*Continued Golden Reference for Water Regulation: the Yangzi River*], ed. Zhongguo shuili shuidian kexue yanjiuyuan and Shuili shi yanjiushi (Wuhan: Hubei renmin chubanshe, 1835/2004).

20 Lin Zexu, "Huguang shuili lun 湖廣水利論 [A Discussion on the Water Control in Huguang]," in He, *Huangchao jingshi wenbian* 117, "Gongzheng" 23.

21 Tao Shu, "Fuzou Jiangsu shangwu zu'e shuidao shazhou zhezi 覆奏江蘇尚無阻遏水道沙洲折子 [Memorial on Sandbars in Waterways of Jiangsu]," in Tao Shu, *Taowenyi gong quanji* 陶文毅公全集 [*The Collection of Essays by Taowenyi Gong*] (1840), 10: 13–18.

The late nineteenth-century official Ma Zhenglin 馬徵麟 studied the Yangzi waterways and wrote *A Pictorial Record of the Yangzi River* (1871), showing detailed geographical features in and along the waterways. In addition to offering information for designing military strategies, he proposed five ways of managing the Yangzi waters: "first, ban mountain reclamation so that the river sources are clear; second, increase the water velocity to scour out the silt in the riverways; third, open the outlets to divert the excess water; fourth, give up some areas to relieve flood waters from the main river course; and fifth, build reservoirs and canals to store excess water."[22] He stressed that there was no better way to manage the Yangzi River floods than implementing these five methods simultaneously.

Late Qing officials' concerns about sedimentation were echoed by contemporary scholars. For example, the historical geographer Lu Xiqi studied management of the Han River and its course changes and asserted that

> the sedimentation in the middle and lower reaches of the Han River remained stable before the mid-Qing. ... After the mid-Qing, the sediment from the mountainous region of the upper Han River valley added an important variable to the relatively stable river ecological system. The quantity of sediment from upstream was not significantly large, but the sediment was made up of coarse and heavy particles moving quickly downstream during a concentrated short time period, and that interrupted the equilibrium of the river system; the impacts were profound.[23]

2.3 *Sacrificing the South for the North*

As mentioned earlier in the chapter, officials' ideas about dealing with Yangzi flooding would clearly have favored the north and damaged the south of the Yangzi, and that was the main reason that the southern communities around the Yangzi constantly rejected government decisions regarding dike construction and the opening or blocking of outlets. An analysis of the social fabric in the northern and the southern communities reveals the rationale in the state's environmental decision making.

---

22 Ma Zhenglin, *Changjiang tushuo* 長江圖說 [*A Pictorial Record of the Yangzi*] (Taipei: Wenhai chubanshe, 1871/1969). Ma was born in Anhui. His lifespan is unknown.

23 Lu and Pan, *Hanshui zhongxiayou hedao bianqian yu difang*, 394–397. He points out that a big turning point in the sedimentation in the Han River probably occurred during the Tang dynasty. Because of the decline of the Nanyang basin during the Northern and Southern dynasties (420–589), a significant area of vegetation recovered, which contributed to a decrease in soil erosion.

Since the mid-Ming, the state had taken the position of protecting the north and gullying the south of the Yangzi (also protecting the north, or left bank, and gullying the south, or right bank, of the Han River). The primary reason was that Zhongxiang County (present-day Jingmen) on the north bank of the Yangzi was the native place of the Jiajing emperor and the location of the tombs of his parents. The second reason was that the Jingzhou area on the north bank of the Yangzi produced many high officials in the Ming government, including Zhang Juzheng 張居正 (1525–1582), who served on the Grand Secretariat. The Jiajing emperor did not ascend the throne following the normal bloodline order; after his enthronement in 1521, he insisted that his father, Prince Xing, posthumously receive the titles and honors due to an emperor.[24] Prince Xing was enfeoffed at Anlu and was buried there after he died in 1519. Anlu was north of both the Han and Yangzi Rivers. To protect Prince Xing's tomb in a location with good *fengshui*, in 1522 the court eunuchs had the left bank of the Han River sealed by building a series of long dikes that blocked all the flood-relief outlets. Many of the blocked outlets were part of the "nine mouths" (*jiukou* 九口, nine outlets that relieved water pressure from the Yangzi River to lakes and wetlands) critical to a healthy river-lake system in the Jianghan Plain.[25]

Zhang Juzheng further diked up the northern bank of the Han River and sealed the northern bank of the Yangzi in Jianli and Mianyang out of the similar motive as the Jiajing emperor: to protect his father's tomb in Jiangling, his native place, and to arrange an auspicious site for the tomb.[26] Often denounced by many later officials when discussing hydraulic issues, Zhang was known to be a very consistent "dike sealer" and was credited with closing the outlets on the Yangzi. Wang Boxin, a firm dike opponent with an interest in diverting the river as discussed earlier, surprisingly endorsed Zhang's dike sealing as "impartial and effective."[27] As Will argues, "The so-called 'hydraulic state,' or its representatives, could also operate a system in an apparently arbitrary way, and, for reasons in fact alien to hydraulics, impose irrational, even nonsensical decisions, as was the case with the diking up of the Han in 1522—or decisions which at the very least were not unanimously accepted."[28]

24 Will, "State Intervention," 311.

25 Will, "State Intervention," 311n27. Will points out that the chronology of the "nine mouths" is not absolutely clear.

26 *Jingmen zhouzhi* (1808), 14; Wang Zhiyi, "Hubei shuili pian 湖北水利篇 [On Water Control in Hubei]," in Yu, *Chubei shuili difang jiyao*.

27 *Jiangling xianzhi* 江陵縣志 [*Gazetteer of Jiangling County*] (1877), 8: 44A–B.

28 Will, "State Intervention," 313.

This rationale was consistently accepted during the Qing. As shown by the Wancheng dike during the reign of Qianlong, the dikes of the north bank were meticulously assigned official projects with carefully divided dike sections, while along the south bank of the Yangzi were large areas of silted shoals in the riverbed with limited dikes maintained by local communities (see Figure 21). This was important because the Jingzhou garrison was located north of the Yangzi. An extreme case of this reasoning was evident during the 1860 flood, in which dikes on both sides of the river were in danger of flooding. Officials on the north bank ordered the firing of a cannon at people who were trying to consolidate the dikes on the south bank. Because people were scared away from their emergency dike work, dikes on the south bank soon collapsed, which relieved the water pressure from the Yangzi. The north bank communities of the river thus were spared from flooding.[29]

In 1709, the opening of the Sigang outlet (to the Han River) stirred up a huge debate between the southern and northern bank communities of the Han River. A petition letter written by Liu Biao, a local literatus from the northern bank, illustrates the geopolitical favoritism embodied in the notion of sacrificing the south for the sake of the north:

> The opening of Sigang was beneficial for the seventy-two *yuan* of the southern bank of the Han River, but was detrimental to the northern bank of the river. However, in terms of taxation, the southern bank *yuan* only contributed two tenths of the total, while the northern bank *yuan* contributed eight tenths. Furthermore, the population of the southern bank was less than a quarter of the total, while the northern bank had more than three-quarters of the total population. On the southern bank, people could take on fishing if their lands were flooded, and they had many lakes to fish. On the northern bank, people were mostly farmers and land was much more available than lakes; if the land was all flooded, local peasants could do nothing, and no taxes could be levied.[30]

The opening of the Sigang outlet was brought up a few times during the eighteenth century, but the outlet remained sealed because of fierce opposition from the northern bank communities.

The official controversies over dike construction, flood control, and sedimentation revealed the organic and holistic interconnections in the river-lake

29 Peng and Zhang, *Mingqing changjiang liuyu*, 220.

30 Peng and Zhang, *Mingqing changjiang liuyu*, 21–34.

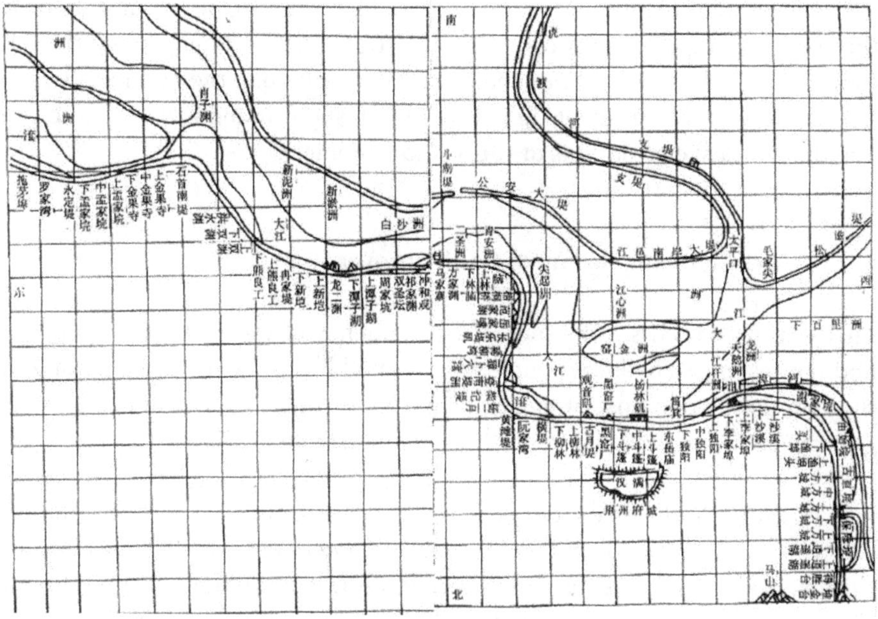

FIGURE 21 The Wancheng dike during the Qing
Note: The image is reversed and reflects a view from the north toward the south. This image shows that shoals spread widely to the south bank of the Yangzi River and that the dike sections were carefully assigned on the north bank of the Yangzi, where the Manchu garrison was located.
SOURCE: NI, *JINGZHOU WANCHENG DIZHI*, 1: 42–43.

system of the central Yangzi. For example, the overexploitation in the upstream mountains led to increased sedimentation of the river, and the blocked outlets compounded the risk of flooding. This view was best described by Hubei governor Emida:

> [The river-lake system] was like a human body; lakes such as the Changhu, Sanghu, Hongma, and Bailu were like the thoracic diaphragm (*xiong ge* 胸膈), the estuary reaches of lakes in Qianjiang, Jianli, and Mianyang were like the sacrum (*wei lǘ* 尾閭), the branch rivers of the Yangzi and the Han were like the veins in the limbs (*sizhi xuemai* 四肢血脈) ... If the diaphragm was broad, and the sacrum was unhindered, the veins of the four limbs would not be blocked.[31]

31 Yu, *Chubei shuili difang jiyao*, 2: 9–10.

However, this organic view of the river-lake system was complicated by the state's strong favoritism toward the north bank of the Yangzi and the left (north) bank of the Han. The increasing conflict among the communities in the region was the result of the private interests of individual communities and the political calculations of various stakeholders.

3 The Changing Nature of Conflicts over Water

This section[32] discusses the increasing frequency of water and land conflicts and the responses by local people to irrational hydraulic decision making by those in power, demonstrating activism from below to choose how they were governed with regard to hydraulic issues on the Jianghan Plain.

3.1 *First, Greater Frequency and on a Larger Scale*

The conflicts over land and water greatly increased on the plain, between upstream and downstream communities, between left-bank and right-bank communities, between fisher folk and merchants, between households that shared an irrigation canal, and between officials and local people. In response, people in local communities resorted more frequently to litigation and violence.[33] As Zhang Jiayan states, "filing lawsuits related to water control became one of the most notorious customs of Hubei Province."[34] Zhang emphasizes four main characteristics of the litigation from the mid-eighteenth century to the twentieth century: the unclear legal ownership of much of the land on the plain, the use of waterways for different purposes, the disputes among the residents of some *yuan* over their own interests, and the involvement of many *yuan* in large, decades-long lawsuits.[35]

32 A portion of this section appears in the article "The Revolt of the Commons" published by *Resilience*, see Gao (2016: 34–70).

33 Thomas M. Buoye, *Manslaughter, Markets, and Moral Economy: Violent Disputes over Property Rights in Eighteenth-Century China* (Cambridge: Cambridge University Press, 2000). Buoye examines the evolution of property rights in Guangdong during the eighteenth century and argues that agricultural commercialization, market incentives, and population growth were the big motivations for changes in Qing institutions. Driven by economic growth, many changes in the land-use system were reflected in the revision of Qing legislation—for example, the abandonment of land redemption and the further practice of topsoil-subsoil division of land rights.

34 Zhang, *Coping with Calamity*, 201.

35 Zhang, *Coping with Calamity*, 197–198.

Even small-scale collaboration among the *yuan* was sometimes problematic in the face of people's self-interest in an individual *yuan*, and conflicts became more frequent after the eighteenth century. For example, a lawsuit on the allocation of dike work between the Bianhe *yuan* and the Wenjia *yuan* in Tianmen County lasted for about sixty years during the eighteenth century. The two *yuan* were geographically connected and were supposed to collaborate on *yuan* dike maintenance. However, the Wenjia *yuan* did not want to cooperate (for reasons unspecified in the sources) and built a separation dam between the two *yuan* in 1701. Afterward, the Wenjia *yuan* did not maintain the dike that mostly surrounded the Bianhe *yuan*, and the Bianhe *yuan* simply could not afford to maintain the dike by itself. As a result, the Bianhe *yuan* sued the Wenjia *yuan* at various levels of government. The case was finally settled in 1759 by the county magistrate, Hu Yi.[36] However, the sources do not specify how it was settled. Presumably, the dike work was divided between the two *yuan* based on their proportional land ownership.

The rifts between lineages also hindered collaboration within and among the *yuan* communities. For example, dike work on the Mutou *yuan* in Qianjiang County was originally allocated between the Zhu and Huang lineages; however, the two lineages held grudges against each other and could not cooperate in dike maintenance. They fought a lawsuit all the way to the capital during the reign of Tongzhi (1862–1874). The solution was to separate the two lineages, merge several other lineages into the *yuan*, divide the dike work (its dike was 4,458.3 meters, or 2,702 *gong*) into three sections (assigned to Zhu, Huang, and other lineages, respectively), and allocate the dike work based on the land owned by each lineage.[37] The Zhu lineage owned 105 hectares of land and therefore had to construct a dike 914 meters long; the Huang lineage owned 171 hectares of land and accordingly took responsibility for 1,490 meters. Other lineages had a total of 235.6 hectares of land, so they were allocated 2,052.6 meters of dike work.[38]

Upstream and downstream *yuan* communities often had conflicts that involved escalating violence. Tragedies happened in the *yuan* in the late nineteenth century. The Lanjia *yuan* was divided in two by an earthen dam: The upstream communities of the *yuan* wanted to destroy it so that the floodwaters could go through, but the downstream communities wanted to retain it so that the area would be free of floods. For generations, the two communities argued over maintaining or destroying the dam, to the point of violence that

36 *Tianmen xianzhi* (1765), 6: 12–15, in *Zhongguo difangzhi jicheng*, 44: 459–460.

37 *Qianjiang xianzhi xu* (1879), 10: 17.

38 *Qianjiang xianzhi xu*, 10: 17.

resulted in numerous deaths. The communities had also fought lawsuits all the way to the capital, where officials in the central government came up with no solution other than sending troops to put down the mass violence.[39]

In other cases, peasants and commoners attacked the heads of dike maintenance (*di zhang* 堤長, or *di tou* 堤頭), usually landlords, rich householders, or officials who were responsible for organizing workers and funding to maintain the dikes. The dike maintenance system was sometimes problematic. Corruption, avoidance of responsibilities, cheating on projects, and refusing collaboration were prevalent in dike construction and maintenance. Rich households, which usually lived far away from the dikes, tried to avoid contributing money and labor to the dike work, and poor peasants were drafted to work on their construction and repairs. Some rich households also cheated in the dike work, for example, by putting a thin layer of soil on the surface of the dike and claiming that they had performed the necessary maintenance. When floods destroyed dikes, sometimes there was not enough money to repair them. Some of the dike funds were embezzled by the dike heads or local officials, leaving insufficient funds for the dike work.[40] Dike workers, usually peasants in the communities, called together groups to rob the dike heads in their homes, especially in the event of big floods that broke the dikes. In the late nineteenth century, a peasant named Tan Jincheng was assigned dike work on the Wujia *yuan*, whose dike head had cut Tan's wages. Tan thereupon stole pigs and cows from the *yuan* in lieu of pay. The dike head sued Tan in the county court. Just before Tan was arrested, he organized hundreds of people to roam around the *yuan* communities, claiming that they were robbing the rich and helping the poor and breaking out in fights.[41] These incidents were usually suppressed by government troops eventually.

These are just a few of the conflicts over water described in local gazetteers and precedential legal cases; many water and land disputes are detailed in the criminal records held by the Board of Punishments. In 1900, Liao Fa'er opened the sluice gate of a public dike for growing crops. When his landlord, Qing Shiguang, found out, he beat Liao to death. Qing was arrested and was sentenced to death in 1902.[42] From 1901 to 1902, a commoner, Xiong Zhijie, fought with his neighbor, Dao Changdian, because of dike construction on land they

---

39 *Qianjiang xianzhi xu* (1879), 10: 5.

40 Hu Zuhe, *Jingchu xiushu zhiyao* 荊楚修疏志要 [*A History of Dike Repairs in Hubei*] (Wuhan: Hubei renmin chubanshe, 1838/1999), 1: 154.

41 Peng and Zhang, *Mingqing changjiang liuyu*, 208.

42 Xingbu: Huguangsi zong'an 湖廣司宗案 [Board of Punishments: Huguang Cases], 16-11412, First Historical Archives of China.

owned in common. The fight resulted in the death of six family members, four in the Xiong family and two in the Dao family.[43] In 1904, Wu Chuanxuan, who lived in Tianmen, falsely accused Xian Chubao, a fellow county resident, of destroying the river dikes. The Board of Punishments investigated and discovered that Wu's accusation was false, and in reality Wu sought revenge in a family conflict.[44] The situation was even worse in the Republican era.

3.2 *Second, Diversifying Stakeholders*

Because of the weakening of the Qing central government, local powers filled the vacuum after the battles with the Taiping rebels and during the attempted restoration period under the reign of Tongzhi (1861–1875). One example was the hydraulic reconstruction in which various stakeholders participated during this period. Although the government insisted on keeping water outlets open, many local communities petitioned, fought for, and even manipulated the blocking of important outlets in their own interest. William T. Rowe examined the Fankou Dam controversy from 1876 to 1883, in the context of reconstruction in the mid-Yangzi region. He found that the controversy over the Fankou Dam construction involved a wide range of stakeholders, including the local and provincial governments, farmers, local elites, intellectual elites, pettifoggers, and fisher folk.[45] Rowe describes Wuchang County as "desperately poor"—the rebels destroyed its once-prosperous commercial sector and the entire area was in an economic depression. By striving for reconstruction, various social groups found a way to express their interests through the controversy over construction of the Fankou Dam.[46] Rowe thus argued that in the nineteenth-century, China had "a remarkably pluralist system of interest group politics, almost precisely the opposite of the despotism that the 'Asiatic mode of production' is said to have spawned."[47]

3.3 *Third, a "Plebeian Culture" in Popular Action*

Mary Rankin writes that, in the half-century after the Taiping Rebellion, in war-devastated Zhejiang Province, local initiatives in public works and services gathered momentum, independent of the state but spearheaded by local elites. In contrast, in other regions, which had less devastation and less

43 Xingbu: Huguangsi zong'an, 16-11415, First Historical Archives of China.

44 Xingbu: Huguangsi zong'an, 16-11700, First Historical Archives of China.

45 William T. Rowe, "Water Control and the Qing Political Process: The Fankou Dam Controversy 1876–1883," *Modern China* 14, no. 4 (1988).

46 Rowe, "Water Control," 354.

47 Rowe, "Water Control," 354.

domination by elites than the lower Yangzi, this rising tide of local initiative may have been less dependent on traditional-style leadership.[48] In contrast to Zhejiang's strongly elite-led initiatives, the conflicts on the Jianghan Plain in the nineteenth-century displayed a remarkable "plebeian culture" in which commoners with various interests competed to obtain hydraulic order and benefits. As E.P. Thompson observed in the various forms of theatrically symbolic actions by the English in their protests against their rulers, the commoners in Jianghan voiced their discontent and took strong action against government decisions in various ways.[49] As Will notes,

> We do not find before the middle of the 19th century such episodes as those of the "monk" Cai Fulong (in 1844) or of the ex-officer Yan Shilian (in 1863–64), who took the lead of the poor peasants of the interior delta in contesting the prevailing "hydraulic order." ... To my knowledge such large-scale movements, apparently not controlled and not manipulated by the gentry, did not have any precedent in the region.[50]

3.4 *Case Study: The Conflicts over the Big and Small Zekou Outlets from the 1840s to the 1910s*

The Zekou outlet gave the Han River a path to its distributary river, the Jing River. In the late nineteenth century, several major outlets were either silted up or converted to farmland, and the Zekou outlet became the only large outlet for relieving the water pressure from the Han River.[51] In 1870, high water in the Han River could not exit the Zekou outlet quickly enough, and a small outlet opened near a silted sandbar within the Zekou outlet. Soon afterward, a tremendous flow of water traveled through the Zekou outlet, swept open the outlet, and eventually changed the course of the Jing River. Because the new outlet went through the land of the Wu family, this change in the course of the river was called *Wujia gaikou* ("outlet change on the Wu family's land").

48 Rankin, *Elite Activism and Political Transformation in China*. See also Rowe, "Water Control," n10.

49 E.P. Thompson uses the plebeian-patrician dichotomy to analyze eighteenth-century English society and points out characteristics of popular action by the working poor as a counterbalance to the cultural hegemony of English gentry, especially those forming a theatrical symbolism of threat and sedition, including "effigy burning, the hanging of a boot from gallows, the illumination of windows ... the untiling of a house which ... had an almost ritualistic significance." E.P. Thompson, "Plebeian Culture, Patrician Society," *Journal of Social History* 7, no. 4 (1974): 400.

50 Will, "State Intervention," 321n57.

51 *Xiangdi cheng'an*, 2: 931–941.

Thereafter, the Han River flowed through the new outlet, instead of the Zekou outlet, and the Zekou outlet gradually silted and dried up.[52] Because the other river outlets were either silted or blocked by people for various purposes, the river now had to flow through *yuan* communities on the south bank of the Han River, which not only inundated the fields and swept away people's homes but also caused serious drainage problems in those *yuan*.[53] Figure 22 shows the locations of the small Zekou, the big Zekou, and the nearby rivers described in the case.

From the 1840s to the 1910s, thirteen conflicts broke out over blocking or opening the Zekou and Wujia outlets, and they all revolved around the conflicting hydraulic interests among four counties on the south bank of the Han River (Mianyang Prefecture, Qianjiang County, Jianli County, and Jiangling County) and ten counties on the north bank of the Han River (including Tianmen, Zhongxiang, and Jingshan Counties). In those conflicts, efforts from below—including local county governments, local literati, and common people—were intense and frequent; the effort was intended to block the two outlets in contravention of the policies from above. The scale and level of violence in these campaigns were unprecedented on the plain. Furthermore, the conflicts demonstrated the strong demand from below for self-governing institutions through which people could make their own decisions based on their hydraulic interests, instead of complying with government decisions.

The main initiators and participants in the campaigns were peasants, commoners, and lower-level gentry. In 1844, Cai Fulong 蔡福隆, a monk in Mianyang, complained that the Wujia outlet was the source of many conflicts among the communities on the south bank of the Han River; in response, he built an earthen embankment near the Wujia outlet. Gentry in Tianmen on the north bank of the river petitioned, and the Mianyang prefectural government ordered, the destruction of the earthen embankment. Cai fled, but returned three years later, circulating pamphlets, collecting fees and grain from local villagers, and trying to organize people in Mianyang to block the outlet again. This effort was dismissed by the prefectural government.[54]

52 *Qianjiang xianzhi xu* (1879), vol. 10; *Xiangdi cheng'an*, 2: 931–941.

53 *Mianyang zhouzhi* (1894), 2: 24, in *Zhongguo difangzhi jicheng*, 47: 49; *Xiangdi cheng'an*, 2: 931–941.

54 Hu Ziming, ed., "Dazekou cheng'an 大澤口成案 (1912–1913) [The Leading Cases of Dazekou, 1912–1913]," in *Zhonghua shanshuizhi congkan* 中華山水志叢刊 [*A Collection of Gazetteers of Mountains and Waters of China*] 18, ed. Shi Guangming, Dongguanghe, and Yang Guanghui (Beijing: Xianzhuang shuju, 2004), 25.

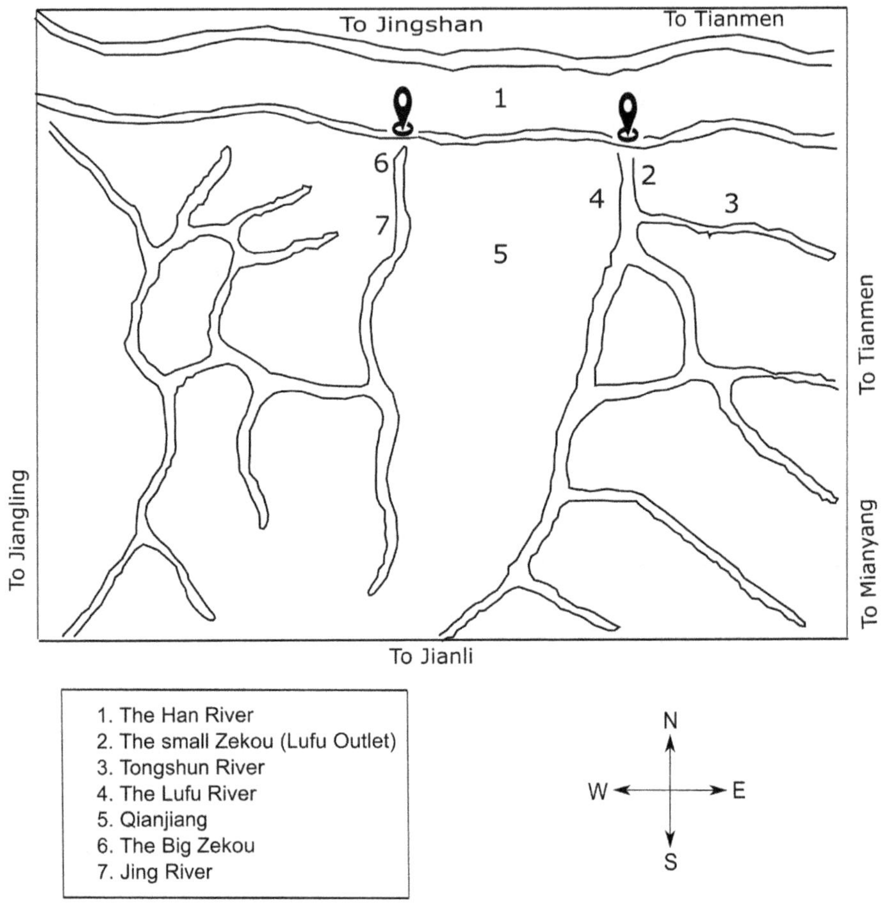

FIGURE 22 The small Zekou, the big Zekou, and the Han River in Qianjiang County during the Daoguang reign (1820–1850)
Note: The location symbols were added to indicate the two outlets in Qianjiang County: one on the left is Zekou, the big Zekou outlet; the one on the right is Lufu Kou, the small Zek*ou* outlet. This map is not to scale.
SOURCE: MODIFIED FROM YU, *CHUBEI SHUILI DIFANG JIYAO* 1: 40–41.

In 1860, Wang Maoyi 王茂義 mobilized thousands of fellow residents of Mianyang to take up arms, chant slogans, and block the Lufu outlet (the small Zekou outlet). They set out to block first the Lufu outlet and then the big Zekou outlet (before it silted up). Gentry in Tianmen again petitioned the prefectural government, which sent people to destroy the earthen embankment.[55] The

55 Hu, "Dazekou cheng'an," 25–26.

issue of blocking the outlets did not come up again until 1872, possibly because of extensive warfare between local militia (which, to some extent, was organized around *yuan* communities) and the Taiping and Nian rebels. These two large-scale peasant rebellions left the hydraulic systems in this region unattended.

Conflicts over the outlets escalated in the 1870s, during the reign of the Tongzhi emperor. In 1873, Liu Yuwen 劉玉文, who was from Qianjiang, and Wang Zifang 王子芳, a military exam degree-holder, distributed pamphlets and organized people to block the Wujia outlet. The Mianyang, the Hanyang, and the Anlu governments all stressed that this outlet had to remain open, and efforts to block it were dismissed. In 1874, Yan Shilian 嚴士連, another commoner in Qianjiang, gathered about two thousand people, marched to the Mianyang prefectural government seat, forced the officials to distribute pamphlets, and took weapons and tools to block the Zekou outlet. They even established a dike bureau to collect fees from the community. This blocking campaign was eventually ended by government troops. Yan Shilian, its leader, was sentenced to death in 1874. His compatriots Tian Bincheng and Liu Zicai were exiled. The governments of the three counties destroyed the earthen embankment and erected a stele at the outlet, declaring that the Zekou outlet could not be blocked and that anyone who attempted to do so would receive a death sentence.[56]

Apparently, the south-bank residents did not take the government warning very seriously. They tried to block the outlets in other ways. Two years later, in 1876, Guan Juncai 關俊才, a resident of Qianjiang, persuaded the Mianyang magistrate to repair the dikes, though his true goal was to block the outlet. The Mianyang magistrate allocated approximately 49,000 *chuan* for the river dike repairs, and the people in the community also donated 60,000 *chuan* for the proposed project.[57] After accepting the funds, Guan did not start to repair the dikes; instead, he instructed his team to build an earthen embankment to block the Wujia outlet. Furthermore, Guan embezzled so much of the repair funds that his colleague, Zhang, sued him in the provincial court. Guan somehow avoided facing the lawsuits. In 1880, Hubei provincial administrative advisers suggested that blockage of the outlet be banned forever.[58] However, as before, the ban did not have any substantial effect; soon thereafter, in 1886, Mianyang residents Wei Fengchi and Chen Huanzao set up a private bureau to collect dike fees and other miscellaneous fees ostensibly for building a dike near Zibeiyuan (in Jianli County). In fact, they intended to block the Wujia outlet, and by the time

56 Hu, "Dazekou cheng'an," 26.
57 One *chuan* is a string of (theoretically) one thousand copper coins.
58 Hu, "Dazekou cheng'an," 26–27.

they started to do so, they had collected over three thousand *chuan*, of which a third was used for other purposes.[59]

In 1888, Yan Xianshan, the son of Yan Shilian, plotted another campaign to block the outlet in the name of the capital officials from the central government who were inspecting the area near the outlet after a flood there. Yan proposed that the capital officials repair the dikes along the Han River. While the officials were still investigating and making a decision, Yan flew a yellow flag with the slogan "Supervising work according to the edict" and started to collect funds. Officials soon learned of Yan's activities and accused him of being greedy and acting under the influence of his father. The Anlu and Hanyang prefectural governments ruled again that the Wujia outlet had become a critical path for the Han River and could not be blocked.[60]

Campaigns like these continued in the last decade of the nineteenth century and the first decade of the twentieth century. In 1893 and 1896, several commoners either petitioned the government or simply called on people to block the outlet. The Qianjiang County government even sent troops to prevent another attempt at blocking the outlet in 1896. In 1903, more than a thousand people from Jiangling, Jianli, and Mianyang gathered together to build an earthen embankment to block the Zekou outlet. The governments of these three regions had to send troops to prevent them from doing so. After another attempt in 1908, the county and prefectural governments of both banks of the Han River came up with seven rules regarding the outlets. The first was that the Zekou outlet should never be blocked. The next four limited the height of the dikes. The sixth required digging trenches to relieve the river's water pressure. And the seventh forbade any private construction.[61]

These rules bought only four years of peace. In 1912, controversy over the Zekou outlet emerged again. In December of that year, representatives of Mianyang Prefecture, along with Jianli residents Tang Huanzhang and Tan Fangpeng, proposed that the Hubei provincial government, newly established after the 1911 Revolution overthrew the Qing dynasty, repair the dikes along the Wujia outlet, and this proposal was allowed to proceed. However, residents of Tianmen soon sent a petition to the provincial government saying that the real purpose of the proposal from the people in Mianyang and Jianli was to block the Wujia outlet, not repair it. They insisted that if the provincial government did not stop them, the ten counties on the north bank would send armed

59 Hu, "Dazekou cheng'an," 27.
60 Hu, "Dazekou cheng'an," 27.
61 Hu, "Dazekou cheng'an," 28.

forces to do so.[62] The conflict escalated a month later. Mianyang and Qianjiang residents gathered at the Wujia outlet and built an earthen embankment to block it. The Hubei provincial government sent troops, arrested their leader, and destroyed the embankment.[63] This was not the end of the conflict. Three months later, in April, Qianjiang and Mianyang residents again organized militia, attacked government troops at the outlet, injured government soldiers, and burned down the official inspection camp at Shayang (a critical section of the Han River). Likewise, Tianmen, Zhongxiang, and Jingshan residents from the north bank organized a local militia numbering tens of thousands to fight people from the south bank. It was noted that "many bandits blended into the militia to rob houses and communities were in chaos."[64] The Hubei provincial government dispatched troops, but the army failed to put down the mass violence, and the provincial government had to ask Tianmen County officials as well as local elites for help.[65] Afterward, the Hubei provincial government launched an investigation of the outlets, sending hydraulic experts to examine the hydromorphological condition of the outlets, in search of a solution that would benefit the people in the communities on both the north and south banks.[66]

This local activism shows that various lower-status social groups—especially farmers, commoners, local literati, and monks from the south bank, rather than powerful lineages, rich families, or gentry who had served in or had official connections to the government—tried to counter the policy-making from above by various levels of government. The residents of the south bank communities of the Han River believed that the changed course of the river greatly affected their lives, and they fought to manage the hydraulic infrastructure in the area in order to serve their interests, in the process manipulating government officials and twisting officials' decisions. They went so far as establishing dike bureaus to collect fees and organize large campaigns. At the same time, local elites, degree holders, and officials in the north bank communities of the Han River did not hesitate to petition against the blocking attempts by communities on the south bank. Although different levels of government had decision-making authority as well as military power, they did not demonstrate strong governance in that situation. The seemingly powerless government at

62 Hu, "Dazekou cheng'an," 17–18.
63 Hu, "Dazekou cheng'an," 23.
64 Hu, "Dazekou cheng'an," 23.
65 Hu, "Dazekou cheng'an," 23.
66 Hu, "Dazekou cheng'an," 24.

subnational levels was characteristic of official and military failures of the regime overall in the late nineteenth and early twentieth century.

4 Changes in Hydrotopography of the Jianghan Plain

The hydrotopography of the Jianghan Plain underwent drastic changes between the Ming dynasty and the 1870s, when the four-outlet-diversion system came into being (see discussion at the beginning of this chapter). The constant dike building and maintenance, along with the hydrogeomorphological movements of the rivers, caused a continual rise of the riverbed. Building dikes usually required a large amount of earth, which came from the land inside and outside the *yuan*. As more earth was taken to strengthen the dikes, the ground level sank lower, and the dikes grew higher. The riverbeds increased as a result, making the area more prone to flooding.[67]

Moreover, because of the long-term strategy of protecting the north and gullying the south, the dikes on the northern bank of the Yangzi and on the left bank of the Han were continually strengthened and the outlets sealed. The likelihood of breaches increased over time on the southern bank of the Yangzi and the right bank of the Han, leading to serious drainage problems in counties such as Jianli, Mianyang, and Qianjiang, the south of the Han and downstream of the Jing River. Furthermore, when the four outlets carried a large amount of sand and soil each year into Dongting Lake, the lakebed grew higher and silted more quickly.[68] Dongting Lake became an aboveground lake, and the Jianghan Plain was at sea level, now lower than the Yangzi and Han Rivers. On average, the Jianghan Plain is about 24–25 meters above sea level; the bottom of the western part of Dongting is about 28.1 meters above sea level, higher than the lake surface in the northern Jianghan Plain; and the bottom of the southern side of Dongting is 26.7 meters above sea level, as high as the land surface of Honghu, north of the Yangzi.[69] During flood season, the water level of the rivers is about 5–10 meters higher than the land surface. The Wanshou

67 Yu, *Chubei shuili difang jiyao*, 2: 7.

68 Chinese historical geographer Zhang Xiugui estimates that the average amount of sand and soil entered from the Yangzi River to Dongting each year increased more than three times since 1870, when two outlets, Ouchi and Songzi, were formed. Zhang calculates that about 76.9 percent of those sand and soil stayed in Dongting in 1934–1936 and 1951–1964, causing rapid siltation of the lake. Zhang Xiugui, "Dongtinghu yanbian de lishi guocheng 洞庭湖演變的歷史過程 [The Historical Changes of the Dongting Lake]," *Lishi dili* 1 (1981).

69 Zhang, "Dongtinghu yanbian de lishi guocheng."

Pagoda 萬壽寶塔 (Figure 23) on the bank of the Jingzhou section of the Yangzi River is an example of the sinking of the plain—it sank 7.5 meters below the Yangzi River main dike base from the mid-16th century to the present. The lower part of the pagoda is shown in Figure 24, indicating that the entrance to the pagoda is below the ground level. Chinese historical geographer Zhang Xiugui views the relationship among the Jianghan Plain, the Jing River, and Dongting Lake as a seesaw: the Jing River was the fulcrum, and the Jianghan area and Dongting Lake were the two ends of a plank centered on it. When Dongting's water level rose, the Jianghan area sank, and vice versa.[70] These hydrotopographical changes resulted from a variety of factors, including the state's continuous favoritism of the north at the expense of the south, intensive deforestation in the upstream rivers, constant diking and diverting of water, and the hydrogeomorphological movements of the rivers.

In her recent book on the Yellow River, Ling Zhang discusses similar gullying of the Hebei Plain during the Northern Song period (960–1127). She argues that the Northern Song government's security strategy pushed the course of the Yellow River toward the central Hebei Plain, which caused a major shift in the river course and catastrophic flooding on the central plain. Over the long run, this geopolitical favoritism by the state slowly led to environmental degradation and economic decline on the Hebei Plain.[71] The Jianghan Plain experienced a similar trajectory. As Chapter 6 shows, most households there were in a state of subsistence. The vast central Chinese hinterland (except for Hankou) were at the brink of economic collapse.

5 Conclusion

In the late nineteenth century, the Jianghan Plain had a water regime in transition: an escalating environmental crisis and intensified local violence over water and land. The continuously sinking Jianghan Plain resulted from the combined effects of state politics, excessive dike building, land reclamation, and the natural movement of water and sediment. The hydrotopography of the plain made it more difficult for the floodwaters to flow through the river-lake systems in the region, not only becoming an endemic threat to

70 Zhang Xiugui, *Zhongguo lishi dimao yu gu ditu yanjiu* 中國歷史地貌與古地圖研究 [*Studies on Historical Geomorphology and Ancient Maps of China*] (Beijing: Shehui kexue wenxian chubanshe, 2006), 64.

71 See Zhang, *The River, the Plain, and the State*.

FIGURE 23
Wanshou Pagoda in Jingzhou, Hubei, on the bank of the Yangzi River
PHOTO BY THE AUTHOR IN 2015.

the livelihood of the local communities but also prompting more conflicts over land and water.

The late Qing management of the water-control system in the Jianghan Plain illustrates not only the central and provincial governments' concerns with a functional hydraulic system but also the rise of various social groups competing for their own interests, to the point of manipulating provincial and national power. The conflicts over the Zekou outlet discussed in this chapter show that multiple layers of society—the central, provincial, and local government and local gentry, hydraulic experts, peasants, commoners, and monks—all participated in the decision-making process. The final decisions came out of a long process of negotiation, conflict, reconciliation, manipulation, and compromise among different stakeholders, and the interplay among nature, local communities, and the state revealed a pattern in which forces of change and resistance clashed swiftly and maintained a subtle balance.

The main participants in the conflicts over water were members of the community, mostly commoners and peasants. They were mobilized by local elites,

FIGURE 24 Wangshou Pagoda in Jingzhou (the lower part)
Note: Built in 1548–1552, the pagoda had sunk 7.5 meters below the Yangzi River main dike base. It is a manifestation of the hydrogeomorphological movement of the Yangzi River over the past few centuries.
PHOTO BY THE AUTHOR IN 2015.

equipped with weapons, drafted into local militias, and fought fiercely for their interests. In some cases, they joined petitions and group fighting on their own. Therefore I emphasize the existence of a "plebeian culture" that was evident in various water conflicts on the plain in the late nineteenth and early twentieth centuries. This culture also played a pivotal role in the interprovincial hydraulic conflicts during the Republican period, discussed in Chapter 6.

During this period, the local gentry also played an important role in leading charity activities and voluntary associations in the Jianghan communities. Many scholars have discussed the role of the gentry in charitable and philanthropic activities at the local level. For example, Mary Rankin argues that some members of the Zhejiang gentry gained political power after the Taiping Rebellion and had an important role in the political process and public activities in the late Qing.[72] Prasenjit Duara wrote that in the Republican period, the locally powerful lineages served as brokers between the state and society on the North China Plain and formed a "cultural nexus" among the local communities.[73] A similar local activism took place on the Jianghan Plain. Local gentry

72 See Rankin, *Elite Activism and Political Transformation in China.*

73 See Duara, *Culture, Power, and the State.*

organized various voluntary activities to help people recover from disasters. For example, in 1849, Pan Zhenkui 潘振魁, a member of the elite, opened an orphanage to take care of babies abandoned after a flood in Qianjiang County.[74] Some established a lifeboat team to rescue people from floodwaters or to collect corpses in rivers and lakes after similar disasters in the late Qing. Those lifeboats usually flew a red flag, so they were called "lifesaving red boats."[75] Many voluntary activities to help save lives after disasters were spontaneous and gave community recovery critical momentum. These were positive social responses from the local communities to a worsening environmental crisis in the post-Taiping era.

74 *Qianjiang xianzhi xu* (1879), 4: 356.

75 More detailed studies on the red lifesaving boats include: Yang Guo'an, "Jiusheng chuanju yu qingdai lianghu shuishang jiusheng shiye 救生船局與清代兩湖水上救生事業 [Lifeboats and Lifesaving Cause of Hubei and Hunan in Qing Dynasty]," *Wuhan daxue xuebao* 59, no. 1 (2006); Lan Yong, "Qingdai changjiang shangyou jiusheng hongchuan zhi chutan 清代長江上游救生紅船初探 [The Life-Saving Red Boats in the Upper Yangzi during the Qing Dynasty]," *Zhongguo shehui jingjishi* 4 (1995); Lan Yong, "Qingdai changjiang shangyou jiusheng hongchuan zhi xukao 清代長江上游救生紅船制續考 [A Continuous Study on the Life-Saving Red Boats in the Upper Yangzi during the Qing Dynasty]," *Zhongguo shehui jingjishi* 3 (2005).

CHAPTER 6

Centering the Plain

In 1924, the Republican government decided to construct a sluice at Jinkou 金口, where the Jinshui 金水 River empties into the Yangzi, to relieve the drainage problem of Jinkou township in the mid-Yangzi river basin. When the sluice was finally completed in 1935, Chiang Kai-shek had a stele erected to commemorate this engineering achievement. The sluice is no longer in use, and a new sluice was built in the 1960s not far from the old one; the stele, however, still stands at the Jinshui River's mouth to the Yangzi River (Figure 25). The uniqueness of the Jinshui Sluice is not in its size (it was only 20 meters long, compared with the Three Gorges Dam, which is 2,335 meters long), or its expenditure, surprisingly expensive at almost 1 million taels for a project of this scale; it is unique in the multinational participation in its design and construction processes. The entire project was supervised by George Gottlieb Stroebe (1880–1973), an American, the principal engineer of the Yangzi River Water Control Commission.[1] An Austrian was appointed as the field general supervisor, Ransomes and Rapier, sluice manufacturers of London, oversaw the construction according to Philippine Navy standard specifications, and a Dutch consultant was brought in at later stages to audit the process of the construction. This hydraulic construction in central China in the 1930s was part of global efforts to build an engineering marvel. One might well ask: What led to the global input into the construction? And what did the global picture of science and technology mean for the dikes and the *yuan* managed by the locals?

The building of the Jinshui Sluice (or the Jinshui Reclamation Project) was but one of the Nationalist government's attempts to "modernize" China. Allegedly, it was the first and the largest sluice built by the Nationalist government during the Republican period. In this chapter, I analyze the state's schemes for reorganizing the *yuan* communities and unifying watersheds nationwide in

1 Stroebe worked as an instructor in descriptive geometry and drawing from 1904 to 1905, instructor in civil engineering from 1906 to 1911, and after 1911 as a principal investigator in Manila. On May 11, 1911, Stroebe submitted his letter of resignation to the Board of Regents at the University of Michigan, explaining that his position "as designing engineer for the Irrigation Division of the Bureau of Public Works of the Philippine Government is much more remunerative than my work at Ann Arbor would be, and is being of much practical benefit to me" (University of Michigan, Faculty History Project, https: //www.lib.umich.edu/faculty-history/faculty/george-gottlieb-stroebe/memoir/).

© KONINKLIJKE BRILL NV, LEIDEN, 2022 | DOI:10.1163/9789004505285_008

the first half of the twentieth century. This water regime in this period was filled with contradictions, tensions, and conflicts—between state programs and local initiatives, between Western technologies and local politics, and between traditional and modern thinking about the environment. The large-scale state hydraulic schemes during the Republican period highlighted the central Yangzi region and its significance for hydroenergy, even though the general planning was just on paper. I also show that large hydraulic schemes based on scientific design and technological means often had little influence on the local communities. In the introduction of this book, I showed that the frequency of the word *yuan* plummeted in the early twentieth century although the number of local gazetteers remained high. As the present state of research, one can propose two explanations for the decline of *yuan* salience: the state was absorbed with top-down modernist projects conducted independently of local input—a trend that gazetteer writers may have followed. Or the *yuan* communities became less significant with their reorganization in the 1930s. The two factors, which are not mutually exclusive, will be examined in this chapter.

1 The Jinshui Reclamation Project

In a document compiled by the National Economic Council, George Stroebe, the principal engineer on the project, discussed the engineering, economic, and social significance of the Jinshui Project. He wrote that it was "very interesting" from the engineering perspective, because

> it has several unique features, one of the most important of which is a large concrete sluice containing three big tunnels driven through a rocky hill through which the entire discharge of the Kinshui River is conveyed. These tunnels are so large that two locomotives could easily pass abreast through each of them. The flow of the river through the tunnels is regulated by three large steel control gates ... [that] are the first sliding gates of this character to be installed in the Yangtse valley.[2]

The German method of tunneling was used, in which the tunnel was securely grouted solid to the rock of the hill to prevent water from the Yangtze from

2 National Economic Council, "Kinshui Sluice: Inaugural Ceremony" (Kinshui, Hupei, April 28, 1935), 2. I am very grateful to David Stroebe, George Stroebe's grandson, for granting me the materials and encouraging me to take a field trip to the sluice.

gaining access to the Jinshui basin when it was at a high level.[3] He further remarked that

> the project is interesting not only engineeringly [sic] and economically but also socially, for on its reclaimed land farmers will be settled according to the plan of General Chiang Kai-shek. This project constitutes one of the far-reaching plans of the Generalissimo for the development of the country. Thus the Kinshui [Jinshui] Project will become a unit in the constructive life of the nation.[4]

Stroebe's words show his confidence in the engineering design and the technology used in the project. He was also very optimistic about the outcome of human engineering on the Yangzi River, which would preserve farmland and create wealth for the national economy.

To initiate this project, a survey by Military Headquarters of the National Government and executed by the Jianghan Conservancy Bureau of Hankow, a branch of the National Economic Council, was conducted to ascertain how much and where there was land suitable for farming in the reclaimed area.[5] In its preliminary report on the Jinshui Project, the Yangzi River Commission stated that, after the completion of the project, the drainage issue in the Jinshui basin could be greatly improved.[6] The Commission also stated in the report that there was no feasible alternative to allowing the submergence of basin lands in these years, as the only way to prevent flooding was the use of pumps, which would be impractical.[7] In the conclusion to the report, the Commission emphasized that the Jinshui Project was not an experiment and that "the Yangtse valley contains many such projects some as large as the Jinshui and many of great age, showing the indisputable value of this class of work in this section of China."[8]

---

3 George G. Stroebe, "The Kinshui Reclamation Project," *Journal of the Association of Chinese and American Engineers* 17, nos. 1–2 (1936): 94.

4 National Economic Council, "Kinshui Sluice," 2.

5 National Economic Council, "Kinshui Sluice," 7.

6 National Economic Council, "Kinshui Sluice," 3. According to the report, the very little land would be submerged by the impounded rainfall in years with minimum rainfall, land between the contours at an elevation between 20.00 and 21.27 meters would be submerged in years of average rainfall, and lands between the contours at an elevation between 20.00 and 24.00 meters (a total of about 550,000 *mu*) would be submerged if heavy rainfall like that of 1889 occurred, when the maximum rainfall at Hankou was 2,105 millimeters.

7 National Economic Council, "Kinshui Sluice," 3.

8 National Economic Council, "Kinshui Sluice," 3.

A project of this scale could hardly be conducted through local initiatives. The project required a double dam—one of stone and one of earth—to close the Yangzi River, and its cost was enormous—approximately $900,000.[9] To close off the river of flowing waters, a stone dam was built to hold back the force of the currents, using great boulders and masses of stones weighing up to two tons each and encased in wire cages. Thus, the discharge of water could only pass through the cracks between the stones. After the completion of the stone dam, an earthen dam was then built completely across the river. According to Stroebe, as many as 2,000 laborers were hired, carrying earth all day and half the night. Some days as much as 80,000 baskets of earth were delivered. In addition, as many as 250 boats brought earth from distant locations, each boat carrying thirty to fifty baskets. The entire dam used over 200,000 cubic meters of earth.[10] The construction of an engineering project of this scale was accomplished much more easily through top-down planning, with the Nationalist government taking an important role in the project. After the sluice's completion, the Nationalist government erected a stele to commemorate the achievement, with the inscriptions on the stele allegedly contributed by Chiang Kai-shek personally (Figure 25).

The sluice's status in the Nationalist government's economic plan was undeniable. Why was this project so important for the Nationalist government, to the point that it "constitutes one of the far-reaching plans of the Generalissimo for the development of the country"?[11] We can understand its significance based on the geopolitical factors of the region, which pointed to the massive hydropower potential of the Yangzi watershed. The Nationalists' recognition of the potential of the upper-mid-Yangzi was deeply rooted in the hydraulic practice as well as the socioeconomic conditions of the Jianghan Plain.

2 The Social, Economic, and Hydraulic Conditions of the Plain

The plain had serious hydraulic, economic, and environmental challenges. The main hydraulic problem during this period was the failure of successive governments to guarantee security in the areas between the Yangzi and the Han by properly reconstructing the long dikes, with their retention ponds along both rivers. After the mid-century disasters, thanks to the expansion of reclaimed agricultural land and the spread of cash crops, the population of the

9 National Economic Council, "Kinshui Sluice," 5.

10 National Economic Council, "Kinshui Sluice," 3–4.

11 National Economic Council, "Kinshui Sluice," 2.

FIGURE 25 The Jinshui sluice stele
PHOTO BY THE AUTHOR IN 2018.

region steadily recovered. But the increased population meant a much greater disaster lay in wait when the poorly maintained long river dikes collapsed in the great flood of 1931. The dependence on cash crops meant that when the Great Depression spread to China, the people in the Jianghan Plain who survived the floods or whose lands could be quickly reclaimed had no market for their cotton, tea, or other products, and they were reduced to a hand-to-mouth existence.

In the early period of the Republic, commercial agriculture reached an exceptional level. According to Loren Brandt, the rate of commercial agriculture in central and eastern China rose from less than 30 percent in the 1890s to 45–50 percent in the 1930s.[12] After World War I, among 2,866 households across seven provinces and seventeen areas, the average rate of commercial agriculture was 46.4 percent; in just one county in Hubei, Yanglou, 30,000

12 Loren Brandt, *Commercialization and Agriculture Development: Central and Eastern China, 1870–1937* (Cambridge: Cambridge University Press, 1989), 15–16.

people produced tea, almost all of which entered the market.[13] Unfortunately, the extensive cash crop cultivation and agricultural commercialization were not unilaterally beneficial for the peasants. Philip C.C. Huang discussed the "involution" in late Qing and Republican agriculture, claiming that the high rate of commercialization did not indicate correspondingly high productivity but, rather, was a result of the intensive labor input to agriculture, which had a high rate of diminishing returns.[14] He noted, "The switch from rice to cotton ... was a big step in further intensification. The cultivation of cotton alone typically required about twice as much labor per unit of land as rice, twenty as opposed to ten days per *mu*."[15] This agricultural involution with extensive commercialization only added to the difficulty faced by rural households—it meant that more people needed to be fed based on fewer resources. This fragile system was bound to collapse under the pressure of a series of natural disasters and the Great Depression.

The growth momentum in the cultivation of cotton, which expanded nationwide in the late Qing and early Republic, ceased in the 1930s. As discussed in Chapter 1, cotton was one of the main crops grown in the *yuan,* and it contributed greatly to the regional agricultural output as well as export totals, so the decline in its production was a heavy blow to the Jianghan region.[16] In many counties on the Jianghan Plain in the Qing, cotton was the most important crop after rice. In the late Qing and early Republic, cotton fields expanded quickly, with the official promotion of cotton production to compete with foreign cotton textiles. The series of natural disasters in the 1930s was an important reason for the decline of cotton production in this region. According to Zhang Jiayan, "Profitable sales of cotton cloth (woven, the description implies, from the cotton grown by locals) required both fertile land and the absence of floods."[17] He concluded that the continuous rise in cotton production in the Jingzhou area in the 1920s was possible because "there was no major break in the Jingjiang Great Lake from 1871 to 1931."[18] This easily explains the sharp

13 Yan Zhongping, ed., *Zhongguo jindai jingjishi tongji ziliao xuanji* 中國近代經濟史統計資料選輯 [*Selected Statistical Sources of Economic History in Pre-1949 China*] (Beijing: Kexue chubanshe, 1955), 328.

14 For a more detailed discussion, see Huang, *The Peasant Economy* (*1985*) and *The Peasant Family* (*1990*).

15 Philip C.C. Huang, "Development or Involution in Eighteenth-Century Britain and China? A Review of Kenneth Pomeranz's 'The Great Divergence: China, Europe, and the Making of the Modern World Economy,' " *Journal of Asian Studies* 61, no. 2 (May 2002): 510.

16 For more discussion on cotton production, see Gao, "Transforming the Water Regime" (2012), Chapter 6.

17 Zhang, "Environment, Market, and Peasant Choice," 50.

18 Zhang, "Environment, Market, and Peasant Choice," 50.

decline in cotton cultivation on the Jianghan Plain in the 1930s. In 1931, the plain was inundated with flooding, which spread to forty-six counties/prefectures (out of sixty-nine) in Hubei.[19] Numerous *yuan* were flooded and ceased production. This flooding of the plain lasted three years and devastated the cotton sector. As many rural households had shifted to cotton cultivation, they usually had no grain stored and had to rely on rice from the market, which they could not afford. This further reduced their ability to cope with disasters and hunger.

Another fatal blow to cotton production was dealt by the Great Depression. According to Kenneth Pomeranz, cotton prices "had been rising 40 percent more than wheat prices during the expansionary years from 1913 to 1920," but "fell 13 percent less between 1929 and 1933."[20] The acute crisis in cotton production caused by the depression was intensified by the loss of Manchuria to Japan after 1931, when textile production was interrupted at numerous textile factories, and the demand for cotton plummeted.[21]

A few studies described the extent of poverty among the Jianghan peasants. According to John Buck at Jinling University, who investigated the living standards of peasants in over 300 counties in northern, central, and eastern China, in five of the eight counties in Hubei, living conditions were worse in the 1930s than in previous years, and in the other three counties, their lives did not improve at all.[22] In 1934 Pan Hongsheng 潘洪聲, a professor at the Central Agricultural Experiment Institute, conducted a survey in central China and described the countryside, "People in rural areas of Hubei are more miserable than other regions. ... Owing to constant disasters, people can hardly sustain their lives. Among one hundred households, only a few of them had rice to eat. ... Some rural people were so poor that they had to rely on vegetable roots [for sustenance]. ... All this is hardly conceivable."[23]

The poverty of the Jianghan peasants was exacerbated by the frequent flooding from the Yangzi and Han Rivers. In his 1929 study on flood control in China, the American engineer Oliver Todd wrote extensively about water issues facing the Yellow and Yangzi Rivers. He described the problem with

19 *Hubeisheng jin wubai nian qihou lishi ziliao*, 211.

20 Kenneth Pomeranz, *The Making of a Hinterland: State, Society, and Economy in Inland North China, 1853–1937* (Berkeley: University of California Press, 1993), 98.

21 Jack Shepherd, "Salvaging the Textile Industry in China," *Far Eastern Survey* 8, no. 15 (1939): 171.

22 John Lossing Buck, *Land Utilization in China: A Study of 16,786 Farms in 168 Localities, and 38,256 Farm Families, in Twenty-Two Provinces in China, 1929–1933* (Nanking: University of Nanking, 1937), 104–105, 360, 408–411.

23 *Chusheng* 鋤聲 [*Monthly News about Agriculture*] 1, no. 20 (1934).

Jianghan dike security: "To the layman this question of holding a river within properly defined banks may seem simple enough. In the first place, it requires concentrated authority; and then it needs large sums of money or quantities of labor and materials. China has worked at the job in places, but has effected a mere beginning. One of the main criticisms to be made of much of the river-control work of China is that, as a rule, the factor of safety is altogether too low."[24] Todd then assessed the reasons that the safety standards were not on par with Western engineering standards: "This is partly because hydraulic data have not been carefully compiled over a sufficiently long period of years. ... Then there is the difficulty of adequate funds. Officials have not generally recognized the need for the degree of insurance against flood that Western engineering would dictate."[25] In a side note, Todd acknowledged that the dikes on the northern bank of the Yangzi River were generally in good shape, whereas those on the southern bank were more vulnerable to flooding, needed amending, and should be approached with caution. Todd's observation from an engineering perspective reflected the centuries-long hydraulic practice of protecting the north at the expense of the south discussed in Chapter 5.

One major problem in flood control was the sediment load of the Yangzi. In a 1927 investigation of the dike section near Shishou, Todd found that "the Yangzi had for years been depositing alternate layers of clay and sand across the stretch to be diked; the test pits and borings showed that bad sand-fills ran as deep as 12 to 14 ft. in places."[26] The problem of sediment in the Yangzi River was so prevalent that hydraulic experts had developed various tools and ways to address it. Anthologies related to water management often give clear descriptions of the various dredging tools—such as iron-leaf-hauler (*tieye lulu* 鐵葉軲轆), iron broom (*tie saozhou* 鐵掃帚), dredging-earth-hauler (*gua di long* 刮地龍) (see Figure 26) and iron comb (*tie bi* 鐵篦).[27] The accumulation of sediment in the river and its valley was gradual but by no means trivial. By the end of the eighteenth century, large sandbars had formed in the riverways, causing catastrophic flooding; for example, the 1788 flood was devastating for Jingzhou and many other areas of the mid-Yangzi region. Large sandbars that were reclaimed and cultivated by the Xiao family were the main cause of the flooding because they blocked the flow of the river.[28] In the early twentieth

24 Oliver J. Todd, *Two Decades in China: Comprising Technical Papers, Magazine Articles, Newspaper Stories and Official Reports Connected with Work under His Own Observation* (Beijing: Association of Chinese and American Engineers, 1938), 58.

25 Todd, *Two Decades in China*, 58.

26 Todd, *Two Decades in China*, 59.

27 *Jingzhou wancheng dizhi*, 10: 293–297.

28 A detailed account is in *Jingzhou wancheng dizhi*, 10: 254–256.

century, engineers examined the sandbars and tried to find ways to deal with the Yangzi's sedimentation problem.[29] The damage to the Shishou dike section from sand, mentioned earlier, shows the fragility of the dikes as well as the entire system along the rivers, especially at times when the flood pressure against the dikes was exceedingly high, as in 1931. A plan to rescue the Jianghan Plain from general social and environmental devastation was desperately needed.

3 Reorganizing the *Yuan* System in the Early Republic

In the 1920s, the early Republican government attempted to reorganize the *yuan* system on the Jianghan Plain, in order to improve agricultural production and accommodate the increasing cultivation of cash crops there. Although local lineages carried out the reorganization, the Hubei provincial government initiated and closely supervised the reorganization, which bureaucratized the *yuan* system to some extent.

The various intellectual debates and government programs in the early Republican period demonstrate how constructing structures could ultimately conquer the water flow in a way that was beneficial for communities. The provincial officials favored the concept of water control presented by the Ming hydrologist Pan Jixun 潘季馴: building high and firm dikes to narrow the water flow and making the water run more quickly so that it would sweep away the sediment from the river bed and thereby relieve the water pressure.[30] Qu Deze 屈德澤, the head of Hubei's Bureau of Water Control in the 1920s, wholeheartedly endorsed Pan's method and was a firm advocate of reconstructing the provincial water system.[31] The concept also resonated with a few other officials who objected to destroying dikes for the sake of flood control, calling it "sticking to the old traditions without applying new methods" and being "too

29 Song Xishang analyzed in detail eleven sandbars in the middle and lower reaches of the Yangzi riverway and proposed engineering plans to facilitate riverway transportation in *Changjiang tongkao* 長江通考 [*A General History of the Yangzi River*] (Taipei: Zhonghua congshu bianshen weiyuanhui, 1963), 234–255.

30 Randall A. Dodgen has a detailed discussion of Pan Jixun's idea of water control and its consequences on the flood control of the Yellow River in late imperial China, in *Controlling the Dragon: Confucian Engineers and the Yellow River in Late Imperial China* (Honolulu: University of Hawai'i Press, 2001).

31 "Preface by Qu Deze 屈德泽, Head of Bureau of Water Control," in *Hubei difang jiyao* 湖北堤防紀要 [*Records of Hubei Dikes*] (1926), 6.

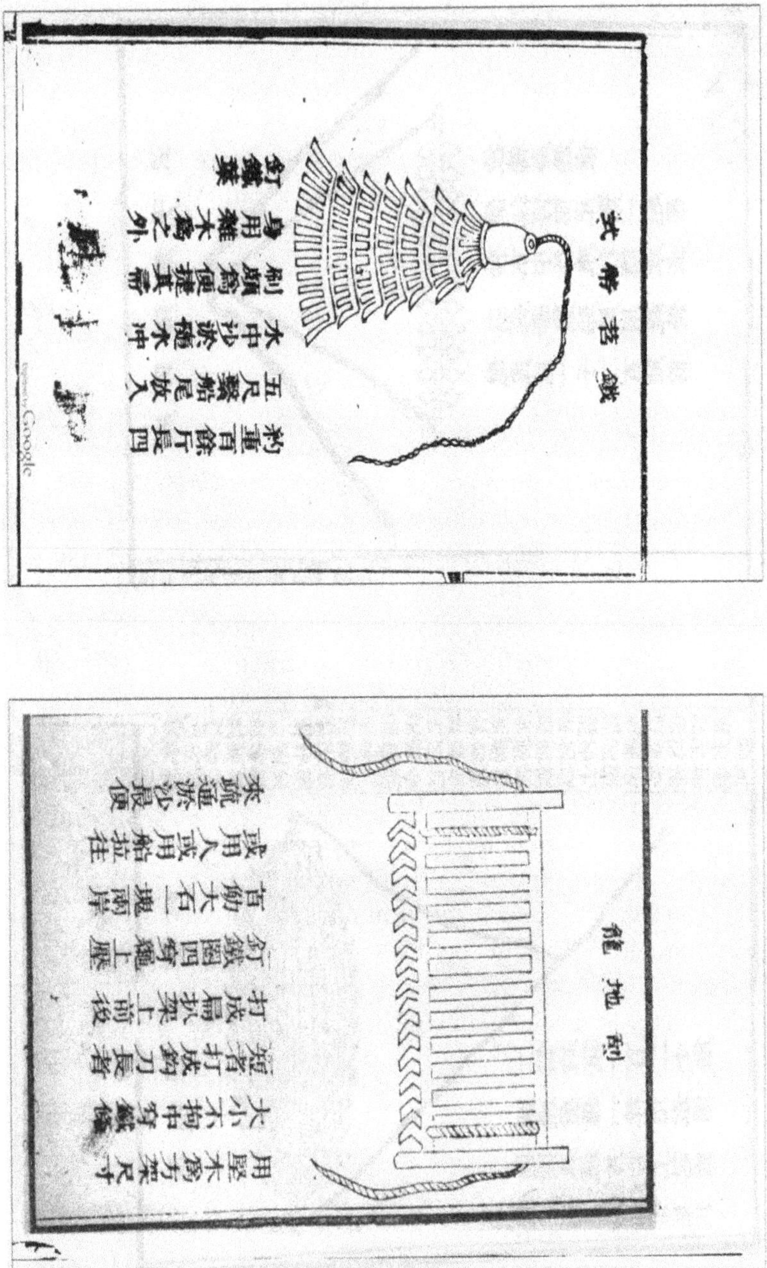

FIGURE 26 Illustration of dredging tools
Left: *tie shaozhou* 鐵掃帚 (iron broom); right: *gua di long* 刮地龍 (dredging-earth-hauler)
SOURCE: YU, *CHUBEI SHUILI DIFANG JIYAO* 2: 38.

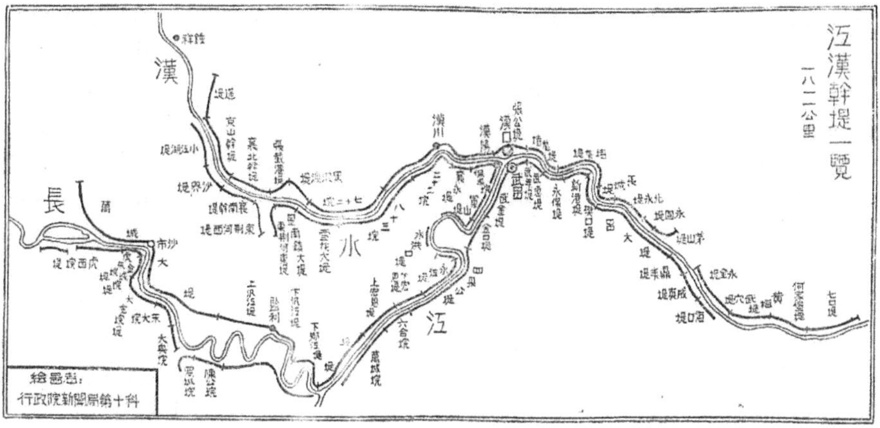

FIGURE 27 *Jianghan gandi yilan* 江漢幹堤一覽 [The dikes along the Yangzi and the Han Rivers] (1947)
Note: Solid lines are dikes along the Yangzi and the Han River arteries. The image shows that the dikes were all built and connected along the rivers, and they were divided into dike sections. It says that the total length of the main dikes was 1,811 km.
SOURCE: XINGZHENGYUAN XINWEN JU 行政院新聞局, *YANGZI JIANG, LUANHE, BAIHE GANZHILIU DUKOU FUDI GONGCHENG* 揚子江、灤河、白河幹支流堵口復堤工程 [*THE PROJECTS OF SEALING AND RESTORING DIKES OF THE MAIN AND BRANCH RIVERS OF THE YANGZI, LUANHE, AND BAIHE*] (1947), 8–9.

conservative to adapt to the new world."[32] Those officials argued that reconstructing a complete dike system was absolutely necessary for flood control and agricultural production in the region.[33] The concept of strengthening dikes was dominant throughout the Republican period: The Nationalist government carried out extensive dike building and restoration in 1920s, 1931–1937, and the 1940s. A 1947 report on the dike work along the major rivers claims that by 1938 the Nationalist government had built and restored dikes along the Yangzi and its branches measuring as much as 2,872 km (see Figure 27).[34]

To restore the local dike system in the region, in March 1924 the provincial government in Hubei conducted a survey of the agricultural land and

32 "Preface by Qu Deze," in *Hubei difang jiyao*, 6.
33 "Preface by Qu Deze," in *Hubei difang jiyao*, 7.
34 *Yangzi jiang, luanhe, baihe ganzhiliu dukou fudi gongcheng* 揚子江、灤河、白河幹支流堵口復堤工程 [*The Projects of Sealing and Restoring Dikes of the Main and Branch Rivers of the Yangzi, Luanhe, and Baihe*], ed. Xingzhengyuan xinwen ju (Xingzhengyuan xinwen ju, 1947), 1.

water control system there. Hubei governor Xiao Yaonan 蕭耀南 explained the rationale for the survey: "Since the warfare [the 1911 Revolution and subsequent conflict among warlords] in this region [the Jingxiang area], the water control system had been largely abandoned. ... It is an urgent issue to assign officials who are familiar with hydrology to investigate the water control system."[35] It took more than two years for the project to collect the land, water, and dike information. The survey results were cataloged and printed in the summer of 1926. Three officials in the Hubei provincial government, who were all trained in hydrology, led the project.[36]

The survey results show some consistency across the institutions within *yuan*. To a large extent, the management of a big *yuan* was based on old rules and hierarchies. Most *yuan* held public elections of the *yuan* heads, and each *yuan* normally had two. If a *yuan* was too big, it was divided into smaller units, called *jia* 甲, *zong wei* 總圩, or *xun* 汛, and was managed hierarchically. For example, the Luzhou *yuan* in Zhijiang County was divided into four *jia*: each *jia* took turns acting as the lead *yuan* (*zong weitou* 總圩頭). In addition, a *yuan* head (*yuan zheng* 垸證) and four *jia* heads (*jiazhang* 甲長) were to assist in the management of a *yuan* comprising more than 2,600 *mu* of land.[37] Another example is the Shangbailizhou *yuan* in Zhijiang County, which was subdivided into *zong* 總. This *yuan* had nine *zong*. As in the Luzhou *yuan*, the nine *zong* took turns acting as the lead *yuan*. The dike works were divided proportionally among the nine *zong*, based on the land owned by each one.[38]

The representatives from these local communities, be they *zongzhang* 总長, *jiazhang* 甲長, *dishou* 堤首 or *yuanzheng* 垸證, were normally publicly elected from among the *yuan* community members. This practice, which had existed in rural central China for a long time (though exactly when it started is hard to pin down; see the analysis in Chapter 2), was well entrenched, as shown by the prevalence of the term *gongju* 公舉 (public election) in the records. For example, the Yangjiao *yuan* in Zhijiang County was composed of nine *zong*, and people from each *zong* publicly elected two *yuan* heads and one dike head to administer dike projects.[39] In the Peixing *yuan* in Songzi County, two *yuan* heads were publicly elected to administer dike projects for a three-year term.[40]

35 "Preface by Xiao Yaonan 蕭耀南, Hubei Governor and Supervisor of military logistics of Hubei," in *Hubei difang jiyao*, 2.

36 "Preface by Xiao Yaonan," in *Hubei difang jiyao*, 3.

37 "Hubeisheng jingjiangduan mindi biao 湖北省荊江段民堤表 [The Chart of Jingjiang People's Dikes in Hubei]," in *Hubei difang jiyao*, 2.

38 "Hubeisheng jingjiangduan mindi biao," in *Hubei difang jiyao*, 3.

39 "Hubeisheng jingjiangduan mindi biao," in *Hubei difang jiyao*, 4.

40 "Hubeisheng jingjiangduan mindi biao," in *Hubei difang jiyao*, 5.

In addition to Zhijiang and Songzi Counties, other counties on the Jianghan Plain, such as Jiangling, Qianjiang, Jianli, and Gong'an, all shared the same feature of *yuan* management. This practice was an important feature of hydraulic communities in rural China in late imperial times.

At the same time, the records also show several major changes in the *yuan* system in the early Republic. First, the distinction between official dikes and people's dikes is very clear in the survey.[41] Previously the distinction between people's dikes and private dikes was not very clear, but under the Republican government, the people's dikes were completely legitimized. The official dikes in this region, called *di* 堤, included major river-long dikes, such as those along the Xiang (Han), the Jing, and the Yangzi Rivers. The people's dikes were circular and surrounded agricultural land, and they were all called *yuan*.[42] The survey also recorded the length of the *yuan* dikes, the land included in the *yuan*, the year that the *yuan* was first constructed and later reconstructed, the institutions established in the *yuan*, the speed of water flow at each dike section, and the dike works shared by various communities. Each dike was rated as "very important" (*zui yao* 最要) or "less important" (*ci yao* 次要): Almost all the official dikes were considered "very important," and the majority of the *yuan* dikes were called "less important."[43] Compared to the *yuan* records in gazetteers during the Ming and Qing dynasties, which were often fragmentary and inconsistent, this survey is indeed systematic and comprehensive.

Second, small *yuan* were merged into big *yuan*; at the same time, a more refined, well-structured, and hierarchical system was established within each enlarged *yuan*. For example, according to the record, the Yunxing *yuan* had been constructed in 1919 and was the result of combining six small *yuan*. In Jiangling County in the 1920s, most of the *yuan* were merged into several big *yuan*, which could consist of three to fifteen small *yuan*. This merging of small *yuan* into big *yuan* dated back to the early Qing (the forming of *yuan* zones, discussed in Chapter 2), but was more thorough. The survey shows that the small *yuan* merged within a big *yuan* to become one entity, in which all the small *yuan* had the same interests, whereas in a *yuan* zone, small *yuan* were still separate entities grouped together, such that they might or might not share the same interests. A cluster of individual *yuan* was concentrated in the border areas of Jiangling and Qianjiang County, probably because those

41 See earlier discussion on official and people's dikes in Chapter 2.

42 "Hubei quansheng guandi biao 湖北全省官堤表 [The Chart of Official Dikes in Hubei]" and "Hubeisheng jingjiangduan mindi biao," *Hubei difang jiyao*.

43 "Hubei quansheng guandi biao" and "Hubeisheng jingjiangduan mindi biao," in *Hubei difang jiyao*.

areas were usually under less government control, enabling local people to maintain their own interests and competitively reclaim wetlands and lakes without government supervision. Therefore, the merging of small *yuan* into big *yuan* was likely a government effort to take some control over the local communities. The consolidation of the *yuan* system went beyond Hubei—a similar process of merging occurred in the Dongting Lake area as well. As shown by the Nanding *yuan* (Figure 28), mergers took place in two periods: the 1920s and the 1950s. The Nanding *yuan* was one of the largest in the Dongting Lake area, and its evolution clearly indicates the trend toward mergers among the small *yuan* and thereby a reduction in the number of *yuan*. This is probably one of the reasons for the minimal appearance of *yuan* in local gazetteers despite the large number of gazetteers in the Republican period (see Figure 2).

The customary method of sharing the dike work among the small *yuan* continued in the reconstructed *yuan* system—allocating dike work among the *yuan* proportionally, based on land ownership. The area of land for each *yuan* was carefully recorded in the survey, and funding for the dike work was allocated among the small *yuan* based on the land owned by each one. For example, Yidu County and Yichang co-managed the *yuan* dikes—Yichang managed the nearly 3,300 meters of dikes on the northern bank, and Yidu County managed the nearly 2,970 meters of dike on the southern bank. They shared a *yuan* that was 5,006 *mu* in size (3,724 *mu* for Yichang and 1,282 *mu* for Yidu). The allocation of dike work between Yichang and Yidu was based on their land ownership.[44]

Third, the Hubei provincial government intervened in the local water management to a much greater degree during the early Republic. A great deal of *yuan* management was directly performed by agents sent by county governments. For example, the county government assigned three agents to administer the Shangbailizhou *yuan*, working with eighteen assistants chosen by the nine *zong*, two for each one. In some *yuan*, an official bureau was established to assist in management, mostly through collecting dike fees and providing technical advice. The Baijiawan river dike was managed by four *yuan* in Gong'an County; *yuan* affairs were reported to county government officials, with a Dike Fee Bureau and a Work Bureau for the four *yuan*.[45] The Tianfu *yuan* in Songzhi County also had a Work Bureau to direct the dike work.[46] The Zhongfan river dike in Jianli was managed by thirteen small *yuan* in three designated zones. The county government supervised dike repairs, and each zone elected one

44 "Hubei jingjiangduan mindi biao," in *Hubei difang jiyao*, 1.

45 "Hubei jingjiangduan mindibiao," in *Hubei difang jiyao*, 13.

46 "Hubei jingjiangduan mindibiao," in *Hubei difang jiyao*, 6.

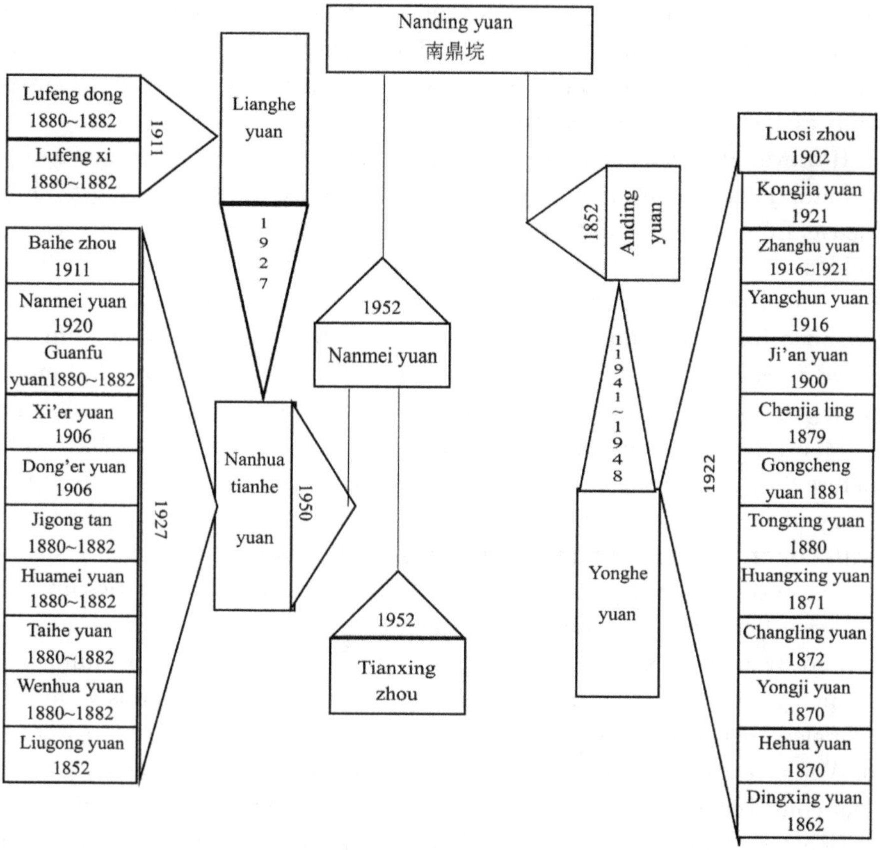

FIGURE 28 The formation of the Nanding *yuan* 南鼎垸
Note: Most *yuan* were built from the 1880s to 1920. Thirteen *yuan* merged to form the Yonghe *yuan* in 1922. Ten *yuan* merged to form the Nanhua Tianhe *yuan* in 1927. The Lianghe *yuan*, which was formed from two small *yuan* in 1911 and also became part of Nanhua Tianhe *yuan* in 1927.
SOURCE: NANXIANZHI BIANWEIHUI, *NANXIAN ZHI* 南縣志 [*THE GAZETTEER OF NANXIAN*] (CHANGSHA: HUNAN RENMIN CHUBANSHE, 1988), 194.

person as head of the zone to assist with the work.[47] In so doing, the provincial government established a joint administration with publicly elected heads of *yuan*. Some of the *yuan* organized a delegation, which was directly associated with the government branches in public works. In this way, whenever flood waters destroyed the boundaries of the *yuan* and caused conflict, the people in

47 "Hubei jingjiangduan mindibiao," in *Hubei difang jiyao*, 17.

the *yuan* elected local gentry with a good reputation to measure the land, and the county government sent officials to investigate. In so doing, they ensured that the *yuan* land was divided clearly and that the tax liability and responsibility of each *yuan* were clear, too.[48]

However, the reconstructed *yuan* communities were devastated in a series of natural disasters from 1931 to 1936: floods from 1931 to 1933 and in 1935, and locusts from 1934 to 1936.[49] According to the records, the long dikes did not hold, and the people's dikes along the Yangzi and the Han Rivers were either flooded or breached in 1931. Forty-five of the sixty-nine counties in Hubei Province had heavy flooding, and as many as thirty-nine of them suffered grave damage.[50] The damage to *yuan* was tremendous—201 *yuan* and more than 900,000 *mu* of land were inundated in Hanchuan County; fifteen *yuan* in Mianyang were flooded for as much as four years and had no harvest.[51] Before they could recover from the severe damage and heavy flooding in 1931, many of those *yuan* communities were hit again in 1935. During these years with abnormally heavy rainfall, the Jianghan Plain's long-time dike systems proved pitifully inadequate. As Lyman P. Van Slyke writes, "Statistics for the '100-year flood' of 1870—one which might be expected once a millennium—are not available, but the '30-year' flood in the summer of 1931 inundated some 8.5 million acres of farmland and cost 150,000 lives; millions were left homeless."[52] Chris Courtney conducted an intriguing study on the 1931 flood in Wuhan, exploring the agricultural, economic, political, and religious factors that contributed to the catastrophe. His argument demonstrates the discrepancy between the government's environmental management and the popular understanding of environmental disaster: whereas the Nationalist government tried to rebuild its infrastructure based on technology, the populace maintained its popular religious conceptualizations of the environment.[53]

---

48 "Shishou xian chengfu linian zaoquan qingxing ji luo heng chen sanyuan tiandi qingzhang shengke banfa 石首縣呈复歷年造券情形及羅横陳三垸田地清丈升科辦法 [Reports on Land in Shishou County and the Proposal of Investigating the Land and Levying the Tax in three *yuan*—Luo, Heng, and Chen *yuan*]" (1932), Hubei Provincial Archives, LS-19-2-3153.

49 *Hubeisheng jin wubai nian qihou lishi ziliao*, 211–236.

50 *Hubeisheng jin wubai nian qihou lishi ziliao*, 211.

51 *Hubeisheng jin wubai nian qihou lishi ziliao*, 213–216.

52 Lyman P. Van Slyke, *Yangtze: Nature, History, and the River* (Boston: Addison-Wesley, 1988), 183.

53 See Courtney, *The Nature of Disaster in China: The 1931 Yangzi River Flood* (Cambridge: Cambridge University Press, 2018); idem, "The Dragon King and the 1931 Wuhan Flood." Kathryn Edgerton-Tarpley, however, has charted how cosmological and moral understandings of disasters became less popular in political discourse, giving way by

A discrepancy also existed between the economic and political pursuits of the local populace and the hydrotechnological needs of the central Yangzi water systems, as shown by the Tiangu *yuan* in a later part of the chapter. Because of this contradiction, the state's large-scale watershed management scheme in the Republican period was not feasible.

4 The Nationalist Government's Scheme of Unifying Watersheds

The Nationalist government tried to implement its own top-down water control reconstruction long before the floods in the 1930s.[54] The initial goal of the reconstruction was to unify the water control systems nationwide, and those who proposed doing so were mainly Western-trained hydraulic experts.[55] Many of them compared China's water management to that in Europe, the United States, and Japan.[56] One article summarized the water control conditions in the 1920s, mentioning that influential officials from the League of Nations, including the heads of its economics, transportation, and public health departments, visited China and inspected the water control conditions in north China. Its author was very optimistic about the visit, although "they [League of Nations officials] did not provide any constructive suggestions."[57]

---

the mid-twentieth century to more technological and nationalistic approaches. Kathryn Edgerton-Tarpley, "From 'Nourish the People' to 'Sacrifice for the Nation': Changing Responses to Disaster in late Imperial and Modern China," *Journal of Asian Studies* 73 (2014): 464. See also the discussion on the religious dimension of irrigation communities in twentieth-century China in Chapter 1.

54 Ruth Gamble and Trevor Hogan explain the origin of the term "watershed": "it was the technical assessment of waterways that led to the coining of the term 'watershed,' from the German Wasserscheide ('water divider') as 19th-century scientists observed the relationship between the water cycle and gravity. The word did not take on its more general meaning of an entire water basin until it began to be used in the United States, and it was not used as a metaphor until decades later (OED Online)"; "Watersheds in Watersheds: The Fate of the Planet's Major River Systems in the Great Acceleration," *Thesis Eleven* 150, no. 1 (2019): 21, note 1.

55 A portion of this section appears in an article published by Environment & Society Portal, *Arcadia*, no. 28. See Gao (2019). doi.org/10.5282/rcc/8747. This article is licensed under a Creative Commons Attribution 4.0 International License (https://creativecommons.org/licenses/by/4.0/).

56 Wang Huzhen, "Yinianlai shijie zhi shuili gongcheng 一年來世界之水利工程 [The Hydraulic Projects around the World in the Past Year]," *Shuili* 1, no. 1 (1931): 57–63; "Shijie shuili jinwen 世界水利近聞 [Recent News on Water Control around the World]," *Shuili* 1, no. 1 (1931): 134–146.

57 Gu Shiji, "Guonei shuili jianshe shiye shuping 國內水利建設事業述評 [A Summary of the Domestic Hydraulic Schemes]," *Shuili* 1, no. 1 (1931): 45–56.

As early as 1931, hydraulic experts suggested unifying water control across China. In a proposal to the Nationalist government, Zhang Zili 張自立 wrote, "Improving water control, focusing on agricultural production, and increasing industrial output shall be the ultimate goal of the government."[58] "Unifying the water control administration is a most important first step" toward achieving those goals.[59] Zhang illustrated the importance of unifying the water control administration by describing the conditions in Hubei: "In terms of financial resources for water control, Hubei Province has the most. The resources all come from the dike fees and donations from local people. … However, the dike work was either passive prevention or a make-up strategy—it only cures the surface but not the root of the problem (*zhibiao bu zhiben* 治標不治本). Hubei's water problem is the water problem of the whole middle Yangzi region; we won't achieve the best result if we manage all the areas separately."[60]

The first thing the Nationalist government did was to establish the Ministry of Water Conservancy (Quanguo shuili weiyuanhui 全國水利委員會) as the highest authority of water control nationwide, directly under the Administrative Yuan (Xingzheng yuan 行政院) and jointly administered by the Ministry of Internal Affairs, Transportation, Industries, the Navy, and Railways.[61] The second was to divide the country into water control regions based on boundaries of natural watersheds (*An hechuan liuyu zhi tianran qingshi jufenzhi* 按河川流域之天然情勢据分之), and to establish an effective water control administrative hierarchy from the central government down to those water control regions. Zhang's proposal created eight of these regions, based on a combination of hydraulic science, administrative convenience, and financial feasibility: Northeast, Shuohai, Yellow River, Huaihe, Yangzi, Donggang (lower Yangzi), and Zhujiang.[62]

Zhang's proposal was well received by the hydraulic engineering community in the government. In April 1931, the Chinese Hydraulic Engineering Society was founded. In March 1932, the association had its first annual meeting. It was a time of "frequent flooding endangering people and [causing] deep concern about the miserable conditions in rural China."[63] Unification of China's water

58 Zhang Zili, "Tongyi shuizheng zhi shangque 統一水政之商榷 [Discussing the Unification of Water Management]," *Shuili* 1, no. 1 (1931): 3.

59 Zhang, "Tongyi shuizheng zhi shangque," 3.

60 Zhang, "Tongyi shuizheng zhi shangque," 5.

61 Zhang, "Tongyi shuizheng zhi shangque," 5–6.

62 Zhang, "Tongyi shuizheng zhi shangque," 6.

63 "Zhongguo shuili gongcheng xuehui diyijue nianhui xuanyan 中國水利工程學會第一屆年會宣言 [Declaration of the First Annual Meeting of Chinese Hydraulic Engineering Society]," *Shuili* 1, no. 5 (1931): 409.

control was again put on the agenda at the meeting. The establishment of an effective organizational system that would connect the central government with local water managers was suggested, as it would enable the central government to be constructive in leading the local water management, and the local management could cooperate with the central government's policies.[64] The association reemphasized that water management needed to be based on watersheds, instead of administrative boundaries such as provinces.[65] That same year, at its national meeting, the head of the Ministry of the Interior (Neizheng bu 內政部) proposed a reorganization of the government branches in charge of water control nationwide and the establishment of a higher authority to manage water affairs from the top down. The meeting approved the proposal and decided that the Ministry of Economic Affairs (Quanguo jingji weiyuanhui 全國經濟委員會) be the authority to manage nationwide water control measures. In 1932, the Nationalist government began preliminary work on a possible dam in the Three Gorges area, which had been proposed by Sun Yat-sen in 1919. In 1935, a Yangzi River Control Commission was established by combining three committees—the Yangzi River Conservancy Agency (Yangzijiang shuidao zhengli weiyuanhui 揚子江水道整理委員會), the Taihu Water Conservancy Agency (Taihu liuyu shuili weiyuanhui 太湖流域水利委員會), and the Xiang'E'Hu Hydrology Station (Xiang'E'Hu shuiwen zhan 湘鄂湖水文站). If the Nationalist government had been more effective and if there had been no interruptions by frequent natural disasters and warfare, this plan for unified water management might have worked. But the Yangzi River projects were all halted first, in 1937, by the outbreak of the Sino-Japanese war and, then, in 1947, by the beginning of the civil war.

5 A Divided Central Yangzi Watershed

In principle, the merging of small *yuan* into big *yuan* and a certain degree of bureaucratization of the *yuan* made top-down administration more convenient and could be seen as a step toward central Yangzi watershed management; however, the conflicts and violence among *yuan* persisted and even escalated. Akira Morita wrote that, during the Republican period, the expansive *yuan* fields took over much of the lake surface of the Dongting, caused frequent floods and led to conflicts over water, mostly between owners of the

64 "Chengqing tongyi quanguo shuili xingzheng wen 呈請統一全國水利行政文 [A Plea to Unify the Water Management Nationwide]," *Shuili* 1, no. 5 (1931): 411.

65 "Chengqing tongyi quangu," 411.

yuan fields.[66] He discussed a water conflict in Yuanjiang, Hunan, in 1932, involving Zeng Yuechuan 曾月川, who was a *yuan* head and member of the Counselor Committee of Hunan (Hunan ziyi ju 湖南谘议局). Having been the head of various bureaus in the Hunan provincial government, Zeng could use his personal power to protect the interests of the *yuan* where his home was, Bao'an, refuse to repair a major sluice gate controlling the waters from a key waterway, and make dozens of other *yuan* suffer from irrigation problems and floods.[67] There were many other conflicts over land and water. In 1934, Guo Dehai, who lived in the Hanyang Xihu *yuan*, sued Xiao Yantang for destroying dikes.[68] And in 1947, Qu Yupin, who lived in Hanchuan, appealed to the high court in Hubei, requesting clarification of the allocation of dike work.[69] Corruption among officials made the situation even worse. For example, the Jiangxi *yuan* in Hanchuan County was flooded in 1931, and it turned out that the dike head, Zhou Tianqu, had embezzled the public dike funds and compromised the dike's quality.[70] The same thing happened in the Wuhe and Hefeng *yuan* in Jiayu County, as well as the Wenhe *yuan* in Mianyang County, and elsewhere.[71]

66 Akira Morita, *Qingdai shuili yu quyu shehui* 清代の水利と地域社会 [*Water Control during the Qing and Regional Societies*], translated into Chinese by Luoshan Lei (Jinan: Shandong huabao chubanshe, 2008), 210, 213.

67 Morita, *Qingdai shuili yu quyu shehui*, 210–233.

68 "Guanyu hubei hanyang xihuyuan xiufangchu zhuren Guo Dehai konggao Xiao Yantang deng pohuai digong de baogao, han 關於湖北漢陽西湖垸修防處主任郭德海控告肖硯堂等破壞堤工的報告、函 [The Report on Guo Dehai of Xihu *yuan* in Hanyang, Hubei Suing Xiao Yantang for Sabotaging the Dike Work]," Hubei Provincial Archives, LS1-5-4967.

69 "Hubeisheng gaodeng fayuan shenli hanchuan xian difang fayuan Qu yuping wei queren yuandi fudan ji gongtong xiufang shangsu 湖北省高等法院審理漢川縣地方法院屈玉屏為確認垸地負擔及共同修防上訴 [Hubei Supreme Court Dealing with Qu Yuping of Hanchuan about Sharing *yuan* Fields and Collaborating in Maintenance]," Hubei Provincial Archives, LS7-2-2707.

70 "Guanyu hubei hanchuan jiangxiyuan kuijue qingkuang ji jianju he chuli digong chuzhang Zou Tianqu deng tanwu gongkuan de baogao yu laiwang wenshu 關於湖北漢川縣江西垸潰決情況及檢舉和處理堤工處長鄒天衢等貪污公款的報告與來往文書 [Correspondences on the Collapse of Jiangxi *yuan* and on Investigating the Case of Zou Tianqu Embezzling Public Funds]," Hubei Provincial Archives, LS1-5-4983.

71 "Guanyu chachu hubei jiayu wuhe yuan, hefeng yuan difang gongcheng zhong toujianliao ji kekou gongzi deng wenti de laiwang wenshu 關於查處湖北嘉魚五合垸、合豐垸堤防工程中偷減料及剋扣工資等問題的來往文書 [Correspondences on Investigations into Cheating on Construction Materials and Wages in the Dike Work of Wuhe *yuan* and Hefeng *yuan* of Jiayu, Hubei]," Hubei Provincial Archives, LS1-5-5030; "Guanyu chakan hubei jiayu, mianyang wenhe yuan difang gongcheng zhiliang wenti de laiwang wenshu 關於查勘湖北嘉魚、沔陽文合垸堤防工程質量問題的來往文書 [Correspondences on the Construction Quality of Wenhe *yuan* in Jiayu and Mianyang, Hubei]," Hubei Provincial Archives, LS1-5-5031.

One of the largest conflicts was in the Tiangu *yuan* between Hubei and Hunan, which lasted from the 1930s to the 1940s. The interests of the communities around the Yangzi-Dongting Lake system were obviously divided. Although hydraulic experts joined in the discourse of the conflict resolution, their hydrotechnological opinions were largely ignored by local communities.

The conflicts over the Tiangu *yuan* began when the Hunan provincial government combined a few small *yuan* along the Dongting Lake and turned them into the Tiangu *yuan* in the early 1930s. After the Tiangu *yuan* was constructed, it separated Datong Lake from Dongting Lake, which sharply reduced the capacity of Dongting Lake to relieve the flood pressure from the Yangzi River. If the floodwaters were not relieved in time, the excessive waters would flood more than ten counties in Hubei Province in the flood season. This endeavor was thus fiercely opposed by the people in Hubei.

The dispute started in 1936. The Tiangu *yuan* had already been constructed, and the people in Hubei demanded the destruction of the *yuan* dikes. Because of the acute tension between Hunan and Hubei over the *yuan*, the National Economic Council conducted a thorough investigation, concluding that the past experience suggested that the Datong Lake remain connected to the Dongting Lake as an important channel for floodwaters and that the Tiangu *yuan* be destroyed.[72] In addition, hydrologists calculated the water level in the Jianghan-Dongting region and found that the Tiangu *yuan* would make the water level of Hankou as much as one *chi* (approximately 0.3 meters) higher than it had been in 1931 if this region had a flood similar to the one that year. This would be catastrophic not only for Hankou but also for the vast Jianghan Plain downstream areas.[73] After careful investigation, the Nationalist government sent orders to destroy the Tiangu *yuan*.[74]

The outbreak of the Sino-Japanese war put that plan on hold. The issue was not brought up again until 1947, when the debate was based on a different argument. Two different arguments emerged among people in Hubei. The first one was made mostly by Western-trained hydraulic experts who claimed that the Tiangu *yuan* had already existed for over ten years, and destroying it not only would be very costly but would not solve the problem of flood relief in the

72 Jiang Hong, "Paohui tianguyuan zhi shangque 刨毀天祜垸之商榷 [A Discussion on Destroying the Tiangu *yuan*]," *Wuhan ribao*, March 24 and 25, 1947.

73 Jiang, "Paohui tianguyuan zhi shangque."

74 "Wuhan tongxianghui duncu zhongyang paohui Tianguyuan lianhehui huyu dianwen 武漢同鄉會敦促中央刨毀天祜垸聯合會呼籲電文 [A Telegraphy on Wuhan Native-Place Associations Urging the Central Government to Destroy the Tiangu *yuan*]," *Wuhan ribao*, July 21, 1947.

region; the second was presented by people in the local communities, many of whom were merchants, who insisted that the Tiangu *yuan* be removed based on the prewar decision.[75]

Hydraulic experts such as Jiang Hong 江鴻 proposed a revision of the project. From 1944 to 1945 Jiang served as the head of the Engineering School at Tongji University in Shanghai, which was established in 1907 by the German doctor Erich Paulun and taken over in 1927 by the Nanjing government. It had strong German academic influence in many fields, including medicine, science, and engineering. This indicated that Jiang had most likely received Western training in engineering. In 1936, Jiang was sent by the Nanjing government to investigate the Tiangu *yuan* situation and initially agreed that the *yuan* dikes be removed.[76] But in March and August 1947, he reexamined the situation and decided that "destroying the Tiangu *yuan* only solved the problem from the surface, not from the root, and it could not stop the fast siltation in the Dongting Lake."[77] He quoted research by Sun Feichen 孫斐忱, the head of the Yangzi River Control Commission, about the siltation in the Dongting area:

> Within the past 10 years, the Dongting Lake surface area decreased from 4,700 sq. kilometers to 3,100 sq. kilometers [about two-thirds of its previous lake surface]; the Datong Lake surface decreased from 403 sq. kilometers of 1936 to 300 sq. kilometers of 1947. If the Dongting area kept on silting at such a speed, within twenty years the Dongting and Datong Lakes would both become silted land. During flood seasons of the Yangzi River, the floodwaters had nowhere to go but to burst into new water routes and the vast Jianghan Plain would be seriously in jeopardy. When that day comes, we would see a new Dongting Lake in Hubei instead of Hunan.[78]

Jiang thus proposed that, instead of destroying the Tiangu *yuan*, solving the the Dongting Lake's siltation problem took higher priority in effective flood control in the mid-Yangzi region. In addition, he advocated regional management of the entire mid-Yangzi region (by this, he meant Hunan and Hubei, excluding Jiangxi) and the establishment of a regional commission between

75 "Wuhan tongxianghui … dianwen"; Jiang Hong, "Cong tianguyuan kan hubei shuihuan 從天祜垸看湖北水患 [Understanding Hubei Floods from the Case of Tiangu *yuan*]," *Wuhan ribao*, August 10, 1947.

76 Jiang, "Paohui tianguyuan zhi shangque."

77 Jiang, "Paohui tianguyuan zhi shangque."

78 Jiang, "Cong tianguyuan kan hubei shuihuan."

Hunan and Hubei to manage the water resources collectively.[79] In Jiang's view, the flooding problem in the Yangzi-Dongting area could not be solved with a divided watershed; effective regional collaboration was absolutely essential.

Research and advice from the engineers added a technical perspective to the debate but failed to steer the conflict to an objective solution. The protests against the Tiangu *yuan* in Hubei became more heated by the day. In July 1947, the people in Hubei established an anti-Tiangu *yuan* committee and petitioned the Nationalist government to destroy the Tiangu *yuan* as scheduled. Hankou merchants, and *tongxiang hui* (native-place organization) also sent telegraphs to the government in support.[80] Powerful landlords in the Tiangu *yuan* organized local peasants to protect the *yuan*. By mid-August 1947, the tension between Hubei and Hunan rose to an unprecedented level. Some people from Hunan even traveled to Hubei and distributed handbills in the street to protest the destruction. Hubei organized a large-scale movement "calling on millions of people to destroy the *yuan* with armed force." A Hubei official assembled two battalions of troops with boats and gunpowder, claiming to tamp down the Tiangu *yuan*, with a heroic slogan: "heads may roll, and blood can drain away, but the *yuan* had to go." Hunan was not afraid of the power held by Hubei and continued its protection of the *yuan* with the slogan of "turning the flesh to earth, and bones to sands."[81] An interprovincial fight seemed inevitable. However, things took an unexpected turn. In late August, the communist troops suddenly attacked eastern Hubei and the business harbor in Hankou. The Hubei provincial government declared a curfew in Hankou on the evening of August 31. This emergency diverted the attention of the people in Hubei from the *yuan*'s destruction. For two weeks, the Hubei anti-*yuan* movement was quiet.[82] The conflict resumed on September 20, when Mao Qinwu, the head of Longqing Farm in Hunan, gathered together some peasants in Hunan and used armed force to protect the Tiangu *yuan*. The destruction was delayed again, and no one knew when it would restart.[83]

The situation in the Tiangu *yuan* was not discussed much after 1947, probably because the civil war between the Nationalists and the Communists became more intense, diverting attention from any other issues. In the 1950s, the newly established People's Republic combined a group of small *yuan* around Dongting Lake into the Tiangu *yuan*, completely separating Datong Lake from

79 Jiang, "Paohui tianguyuan zhi shangque"; idem, "Cong tianguyuan kan hubei shuihuan."

80 "Wuhan tongxianghui … dianwen."

81 *Xinwen tiandi* 新聞天地 [*Newsdom*], no. 28 (October 1, 1947).

82 *Xinwen tiandi*, October 1, 1947.

83 *Xinwen tiandi*, October 1, 1947.

Dongting Lake. In addition, several reservoirs were added south of the lake, with sluices to take up the Yangzi flood waters. Similar actions were undertaken in Hubei on the north bank. It seems to me, that was the final solution to the Tiangu controversy.

6 Hydropower: Centering the Yangzi

The large conflicts over the Tiangu *yuan* show that, during the Republican period, managing a divided central Yangzi watershed was unrealistic; the eventual force of unifying the watershed management would come from the huge hydropower potential of the Yangzi (and its branch rivers), especially its middle reaches.

The idea of building a dam on the Yangzi for hydropower goes back to Sun Yat-sen. In 1920, he wrote *The International Development of China*, in which he proposed using Western capital and technology for China's industrialization and pledged to recruit international cooperation to help build China's infrastructure. His proposal described grand schemes in six major areas, including harbors, railways, roads, mining, and waterways. His analysis on the industrial potential of the rivers mentioned "sluices" (*shui zha* 水閘) eleven times, proposing that they be built on various rivers, including the Bei (in the Guangzhou area), Xiang (in the Hunan area), Han, and Yangzi Rivers. Instead of focusing on irrigation and flood control, he was interested in the river capacity for water transport and hydropower. In his proposal on the Yangzi River, he stated that the waterways from Yichang to Sichuan were treacherous to sail on—they were firmly constrained by mountain cliffs and were narrow and deep; the waterways had numerous rapids, sand bars, and rocks. Thus, he suggested removal of the rocks blocking the waterways and the building of a dam to facilitate transportation and generate hydropower.[84]

Sun's dream of a dam on the Yangzi was echoed in *A Single Pebble,* a novel by the American writer John Hersey in 1956. The protagonist of Hersey's novel was a young American engineer, who travels in China and embarks an upstream journey through the Three Gorges on a *kwa-tzu,* a traditional small junk, to survey possible locations for a dam, eventually finding the site where the Three Gorges Dam was constructed. In the end, the young engineer, "stunned and sobered by the gulf separating his callow notion of progress from

84 Sun Yat-sen, *Shiye jihua* 實業計劃 [*International Development of China*] (1920), "Part 4: Improve Extant Waterways and Canals," http: //www.gzmg.gov.cn/Article/szs/szswx/200811/32. html.

a deeper Chinese attachment to the ways of nature, abandons the dream not as technically impossible but as somehow profoundly wrong."[85]

> How could I, in the momentary years of my youth, have a part in persuading these people to tolerate the building of a great modern dam that would take the waters ..., with their age-old furies, on its back, there to grow lax and benign? How could I span a gap of a thousand years—a millennium in a day? These people on the junk could be said to be living in the era between Charlemagne and William the Conqueror, in the time of serfs and villains, before the Crusades, before Western printing and gunpowder, long, long before Chaucer and Giotto and Thomas Aquinas and Dante. And they were satisfied (or so I thought) to exist in the Dark Ages, while I lived in a time of enlightenment and was not satisfied. ... [I began to] wonder whether a dam was the right thing with which to start closing the gap.[86]

With much compassion for the riverine communities along the Yangzi River gorges, the American engineer reminisces about the Chinese appreciation of nature, albeit with a hint of Western superiority. This mixture of romanticism and great faith in technology was not uncommon in the numerous travelogues and accounts by Western travelers in China in the first few decades of the twentieth century.

At the same time, the Nationalist government did not have the capacity or sensitivity for dealing with rivers or the ecological impacts associated with modifying them. For instance, the 1938 Yellow River flood at Huayuankou was deliberately caused by the Nationalist government in an attempt to prevent the movement of the Japanese army. It caused massive waves of refugees from Henan to Shanxi and had disastrous environmental consequences in numerous local environments.[87]

Hydraulic experts had been interested in investigating the mid-Yangzi and Han River valley as early as the 1930s. A group of hydrologists and engineers surveyed the Han River to determine its irrigation, transportation, and hydropower capacity in 1932. Li Yizhi 李儀祉, a hydrologist and a board member of Chinese Hydraulic Engineering Society, noted in a report that "approximately as high as 1,800 megawatts of hydroelectricity can be generated annually by

85 Van Slyke, *Yangtze*, 182.

86 John Hersey, *A Single Pebble* (New York: Vintage, 1989), 138–139.

87 For an in-depth study on refugees and environmental impacts after the 1938 flood, see Muscolino, *The Ecology of War in China*.

the Han River and its branches" and that "the hydroelectricity could tremendously benefit the industries and river transportation along the Han River."[88] Although Li made only a rough estimate, he was keenly aware of the economic significance of the Han River valley.[89]

A survey by the Nationalist Resource Committee (Ziyuan weiyuanhui 資源委員會) in May 1949 sheds some light on the government's enthusiasm on using water resources in central China:

> Wuhan is a core industrial city that needs a sufficient energy supply. It is urgent to investigate the potential hydropower in all rivers of central China. For the time being, the Three Gorges Dam project is too gargantuan to be carried out, so we decided to change the Three Gorges Survey Department to Central China Survey Department in order to study the hydraulic resources of all rivers in central China.[90]

Table 16 presents information compiled by Zhang Guangdou 張光斗, the chief engineer of the Resource Committee, about the potential hydropower in various major watersheds as of May 1949.

The table shows that as of mid-1949, the Yangzi River watershed had the largest hydropower potential; the entire watershed could generate as much as 24,349.6 MW of electricity, exceeding the amount that could be generated by all the other rivers listed here in the country, combined. The hydropower capacity of the central Yangzi watershed alone was close to half that of the entire Yellow River artery. Fifty-four hydropower projects were built or were planned to be built in the central Yangzi watershed, nearly equivalent to the number of projects—fifty-seven, in the Yellow River, Pearl River, and Southeastern watersheds, combined.

Table 17 shows the hydropower potential of Hubei in central China in 1945, showing that the combined potential hydroelectric power in Hubei was twice that of all other rivers listed here in central-south China, and a power station on a single river—Sanxia on the Yangzi—was believed able to generate the

88 Li Yizhi, "Hanjiang shangyou zhi gaikuang ji xiwang 漢江上游之概況及希望 [The Current Conditions and Hopes of the Upstream Han River]," *Shuili* 4, nos. 5–6 (1932): 181.

89 Li, "Hanjiang shangyou," 182.

90 "Zhongyuan gongyebu: qian quanguo shuili fadian gongcheng gaikuang ji huazhong kancechu gongzuo jihua baogao 中原工業部：前全國水力發電工程概況及華中勘測處工作計劃報告 [Central China Department of Industry: Previous National Hydropower Projects and Central China Survey Department Work Plan Report]," Hubei Provincial Archives, GM 9-1-84.

TABLE 16 Comparative potential hydropower in major watersheds (May 1949)

	Yangzi River Watershed					Yellow River Watershed		Pearl River Watershed	Southeastern Watersheds	Total
	Central Yangzi	West Sichuan	East Sichuan	Yunnan	Yangzi (other)	Branch Rivers	Yellow River			
Hydropower projects	54	13	13	28	11	23	6	10	18	179
Hydropower potential (MW)	3,063	2,434.5	2,434.5	417.6	16,000	1,291.8	7,500	176	1,259	30,817.8

SOURCE: "ZHONGYUAN GONGYEBU: QIAN QUANGUO SHUILI FADIAN GONGCHENG GAIKUANG JI HUAZHONG KANCECHU GONGZUO JIHUA BAOGAO 中原工業部: 前全國水力發電工程概況及華中勘測處工作計劃報告 [CENTRAL CHINA DEPARTMENT OF INDUSTRY: PREVIOUS NATIONAL HYDROPOWER PROJECTS AND CENTRAL CHINA SURVEY DEPARTMENT WORK PLAN REPORT]," MAY 1949, HUBEI PROVINCIAL ARCHIVES, GM 9-1-84.

TABLE 17 Comparative hydropower resources in Central-South China (1945)

Province	Rivers	Max. flow	Max. hydropower (kW)	Total (kW)
Henan	**Yellow**, Ru, Huai, Dan, Shi, Huang	1,200	2,177,000	2,263,500
Hubei	**Yangzi**, Han, Qing, Qu, Lu.	6,000	10,560,000	12,708,800
Hunan	Wu, **Yuan**, Fu, Li, Zi, Xiang, Dafu	400	479,000	1,029,400
Jiangxi	Xiu, Rao, Wuyang, **Gan**	300	170,000	238,200
Guangdong	Ji, Dong, **Bei**, Xi, Neihe, Changbei	400	235,000	862,500
Guangxi	**Hongshui**, Liu, Ying, Nanpan	600	650,700	1,772,900

Note: The maximal flow and maximal hydropower refer to one river (in bold) with the highest number in a province.

SOURCE: "HUAZHONG NANQU SHUILI FADIAN ZIYUAN TONJI BIAO 華中南區水力發電資源統計表 [THE STATISTICS OF CENTRAL-SOUTH CHINA HYDROELECTRICITY RESOURCES]," HUBEI PROVINCIAL ARCHIVES, GM 9-1-000007-002-0004, GM 9-1-000007-002-0005, AND GM 9-1-000007-002-0006.

most hydroelectric power among all the rivers. It is not surprising that the Nationalist government placed tremendous emphasis on water management in central China.

In his general history of the Yangzi River, Song Xishang 宋希尚 extensively analyzed the significance of hydroelectric power on the Yangzi. He wrote, "Electricity was the foundation of industries; no electricity, then no national defense, and no industrial strength."[91] In addition, he emphasized the advantages of hydroelectric power development—it provided endless energy, at low cost after the initial technological input and construction.[92] Song, who first studied at the Hehai Engineering School under the National Bureau of Water Conservancy, received advanced training in engineering at MIT and then Brown University in the US. After obtaining his master's degree in engineering,

91 Song, *Changjiang tongkao*, 223.
92 Song, *Changjiang tongkao*, 223.

he investigated hydraulic works in various European countries, including Germany, the Netherlands, Belgium, Britain, France, and Switzerland. He worked on the Yangzi River extensively under the Nationalist government starting in 1928. His vision for development of the Yangzi River basin was greatly shaped by his engineering training in the US and Europe, and he advocated a comprehensive hydropower development plan for the Yangzi, including the construction of the Three Gorges Dam (Sanxia Dam). Working with three other engineers—Yun Zhen 恽震, Cao Ruizhi 曹瑞芝, and George Stroebe—he conducted a field investigation in the Three Gorges area in the early 1930s. After months of surveys, the team proposed building a hydropower dam at one of two ideal locations, Gezhou Ba or Huangling Miao, approximately where the Yangzi's mega-dams are currently located. They also proposed a multistage project, the first stage of which would generate 320 kW hydroelectricity.[93]

Song's ideas about managing the Yangzi, to a large extent, derived from the management of the Tennessee Valley watershed by the Tennessee Valley Authority (TVA). He enthusiastically endorsed the TVA project and discussed its potential in the Yangzi valley. He wrote, "Since [undertaking] the initiative of the TVA in the 1930s, the Tennessee Valley realized its electrification and eliminated the potential threat of flooding; its generation of wealth and public service in a river valley was exemplary to the whole world."[94] He then suggested that China could learn from the TVA project and create a Yangzi Valley Authority to make use of the vast natural resources in the Yangzi valley.[95]

This grand scheme was well on its way to being implemented in the 1930s and 1940s. In 1944, the American economist G.R. Passhal suggested turning the entire Sanxia area into an industrial region—including a dam with a capacity of 10,500 kW of hydroelectricity and chemical fertilizer factories powered by hydroelectricity. The proposal would receive US investment and the fertilizers produced would be sent to the US as well.[96] In May 1944, the Nationalist government's Resource Committee invited the chief design engineer, Dr. John L. Savage, from the US Bureau of Reclamation to investigate various watersheds along the Yangzi, including the Sanxia area near Yichang. After the survey, Dr. Savage drafted a report on the potential for building a dam at Sanxia and its comprehensive benefits for agricultural irrigation, flood control, hydroelectricity generation, river transportation, industrial power (especially for chemical

93 Song, *Changjiang tongkao*, 224.

94 Song, *Changjiang tongkao*, 223.

95 Song, *Changjiang tongkao*, 223–224.

96 Song, *Changjiang tongkao*, 224.

TABLE 18 Estimated gains from the proposed Sanxia project (US dollars per year)

	Gross profit	Net profit
Hydroelectricity	143,450,000	50,660,000
Irrigation	37,000,000	18,500,000
Flood control	38,240,000	38,240,000
Navigation	192,500,000	3,000,000
Drinking water	56,600,000	5,000,000
Tourism	50,000,000	5,000,000
Total	527,790,000	153,900,000

SOURCE: SONG, *CHANGJIANG TONGKAO*, 234.

fertilizer factories), and drinking water.[97] According to his optimistic report, after the project was completed, it would generate as much as four times more electricity than the TVA project.[98] Song then listed the benefits of the Sanxia project (see Table 18).

Table 18 shows that Song estimated gains from the proposed Sanxia project in hydroelectricity, irrigation, flood control, navigation, drinking water and tourism, with the highest net profit in hydroelectricity. This project would no doubt have tremendous economic benefits for the country. Although Song and his engineering team recognized the potential harm to certain communities along the Yangzi River, no specific plans were drawn up to deal with the potential losses, except for a brief statement—"information [on such losses] can be obtained only after field investigations."[99] Along those lines, Song mentions that the Resource Committee surveyed the communities along the Yangzi River in 1946–1947 and carefully recorded the data on population, agriculture, industries and mines, businesses, and transportation, especially from the areas slated to benefit in the mid- and lower Yangzi valley.[100] Despite the optimism and preparation leading up to the actual Sanxia dam, the project was halted by internal warfare in China.

97 Song, *Changjiang tongkao*, 230.
98 Song, *Changjiang tongkao*, 225.
99 Song, *Changjiang tongkao*, 228.
100 Song, *Changjiang tongkao*, 228.

7 Conclusion

From a materialist perspective, reconceptualizing nationwide water management based on watersheds was one step toward consolidating power during the Republican period. Like many of their predecessors, the Republican leaders in China represented yet another attempt to order nature in the pursuit of political power. From the Jinshui Reclamation Project to reorganization of the dike systems, to unification of the watersheds, and the proposal of a multifunctional dam at Sanxia, all the proposals demonstrated the Chinese state's goal to increase national wealth and to industrialize and stabilize the regions. By taking a technological and nationalist approach, the hydraulic schemes during the Republican period were fully geared toward strengthening the country, using hydroelectricity to fuel industries, and so on. Nature was the venue for achieving power and wealth. As David Pietz writes in his study of the twentieth-century Yellow River valley, "from the broadest perspective, the developmental regime adopted in many polities by the mid-twentieth century was a 'high-modernist' vision of economic development and state capacity that sought to efficiently and rationally exploit resources to power an industrial economy."[101] The mid-Yangzi, which has enormous hydropower potential, won its centrality in building a modern and wealthy nation in the first half of the twentieth century.

The unification of the watershed management and the shift of focus in hydraulic management from irrigation to hydropower generation showed the national pursuit of modernity in the central Yangzi Valley in the Republican period. In his 2002 book, David Pietz discusses the attempts of the Nationalist government to reestablish central control over Huai River management as part of its national reconstruction program, stating that its hydraulic policies exemplified "a centralizing and modernizing administration based on a faith in technology, industry, and international cooperation."[102] Unlike in other regions, the state resource management on the Jianghan Plain showed some penetration of state power into the grassroots-level hydraulic unit and an effort to incorporate the *yuan* system into the government system during the Republican period. Although the state scheme was not completely effective or successful, as shown in the large-scale conflict over the Tiangu *yuan*, the state's ideas about managing water control based on watersheds and setting up regional water

101 Pietz, *The Yellow River*, 94.

102 Introduction to David Pietz, *Engineering the State: The Huai River and Reconstruction in Nationalist China, 1927–1937* (New York: Routledge, 2002). This theme is also explored in Chapter 3 of his book *The Yellow River* (2015).

management were still constructive.[103] As Pietz asserted, "Although there were few accomplishments in 'ordering the waters' during the Republican period because of limited central political control, administrative fractionalization and Japanese invasion, these forces were further structured by the Chinese Communist Party after 1949 and ultimately shaped the management of water in the Maoist (1949–1976) and post-Maoist periods (1976–)."[104]

Moreover, the reliance in China on international engineers and a hybridity of expertise and approaches showed little concern for local communities, especially those whose location was deemed less important than others. The scientific advice from the engineering community about the Tiangu *yuan* mattered little during the conflicts between Hubei and Hunan. The early twentieth-century watershed management scheme at the state level and the *yuan* reorganization at the community level were parallel activities that had minimal influence on each other. The state plan to build the Sanxia dam had the potential to harm certain communities along the Yangzi River, as acknowledged by Song Xishang and his team of engineers, but no specific plan was considered to deal with the potential losses of the local communities.

I have shown that the *yuan* was highly significant in the control of floods, that communities that formed in and around them had lasting importance, and that officials long made use of the term. Why then is *yuan* much less mentioned in Republican local gazetteers? Undoubtedly early 20th century gazetteer writers did not take *yuan* to be central players. The state was intervening

103 Although the general retreat of state power during the late Qing and Republican periods has been almost universally recognized among historians, some scholars still see the strengthening of state power in certain domains of the society, such as solving transboundary conflicts, supervising the local market, and distributing the knowledge of modern science and technology. Hydraulic projects, without doubt, were among the most important domains on which governments of the late Qing and the Republic worked. Micah Muscolino, who conducted extensive research on fisheries in the coastal areas of Republican China, emphasized the state's (the Nanjing government) role in settling the Sino-Japanese sea-fishing dispute, in *Fishing Wars and Environmental Change in Late Imperial and Modern China* (Cambridge: Harvard University Press, 2009). Keith Schoppa examined cases of land reclamation in Hangzhou Bay from 1866 to 1936 and showed a state with changing perceptions of and approaches to society. He suggested that even though those cases revealed efforts at state-making, they were hollow achievements. He also reveals "a defensive Nationalist state in the late 1920s and 1930s attempting, despite increasingly tenuous ties to local society, to assert its power and strengthen its role there, most often through increased use of military and police powers. However, for local elites and masses, such attempts tended to diminish the state's moral authority and to undercut efforts to foster its legitimacy." R. Keith Schoppa, "State, Society, and Land Reclamation on Hangzhou Bay during the Republican Period," *Modern China* 23, no. 2 (1997): 249.

104 Pietz, *The Yellow River*, 79.

directly, this time focusing on large scale model projects that were high modernist in nature, with ultimate emphasis on watershed management and electrification. The local dikes and *yuan* thus received much less attention. Meanwhile, there is some evidence of *yuan* consolidation in the early twentieth century, for example, the merging of a group of small *yuan* into a big *yuan* that was discussed earlier in this chapter, possibly reducing their prevalence in the records. Although big conflicts continued over water and land among the *yuan* in various records, in general *yuan* became much less important as a framework for local belonging or a focus of state action. This shift in water management foreshadowed the new authoritarian, highly modernist hydraulic schemes in the second half of the twentieth century.

Conclusion

In her 2015 work, the environmental historian and philosopher of nature Carolyn Merchant notes the philosophical distinction between two types of nature: *natura naturans* (nature as creator) and *natura naturata* (created nature), with the former indicating the unpredictability and uncontrollability of nature.[1] Merchant's conceptualization of nature implies the three characteristics of the water regime discussed in this book: it was autonomous, cultural, and amphibious. Water oscillated between culture and nature and connected people's everyday experience with the operation of state power. As Merchant points out, "the way in which nature as an autonomous system behaves depends on how humans behave in relation to it."[2] By analyzing the transformation of the water regime on the Jianghan Plain from the seventeenth to the early twentieth centuries, this book departs from a dialectics of state and society and focuses, instead, on the interactions between society and nature in an environmental network. As argued in earlier chapters, changes in water systems are the result of an intricate interplay among state and local politics, cultural practices, hydraulic engineering, and the particular hydrogeomorphology of the rivers and the geography and ecology of the Jianghan Plain. In this way, the landscape and waterscape of the plain were a kind of "socionature" produced through the interactions between the materiality of water and the state and social powers that acted upon it.[3]

The hydrosocial structure, the *yuan*, was a pivotal part of the water regime of the Jianghan Plain—the node between land and water and a hybrid of nature and culture. Originating as the key hydraulic strategy for fending off excessive floodwaters and irrigating agricultural lands, the *yuan* in the central Yangzi region enabled people to live in a flood-prone environment. After sophisticated institutions were developed to regulate local communities' activities, it continued to be the venue through which state politics interacted with the materiality of water. Centering on an analysis of the *yuan*, the book demonstrates the continuity from the early economic water regime to the later ethnic, military, and hydrotechnological regimes. In successive water regimes, the *yuan* persisted as the site where politics and ecology collided.

1 See Carolyn Merchant, *Autonomous Nature: Problems of Prediction and Control from Ancient Times to the Scientific Revolution* (London: Routledge, 2015).

2 Merchant, *Autonomous Nature*, 150.

3 Swyngedouw, "Modernity and Hybridity," 448.

© KONINKLIJKE BRILL NV, LEIDEN, 2022 | DOI:10.1163/9789004505285_009

Yet the *yuan* was not unchanging. It started as a military-economic structure and was the domain of social, economic, and military state schemes to be implemented at the local level. Floods changed and destroyed them, and so did the official management of land and water—smaller *yuan* merged with bigger ones (Chapters 2 and 6). Local people constructed and disputed *yuan*, and officials at various levels destroyed or protected them based on different interests. In the twentieth century, *yuan* went through a process of bureaucratization and became less important as a frame for local belonging or a focus of state action. The changes in the *yuan* reflected the shifting complex relationships within an environmental network in different historical periods.

1 An Autonomous Water Regime

In conformance with Merchant's distinction between two "natures," I emphasize the unintended consequences of the interplay of human action and non-human processes in transforming the plain. In several examples, I show that dikes and land reclamation could be sources of conflict: the blocking or releasing of water could be disastrous for those who were adjacent or downstream and produced violent struggles over water and land (Chapter 2). In other examples, I demonstrate that the state's environmental favoritism could have lasting environmental effects: for instance, the favoring of the north bank of the Yangzi River, where ancestral tombs of high officials and the garrison were located, at the expense of the south bank, where the people managed the *yuan* themselves (Chapter 5), contributed to a severe drainage problem in the low-land Jianghan Plain, an issue that remains troublesome.

Natural systems involving wetlands, horses, forests, soil, and sediment continually shaped and reshaped the plain, never in isolation from human activity. Sedimentation is a case in point. Until the end of the eighteenth century, it was not a salient problem, but in the nineteenth century, the literature is filled with concern. Presumably, the sedimentation that blocked river-lake systems was the result of long-term denuding of upland forest cover, so its origin was partly social. Conversely, consideration of the natural processes of sedimentation and the outlet blocking in the river-lake systems in the region helps us capture the full story behind the increasing local violence over water and land, so conflicts had a partly natural cause. The expansion of agriculture was another case of the "two natures" working in tandem. The reclamation of horse pastures for grain production (Chapter 3), despite the high priority of Manchu calvary for the ruling elite, reflected the enormous population pressures in the eighteenth century, but it could never have occurred without the combination of a humid environment and suitable varieties of grain.

The local ecosystems were the key actors in a complex environmental network, affecting the plain's landscape and waterscape in unexpected ways, such as the frequent emergence and expansion of sandbars in the rivers, the blockage of outlets from the rivers to flood-relieving lakes, or the siltation of lakes (i.e., Dongting Lake), which prevented the relief of any water pressure from the main riverbed. The lowland hydrogeographic feature of the plain and its compromised capacity for relieving floods today is an environmental legacy of the historical and long-term operation of a semiautonomous water regime. The various human actors interacted within an environmental network full of tension and contradiction. The more they tried to hold back the waters, the more they aggravated the general flooding problem. Agriculture thus became more hazardous, prompting more diking; more settlers and building reduced the upstream forest cover, which inevitably worsened downstream flooding and sedimentation. Therefore, the intensification of agriculture and population did not make for greater security but, rather, less. The efforts of the local lineages and local officials, sometimes at odds, did not solve these problems. The state's military and political schemes often worsened the situation, simply making the problems larger. Without a deep understanding of the interconnectedness of various factors in a water regime, or a holistic approach to interlocking issues, the effort to solve ecological problems was like the work of the sorcerer's apprentice, with one disaster leading to another.

2 An Amphibious Water Regime

In addition to asserting the autonomous functioning of the water regime, this book emphasizes the community dynamism and local initiative. In a large-scale river valley, where wetlands, lakes, and rivers supplied multiple opportunities for land reclamation and economic gain, the *yuan* was of pivotal significance. As shown in Chapter 1, the early *yuan* on the Jianghan Plain provided a flexible space for people to maintain an amphibious lifestyle, shifting their livelihood between land and water, building and altering the dikes, and thereby manipulating the physical nature of the *yuan*. The *yuan* communities arose from local struggles with water disasters. The *yuan* permitted a degree of local autonomy (Chapters 1 and 2). Localization enabled communities to form their own systems for managing water resources and cooperating with one another. Despite the eighteenth-century emergence of lineage management and collaboration with county and prefectural officials, strong local attachments persisted. When state authorities tried to intervene in local management, the communities devised strategies to evade intervention, satisfy their own interests, limit their concessions to the state, and even manipulate state authorities to achieve their own goals. The conflicts between divergent hydrogeopolitical interests over the big Zekou (Chapter 5) and the Tiangu *yuan* (Chapter 6) showed extraordinary local resourcefulness in community mobilization and collaboration. In both cases, the common people were the main actors in local hydraulic dramas, and their local interests often overrode regional hydraulic interests. When hydraulic experts devised a watershed unification scheme that failed to take into account the views of local *yuan* communities, such as the Tiangu *yuan*, interprovincial conflicts over the *yuan* persisted, and the experts played little role in either resolving them or addressing the underlying hydraulic problems.

The *yuan*, as an agricultural and social unit, maintained a certain stability as the identifying marker of a hydraulic community over the centuries. The stability did not depend on the dike boundaries, which shifted over time, but, instead, on the consistency in their institutional management and cultural practices. Floods could easily destroy the dikes, and they often did; however, the *yuan* communities were not defined by the dikes—the residents of any given *yuan* knew to which *yuan* they belonged even after the dikes washed away. For officials, it did not matter whether the *yuan* was flooded—taxes could be levied on both agriculture and fishing. Chapter 3 discusses a case in which officials suggested lowering the *yuan* dikes so that people could live by fishing instead of cultivating crops. Thus, despite physical changes, *yuan* were a durable social structure between land and water. They represented a cultured nature as well as a natured culture.

3 The Role of the State

Perdue's point bears repeating here: "Studies of the Middle Yangzi must at least consider the role of the 'hydraulic state,' even if they ultimately reject its importance."[4] This study of the Jianghan Plain shows the state's governing strategies through the manipulation of water and the "ordering" of nature. The early Qing state took a laissez-faire approach in the central Yangzi region, largely because of the complex hydrogeographical conditions of the landscape and waterscape. The economic and political status of the region grew over time: the initial war against the Mongols kickstarted massive land reclamation

4 Perdue, "Lakes of Empire," 124.

in the plain; a military garrison was established in Jingzhou after the Revolt of the Three Feudatories; the *jianbi qingye* policy was implemented to suppress the White Lotus rebels and later the Taipings who rampaged over large areas of the central Yangzi region; and large-scale hydroengineering schemes were contemplated in the midst of the catastrophic flood of 1931, which laid the groundwork for massive hydraulic construction in the same region decades later. In each of these cases, local environments were altered to suit the needs of the state, whether reclaiming lands, building dikes, removing horses, building forts, or constructing dams. By working through the local environments, the state gradually turned the Jianghan Plain from hydraulically marginal (as discussed in Chapter 2) to a hydraulic center in the twentieth century (Chapter 6). The hydrogeographic features of the Jianghan Plain were a key consideration in imperial rulers' regional governance, military plans, and national politics. Nature (specifically, water) was the stage on which power was exercised.

The trajectory of the Jianghan Plain from hydraulically marginal to hydraulic center over seven centuries was the result of the long-term interplay among water politics, cultural practices, and the hydrogeography and ecology of the plain. This transformation suggests the complexity of managing small, dispersed, self-interested hydraulic units at a local level. Unlike the Yellow River valley, where centralized management had always been in practice—for instance, in the establishment of the Yellow River Commission and the direct control of finance by the imperial court—the Yangzi River was never under central control in imperial times. No evidence has been found that the late imperial rulers ever thought of establishing a Yangzi River Commission.[5] Maybe the paramount difficulty of overcoming the precarious hydrogeomorphology of the central Yangzi and the dispersed, flexible, and manipulative nature of local hydraulic communities together discouraged thoughts of unifying water control there. The Nationalist government did try to unify water control nationwide, an important component of which was unified Yangzi River management. However, the Yangzi River Commission that it established was compromised by an ineffective government, warfare, and the continual disasters in the 1930s (Chapter 6). It is doubtful that such a unification plan could have been realized without a strong interventionist government. Early on, the Chinese communist government set up a Yangzi Water Resources Commission, and over the years, it has proposed and constructed numerous projects, including the controversial Three Gorges Dam.

5 For further discussion, see Will, "Zhonghua diguo wanqi guojia dui shuili de guanli."

The response to ongoing environmental crises shows a discrepancy between the ideals of "statecraft" and the reality of actions by ordinary people, as well as a gap between people's awareness of environmental problems and the realities of nature. The imperial governments inherited a long tradition of expertise in water control but drew different lessons from it. Eighteenth-century state officials argued among themselves about strategies for managing the *yuan* amid the plain's land and water. Nineteenth-century officials tended to see the rivers as an organic system and argued for a holistic solution to issues with rivers. Early twentieth-century Western-trained hydraulic experts proposed grand schemes to alleviate the hydraulic pressure in the central Yangzi region. Meanwhile, local communities reacted to water crises with proactive strategies that conflicted with the state's hydraulic decisions (Chapters 3 and 5). The holistic vision adopted by many late Qing officials anticipated their twentieth-century successors, who combined centralized watershed management with brute-force technologies.[6]

4 Environmental Changes in the *Longue Durée*

The case of the Jianghan Plain suggests the need to think about environmental change over the long term. In the postscript to his book on the Yangzi River, Van Slyke exclaimed: "The Yangtze River does seem to be changing in 'the blinking of an eye.'… Yet from the other perspective, it seems to have gone on forever … changes in the river during a generation or two were so trivial as to be insignificant."[7] He captured two types of temporality in environmental change perfectly. Quiet changes might incubate powerful destructiveness. Van Slyke quoted T.S. Eliot's poem "The Dry Salvages" to suggest that perhaps the river was waiting:

> I think that the river
> Is a strong brown god—sullen, untamed and intractable,
> Patient to some degree, at first recognized as a frontier;
> Useful, untrustworthy, as a conveyor of commerce;
> Then only a problem confronting the builder of bridges.

6 Paul Josephson uses the term "brute force" technologies to describe the large destructive resource management technologies, such as hydropower dams and forest and fishery management in the US, Canada, Norway, and other countries, in *Industrialized Nature: Brute Force Technology and the Transformation of the Natural World* (Washington, DC: Island Press, 2002).

7 Van Slyke, *Yangtze*, 193.

> The problem once solved, the brown god is almost forgotten
> By the dwellers in cities—ever, however, implacable,
> Keeping his seasons and rages, destroyer, reminder
> Of what men choose to forget. Unhonoured, unpropitiated
> By worshippers of the machine, but waiting, watching and waiting.[8]

We can never know how long the river will wait before it swings into action again. Over the span of seven centuries, the Jianghan Plain has gone through profound changes.

4.1 *Hydrogeographic Changes*

Until the twentieth century, almost the only hydrographic constant was the massive floodwater to be expected seasonally from the upstream waterways, which swelled from time to time—but unpredictably—into disastrous floods. Even in recent years, such as in 1998, 2016 and 2020, serious floods affected the region. Despite the completion of the Three Gorges Dam in 2012, Wuhan, at the juncture of the Han and Yangzi Rivers, is still subject to flooding. In the absence of significant institutional change, piecemeal human attempts to cope with small seasonal and large periodic floods cannot be effective in the long run; in fact, they transformed the plain's hydrography in unhelpful ways. Land reclamation and population increases reduced the capacity of floodplains, ponds, and lakes to relieve flood pressure. The multiplication and then consolidation of *yuan* had the same effect. A short time frame, such as a few years or decades, is insufficient for discerning the transformative effects of a government's geopolitical favoritism. However, several centuries of dike strengthening on the northern bank of the Yangzi and the left (northern) bank of the Han river worsened flooding on the opposite banks of both rivers. Vanishing vegetation cover in the plain and its hinterland watershed increased sedimentation, which, along with the continuous sinking of the central plain, intensified the impact of the periodic floods. Some modern observers described what they saw as the "Netherlands of Central China." The implied comparison dwelt on the impressive visible impact of human activity and dense population on the plain's hydrogeography but failed to account for the unintended consequences of all these efforts at water control and ignored the continuing insecurity in the face of flooding.

Land reclamation over the centuries turned thousands of lakes, vast floodplains, and wetlands into agricultural fields. By the mid-twentieth century,

8 Van Slyke, *Yangtze*, 193–194.

Hubei Province was no longer the "thousand-lake province": 60 to 70 percent of the lakes and wetlands had shrunk or completely disappeared, and the *yuan* had long since ceased to be a significant territorial division or a local force. Rivers, containing large quantities of soil and sand from upstream, are constrained within strong, high dikes along the riverbanks and have nowhere to release their excess water because important river and lake outlets have been blocked. The interrupted river-lake system was both the cause and the effect of the frequent flooding of the plain. In the event of excessive floodwaters from the Yangzi and Han Rivers, the river water level often easily rose above the street level in Wuhan, placing enormous pressure on the long dikes along the rivers and threatening the safety of the city. More unintended consequences will unfold in the years to come. Local decision making, with its problematic aspects, is no more, along with the *yuan* society, but the large-scale problem of Yangzi/Han control has not been fully addressed.

4.2 *Loss of Biodiversity*

The initial footprint of settlement in the Song and Yuan periods was seasonal reclamation and temporary walling off of flooded lands, a cyclical process that brought little permanent security for settlers but, by the same token, created minimal disruption of avian life and fauna and flora. But population growth and land clearance for agriculture gradually destroyed the marsh and forest habitat. By the end of the tenth century, Asian elephants and rhinoceroses were no longer found.[9] At the end of the nineteenth century, tigers, which still lived in large numbers in the downstream valley of the Han River at the end of the twelfth century, were observed only around Changjia Lake and Dabian Lake in Gong'an County on the lower Jianghan Plain.[10] Excessive human activity had led to ecological exhaustion. Waterfowl gradually lost their wetland habitats, and many species became extinct after the eighteenth century. For example, wild swans had once visited Taibai Lake in Hanyang County in large

9 Wen Huanran and Wen Rongsheng, ed., *Zhongguo lishi shiqi zhiwu yu dongwu bianqian yanjiu* 中國歷史時期植物與動物變遷研究 [*Changes in Flora and Fauna in Historical China*] (Chongqing: Chongqing chubanshe, 1995), 186–225; see also Elvin, *The Retreat of the Elephants*.

10 He Yeheng, *Zhongguo zhenxi shoulei de lishi bianqian* 中國珍稀獸類的歷史變遷 [*The Historical Changes of Rare Wildlife in China*] (Changsha: Henan kexue jishu chubanshe, 1993), 141–145. Gong Shengsheng analyzed the transformations in historical wetlands of the Jianghan-Dongting Lake area, in "Jianghan-Dongtinghu pingyuan shidi de lishi bianqian yu kechixu liyong 江漢—洞庭湖平原濕地的歷史變遷與可持續利用 [Historical Changes and Sustainable Utilization of the Jianghan-Dongting Plain's Wetlands]," *Changjiang liuyu ziyuan yu huanjing* 11, no. 6 (2002).

numbers, but after 1818, they vanished. The famous cranes of Jiangling survived a few more decades but were no longer seen in the 1880s.[11]

Other long-extant species succumbed to human pressure. The bounty and diversity of ecological resources, including birds, fish, and other animals, had visibly diminished by the end of the nineteenth century. The Yangzi alligator (*Alligator sinensis* 揚子鱷), a "living fossil" in Yangzi waters once reported in more than thirty counties on the Hubei plain, is now nowhere to be found.[12] The Chinese paddlefish (*Psephurus gladius, baixun* 白鱘), one of the largest freshwater fish, which had lived for 34–75 million years, went extinct by 2005–2010.[13] In 2006–2007, a six-week expedition to the Yangzi River by thirty scientists failed to detect any Yangzi dolphins (*Lipotes vexillifer, baiji* 白暨豚) and concluded that it was extinct, largely due to human activity.[14] This extinction "represents not only the first documented global extinction of a 'megafaunal' vertebrate for over fifty years, but also the disappearance of an entire mammal family (*Lipotidae*)."[15] A 2003 study of the entire Yangzi River basin found that "hydrological alterations" were the largest threat to fish biodiversity and recommended reconnection of the river with neighboring lakes and habitats for the spawning and feeding of migratory fish.[16] Numerous human activities, such as excessive fishing, factory operation, dam construction, sewage, and chemical pollution, also contributed to the deterioration of the Yangzi basin biota, once one of the richest in the world.

---

11 He Yeheng, *Zhongguo zhenxi niaolei de lishi bianqian* 中國珍稀鳥類的歷史變遷 [*The Historical Changes of Rare Birds in China*] (Changsha: Henan kexue jishu chubanshe, 1994), 32–34, 176–178.

12 Wen Rongsheng, "Xiancun e'lei yu Yangzi e shengshuai 現存鱷類與揚子鱷盛衰 [The Existent Allegators and the Rise and Fall of the Yangzi Allegator]," in Wen and Wen, *Zhongguo lishi shiqi zhiwu yu dongwu bianqian yanjiu*, 269.

13 Based on 210 sightings of Chinese paddlefish during the period 1981–2003, the researchers estimated the timing of its extinction to be by 2005, and no later than by 2010. Zhang Hui et al., "Extinction of One of the World's Largest Freshwater Fishes: Lessons for Conserving the Endangered Yangtze Fauna," *Science of the Total Environment* 710 (2020), Douglas Main, "The Chinese Paddlefish, One of World's Largest Fish, Has Gone Extinct," *National Geographic* (January 8, 2020), https: //www.nationalgeographic.com/animals/2020/01/chinese-paddlefish-one-of-largest-fish-extinct/#close/.

14 For more discussion on the extinction of the Yangzi dolphin, see Samuel Turvey, *Witness to Extinction: How We Failed to Save the Yangzi Dolphin* (Oxford: Oxford University Press, 2008).

15 "Baiji," IUCN SSC–Cetacean Specialist Group, http: //iucn-csg.org/baiji/.

16 Fu Cuizhang et al., "Freshwater Fish Biodiversity in the Yangtze River Basin of China: Patterns, Threats and Conservation," *Biodiversity and Conservation* 12 (2003): 1657.

5 Hopes and Challenges in the Jianghan Plain

The Jianghan Plain is yet another declensionist story of environmental degradation, but its people continue to show resilience. The local initiatives in hydraulic management on the historical Jianghan Plain could offer a model for the sporadic but persistent antipollution activities in the present. In the fall of 2007, I went to a village in the Zibeiyuan area, near the border of Jianli and Honghu Counties. The villagers were talkative and showed great interest in my research. One woman whose family had migrated from Jiangling County told me about an ongoing lawsuit over pollution caused by the cultivation of jute (*Corchorus capsularis Linn, Huangma* 黄麻), one of the main cash crops on the Jianghan Plain. After being harvested, jute is soaked in local lakes and rivers to extract the fibers. The chemicals in the jute turned the water black and posed a threat to the water quality and the fish stock in the region. Complaining about the poor water quality and decreasing fish populations, local residents sued the jute farmers at the county level. Her story was filled with concern over the environment and frustration at the pollution created by jute production. In 2011, professors and students at Changjiang University protested the hazard to people's health and livelihood from the pollutants released into the air by a Jingzhou chemical factory. A dozen professors led the students in kneeling in front of the main gate of the factory in silent protest. The government stepped in to investigate and forced the chemical factory to take measures to clean up the pollution.[17] In another example, in the summer of 2018, I visited the Jinshui Dam in Jinshui County, Hubei. The local people there were concerned about the spread of the common water hyacinth (*Eichhornia crassipes, shui hulu* 水葫蘆) in the Jinshui River, which affected the water quality as well as biodiversity of the river. For me, it was quite encouraging to see the rise in people's environmental consciousness at the grassroots level.

The activities by the university community inspired different reactions in the media. Some people agreed with the professors and students, while others argued that they should have taken a more laid-back approach. In a society in which public protests are closely monitored by the government, the passive-aggressive approach of public kneeling may have been more effective

17 He Qinglian, "Dianping Zhongguo: Jiaoshou xiagui, kongqi tegong yu zhengfu zeren 點評中國：教授下跪，空氣特供與政府責任 [Commenting on China: Professors Kneeling Down, Air Supply and Governmental Responsibility]," BBC China, November 17, 2011, http: //www.bbc.co.uk/zhongwen/simp/focus_on_china/2011/11/111114_cr_airpollution_byheqinglian.shtml.

in making their voices heard than more confrontational methods.[18] It could be argued that these public protests arose more out of pragmatic economic concerns than interest in environmental protection. However, the social significance of raising environmental consciousness should not be underestimated.

The commercial interest in nature is a recent trend. Hong Lake, at the border of Jianli and Honghu Counties, is now the largest wetland conservation area in Hubei.[19] People fish and harvest lotus roots in the lake, and beautiful lotus flowers, with their large leaves, cover its surface. Aquatic products processed in local industries are marketed as "natural" and "healthy." Tourism companies offer tours to multiple well-managed wetland parks in or near Wuhan and advertise guided tours of "pristine, undisturbed landscapes," including visits to ancient sites. Although ecological tourism makes up a small share of the tourism industry, its organizers are striving to make nature a commodity. But nature has sounded a warning bell. After centuries of population growth and agrarian transformation in the old land of the *yuan*, the massively expanding market economy has permanently altered the "two natures" and the balance between them. An observer might question whether any "pristine, undisturbed landscapes" survive for tourist enjoyment on the Jianghan Plain.

18 Kate Merkel-Hess, Kenneth L. Pomeranz, and Jeffrey Wasserstrom, ed., *China in 2008: A Year of Great Significance* (Lanham: Rowman & Littlefield, 2009), chap. 1.

19 For further discussion on China's wetlands, see An Shuqing et al., "China's Natural Wetlands: Past Problems, Current Status, and Future Challenges," *Ambio* 36, no. 4 (2007).

Appendix: Glossary of Chinese Measurement Terms

Chinese measurement	English-language equivalents
chao 抄	0.0015 kg (1.5g)
chi 尺	⅓ meter; 1.07 feet
cun 寸	1.3 inch
dan 担	50 kg
dou 斗	15 kg
dun 吨	1 ton; 1,000 kg
gong 弓	1.65 meters
he 合	0.15 kg (150 g)
jin 斤	½ kg; 1.1 pounds
li 里	½ kilometer; 0.311 mile
liang 两	50 grams
mu 畝	⅙ acre; 1⁄15 hectare
qing 頃	About 3.33 hectare
qian 錢	5 grams
shao 勺	0.015 kg (15 g)
sheng 升	1.5 kg
shi 石	About 150 kg
zhang 丈	10.3 meters; 10.7 feet
chuan 串	1,000 copper coins
wen 文	1 copper coin

SOURCE: FANG JIQING AND MICHAEL CONNELLY, ED., *CHINESE MEASURE WORD DICTIONARY* (BOSTON: CHENG & TSUI, 2008), 181. THE AUTHOR ADDED ADDITIONAL MEASUREMENT WORDS TO THE ORIGINAL GLOSSARY.

© KONINKLIJKE BRILL NV, LEIDEN, 2022 | DOI:10.1163/9789004505285_010

Works Cited

Gazetteers, Archives, and Other Manuscript Sources (Arranged by Title)

Baqi tongzhi chuji 八旗通志初集 [*A Collective Record of the Eight Banners*]. E'ertai 鄂爾泰. Changchun: Dongbei shifan daxue chubanshe. 1739/1985.

Bojian shanfang wenji 柏梘山房文集 [*The Anthology of Mei Zengliang*]. Mei Zengliang 梅曾亮 (Qing). Taipei: Huawen shuju. 1968.

Changjiang tushuo 長江圖說 [*A Pictorial Record of the Yangzi*]. Ma Zhenglin 馬徵麟. Taipei: Wenhai chubanshe. 1871/1969.

Chubei shuili difang jiyao 湖楚北水利堤防紀要 [*Dike Management in Hubei*]. Yu Changlie 俞昌烈. Hubei: Hubei fanshu keben. 1865.

Chusheng 鋤聲 [*Monthly News about Agriculture*]. Vol. 1, no. 20. 1934.

Daqing huidian (Kangxi) 大清會典(康熙朝) [*Qing Collected Statues in the Kangxi Reign*]. Taipei: Taiwan wenhai chubanshe. 1690/1992.

Daqing huidian (Yongzheng) 大清會典(雍正朝) [*Qing Collected Statues in the Yongzheng Reign*]. Taipei: Taiwan wenhai chubanshe. 1732/1990.

Daqing huidian (Guangxu) 大清會典(光緒朝) [*Qing Collected Statues in the Guangxu Reign*]. In *Xuxiu siku quanshu* 續修四庫全書 [*Complete Collection in Four Treasuries*]. Shanghai: Shanghai guji chubanshe. 1899/1994.

Daqing huidian shili (Jiaqing) 大清會典事例 (嘉慶朝) [*Cases on Qing Collected Statues*]. Taipei: Wenhai chubanshe. 1818/1991.

Daqing huidian shili (Guangxu) 大清會典事例 (光緒朝) [*Cases on Qing Collected Statues*]. Beijing: Zhonghua shuju. 1899/1991.

Daqing gaozong chun (Qianlong) huangdi shilu 大清高宗純（乾隆）皇帝實錄 [*A Veritable Record of the Qianlong Emperor*]. Taipei: Hualian chubanshe. 1964.

Daqing shengzu ren (Kangxi) huangdi shilu 大清聖祖仁（康熙）皇帝實錄 [*A Veritable Record of the Kangxi Emperor*]. Taipei: Hualian chubanshe. 1964.

Daqing shizong xian (Yongzheng) huangdi shilu 大清世宗憲（雍正）皇帝實錄 [*A Veritable Record of the Yongzheng Emperor*]. Taipei: Hualian chubanshe. 1964.

Daqing wenzong xian (Xianfeng) huangdi shilu 大清文宗顯（咸豐）皇帝實錄 [*A Veritable Record of the Xianfeng Emperor*]. Taipei: Hualian chubanshe. 1964.

Daqing xuanzong cheng (Daoguang) huangdi shilu 大清宣宗成（道光）皇帝實錄 [*A Veritable Record of the the Daoguang Emperor*]. Taipei: Hualian chubanshe. 1964.

Dazekou cheng'an (1912–13) 大澤口成案 [*The Leading Cases of Dazekou, 1912–13*]. Comp., Hu Ziming 鬍子明, 民國鉛印本. In *Zhonghua shanshuizhi congkan* 中華山水志叢刊 [*A Collection of Gazetteers of Mountains and Waters of China*] 18, ed. Shi Guangming

石光明, Dong Guanghe 董光和, and Yang Guanghui 楊光輝. Beijing: Xianzhuang shuju. 2004.

"Dr. John Dudgeon's Report on the Health of Peking for the Half-Year Ended 31st March 1871." *Customs Gazette*. no. 10. September 11, 1871.

Gongzhongdang kangxichao zouzhe 宮中檔康熙朝奏摺 [*Memorials of the Kangxi Reign*]. Taipei: Guoli gugong bowuyuan, 1976.

Hanchuan tuji zhengshi 漢川圖記徵實 [*A Pictorial Record of Hanchuan County*]. 1895.

Hanchuan xianzhi 漢川縣志 [*Gazetteer of Hanchuan County*]. 1873.

Hanyang fuzhi 漢陽府志 [*Gazetteer of Hanyang Prefecture*]. 1747.

Hu Linyi ji 胡林翼集 [*The Collection of Hu Linyi's Writings*]. Hu Linyi 胡林翼. Changsha: Yuelu shushe. 1999.

Hu wenzhong gong fu'e ji 胡文忠公撫鄂記 [*Hu Linyi Pacifying Hubei*]. Wang Shiduo 汪士鐸 (Qing). Changsha: Yuelu shushe. 1988.

Hu wenzhonggong yiji 胡文忠公遺集 [*A Compilation of Hu Linyi's Writings*]. Hu Linyi 胡林翼. 1864.

Huangchao jingshi wenbian 皇朝經世文編 [*Collected Essays about Statecraft of the Qing*]. ed. He Changling 賀長齡 (Qing). Taiwan Academia Sinica online database.

Huangchao jingshiwen xubian 皇朝經世文續編 [*A Continued Collection of Statecraft Writings*]. ed. Rao Yucheng 繞玉成 (Qing). Taiwan Academia Sinica online database.

Huangchao jingshiwen xubian 皇朝經世文續編 [A *Sequel to Collected Essays about Stateccraft of the Qing*]. ed. Ge Shirui 葛士濬 (Qing). Taiwan Academia Sinica online database.

Huangchao jingshiwen xubian 皇朝經世文續編 [*A Continued Collection of Statecraft Writings*]. ed. Sheng Kang 盛康 (Qing). Taiwan Academia Sinica online database.

Huangchao jingshiwen tongbian 皇朝經世文統編 [*A Comprehensive Collection of Statecraft Writings*]. ed. Shao Zhitang 邵之棠 (Qing). Taiwan Academia Sinica online database.

Huangqing zouyi 皇清奏議 [*Memorials of the Qing Dynasty*], vol. 56. Renhe qinchuan jushi 仁和琴川居士. Taipei: Wenhai chubanshe. 1765/1968.

Huangzhou fuzhi 黃州府志 [*Gazetteer of Huangzhou Prefecture*]. 1884.

Hubei anxiangyundao shuiliji'an 湖北安襄鄖道水利集案 [*Leading Cases of Anxiangyun Dao in Hubei*]. Comp., Wang Gai 王概 and Zhang Zhiyun 張志雲. In *Zhonghua shanshuizhi congkan* 中華山水志叢刊 [*A Collection of Gazetteers of Mountains and Waters of China*] 17, ed. Shi Guangming 石光明, Dong Guanghe 董光和, and Yang Guanghui 楊光輝. Beijing: Xianzhuang shuju. 2004.

Hubei difang jiyao 湖北堤防紀要 [*A History of Hubei Dikes*]. 1926.

Hubei Provincial Archives. LS-19-2-3153. "Shishou xian chengfu linian zaoquan qingxing ji luo heng chen sanyuan tiandi qingzhang shengke banfa 石首縣呈复歷年造券情形及羅橫陳三垸田地清丈升科辦法 [The Land Registration in Shishou County and the Proposal of Investigating the Land and Levying the Tax in three *yuan*—Luo, Heng, and Chen *yuan*]." 1932.

Hubei Provincial Archives. LS1-5-4967. "Guanyu hubei hanyang xihuyuan xiufangchu zhuren Guo Dehai konggao Xiao Yantang deng pohuai digong de baogao, han 關於湖北漢陽西湖垸修防處主任郭德海控告肖硯堂等破壞堤工的報告、函 [The Report on Guo Dehai of Xihu *yuan* in Hanyang, Hubei Suing Xiao Yantang for Sabotaging the Dike Work]." 1934.

Hubei Provincial Archives. LS7-2-2707. "Hubeisheng gaodeng fayuan shenli hanchuan xian difang fayuan Qu yuping wei queren yuandi fudan ji gongtong xiufang shangsu 湖北省高等法院審理漢川縣地方法院屈玉屏為確認垸地負擔及共同修防上訴 [Hubei Supreme Court Dealing with Qu Yuping of Hanchuan about Sharing *yuan* Fields and Collaborating in Maintenance]." 1947.

Hubei Provincial Archives. LS1-5-4983. "Guanyu hubei hanchuan jiangxiyuan kuijue qingkuang ji jianju he chuli digong chuzhang Zou Tianqu deng tanwu gongkuan de baogao yu laiwang wenshu 關於湖北漢川縣江西垸潰決情況及檢舉和處理堤工處長鄒天衢等貪污公款的報告與來往文書 [Correspondences on the Collapse of Jiangxi *yuan* and on Investigating the Case of Zou Tianqu Embezzling Public Funds]." 1931.

Hubei Provincial Archives. LS1-5-5030. "Guanyu chachu hubei jiayu wuhe yuan, hefeng yuan difang gongcheng zhong toujianliao ji kekou gongzi deng wenti de laiwang wenshu 關於查處湖北嘉魚五合垸、合豐垸堤防工程中偷減料及剋扣工資等問題的來往文書 [Correspondences on Investigations into Cheating on Construction Materials and Wages in the Dike Work of Wuhe *yuan* and Hefeng *yuan* of Jiayu, Hubei]."

Hubei Provincial Archives. LS1-5-5031. "Guanyu chakan hubei jiayu, mianyang wenhe yuan difang gongcheng zhiliang wenti de laiwang wenshu 關於查勘湖北嘉魚、沔陽文合垸堤防工程質量問題的來往文書 [Correspondences on the Construction Quality of Wenhe *yuan* in Jiayu and Mianyang, Hubei]."

Hubei Provincial Archives. GM 9-1-000007-002-0004, GM 9-1-000007-002-0005, and GM 9-1-000007-002-0006. "Huazhong nanqu shuili fadian ziyuan tonji biao 華中南區水力發電資源統計表 [The Statistics of Central-South China Hydroelectricity Resources]." 1945.

Hubei Provincial Archives. GM 9-1-84. "Zhongyuan gongyebu: qian quanguo shuili fadian gongcheng gaikuang ji huazhong kancechu gongzuo jihua baogao 中原工業部：前全國水力發電工程概況及華中勘測處工作計劃報告 [Central China Department of Industry: Previous National Hydropower Projects and Central China Survey Department Work Plan Report]." 1949.

Hubei shengzhi 湖北省志 [*Gazetteer of Hubei Province*]. Hubeisheng dang'anju 湖北省檔案局. Wuhan: Hubei renmin chubanshe. 1994.

Hubei xianzheng gaikuang 湖北县政概况 [*The Basic Situation of Hubei Administration*]. Hubeisheng minzhengting 湖北省民政廳. Vol. 1, 1934.

Hubeisheng jin wubai nian qihou lishi ziliao 湖北省近五百年氣候歷史資料 [*Historical Climates of Hubei in the Most Recent Five Hundred Years*]. Wuhan zhongxin qixiangtai 武漢中心氣象台. Wuhan: Wuhan zhongxin qixiangtai. 1978.

Hubeisheng ziran zaihai lishi ziliao 湖北省自然災害歷史資料 [*Historical Records of Natural Disasters in Hubei Province*]. Hubeisheng wenshi yanjiu guan 湖北省文史研究館. Wuhan: Hubeisheng wenshi yanjiu guan. 1955.

Huguang zongzhi 萬曆湖廣總志 [*General Gazetteer of Huguang*], in *Siku quanshu* 四庫全書 (History 195). 1586.

Hushi zongpu 胡氏宗谱 [*The Genealogy of the Hu Lineage*]. Tongzhi.

Jianli xianzhi 監利縣志 [*Gazetteer of Jianli County*]. 1872.

Jiangling xianzhi 江陵縣志 [*Gazetteer of Jiangling County*]. 1877.

Jingchu xiushu zhiyao 荊楚修疏志要 [*A History of Dike Repairs in Hubei*]. comp. Hu Zuhe 胡祖翮. Wuhan: Hubei renmin chubanshe. 1838/1999.

Jingmen zhouzhi 荊門州志 [*Gazetteer of Jingmen Prefecture*]. 1808.

Jingshan xianzhi 京山縣志 [*Gazetteer of Jingshan County*]. 1882.

Jingzhou fuzhi 荊州府志 [*Gazetteer of Jingzhou Prefecture*]. 1757.

Jingzhou fuzhi 荊州府志 [*Gazetteer of Jingzhou Prefecture*]. 1880.

Jingzhou shishou 荊州十首 [*Ten Poems on Jingzhou*]. Su Dongpo 蘇東坡. ca. 1060.

Jingzhou wancheng dizhi 荊州萬城堤志 [*A Record of the Jingzhou Wancheng Dike*]. Ni Wenwei 倪文蔚. Wuhan: Hubei jiaoyu chubanshe. 1876/2002.

Jingzhou zhufang zhi 荊州駐防志 [*Gazetteer of the Jingzhou Garrison*]. Comp., Xiyuan 希元. Wuhan: Hubei jiaoyu chubanshe. 1879/2002.

Kanjing jiaofei shubian 堪靖剿匪述編 [*Chronicles of Exterminating the Rebels*]. Shixiangcun jushi 石香村居士. Jingdu liulichang kanben 京都琉璃廠刊本. 1826.

Kangxichao hanwen zhupi zouzhe huibian 康熙朝漢文硃批奏摺匯編 [*Chinese Annotated Memorials of the Kangxi Reign*]. Beijing diyi lishi dang'an guan 北京第一歷史檔案館. Beijing: Dang'an chubanshe, 1985.

Kuangshi tanyuan 匡氏探源 [*Origins of the Kuang Lineage*]. Kuang Sihong 匡祀鴻. 2001.

Gongzhongdang kangxichao zouzhe 宮中檔康熙朝奏摺 [*Memorials of the Kangxi Reign*]. Taipei: Guoli gugong bowuyuan. 1719/1976.

Grand Council Memorial. "Huikan jingzhou machang dimu biantong zengjian kezu 會勘荊州馬廠地畝變通增減課租 [Changes in Acreages of Jingzhou Horse Pastureland and Increase in Land Taxation]," by Bayang'a 巴揚阿. Harvard Yenching Database.

Liushi zongpu 劉氏宗譜 [*The Genealogy of the Liu Lineage*]. 1948.

Lixu zouzhe 李煦奏摺 [*Memorials of Lixu*]. Gugong bowuyuan mingqing dang'an bu 故宮博物院明清檔案. Beijing: Zhonghua shuju. 1976.

Mianyang zhouzhi 沔陽州志 [*Gazetteer of Mianyang Prefecture*]. 1530.

Mianyang zhouzhi 沔陽州志 [*Gazetteer of Mianyang Prefecture*]. 1894.

Nanxian zhi 南縣志 [*The Gazetteer of Nanxian*]. Nanxianzhi bianweihui 南縣志編委會. Changsha: Hunan renmin chubanshe. 1988.

Peishi zupu 裴氏族谱 [*The Genealogy of Pei Lineage*]. n.d.

Qianjiang jiuwen lu 潛江舊聞錄 [*Old Stories of Qianjiang*]. Gan Pengyun 甘雲鵬. 1934.

Qianjiang xianzhi 潛江縣志 [*Gazetteer of Qianjiang County*]. 1694.

Qianjiang xianzhi xu 潛江縣志續 [*Gazetteer of Qianjiang County*]. 1879.

Qianjiangxian taihexiang shizheng dice: Liutanzi yuan 潛江縣太和鄉實證底冊：流灘子垸 [The Tax Catalog of Taihexiang, Qianjiang County: Liutanzi yuan]. 1889.

Qianjiangxian taihexiang shizheng dice: zhuantangwai yuan 潛江縣太和鄉實證底冊：磚淌外垸 [The Tax Catalog of Taihexiang, Qianjiang County: Zhuantangwai yuan]. 1889.

Qingdai zouzhe huibian—nongye, huanjing 清代奏摺匯編—農業、環境 [*A Compilation of Memorials of the Qing Dynasty—Agriculture and Environment*]. Zhongguo kexueyuan dili kexue yu ziyuan yanjiusuo and zhongguo diyi lishi dang'an guan 中國科學院地理科學與資源研究所和中國第一歷史檔案館. Beijing: Shangwu yinshu guan. 2005.

Qingshi gao 清史稿 [*A Draft History of the Qing*]. Zhao Er'xun 趙爾巽, in *Xuxiu siku quanshu* 續修四庫全書 [*Complete Collection in Four Treasures*]. Shanghai: Shanghai guji chubanshe. 1928/1998.

Qizhou zhi 蘄州志 [*Gazetteer of Qi Prefecture*]. 1882.

Rushu ji 入蜀記 [*Traveling to Shu*]. Lu You 陸游. 1170.

Sanguo zhi 三國志 [*Records of the Three Kingdoms*]. Beijing: Zhonghua shuju. Chen Shou 陳壽 (Western Jin). 1969.

Sansheng bianfang beilan 三省邊防備覽 [*A Survey of the Borderland among Hubei, Shaanxi and Sichuan*]. Yan Ruyi 嚴如熤. 1843.

Shengwu ji 聖武記 [*A Military History of the Qing Period*]. Wei Yuan 魏源. Beijing: Zhonghua shuju. 1842/1984.

Shuili 水利 [*Water Control Monthly*]. Vol. 1, 2, 3, 4. 1931&1932.

Sunshi zupu 孫氏族譜 [*Genealogy of the Sun Lineage*]. n.d. (Republican period).

Taowenyi gong quanji 陶文毅公全集 [*Collection of Essays by Mr. Tao Wenyi*]. Tao Shu 陶澍. Lianghuai huaibei shimin gongkan 兩淮淮北士民公刊. 1840.

Tianmen xianzhi 天門縣志 [*Gazetteer of Tianmen County*]. 1765.

Wang Zhen nongshu 王禎農書 [*The Treatises of Agriculture by Wang Zhen*]. Wang Zhen 王禎. Yuan Dynasty.

Wuchuan lu 吳船录 [*A Record of Wuchuan*]. Fan Chengda 范成大. 1177.

Wuchang fuzhi 武昌府志 [*Gazetteer of Wuchang Prefecture*]. 1687.

Wuchang xianzhi 武昌縣志 [Gazetteer of Wuchang County]. 1763.

Wuhan ribao 武漢日報 [*Wuhan Daily*]. March 24&25, July 21, August 10. 1947.

Wusheng gouxu shuidao tushuo 五省溝洫水道圖說 [*An Illustration of the Irrigation Aqueducts and Waterways of Five Provinces*]. Shen Menglan 沈夢蘭. 1879.

Xia Jingnan dao zhi 下荊南道志 [*The Gazetteer of the Lower Jingnan Circuit*]. Comp., Jing Daomo 靖道謨 and Lu Zhiyu 魯之裕. 1816.

Xiangdi cheng'an 襄堤成案 [*Leading Cases on the Xiang Dike*]. Comp., Chen Guangwen 陳广文and Hu Zixiu 胡子修, comp. Taipei: Wenhai chubanshe. 1894/1969.

Xiangyang xianzhi 襄陽縣志 [*Gazetteer of Xiangyang County*]. 1874.

Xiaoshi zupu 蕭氏族譜 [*Genealogy of the Xiao Lineage*]. n.d.

Xingbu: Huguangsi zong'an 湖廣司宗案 [Board of Punishments: Huguang Cases]. First Historical Archives of China.

Xinwen tiandi 新聞天地 [*Newsdom*], no. 28. 1947.

Xu Xiake youji 徐霞客遊記 [*The Travelogue of Xu Xiake*]. Vol. 1. Xu Xiake 徐霞客 (Ming). Taipei: Shijie shuju. 1999.

Yangzi jiang, luanhe, baihe ganzhiliu dukou fudi gongcheng 揚子江、灤河、白河幹支流堵口復堤工程 [*The Projects of Sealing and Restoring Dikes of the Main and Branch Rivers of the Yangzi, Luanhe, and Baihe*]. Xingzhengyuan xinwen ju 行政院新聞局. 1947.

Yunxi xianzhi 鄖西縣志[*Gazetteer of Yunxi County*]. 1757.

Zai xu xingshui jinjian (*Changjiang*) 再續行水金鑒 [*Continued Golden Reference for Water Regulation: The Yangzi River*]. Zhongguo shuili shuidian kexue yanjiuyuan and Shuili shi yanjiushi 中國水利水電科學研究院和水利史研究室. Wuhan: Hubei renmin chubanshe. 1835/2004.

Zhongguo difangzhi jicheng: Hubei fuzhi ji 中國地方志集成·湖北府縣志輯 [*A Collection of Chinese Local Gazetteers: Hubei*]. Nanjing: Jiangsu guji chubanshe. 2001.

Zhongguo fangzhi congshu: huazhong difang 中國方志叢書· 華中地方 [*A Compilation of Chinese Local Gazetteers: Central China*]. Taipei: Chengwen chubanshe, 1975.

Zhongguo lishi dahongshui diaocha ziliao huibian 中國歷史大洪水調查資料彙編 [*A Collection of Surveys on Historical Floods in China*]. ed. Luo Chengzheng 駱承政. Beijing: Zhongguo shudian chubanshe. 2006.

Zhongxiang xianzhi 鍾祥縣志 [*Gazetteer of Zhongxiang County*]. 1937.

Zhushan xianzhi 竹山縣志 [*Gazetteer of Zhushan County*]. 1807.

Databases

CHGIS, Version 4.0 (1820 historical data). 2007. Cambridge: Harvard Yenching Institute.

Taiwan Academia Sinica online database (Scripta Sinica) 台灣漢籍電子文獻資料庫, https://hanji.sinica.edu.tw/.

LoGaRT, Local Gazetteer Research Tools, Max Planck Institute for the History of Science, Berlin, February 2017.

Books and Articles

An Shuqing et al. 2007. "China's Natural Wetlands: Past Problems, Current Status, and Future Challenges." *Ambio* 36, no. 4: 335–342.

Bai Liping. 2006. "Qingdai lianghu pingyuan de shecang jianshe 清代兩湖平原的社倉建設 [The Granaries in the Lianghu Plain during the Qing Dynasty]." *Wuhan daxue xuebao* 59, no. 1. 75–81.

Bai Shouyi, ed. 1999. *Zhongguo tongshi* 中國通史 [*A History of China*]. Shanghai: Shanghai renmin chubanshe.

Bankoff, Greg. 2003. *Cultures of Disaster: Society and Natural Hazard in the Philippines.* London: Routledge Curzon.

Bello, David. 2010. "The Cultured Nature of Imperial Foraging in Manchuria." *Late Imperial China* 31, nos. 2: 1–33.

Bingdaodunjun. 2005. "Nongcun shehui: yanjiu biji 農村社會研究筆記 [Notes on the Study of Rural Society]." In *Jingdai Zhongguo de xiangcun shehui* 近代中國的鄉村社會 [*Rural Society of Modern China*], ed. History Department of Fudan University, 255–279. Shanghai: Shanghai guji chubanshe.

Blackbourn, David. 2006. *The Conquest of Nature: Water, Landscape, and the Making of Modern Germany.* New York: W. W. Norton.

Brandt, Loren. 1989. *Commercialization and Agriculture Development: Central and Eastern China, 1870–1937.* Cambridge: Cambridge University Press.

Brook, Timothy. 1996. "In Memoriam: The Sinology of Joseph Needham." *Modern China* 22, no. 3: 340–348.

Buck, John L. 1937. *Land Utilization in China: A Study of 16,786 Farms in 168 Localities, and 38,256 Farm Families, in Twenty-Two Provinces in China, 1929–1933.* Nanking: University of Nanking.

Buoye, Thomas M. 2000. *Manslaughter, Markets, and Moral Economy: Violent Disputes over Property Rights in Eighteenth-Century China.* Cambridge: Cambridge University Press.

Changjiang liuyu guihua bangongshi. 1978. *Changjiang shuili shilue* 長江水利史略 [*A Brief History of the Yangzi River*]. Beijing: Shuili shuidian chubanshe.

Chen Feng. 2006. *Mingqing yilai changjiang liuyu shehui fazhan shilun* 明清以來長江流域社會發展史論 [*Studies on the Social Development of the Yangzi Valley since the Ming and Qing Times*]. Wuhan: Wuhan daxue chubanshe.

Chen Tao. 2007. "Hongshui cunluo kongjian jiegou de yanbian 洪水與村落空間結構的演變—江漢平原楊馬村的台子的社會學考察 [Floods and Transformation in the Spatial Pattern of Villages: A Sociological Analysis of Tai in Yangjia Village of the Jianghan Plain]." *Gujin nongye* 2: 9–14.

Chen Xi and Yang Guo. 2008. *Jingji kaifa yu huanjing bianqian yanjiu: Song, Yuan, Ming, Qing shiqi de Jianghan pingyuan* 經濟開發與環境變遷研究：宋元明清時期的江漢

平原 [*Economic Development and Environmental Changes: The Jianghan Plain during the Song, Yuan, Ming and Qing Periods*]. Wuhan: Wuhan daxue chubanshe.

Chen Yue. 2009. "Qingdai jingzhou mancheng chutan 清代荊州滿城初探 [An Analysis of the Manchu City of Jingzhou in Qing Dynasty]." *Sanmenxia zhiye jishu xueyuan xuebao* 8, no. 1: 55–59.

Chi, Ch'ao-Ting. 1963. *Key Economic Areas in Chinese History; As Revealed in the Development of Public Works for Water-Control.* New York: Paragon Book Reprint.

Ch'ü T'ung-tsu. 1962. *Local Government in China under the Ch'ing*. Stanford: Stanford University Press.

Clausewitz, Carl von. 1873. *On War*, translated by J.J. Graham. London: N. Trübner.

Closmann, Charles E., ed. 2009. *War and the Environment: Military Destruction in the Modern Age.* College Station: Texas A&M University Press.

Courtney, Chris. 2015. "The Dragon King and the 1931 Wuhan Flood: Religious Rumors and Environmental Disasters in Republican China." *Twentieth-Century China* 40, no. 2: 83–104.

Courtney, Chris. 2018. *The Nature of Disaster in China: The 1931 Yangzi River Flood.* Cambridge: Cambridge University Press.

Crossley, Pamela Kyle. 1999. *A Translucent Mirror: History and Identity in Qing Imperial Ideology*. Berkeley: University of California Press.

Davis, Mike. 2002. *Late Victorian Holocausts: El Niño Famines and the Making of the Third World.* London: Verso.

Dean, Kenneth. 2003. "Lineage and Territorial Cults: Transformations and Interactions in the Irrigated Putian Plains." In *Belief, Ritual, and Society: Papers from the Third International Conference on Sinology*, ed. Meirong Lin, 87–129. Taipei: Institute of Ethnology, Academia Sinica.

Dean, Kenneth and Zheng Zhenman. 2009. *Ritual Alliances of the Putian Plain,* vol. 1: *Historical Introduction to the Return of the Gods.* Leiden: E. J. Brill.

Diamond, Jared. 1997. *Guns, Germs, and Steel: The Fates of Human Societies*. New York: W. W. Norton.

Ding Yizhuang. 2003. *Qingdai baqi zhufang yanjiu* 清代八旗駐防研究 [*A Study on the Qing Banner Garrison System*]. Shenyang: Liaoning minzu chubanshe.

Dodgen, Randall A. 2001. *Controlling the Dragon: Confucian Engineers and the Yellow River in Late Imperial China.* Honolulu: University of Hawai'i Press.

Dong Xiaoping and Christian Lamouroux. 2003. Buguan er zhi—Shanxi sishe wucun shuili zuzhiguanli wenxianyuminsu 不灌而治-山西四社五村水利組織管理文獻與民俗 [Water Management without Irrigation—Hydraulic Organization "Four Communities and Five Villages" in Shanxi Province]. In *Shanshaan diqu shuiliziyuan yu minjian shehui diaocha ziliaoji* 陝山地區水資源與民間社會調查資料集 [*A Compilation Record of Water Resources and Local Society in Shan-Shaan Region*]. Beijing: Zhonghua shuju.

Downs, James F. 1961. "The Origin and Spread of Riding in the Near East and Central Asia." *American Anthropologist* 63, no. 6: 1193–1203.

Duara, Prasenjit. 1988. *Culture, Power, and the State: Rural North China, 1900–1942*. Stanford: Stanford University Press.

Duara, Prasenjit. 1988. "Superscribing Symbols: The Myth of Guandi, Chinese God of War." Journal of Asian Studies 47, no. 4: 778–795.

Eastman, Lloyd E. 1988. Family, Fields, and Ancestors: Constancy and Change in China's Social and Economic History, 1550–1949. New York: Oxford University Press.

Edgerton-Tarpley, Kathryn. 2008. *Tears from Iron: Cultural Responses to Famine in Nineteenth-Century China*. Berkeley: University of California Press.

Edgerton-Tarpley, Kathryn. 2014. "From 'Nourish the People' to 'Sacrifice for the Nation': Changing Responses to Disaster in Late Imperial and Modern China." *Journal of Asian Studies* 73: 447–469.

Elliott, Mark C. 2001. *The Manchu Way: The Eight Banners and Ethnic Identity in Late Imperial China.* Stanford: Stanford University Press.

Elvin, Mark. 1973. *The Pattern of the Chinese Past.* Stanford: Stanford University Press.

Elvin, Mark. 1977. "Market Towns and Waterways: The County of Shang-hai from 1480 to 1910," in *The City in Late Imperial China*, ed. G. William Skinner. Stanford: Stanford University Press. 441–474.

Elvin, Mark. 1993. "Three Thousand Years of Unsustainable Growth: China's Environment from Archaic Times to the Present." *East Asian History* 6: 7–46.

Elvin, Mark. 1998. "Who Was Responsible for the Weather? Moral Meteorology in Late Imperial China." *Osiris* 13: 213–237.

Elvin, Mark. 1998. "The Environmental Legacy of Imperial China." *China Quarterly* 156: 733–756.

Elvin, Mark. 2004. *The Retreat of the Elephants: An Environmental History of China.* New Haven: Yale University Press.

Elvin, Mark et al., ed. 1994. *Japanese Studies on the History of Water Control in China: A Selected Bibliography* [*Chugoku suirishi kenkyu: nihongo bunken mokuroku*]. Tokyo: Centre for East Asian Cultural Studies for UNESCO, Toyo Bunko.

Elvin, Mark, and Liu Ts'ui-jung. 1998. *Sediments of Time: Environment and Society in Chinese History.* Cambridge: Cambridge University Press.

Esherick, Joseph. 1987. *The Origins of the Boxer Uprising*. Berkeley: University of California Press.

Fang Jingyun, Rao Sheng, and Zhao Shuqing. 2005. "Human-Induced Long-Term Changes in the Lakes of the Jianghan Plain, Central Yangtze." *Frontiers in Ecology and the Environment* 3, no. 4: 186–192. https://doi.org/10.1890/1540-9295(2005)003[0186:HLCITL]2.0.CO;2.

Fang Jiqing and Michael Connelly, ed. 2008. *Chinese Measure Word Dictionary.* Boston: Cheng & Tsui.

Feng Tianyu, He Xiaoming, and Zhou Jiming. 2005. *Zhonghua wenhua shi* 中華文化史 [*The History of Chinese Culture*]. Shanghai: Shanghai renmin chubanshe.

Feuerwerker, Albert. 1984. "The State and the Economy in Late Imperial China." *Theory and Society* 13, no. 3: 297–326.

Finlay, Robert. 2000. "China, the West, and World History in Joseph Needham's 'Science and Civilization in China'." *Journal of World History* 11, no. 2: 265–303.

Flad, Rowan K. and Pochan Chen. 2013. *Ancient Central China: Case Studies in Early Societies*. Cambridge: Cambridge University Press.

Fu Cuizhang et al. 2003. "Freshwater Fish Biodiversity in the Yangtze River Basin of China: Patterns, Threats and Conservation." *Biodiversity and Conservation* 12: 1649–1685.

Furnivall, John S. 1939/1991. *The Fashioning of Leviathan: The Beginnings of British Rule in Burma*, ed. Gehan Wijeyewardene. Canberra: Department of Anthropology, Research School of Pacific Studies, Australian National University.

Gamble, Ruth, and Trevor Hogan. 2019. "Watersheds in Watersheds: The Fate of the Planet's Major River Systems in the Great Acceleration." *Thesis Eleven* 150, no. 1: 3–25.

Gao Yan. 2012. Transforming the Water Regime: State, Society, and Ecology of the Jianghan Plain in Late Imperial and Modern China. PhD Dissertation, Carnegie Mellon University.

Gao Yan. 2014. "The Retreat of the Horses: The Manchus, Land Reclamation, and Local Ecology in the Jianghan Plain (ca. 1700s–1850s)," in *Environmental History in East Asia: Interdisciplinary Perspectives*, ed. Ts'ui-jung Liu. New York: Routledge. 100–125.

Gao Yan. 2016. "'The Revolt of the Commons': Resilience and Conflicts in the Water Management of the Jianghan Plain in Late Imperial China." *Resilience: A Journal of the Environmental Humanities* 3: 34–70.

Gao Yan. 2019. "Unifying the Yangzi Watershed in Early Twentieth-Century China." Environment & Society Portal, *Arcadia*, no. 28. Rachel Carson Center for Environment and Society. doi.org/10.5282/rcc/8747.

Geertz, Clifford. 1972. "The Wet and the Dry: Traditional Irrigation in Bali and Morocco." *Human Ecology* 1, no. 1: 23–39.

Gong Shengsheng, 1996. *Qingdai lianghu nongye dili* 清代兩湖農業地理 [*Agricultural Geography in Hunan-Hubei during the Qing Dynasty*]. Wuhan: Huazhong shifan daxue chubanshe.

Gong Shengsheng. 2002. "Jianghan-Dongtinghu pingyuan shidi de lishi bianqian yu kechixu liyong 江漢-洞庭湖濕地的歷史變遷與可持續利用 [Historical Changes and Sustainable Utilization of the Jianghan-Dongting Plain's Wetlands]." *Changjiang liuyu ziyuan yu huanjing* 11, no. 6: 569–574.

Gunderson, Lance and C.S. Holling. 2002. *Panarchy: Understanding Transformations in Human and Natural Systems.* Washington, D.C.: Island Press.

He Yeheng. 1993. *Zhongguo zhenxi shoulei de lishi bianqian* 中國珍稀獸類的歷史變遷 [*The Historical Changes of Rare Wildlife in China*]. Changsha: Henan kexue jishu chubanshe.

He Yeheng. 1994. *Zhongguo zhenxi niaolei de lishi bianqian* 中國珍稀鳥類的歷史變遷 [*The Historical Changes of Rare Birds in China*]. Changsha: Henan kexue jishu chubanshe.

Henderson, Mark, G. William Skinner, and Lawrence W. Crissman. 1999. "A Hierarchical Regional Space Model for Contemporary China: Conceptualizing HRS and Constructing Tabular and Spatial Datafiles." Paper presented at the Geoinformatics conference, University of Michigan, Ann Arbor, MI.

Henderson, Mark. 2013. "Macroregions." *Oxford Bibliographies* (last modified April 22, 2013). DOI: 10.1093/obo/9780199920082-0055.

Hersey, John. 1989. *A Single Pebble.* New York: Vintage.

Ho, Ping-ti. 1959. *Studies on the Population of China, 1368–1953*. Cambridge: Harvard University Press.

Ho, Ping-ti. 1967. "The Significance of the Ch'ing Period in Chinese History." *Journal of Asian Studies* 26, no. 2: 189–195.

Ho, Ping-ti. 1998. "In Defense of Sinicization: A Rebuttal of Evelyn Rawski's 'Reenvisioning the Qing'." *Journal of Asian Studies* 57, no. 1: 123–155.

Hsiao, Kung-ch'üan. 1960. *Rural China: Imperial Control in the Nineteenth Century.* Seattle: University of Washington Press.

Hua Qiang. 1991. *Taiping tianguo dili zhi* 太平天國地理志 [*A Geographical Catalog of the Taiping Rebellion*]. Nanning: Guangxi renmin chubanshe.

Huang Limin and Liu Chengwu. 2006. "Hubeisheng jindai honglao zaihai de tedian jiqi chengyin fenxi 湖北省近代洪澇災害的特點及其成因分析 [The Characteristics and Reasons of Floods in Modern Hubei]." *Huazhong shifan daxue xuebao* 40, no. 1: 115–123.

Huang, Philip C. C. 1985. *The Peasant Economy and Social Change in North China.* Stanford: Stanford University Press.

Huang, Philip C. C. 1990. *The Peasant Family and Rural Development in the Yangzi Delta, 1350–1988.* Stanford: Stanford University Press.

Huang, Philip C. C. 2002. "Development or Involution in Eighteenth-Century Britain and China? A Review of Kenneth Pomeranz's 'The Great Divergence: China, Europe, and the Making of the Modern World Economy.' " *Journal of Asian Studies* 61, no. 2: 501–538.

Hubei shuilizhi bianzhuan weiyuanhui. 2000. *Hubei shuili zhi* 湖北水利史 [*A History of Water Control in Hubei*]. Beijing: Zhongguo shuili shuidian chubanshe.

Janku, Andrea. 2007. "Towards a History of Natural Disasters in China: The Case of Linfen County." *Medieval History Journal* 10, nos. 1–2: 267–301.

Janku, Andrea. 2009. "'Heaven-Sent Disasters' in Late Imperial China: The Scope of the State and Beyond," in *Natural Disasters, Cultural Responses: Case Studies Toward a Global Environmental History*, ed. Christof Mauch and Christian Pfistr. Lanham: Lexington Books. 233–264.

Janku, Andrea. 2018. "Drought and Famine in Northwest China: A Late Victorian Tragedy?" *Journal of Chinese History* 2: 373–391. https://doi.org/10.1017/jch.2018.4.

Josephson, Paul. 2002. *Industrialized Nature: Brute Force Technology and the Transformation of the Natural World.* Washington, DC: Island Press.

Kuhn, Philip A. 1970. *Rebellion and Its Enemies in Late Imperial China.* Cambridge, MA: Harvard University Press.

Kuhn, Philip A. 1990. *Soulstealers: the Chinese Sorcery of 1768.* Cambridge: Harvard University Press.

Lan Yong. 1995. "Qingdai changjiang shangyou jiusheng hongchuan zhi chutan 清代長江上游救生紅船初探 [The Life-Saving Boats in the Upper Yangzi during the Qing Dynasty]." *Zhongguo shehui jingjishi* 4: 37–43.

Lan Yong. 2005. "Qingdai changjiang shangyou jiusheng hongchuan zhi xukao 清代長江上游救生紅船制續考 [A Continuous Study on the Life-Saving Red Boats in the Upper Yangzi during the Qing Dynasty]." *Zhongguo shehui jingji shi* 3: 53–57.

Lander, Brian. 2014. "State Management of River Dikes in Early China: New Sources on the Environmental History of the Central Yangzi Region." *T'oung Pao* 100, nos. 4–5: 325–362.

Lansing, J. Stephen. 1987. "Balinese 'Water Temples' and the Management of Irrigation." *American Anthropologist*, n.s., 89, no. 2: 326–341.

Lansing, J. Stephen and John H. Miller. 2003. "Cooperation in Balinese Rice Farming." SFI Working Paper, Santa Fe Institute. https: //sfi-edu.s3.amazonaws.com/sfi-edu/production/uploads/sfi-com/dev/uploads/filer/69/b3/69b31b20-00af-4a55-947a-d47e32cd2276/03-05-030.pdf.

Lansing, Stephen. 2007. *Priest and Programmers: Technologies of Power in the Engineered Landscape.* Princeton: Princeton University Press.

Latour, Bruno. 1993. *We Have Never Been Modern.* Translated by Catherine Porter. Cambridge: Harvard University Press.

Latour, Bruno. 1996. "On Actor-Network Theory. A Few Clarifications Plus More Than a Few Complications." *Soziale Welt* 47: 369–381. http://www.bruno-latour.fr/sites/default/files/P-67%20ACTOR-NETWORK.pdf.

Latour, Bruno. 2007. *Reassembling the Social: An Introduction to Actor-Network-Theory.* Oxford: Oxford University Press.

Leung, Angela Ki Che. 2009. *Leprosy in China: A History.* New York: Columbia University Press.

Lewis, Simon L. and Mark A. Maslin. 2015. "Defining the Anthropocene." Nature 519: 171–180.

Li, Lilian M. 2007. *Fighting Famine in North China: State, Market, and Environmental Decline, 1690s–1990s*. Stanford: Stanford University Press.

Little, Daniel. 1989. *Understanding Peasant China.* New Haven: Yale University Press.

Liu Ts'ui-jung. 1970. "Dike Construction in Ch'ing-Chou, A Study Based on the 'Ti-Fang Chih' Section of the Ching-Chou Fu-Chih." *Papers on China* 23: 1–28.

Liu Ts'ui-jung. 1974. "Trade on the Han River and Its Impact on Economic Development, c. 1800–1911." PhD dissertation, Harvard University.

Liu Ts'ui-jung and John C.H. Fei. 1978. "The Public Granary Institutions of the Ch'ing Dynasty, 1644–1911." Center Discussion Paper, No. 299, Economic Growth Center, Yale University.

Liu Xiusheng. 2007. "Qingdai xianzheng guanli de baike quanshu–ping Huang Liuhong <Fuhui quanshu> jiqi weiguan zhidao 清代縣政管理的百科全書—評黃六鴻《福惠全書》及其為官之道 [An Encyclopedia of the Qing County Administration: Evaluating Fuhui quanshu and Huang's Way of Being an Official]." In *Zhongguo shehui jingjishi luncong: Wu Chengming jiaoshou jiushi huadan jinian wenji* 中國社會經濟史論叢：吳承明教授九十華誕紀念文集 [*An Anthology on Chinese Social and Economic History: In Celebration of the Ninetieth Birthday of Professor Wu Chengming*], ed. Fang Xing. Beijing: Zhongguo shehui kexue chubanshe. 762–769.

Lu Xiqi. 2004. "Tai, yuan, dadi: Jianghan pingyuan shehui jingji quyu de xingcheng, kuozhan yu zuhe 台、垸、大堤：江漢平原社會經濟區域的形成、擴展與組合 [Tai, Yuan, and Dikes: The Formation, Expansion and Combination of Socio-Economic Units in the Jianghan Plain]." *Shixue yuekan* 4.

Lu Xiqi. 2005. "Shi Quan jiaoshou de daode wenzhang: 'Shi Quan Wenji' bianhou ganyan 石泉教授的道德文章—《石泉文集》編後感言 [The Morals and Research of Professor Shi Quan—Postscript to A Collection of Shi Quan's Writings]." Personal communication. Also available at: https: //site.douban.com/228138/widget/notes/15538304/note/565582902/.

Lu Xiqi. 2011. "Mingqing shiqi Jianghan pingyuan de weiyuan: cong 'shuili gongcheng' dao 'shuili gongtongti' 明清時期江漢平原的圍垸：從"水利工程"到"水利共同體" [Yuan in the Jianghan Plain during the Ming and Qing Periods: From 'Hydraulic Construction' to 'Hydraulic Collectivity']." In *Lishi shiqi Changjiang zhongyou diqu renlei huodong yu huanjing bianqian zhuanti yanjiu* 歷史時期長江中游地區人類活動與環境變遷專題研究 [*Human Activities and Environmental Changes in Historical Middle Yangzi Region*], ed. Zhang Jianmin and Lu Xiqi, 348–439. Wuhan: Wuhan daxue chubanshe.

Lu Xiqi. 2013. "Shuili shehui de xingcheng: yi mingqing shiqi jianghan pingyuan de weiyuan wei zhongxin 水利社會的形成：以明清時期江漢平原的圍垸為中心 [The Making of Water Community in the Traditional China: Discussion around the 'Enclosed Embankment' in Jianghan Plain during the Ming-Qing Period]." *Zhongguo jingjishi yanjiu* 2: 122–140.

Lu Xiqi. 2016. *Changjiang zhongyou de rendi guanxi yu diyu shehui* 長江中游的人地關係與地域社會 [*The Human-Land Relationship and Local Society in the Middle Yangzi Region*]. Xiamen: Xiamen daxue chubanshe.

Lu Xiqi and Pan Sheng. 2004. *Hanshui zhongxiayou hedao bianqian yu difang* 漢水中下游河道變遷與堤防 [*River Course Changes and Dike Construction in the Middle and Lower Reaches of the Han River*]. Wuhan: Wuhan University Press.

Marks, Robert. 1998. *Tigers, Rice, Silk, Silt: Environment and Economy in Late Imperial South China.* Cambridge: Cambridge University Press.

Marks, Robert. 2012. *China: Its Environment and History.* Lanham: Rowman & Littlefield.

Main, Douglas. 2020. "The Chinese Paddlefish, One of World's Largest Fish, Has Gone Extinct." *National Geographic*. https: //www.nationalgeographic.com/animals/2020/01/chinese-paddlefish-one-of-largest-fish-extinct/#close/.

Mauch, Christof, and Christian Pfister, ed. 2009. *Natural Disasters, Cultural Responses: Case Studies toward a Global Environmental History*. Lanham: Rowman & Littlefield.

McNeill, William H. 1976. *Plagues and Peoples.* New York: Anchor Press.

Mei Li, Zhang Guoxiong, and Yan Changgui. 1995. *Lianghu pingyuan kaifa tanyuan* 兩湖開發探源 [*Exploring the Origins of Opening the Hunan-Hubei Plain*]. Jiangxi: Jiangxi jiaoyu chubanshe.

Menzies, Nicholas K. 1992. "Strategic Space: Exclusion and Inclusion in Wildland Politics in Late Imperial China." *Modern Asian Studies* 26, no. 4: 719–733.

Merchant, Carolyn. 2015. *Autonomous Nature: Problems of Prediction and Control from Ancient Times to the Scientific Revolution*. London: Routlege.

Merkel-Hess, Kate, Kenneth L. Pomeranz, and Jeffrey Wasserstrom, ed. 2009. *China in 2008: A Year of Great Significance*. Lanham: Rowman & Littlefield.

Min Zongdian. 2004. "Qingdai suzhewan huangzai yanjiu 清代蘇浙皖蝗災研究 [A Study on the Locust Disaster in Jiangsu, Zhejiang and Anhui Provinces during the Qing Dynasty]." *Zhongguo nongshi* 2: 56–62.

Morita Akira. 1960. "Shindai Kokō ni okeru chisui kakai no tenkai [The Development of Water Control and Irrigation in Huguang under the Qing]." *Tōhōgaku* 20: 63–76.

Morita Akira. 1974. *Shindai suirishi kenkyu* [*Research on the History of Water Control in the Qing Dynasty*]. Tokyo: Aki shobo.

Morita Akira. 2008. *Qingdai shuili yu quyu shehui* 清代の水利と地域社会 [*Water Control during the Qing and Regional Societies*], translated into Chinese by Luoshan Lei. Jinan: Shandong huabao chubanshe.

Mote, F. W. 1961. "The Growth of Chinese Despotism; A Critique of Wittfogel's Theory of Oriental Despotism as Applied to China." *Oriens extremus* 8, no. 1: 1–41.

Mukerji, Chandra. 1994. "The Political Mobilization of Nature in Seventeenth-Century French Formal Gardens." *Theory and Society* 23, no. 5: 651–677.

Muscolino, Micah. 2009. *Fishing Wars and Environmental Change in Late Imperial and Modern China.* Cambridge: Harvard University Asia Center.

Muscolino, Micah. 2014. *The Ecology of War in China: Henan Province, the Yellow River, and Beyond 1938–1950.* Cambridge: Cambridge University Press.

Myers, Ramon H. and Yeh-Chien Wang. 2002. "Economic Developments, 1644–1800," in *The Cambridge History of China*, vol. 9, ed. Willard J. Peterson, part 1, The Ch'ing Empire to 1800. Cambridge: Cambridge University Press. 563–645.

National Economic Council. 1935. "Kinshui Sluice: Inaugural Ceremony." Kinshui, Hupeh. April 28.

Needham, Joseph. 1965. *Science and Civilization in China,* vol. 4, part 2. Cambridge: Cambridge University Press.

Niu Guanjie. 2006. "Qingdai mazheng chutan 清代馬政初探 [A Study on the Horse Administration in Qing Dynasty]." *Yanshan daxue xuebao* 2: 57–63.

O'Connor, Richard A. 1995. "Agricultural Change and Ethnic Succession in Southeast Asian States: A Case for Regional Anthropology." *Journal of Asian Studies* 54: 988n11.

Osborne, Anne. 1994. "The Local Politics of Land Reclamation in the the Lower Yangzi Highlands." *Late Imperial China* 15, no. 1: 1–46.

Osborne, Anne. 2004. "Property, Taxes, and State Protection of Rights." In *Contract and Property in Early Modern China*, ed. Jonathan Ocko, Robert Gardella, and Madeleine Zelin, 120–158. Stanford: Stanford University Press.

Pan Honggang. 2005. "Qingdai zhufang baqi de minzu guanxi wenti yanjiu–cong jingzhou qi/min de jici dou'ou shijian rushou de tantao 清代駐防八旗的民族關係問題研究—從荊州旗、民的幾次鬥毆事件入手的探討 [A Study on the Ethnic Relations of the Jingzhou Garrison of the Qing Dynasty with Case Studies on the Banner and Han Conflicts of Jingzhou]." *Jianghan luntan* 2: 72–76.

Parker, Geoffrey. 2008. "Crisis and Catastrophe: The Global Crisis of the Seventeenth Century Reconsidered." *American Historical Review* 113, no. 4: 1053–1079.

Peng Yuxin and Zhang Jianmin. 1993. *Mingqing shijqi changjiang liuyu de nongtian shuili* 明清時期長江流域的農田水利 [*Agriculture and Water Conservation in the Yangzi Valley in Ming and Qing Dynasty*]. Wuhan: Wuhan daxue chubanshe.

Perdue, Peter C. 1982. "Official Goals and Local Interests: Water Control in the Dongting Lake Region during the Ming and Qing Periods." *Journal of Asian Studies* 41, no. 4: 747–765.

Perdue, Peter C. 1987. *Exhausting the Earth: State and Peasant in Hunan, 1500–1850.* Cambridge: Harvard University Press.

Perdue, Peter C. 1990. "Lakes of Empire: Man and Water in Chinese History." *Modern China* 16, no. 1: 119–129.

Perdue, Peter C. 2010. *China Marches West: The Qing Conquest of Central Eurasia.* Cambridge: Harvard University Press.

Perry, Elizabeth J. 1980. *Rebels and Revolutionaries in North China, 1845–1945*. Stanford: Stanford University Press.

Pietz, David. 2002. *Engineering the State: The Huai River and Reconstruction in Nationalist China 1927–1937*. New York: Routledge.

Pietz, David. 2015. *The Yellow River: The Problem of Water in Modern China*. Cambridge: Harvard University Press.

Pomeranz, Kenneth. 1993. *The Making of a Hinterland: State, Society, and Economy in Inland North China, 1853–1937*. Berkeley: University of California Press.

Qiang Hua. 1991. *Taiping tianguo dili zhi* 太平天國地理志 [*A Geographical Record of Taiping Rebellion*]. Nanning: Guangxi renmin chubanshe.

Qin Jianming and Marianne Bujard, ed. 2003. *Yaoshan shengmumiao yu shenshe* 堯山聖母廟與神社 [*The Temple of Empress of the Yao Mountain and Shrine*]. In *Shanshaan diqu shuiziyuan yu minjian shehui diaocha ziliaoji* 陝山地區水資源與民間社會調查資料集 [*A Compilation Record of Water Resources and Local Society in Shan-Shaan Region*]. Beijing: Zhonghua shuju.

Radkau, Joachim. 2008. *Nature and Power: A Global History of the Environment*. Cambridge: Cambridge University Press.

Rankin, Mary. 1986. *Elite Activism and Political Transformation in China: Zhejiang Province, 1865–1911*. Stanford: Stanford University Press.

Rawski, Evelyn S. 1975. "Agricultural Development in the Han River Highland." *Ching shih wen-t'i* 3, no. 4: 63–81.

Rawski, Evelyn S. 1996. "Reenvisioning the Qing: The Significance of the Qing Period in Chinese History." *Journal of Asian Studies* 55, no. 4: 829–850.

Ren Fang. 2003. *Mingqing Changjiang zhongyou shizhen jingji yanjiu* 明清長江中游市鎮經濟研究 [*Township Economy in the Mid-Yangzi Region*]. Wuhan: Wuhan University Press.

Rowe, William T. 1983. "Hu Lin-i's Reform of the Grain Tribute System in Hupeh, 1855–1858." *Ch'ing-shih wen-t'i* 4, no. 10: 33–86.

Rowe, William T. 1984. *Hankow: Commerce and Society in a Chinese City, 1796–1889*. Stanford: Stanford University Press.

Rowe, William T. 1988. "Water Control and the Qing Political Process: the Fankou Dam Controversy 1876–1883." *Modern China* 14, no. 4: 353–387.

Rowe, William T. 2002. *Saving the World: Chen Hongmou and Elite Consciousness in Eighteenth-Century China*. Stanford: Stanford University Press.

Rowe, William T. 2008. *Crimson Rain: Seven Centuries of Violence*. Stanford: Stanford University Press.

Rowe, William T. 2012. *China's Last Empire: The Great Qing*. Cambridge: Harvard University Press.

Schoppa, R. Keith. 1982. *Chinese Elites and Political Change: Zhejiang Province in the Early Twentieth Century*. Cambridge: Harvard University Press.

Schoppa, R. Keith. 1989. *Song Full of Tears—Xiang Lake: Nine Centuries of Chinese Life.* New Haven: Yale University Press.

Schoppa, R. Keith. 1997. "State, Society, and Land Reclamation on Hangzhou Bay during the Republican Period." *Modern China* 23, no. 2: 246–271.

Schoppa, R. Keith. 2002. *Song Full of Tears: Nine Centuries of Chinese Life around Xiang Lake.* New York: Basic Books.

Scott, James C. 2009. *The Art of Not Being Governed: An Anarchist History of Upland Southeast Asia.* New Haven: Yale University Press.

Shabad, Theodore. 1959. "Non-Western Views of the 'Hydraulic Society'." *Annals of the Association of American Geographers* 49, no. 3: 324–325. https://doi.org/10.1111/j.1467-8306.1959.tb01617.x.

Shepherd, Jack. 1939. "Salvaging the Textile Industry in China." *Far Eastern Survey* 8, no. 15: 171–175.

Shi Quan and Zhang Guoxiong. 1988. "Jianghan pingyuan de yuantian xingqiyu heshi 江漢平原的垸田興起於何時 [When Did *Yuan* Fields Start in the Jianghan Plain?]." *Zhongguo lishi dili luncong* 1: 131–140.

Shiue, Carol H. 2004. "Local Granaries and Central Government Disaster Relief: Moral Hazard and Intergovernmental Finance in Eighteenth and Nineteenth-Century China." *Journal of Economic History* 64, no. 1: 100–124.

Skinner, G. William, ed. 1977. *The City in Late Imperial China.* Stanford: Stanford University Press.

Skinner, G. William, Mark Henderson, and Yuan Jianhua. 2000. "China's Fertility Transition through Regional Space: Using GIS and Census Data for a Spatial Analysis of Historical Demography." *Social Science History* 24: 613–652.

Song Xishang. 1963. *Changjiang tongkao* 長江通考 [*A General History of the Yangzi River*]. Taipei: Zhonghua congshu bianshen weiyuanhui.

Spence, Jonathan D. 1980. *To Change China: Western Advisers in China 1620–1960.* New York: Penguin Books.

Spence, Jonathan D. 1998. *Emperor of China: Self-Portrait of Kang-Hsi.* New York: Vintage Books.

Stroebe, George G. 1936. "The Kinshui Reclamation Project." *Journal of the Association of Chinese and American Engineers* 17, nos. 1–2: 1–21, 88–98.

Sun Yat-sen. 1920. *Shiye jihua* 實業計劃 [*International Development of China*]. http: // www.gzmg.gov.cn/Article/szs/szswx/200811/32. html.

Sutton, Donald S. 1989. "A Case of Literati Piety: the Ma Yuan Cult from High-Tang to High-Qing." *Chinese Literature: Essays, Articles, Reviews* 11: 79–114.

Sutton, Donald S. 2004. "Prefect Feng and the Yangzhou Drought of 1490: A Ming Social Crisis and the Rewards of Sincerity." *Min-su ch'u-i* 143: 19–55.

Swyngedouw, Erik. 1999. "Modernity and Hybridity: Nature, *Regeneracionismo*, and the Production of the Spanish Waterscape, 1890–1930." *Annals of the Association of American Geographers* 89, no. 3: 443–465.

Thompson, E. P. 1974. "Plebeian Culture, Patrician Society." *Journal of Social History* 7, no. 4: 382–405.

Todd, Oliver J. 1938. *Two Decades in China: Comprising Technical Papers, Magazine Articles, Newspaper Stories and Official Reports Connected with Work under His Own Observation.* Beijing: Association of Chinese and American Engineers.

Turvey, Samuel. 2008. *Witness to Extinction: How We Failed to Save the Yangzi Dolphin.* Oxford: Oxford University Press.

Tvedt, Terje. 2015. *Water and Society: Changing Perceptions of Societal and Historical Development.* London: I. B. Tauris.

Van Slyke, Lyman P. 1988. *Yangtze: Nature, History and the River.* New York: Addison Wesley.

Waley-Cohen, Joanna. 2004. "The New Qing History." *Radical History Review* 88: 193–206.

Wan Qian. 2006. "Wanqing jingzhou mancheng jiating jiegou fenxi yu dianxing juzhu moshi tuice 晚清荊州滿城家庭結構分析與典型居住模式推測 [Analysis of the Family Structures and Inhabitancy Pattern of Jingzhou "Man"-district of Late Qing Dynasty]." *Xin jianzhu* 1: 23–26.

Wang Shufen. 1995. "Qingdai zhishan fanghong huanbao celue zhi tantao: yi changjiang liuyu wei zhongxin 清代治山防洪環保策略之探討：以長江流域為中心 [A Study on the Mountain Management and Flood Control during the Qing: A Case Study of the Yangzi River]." *Guoli Taibei jiaoyu daxue xuebao* 19, no. 1: 51–78.

Watson, James L. 1985. "Standardizing the Gods: The Promotion of T'ien Hou ('Empress of Heaven') along the South China Coast, 960–1960." in *Popular Culture in Late Imperial China*, ed. David Johnson, Andrew J. Nathan, and Evelyn S. Rawski. Berkeley: University of California Press. 292–324.

Weber, Max. 1951. *Religions of China: Confucianism and Taoism.* New York: The Free Press.

Wen Huanran and Wen Rongsheng, ed. 1995. *Zhongguo lishi shiqi zhiwu yu dongwu bianqian yanjiu* 中國歷史時期植物與動物變遷研究 [*Changes in Flora and Fauna in Chinese History*]. Chongqing: Chongqing chubanshe.

White, Richard. 1995. *The Organic Machine: The Remaking of the Columbia River.* New York: Hill and Wang.

Whitfield, Susan. 1999. *Life along the Silk Road.* Berkeley: University of California Press.

Will, Pierre-Etienne. 1985. "State Intervention in the Administration of a Hydraulic Infrastructure: The Example of Hubei Province in Late Imperial Times." In *The Scope of State Power in China*, ed. Stuart R. Schram, 295–347. Hong Kong: Chinese University Press.

Will, Pierre-Etienne. 1990. *Bureaucracy and Famine in Eighteenth-Century China.* Stanford: Stanford University Press.

Will, Pierre-Etienne. 2006. "Zhonghua diguo wanqi guojia dui shuili de guanli [State's Water Management in Late Imperial China]." In *Mingqing yilai changjiang liuyu shehui fazhan shilun* [*Social Development of the Yangzi River Valley since Ming and Qing Dynasties*], ed. Chen Feng, 796–810. Wuhan: Wuhan University Press.

Will, Pierre-Etienne, R. Bin Wong et al. 1991. *Nourish the People: The State Civilian Granary System in China, 1650–1850.* Ann Arbor: University of Michigan Press.

Winiwarter, Verena. 2014. "The Emerging Long-Term View: Challenges and Opportunities of Writing Environmental Histories in Central Europe," in Man, Nature and Environment between the Northern Adriatic and the Eastern Alps in Premodern Times, ed. Peter Štih and Žiga Zwitter. Ljubljana: Znanstvena založba Filozofske fakultete. 8–23.

Wittfogel, Karl A. 1957. "Chinese Society: An Historical Survey." *Journal of Asian Studies* 16, no. 3: 343–364.

Wittfogel, Karl A. 1957. *Oriental Despotism.* New Haven: Yale University Press.

Wolfganger, Louis A. 1929. "Major World Soil Groups and Some of Their Geographic Implications." *Geographical Review* 19, no. 1: 94–113.

Wong, R. Bin. 1982. "Food Riots in the Qing Dynasty." *Journal of Asian Studies* 41, no. 4: 767–788. https://doi.org/10.2307/2055449.

Wong, R. Bin, and Peter C. Perdue. 1983. "Review: Famine's Foes in Ch'ing China." *Harvard Journal of Asiatic Studies* 43, no. 1: 291–332.

Wong, Youngtsu. 2010. "'Tiandi zhidao': mingqing diguo shengtai weiji zongshuo 天地之盜：明清帝國生態危機綜說 ['Rob the Wealth of the Earth': The Ecological Crisis in Late Imperial China]." *Zhongguo wenhua yanjiusuo xuebao* no. 51: 87–115. https://www.cuhk.edu.hk/ics/journal/articles/v51p087.pdf.

Wood, Frances. 2002. *The Silk Road: Two Thousand Years in the Heart of Asia.* Berkeley: University of California Press.

Worster, Donald. 1985. *Rivers of Empire: Water, Aridity, and the Growth of the American West.* New York: Pantheon Books.

Wu Chengming. 2004. "18 yu 19 shiji shangye de zhongguo shichang 18 與 19世紀上葉的中國市場 [China's Market during the Eighteenth Century and the First Half of the Nineteenth Centuries]." China Forum of Economic History.

Xia Mingfang. 1998. "Cong qingmo zaihai qunfaqi kan zhongguo zaoqi xiandaihua de lishi tiaojian 從清末災害群發期看中國早期現代化的歷史條件—災荒與洋務運動研究之議 [A Study on the Historical Condition of Early Modernization during the Disaster Cluster of the Late Qing]." *Qingshi yanjiu* 1: 70–82.

Xu Bin. 2003. "Mingqing shiqi lianghu diqu yuye shengchan yu guanli 明清時期兩湖地區漁業生產與管理 [The Fishery Production and Management of the Hunan-Hubei Region during the Ming and Qing Periods]." MA thesis, Wuhan University. It was later published into a book, Zhidu, jingji yu shehui: *Mingqing lianghu yuye, yumin yu shuiyu shehui* 制度、經濟與社會：明清兩湖漁業、漁民與水域社會 [*Institutions, Economy and Society: Fishery, Fisher Folk and Society in Ming and Qing Dynasties*] (Beijing: Kexue chubanshe, 2018).

Xu Bin. 2010. *Mingqing e'dong zongzu yu difang shehui* 明清鄂東宗族與地方社會 [*The Lineages of Eastern Hubei and Local Society during the Ming and Qing Periods*]. Wuhan: Wuhan University Press.

Xu Bin. 2017. "Yishui wei benwei: Dui 'tudi shiguan' de fansi yu 'xin shuiyu shi' de tichu 以水為本位：對"土地史觀"的反思與"新水域史"的提出 [Rethinking Land and Water: A New Water History]." *Wuhan daxue xuebao* 1: 122–128.

Yan Zhongping, ed. 1955. *Zhongguo jindai jingjishi tongji ziliao xuanji* 中國近代經濟史統計資料選輯 [*Selected Statistical Sources of Economic History in Pre-1949 China*]. Beijing: Kexue chubanshe.

Yang Guo'an. 2001. "Shehui dongdang yu qingdai hubei xiangcunzhong de zhaibao 社會動盪與清代湖北鄉村中的寨堡 [Social Turmoil and *Zhai/Bao* in Rural Hubei of Qing]." *Wuhan daxue xuebao* 54, no. 5: 574–578.

Yang Guo'an. 2004. *Mingqing lianghu diqu jiceng zuzhi yu xiangcun shehui yanjiu* 明清兩湖地區基層組織與鄉村社會研究 [*The Local Social Structure and Rural Society of Hunan-Hubei Region during the Ming and Qing Periods*]. Wuhan: Wuhan daxue chubanshe.

Yang Guo'an. 2006. "Jiusheng chuanju yu qingdai lianghu shuishang jiusheng shiye 救生船局與清代兩湖水上救生事業 [Lifeboats and Lifesaving Cause of the Hubei-Hubei Region in the Qing Dynasty]." *Wuhan daxue xuebao* 59, no. 1: 69–74.

Yang Huairen and Tang Richang, ed. 1998. *Changjiang zhongyou jingjiang bianqian yanjiu* 長江中游荊江變遷研究 [*A Study on the Changes of Middle Yangzi River*]. Beijing: Zhongguo shuili shuidian chubanshe.

Yao Shan-yu. 1942. "The Chronological and Seasonal Distribution of Floods and Droughts in Chinese History, 206 B.C.–A.D. 1911." *Harvard Journal of Asiatic Studies* 6, nos. 3/4: 273–312.

Yin Lingling. 2004. *Mingqing changjiang zhongxiayou yuye jingji yanjiu* 明清長江中下游漁業經濟研究 [*A Study on the Fishery Economy of the Mid- and Lower Yangzi Region in the Ming and Qing Dynasties*]. Jinan: Qilu shushe.

Yin Lingling. 2008. *Mingqing lianghu pingyuan de huanjing bianqian yu shehui yingdui* 明清兩湖平原的環境變遷與社會應對 [*The Environmental Transformation and Social Response in the Hunan-Hubei Plain during the Ming and Qing Dynasties*]. Shanghai: Shanghai renmin chubanshe.

Zhang Guoxiong. 1987. "Mingdai jianghan pingyuan shuihan zaihai bianhua yu yuantian jingji de guanxi 明代江漢平原水旱災害的變化與垸田經濟的關係 [Flood and Drought and the *Yuan* Economy in the Jianghan Plain during the Ming Dynasty]." *Zhongguo nongshi* 4: 28–34, 53.

Zhang Guoxiong. 1989. "Jianghan pingyuan yuantian de tezheng jiqi zai mingqing shiqi de fazhan yanbian 江漢平原垸田的特徵及其在明清時期的發展演變 [The Characteristics of Wet Paddy Rice Fields in Jianghan Plain and Their Transformation in the Ming-Qing Period]." *Nongye kaogu* 1: 227–233; 2: 238–248.

Zhang Guoxiong. 1990. "Jianghan pingyuan de hanlao zaihai yu yuantian shengchan 江漢平原的旱澇災害與垸田生產 [The Droughts and Floods of the Jianghan Plain and the Agricultural Production in the Yuan]." *Zhongguo nongshi* 1: 28–34.

Zhang Guoxiong. 1995. *Mingqing shiqi de lianghu yimin* 明清時期的兩湖移民 [*The Hunan-Hubei Immigration in Ming and Qing Times*]. Xi'an: Shanxi renmin jiaoyu chubanshe.

Zhang Hui et al. 2020. "Extinction of One of the World's Largest Freshwater Fishes: Lessons for Conserving the Endangered Yangtze Fauna." *Science of the Total Environment* 710: 1–7. http://dx.doi.org/10.1016/j.scitotenv.2019.136242.

Zhang Jianmin. 1987. "Qingdai jianghan-dongting huqu diyuan nongtian de fazhan jiqi zonghe kaocha 清代江漢—洞庭湖區堤垸農田的發展及其綜合考察 [The Development of Jianghan-Dongting Lake Yuan Fields of the Qing Dynasty]." *Zhongguo nongshi* 2.

Zhang Jianmin. 1999. *Hubei tongshi* 湖北通史 [*A General History of Hubei: Ming and Qing*]. Wuhan: Huazhong shifan daxue chubanshe.

Zhang Jianmin. 2007. *Mingqing changjiang liuyu shanqu ziyuan kaifa yu huanjing yanbian: yi qinling-daba shanqu wei zhongxin* 明清長江流域山區資源開發與環境演變：以秦嶺—大巴山區為中心 [*Exploration in Mountainous Resources and Environmental Changes during the Ming-Qing Periods: Studies on Qinling-Daba Mountain Areas*]. Wuhan: Wuhan daxue chubanshe.

Zhang Jianmin and Lu Xiqi, ed. 2011. *Lishi shiqi changjiang zhongyou diqu renlei huodong yu huanjing bianqian zhuanti yanjiu* 歷史時期長江中游人類活動與環境變遷專題研究 [*Human Activities and Environmental Change in Historical Middle Yangzi Region*]. Wuhan: Wuhan daxue chubanshe.

Zhang Jiayan. 2001. "Qingdai jianghan pingyuan yuantian nongye jingji texing fenxi 清代江漢平原垸田農業經濟特性分析 [The Agricultural and Economic Characteristics of the *Yuan* Fields in the Jianghan Plain during the Qing Dynasty]." *Zhongguoshi yanjiu* 1: 134–143.

Zhang Jiayan. 2006. "Environment, Market, and Peasant Choice of the Jianghan Plain." *Modern China* 32, no. 1: 31–63.

Zhang Jiayan. 2006. "Water Calamities and Dike Management in the Jianghan Plain in the Qing and the Republic." *Late Imperial China* 27, no. 1: 66–108.

Zhang Jiayan. 2014. *Coping with Calamity: Environmental Change and Peasant Response in Central China, 1736–1949*. Vancouver: UBC Press.

Zhang Jiayan. 2016. "Water, Dike, and Temple: Water Deity Worship and Dike Management in the Jianghan Plain, 1788–2013." *Journal of Social History* 50, no. 1: 120–147. https://doi.org/10.1093/jsh/shv086.

Zhang Ling. 2016. *The River, the Plain, and the State: An Environmental Drama in Northern Song China, 1048–1128*. Cambridge: Cambridge University Press.

Zhang Xiangwen and Hui Fuping. 2006. "Qingdai zhongwanqi shandi zhongzhi yumi yinfa de shuitu liushi jiqi e'zhi cuoshi 清代中晚期山地種植玉米引發的水土流失及其遏制措施 [Soil Erosion Caused by Maize Cultivation and Its Preventive Measures in the Mid- and Late Qing]." *Zhongguo nongshi* 25, no. 3: 13–21.

Zhang Xiaohong, Man Zhimin, and Ge Quansheng. 2002. "Qingdai Shannan tudi liyong bianqian qudongli yanjiu 清代陝南土地利用變遷驅動力研究 [A Study on the Changes in Land Utilization of Shannan Region during the Qing]." *Zhongguo lishi dili luncong* 17, no. 4: 114–125.

Zhang Xiugui. 1981. "Dongtinghu yanbian de lishi guocheng 洞庭湖演變的歷史過程 [The Historical Changes of the Dongting Lake]." *Lishi dili* 1: 99–116.

Zhang Xiugui. 2006. *Zhongguo lishi dimao yu gu ditu yanjiu* 中國歷史地貌與古地圖研究 [*Studies on Historical Geomorphology and Ancient Maps of China*]. Beijing: Shehui kexue wenxian chubanshe.

Zhang Zhi, ed. 2003. *Huayi fengtu zhi* 華夷風土志 [*A History of Customs in China*]. Yangzhou: Guangling shushe.

Zhao Gang. 1995. "Qingdai de kenzhi zhengce yu pengmin huodong 清代的墾殖政策與棚民活動 [Land Reclamation and the Shack People during the Qing Dynasty]." *Zhongguo lishi dili luncong* 3: 27–46.

Zhao Zhui. 2007. "Qiangshi yu huayu: qingdai pengmin lishi diwei zhi fansi 強勢與話語：清代棚民歷史地位之範式 [Power and Dialogues: A Reflection on the Historical Significance of the Shack People during the Qing]." *Zhongguo nongshi* 3: 113–122.

Zhou Rong. 2006. *Mingqing shehui baozhang zhidu yu lianghu jiceng shehui* 明清社會保障制度與兩湖基層社會 [*Social Welfare System and the Local Society of Hunan-Hubei Region during the Ming and Qing Periods*]. Wuhan: Wuhan daxue chubanshe.

Zhu Kezhen. 1972. "Zhongguo jin wuqiannianlai qihou bianqian de chubu yanjiu 中國近五千年來氣候變遷的初步研究 [Preliminary Study of the Changes in China's Climate in the Past 5,000 Years]." *Kaogu xuebao* 1: 15–38.

Index

www.ingramcontent.com/pod-product-compliance
Lightning Source LLC
Chambersburg PA
CBHW071324230926
51849CB00002B/312
* 9 7 8 9 0 0 4 5 0 5 2 7 8 *